JUST BEFORE BRETTON WOODS:

THE ATLANTIC CITY CONFERENCE,

JUNE 1944

Just Before Bretton Woods: The Atlantic City Conference, June 1944

Edited by

Kurt Schuler
and
Gabrielle Canning

CENTER FOR FINANCIAL STABILITY

NEW YORK

E-book and print editions published 2019 by the Center for Financial Stability, 1120 Avenue of the Americas, 4th floor, New York, NY 10036

Online companion files to this book are available at the Web site of the Center for Financial Stability, <www.centerforfinancialstability.org>

Cataloging data available from the Library of Congress

ISBN 978-1-941801-04-8 (e-book), 978-1-941801-05-5 (hardcover)

Contents

CONTENTS

CONTENTS

About the Editors

Kurt Schuler is an economist in the Office of International Affairs at the U.S. Department of the Treasury in Washington, D.C. In his spare time he is Senior Fellow in Financial History at the Center for Financial Stability. He is the editor of the Center's Historical Financial Statistics, a free online database. His previous books include *The Bretton Woods Transcripts,* edited with Andrew Rosenberg and published by the Center in 2012.

Gabrielle Canning is a recent graduate of the College of William and Mary, where she earned her B.A. in history and theatre. She did part of her work on this book as a senior independent study under the mentorship of Professor Michael Butler.

The views here are ours alone and should not be attributed to the institutions we are connected with.

1

Introduction

Background to the conference • The presuppositions of Bretton Woods • The Bretton Woods conference and the Atlantic City preconference • American goals and preparations • British goals and preparations • Conference organization and schedule • Meetings of the partial conference • Meetings of the full conference • What the conference accomplished • The documents • Our editorial changes • Online companion files • Acknowledgments • References • Sources of chapters

During and shortly after World War II, the Allied nations created a number of institutions aimed at promoting international cooperation and preventing a World War III. Of these, the International Monetary Fund (IMF) and the International Bank for Reconstruction and Development (IBRD or World Bank) are the most influential and successful, arguably surpassing the United Nations. Now 75 years old, they remain important in the world financial system, for their own ability to lend to countries in distress; their role in catalyzing other official and private funding for such countries; and their authority as promoters of best practices in many areas of finance and economic development.

The durability of the IMF and the World Bank has made the process that created them a subject of persistent fascination. Some parts of the process have received far more attention than others. The rival monetary proposals of the U.S. Treasury official Harry Dexter White and the British Treasury adviser John Maynard Keynes have been discussed in hundreds of publications. The July 1944 conference in Bretton Woods, New Hampshire that created the IMF and the World Bank is so well known that the IMF and World Bank are nicknamed the Bretton Woods institutions. Periodically, proposals arise for a "new Bretton Woods," trying to borrow the luster of the original to promote some would-be present-day policy to reform the world economy. The Bretton Woods conference and its effects have been the subject of a number of books and thousands of articles.

Table. Chronology

September 1, 1939	World War II begins in Europe; United States enters the war on December 7, 1941
1940-1941	Harry Dexter White (U.S.) and John Maynard Keynes (UK) begin thinking about postwar world finance
January 1942	United States informally presents proposal for an international stabilization fund at inter-American conference in Rio de Janeiro
April-July 1943	Keynes, White, French, and Canadian plans for an international monetary organization released; Chinese and Norwegian plans not publicly released; informal multinational conference in Washington, June 15-17
April 21, 1944	Joint Statement by Experts on the Establishment of an International Monetary Fund (IMF)
May 26, 1944	United States invites 43 countries to international conference on IMF and Bank for Reconstruction and Development
June 6, 1944	D-Day: Allied liberation of mainland France begins
June 10, 1944	U.S. telegram invites select countries to Atlantic City
June 14, 1944	American delegation arrives in Atlantic City
June 16, 1944	British and other European delegations leave London to board *Queen Mary* bound for New York
June 19, 1944	Many foreign delegations arrive in Atlantic City; informal deliberations begin
June 23, 1944	*Queen Mary* arrives in New York City and the delegations aboard travel to Atlantic City
June 24, 1944	More formal conference deliberations begin
June 30, 1944	Atlantic City conference ends, having developed draft agreements on the IMF and the Bank for Reconstruction and Development; delegates leave for Bretton Woods
July 1, 1944	Bretton Woods conference begins
July 22, 1944	Bretton Woods conference ends with signature of Articles of Agreement for the IMF and the International Bank for Reconstruction and Development (World Bank)

Far less known is the Atlantic City, New Jersey conference in June 1944 that immediately preceded Bretton Woods and established the draft agreements from which Bretton Woods started. A few short summaries of the Atlantic City conference are the total of previous serious writing on the subject.[1] One reason for the lack of attention to Atlantic City has been the lack of published material from the conference. This book fills in a previously sketchy part of the story of the origins of the Bretton Woods institutions. It contains an extensive set of documents from the Atlantic City conference, as well as some relevant preconference documents. Online files contain photographs of the source documents and ancillary material.

Background to the conference

Many accounts exist of British and American planning for the post-World War II international monetary system, with, as we have said, a notable gap concerning the Atlantic City conference. We will just briefly summarize events before mid 1944.

The historical backdrop to the postwar planning of 1944 was a generation of political and financial tumult resulting from World War I (1914-1918) and its aftermath. The war proved devastatingly costly. The countries that fought financed their war spending partly by inflation, whose effects they suppressed through controls on prices of domestic goods. Most had been on some type of gold standard before the war, and during the war most suspended adherence to the gold standard and imposed exchange controls, preventing people from buying or selling foreign currencies without government permission. The money they created to finance their war spending presented them with an unpleasant choice afterwards: devaluing and letting suppressed inflation come out

---

[1] Horsefield (1969, v. 1: 79-88); Bittermann (1971: 68-69); Van Dormael (1978: 156-167), Steil (2013: 192-199); Conway (2014: 183-198). Reinertsen (2017) focuses on the voyage of British and other delegations to the United States aboard the *Queen Mary*, discussed more below. For accounts of some incidents at the conference, see Beyen (1949: 169); Black (1991: 42-43); George Bolton diary; Alice Bourneuf papers; Harrod (1951: 577-584); Harry S. Truman Library and Museum [2012]; Howson (2011: 519-524); Keynes (1980b: 59-71); Mikesell (1994: 33-34; 2000: 39-40); Morgenthau Diaries; Robbins and Meade (1981: 156-166); Skidelsky (2001: 343-346); World Bank Archives Oral History Program (1961: 5-8); and Young (1950: 786). Lionel Robbins's diary is notable for its blunt assessments of people. We have not seen George Bolton's diary.

into the open, possibly generating politically uncontrollable pressures leading to further inflation, or deflating to return to prewar gold parities (exchange rates), which would choke growth. Germany suffered hyperinflation that made its currency worthless and wiped out the savings of millions; at the opposite pole, the United States never officially suspended its prewar gold parity and experienced a severe but short deflationary postwar recession. Britain experienced several years of deflation and sluggish growth on the way to eventually restoring its prewar gold parity in 1925, part of a substantial restoration of the gold standard worldwide. Then, from December 1926 to June 1932, France absorbed all of the increase to the world supply of monetary gold plus some more, raising its share of world monetary holdings from 8 percent to 28 percent. Gold flowed in to buy French francs because changes in policy by the French government and the Bank of France (central bank) gave investors confidence that the franc was now cheap compared to other major currencies. Contrary to standard profit-seeking practice, the Bank of France "sterilized" most of the additional gold, in effect locking it up rather than letting it feed through to higher prices. In the key years of 1929 and 1930 the U.S. Federal Reserve System likewise sterilized increases to its gold reserves.[2] These policies created strong deflationary pressure on prices in gold-standard currencies. The Great Depression that began in 1929 created a downward spiral of distress and default. The countries that recovered fastest were those that ended deflation earliest by devaluing or floating their exchange rates against gold.[3]

The Great Depression shrank world trade. Governments responded with "competitive devaluations" of their exchange rate, higher tariffs, and preferential trade agreements with favored countries. The more open trading system before the Depression was more efficient, but proved unable to withstand political pressure for protectionism.

The monetary and trade mistakes of the late 1920s and early 1930s created political turmoil that led to the rise of Nazism in Germany and intensified Japanese militarism. Then came a second world war, more gigantic and destructive than the first.

To prevent a repeat of the mistakes of the interwar period, the

---

[2] Calculations from Center for Financial Stability, Historical Financial Statistics data set, based on Federal Reserve data on gold holdings and balance sheets of the Banque de France and the Federal Reserve System; Irwin (2012).

[3] Eichengreen (1992), currently the standard history of the interwar monetary system, emphasizes this point.

organizers of framework for the post-World War II global economy developed an array of institutions and policies. On the political side, the United Nations would replace the League of Nations. On the economic side there were to be three major institutions. The International Monetary Fund would restrain competitive devaluations by helping countries experiencing temporary currency problems, but would allow more flexibility in exchange rates than the old gold standard so as to avoid harmful deflations. The International Bank for Reconstruction and Development would speed recovery from war damage and foster economic development in poor countries. And the International Trade Organization would promote reductions in trade barriers. Opposition in the U.S. Senate killed the proposed International Trade Organization. The less ambitious General Agreement on Trade and Tariffs substituted for it until 1995, when the World Trade Organization began.[4]

The two outstanding figures who shaped the Fund and the Bank were the English economist John Maynard Keynes (1883-1946) and his American counterpart Harry Dexter White (1892-1948). Keynes's economist father John Neville Keynes was a lecturer at the University of Cambridge, and his mother was a prominent social reformer who became mayor of Cambridge. Keynes attended England's most prestigious boarding school, Eton College, and returned to Cambridge as a student. He mainly studied mathematics, but read widely in economics on his own. After graduating, he joined the British government's London bureaucracy governing India, but it soon bored him, so he returned to the University of Cambridge as a lecturer in economics. In 1915, he went to work in the British Treasury, where his abilities soon made him pre-eminent in international financial matters. After the war he attended the 1919 Paris peace conference as a member of the British delegation, but resigned in disgust at what he saw as the counterproductive terms that the conference imposed on Germany. He became an international celebrity by writing a best-seller critical of the conference, *The Economic Consequences of the Peace.* Keynes later resumed his connection to the Treasury, as an unpaid adviser. He took no salary because his writing and financial speculations had made him independently wealthy, and because being unpaid left him free to express his views without the strictures that applied to civil

---

[4] The United Nations Relief and Rehabilitation Administration, established in 1943, was important at the time but not intended to last long beyond the war; it closed in 1947. There were also ideas about establishing an international commodity council to regulate buffer stocks of key raw materials, but they gained no traction.

servants. His official title was adviser to the Treasury, but in truth during World War II he was the British government's one-man brain trust for wartime finance. In 1942, he was granted a peerage, becoming Baron Keynes of Tilton (the name of the country house he leased near the English Channel). He had long had a lordly manner; now he was officially a lord. Keynes moved across academic, government, business, and artistic circles with ease, having great influence in all as a writer, adviser, or financier. He was renowned for quicksilver intellect and his ability to turn a phrase.

While at the 1919 Paris conference, Keynes wrote a memorandum on a "Scheme for the Rehabilitation of European Credit and for Financing Relief and Reconstruction." The memo proposed multilateral guarantees for bonds that Germany would issue to help pay reparations for World War I.[5] The guarantee principle was an antecedent to the World Bank. Years later, Keynes's 1930 *Treatise on Money* proposed a Supernational Bank issuing Supernational Bank Money (S.B.M.) analogous to what are now the IMF's Special Drawing Rights (SDRs).[6] (Curiously, an international monetary and financial angle is absent from the book that cemented Keynes's status as the world's most famous economist, 1936's *The General Theory of Employment, Interest and Money*.)

Harry Dexter White came from far humbler circumstances than Keynes. He was the son of Lithuanian Jewish immigrants, part of the first generation in his family to attend college. Although he earned a Ph.D. in economics from Harvard University and won its prize for the best publishable work in economics by a student, he lacked the bent for high theory that academics esteem. He was teaching at a small college in Wisconsin in 1934 when he got an opportunity to work at the Department of the Treasury. He seized it and never returned to academia. White worked mainly on domestic and international monetary matters, and showed industry and intelligence. He first crossed paths with Keynes when the Treasury sent him to Europe in 1935 to assess the views of important people on exchange rate issues. He became involved with efforts to stabilize exchange rates informally among the major currencies. In 1938, U.S. Secretary of the Treasury Henry Morgenthau, Jr., made White director of the new Division of Monetary Research. In that job, White was involved in 1939 and 1940 in a proposal for an Inter-American

---

[5] Baker (1923: 336-346) has the memo, its endorsement by British prime minister David Lloyd George, and its rejection by American president Woodrow Wilson.
[6] Keynes (1930, v. 2: ch. 38, sec. 2, p. 400).

Bank, which died because of opposition in the U.S. Senate. Sometime from February to June 1940 he apparently also wrote memos on "Establishment of a bank to permit substantial aid in the post-war reconstruction" and "Payments assistance to the Allies."[7] When the United States entered World War II in December 1941, Morgenthau quickly put White in charge of all of the Treasury's international affairs.[8]

Besides his influence on the IMF and the World Bank, White is best known today for having passed classified information to American Communists who were spying for the Soviet Union. We can discern no advantage that might have arisen to the Soviet Union had he passed information concerning the Atlantic City conference, though.[9]

World War II stimulated Keynes and White to revisit and elaborate on their earlier ideas for international financial cooperation. On July 25, 1940, a month after the German conquest of France, the German minister of the economy, Walther Funk, gave a speech on the economic reorganization of Europe under Nazi rule. Among other things, Funk envisioned the German Reichsmark becoming the basis of a pan-European currency, with a monetary policy independent to any connection with gold. Funk's speech received wide publicity, and it criticized not only Britain, but the United States, which was not yet in the war.[10]

In 1941, Keynes and White independently wrote plans for a body to coordinate the postwar international financial system. Keynes called his ambitious vision the International Clearing Union. It would have been a global bank for clearing trade among nations, and it would have issued its own unit of account, the bancor (from the French *banque or*, "bank gold"), which would have functioned as a global reserve currency accepted by

---

[7] For the proposed agreement for the Inter-American Bank, see the *Federal Reserve Bulletin*, June 1940: 517-525; see also Rees (1973: 138). We have not seen the 1940 memos, which are listed in the Harry Dexter White Papers, Box 4, Folder 13, "Division Memoranda and Reports from February to July 1940": 14. "Division" is the Division of Monetary Research.

[8] Rees (1973: 58-60, 138); U.S. Department of the Treasury (1939: xvi); U.S. Treasury Department Press Service (press release) No. 29-18, December 20, 1941.

[9] Boughton and Sandilands (2003) and Craig (2004: 83-112) make the case for White's innocence or at least naivety. Haynes and Klehr (1999: 129-145) and Haynes and others (2009: 260) make the, to us, more convincing opposite case.

[10] Funk (1940). During the war, Berlin became the clearing center for many transactions among German-occupied countries (BIS 1942: 30).

national central banks. The rules of the Clearing Union would have penalized countries that accumulated large trade and financial surpluses as well as those that ran large deficits. White called his more modest vision the International Stabilization Fund. It would act a kind of credit union for member countries, but would not issue its own unit of account and would not have rules penalizing countries with large surpluses, since the United States was the chief such country. It would also likely involve less expense to the United States than the Clearing Union. The United States informally presented White's idea at an inter-American conference of foreign ministers in Rio de Janeiro in January 1942.

White and Keynes first saw each other's plans in mid 1942. After further changes, both plans were published in April 1943. The Free French and Canadian governments also issued plans. China and Norway wrote plans but did not publish plans. Because none of these plans were proposed by the world's top two financial powers, they received far less consideration.[11] A year of further negotiation and consultation with other World War II Allied governments followed, including a conference in Washington from June 15-17, 1943.[12] On April 21, 1944, a Joint Statement by Experts on the Establishment of an International Monetary Fund (reproduced in chapter 2) was published simultaneously in the United States, Britain, and other countries. It would serve at the starting-point for most discussion at the Atlantic City conference. The Joint Statement mainly reflected White's vision, because the United States was the world's largest and richest economy; the only major belligerent country that had not suffered extensive damage to its territory; the creditor to the rest of the world; the holder of most of the world's reserves of monetary gold; and therefore the only country that could afford to finance the planned agency. Britain had little choice but to acquiesce, especially given that it was seeking further wartime loans from the United States, termed Lend-Lease, in negotiations that would not conclude until after Bretton Woods.

---

[11] For the Keynes, White, French, and Canadian plans, see Horsefield (1969, v. 3: 3-118). The Chinese and Norwegian plans are in the Harry Dexter White Papers, Box 8, Folders 1 and 2, respectively. For commentary on the Chinese plan, see Helleiner (2014: 192-197). John Parke Young, an American adviser who attended the Atlantic City conference, took the lead in drafting the Chinese plan.

[12] The conference was announced in U.S. Department of the Treasury, Press Service (press release) No. 36-3, April 6, 1943. The United States invited 37 countries; 19 attended.

The presuppositions of Bretton Woods

Keynes, White, and their colleagues operated within an intellectual framework that foreclosed some options that previous or later experience has shown to be economically feasible, and it is worth noting them.

It is a commonplace among economists and historians that in the several decades before World War I, the international monetary system worked more smoothly than it did between World War I and World War II.[13] Changes in gold parities were rare compared to later years. Exchange controls were rarer still. An important reason that the system operated smoothly is, we think, that central banks were far fewer before World War I. Most countries outside of Europe did not have them. Among those that did not, for example, were three of the largest and most populous economies, the United States, China, and India. Competitive issue of currency by commercial banks, without any central bank, was widespread.[14] Where central banks existed, many were privately owned and operated more on a strictly commercial basis than they do today. Day-to-day government involvement in monetary policy was rarer.

Economists and policy makers of the time viewed central banking as the most advanced arrangement and did not fully appreciate its possible shortcomings either on a theoretical level or in political practice. Monetary conferences sponsored by the League of Nations in Brussels in 1920 and Genoa in 1922 called for nations that did not yet have central banks to establish them. Central banking was hence one of the presuppositions of Bretton Woods. Not until the 1970s did economists even begin to reconsider whether central banking was in fact better than what it replaced.[15] Today, cryptocurrencies are bringing the question in more immediate form from academic analysis into practice.

Another presupposition of Bretton Woods was that exchange rates should be pegged. Many countries had had individual experience with floating exchange rates, but there was no experience of all the major currencies floating simultaneously.[16] Under the gold standard, floating

---

[13] Keynes (1919: 9-10) himself wrote an eloquent lament for that bygone era.

[14] Schuler (1992).

[15] For an academic summary, see Selgin and White (1994); for up to date discussion on the subject, se the Alt-M Web site, <www.alt-m.org>.

[16] During World War I, most belligerents suspended the gold standard but imposed exchange controls that prevented trading at floating exchange rates. Between World War I and World War II there were periods when among the

was usually associated with currency depreciation and inflation because countries abandoned the gold standard when they lacked the gold reserves or the resolve to maintain the existing pegged parity. The experience of the interwar period was even worse: Germany and some of its neighbors suffered hyperinflations. The Great Depression showed the other side of the coin, the costs of deflation under pegged exchange rates. So, the designers of the Bretton Woods system wanted exchange rates to be adjustable, unlike the expectation for them before World War I, but generally stable. They tended to think in terms of nominal exchange rates rather than in terms of real (inflation-adjusted) exchange rates.

A final important presupposition of Bretton Woods, related to views on exchange rates, was the desirability of capital controls — exchange controls restricting cross-border investment in deposits, stocks, and bonds. The designers of the Bretton Woods system thought that current-account transactions, involving payment for goods and services, should if possible be unrestricted, to promote efficient patterns of international trade. They saw no similar urgency for capital movements, involving the buying and selling of stocks, bonds, deposits, and the like, because they had seen how speculative flows of capital had aggravated the difficulty of preserving pegged exchange rates in the interwar period. Much of the difficulty arose because, as we have mentioned, in the early interwar years the exchange rates in question were not devalued or at least not devalued enough to balance supply and demand; later, French monetary policy put deflationary pressure on other countries and their currencies. The IMF agreement encouraged members to make current transactions free of exchange controls, but did not and still does not do the same for capital transactions.

The result of these presuppositions was what the political scientist John Ruggie later termed embedded liberalism.[17] The pre-World War I era of laissez faire seemed politically infeasible. The interwar practice of every country for itself had been economically disastrous. The Bretton Woods institutions liberalized trade and financial flows compared to the interwar period, but embedded them in a framework that condoned government economic policies far more activist than was typical before World War I.

The system of pegged exchange rates among member currencies that

---

three leading currencies — the U.S. dollar, pound sterling, and French franc — two were floating, but never all three.

[17] Ruggie (1982).

the IMF agreement established at Bretton Woods lasted only a generation. The United States, the key country of the system, was unwilling to restrain monetary policy sufficiently to preserve the exchange rate of the dollar with gold. Starting in 1961, the Federal Reserve System began policies that eroded its gold reserves over the next decade from approximately 500 million troy ounces to 300 million over a decade,[18] even as the world gold supply and the U.S. money supply increased. The United States in effect abandoned the gold standard on August 15, 1971, and all other countries followed. Some currencies continue to have pegged exchange rates to others, but the currencies of the large, rich economies have generally floated.[19] The resulting "nonsystem," as it has been termed, has lasted longer than the Bretton Woods monetary system did, proving to be politically as well as economically durable. Moreover, it has seen a relaxation of capital controls. Full freedom from exchange controls, for capital transactions as well as for current transactions, has spread from the handful of countries where it existed under the Bretton Woods monetary system to many more countries. Without the need to defend a particular exchange rate, it has been easier for governments to relax exchange controls.

Whatever criticisms one might make of the Bretton Woods monetary system today, it was a big improvement over the interwar system. It coincided with rapid, widely shared economic growth; high growth in international trade; and lower volatility in financial systems than its predecessors or successors.[20] Its good record accounts for the continuing interest in it.

The Bretton Woods conference and the Atlantic City preconference

A telegram from U.S. president Franklin Roosevelt to British prime minister Winston Churchill on February 23, 1944 had mentioned "a possible convocation of an United Nations Monetary Conference."[21] ("United Nations" was originally a term for the World War II Allies.) By

---

[18] Bao and others (2018, spreadsheet).
[19] Many European countries have joined in a single currency, the euro. They have fixed exchange rates internally but the euro floats against the U.S. dollar.
[20] Bordo and others (2001: 59). The Great Recession that the North Atlantic economies experienced in 2008-09 strengthens the claim of the Bretton Woods era as the least financially volatile.
[21] Telegram no. 476, Roosevelt to Churchill, February 23, 1944, in U.S. Department of State (1967: Document 9).

March, the U.S. Treasury was already planning for a conference.[22] Roosevelt approved a conference on April 4, in the lead-up to publication of the Joint Statement on the IMF.[23] The next day, U.S. Secretary of the Treasury Henry J. Morgenthau, Jr. sent a telegram to his British counterpart, Chancellor of the Exchequer Sir John Anderson. Morgenthau proposed to convene an international conference on the International Monetary Fund and the Bank for Reconstruction and Development during May.[24] In a follow-up telegram of April 20, Morgenthau specified that he planned to call the conference to begin in the last week of May and that he hoped that the chief financial officer (in Britain's case, Anderson) would head each delegation. Morgenthau also mentioned "a drafting committee to begin work as soon as a conference is officially called." The idea of a drafting committee was not new; it had been broached at least as early as 1943.[25]

The Bank had received less attention than the Fund. Keynes's

---

[22] Telephone call from Henry Morgenthau, Jr. (U.S. Secretary of the Treasury) to William Adams Brown, Jr. (Department of State), March 31, 1944, in Morgenthau Diaries (v. 716: 309). American plans for a conference were of long standing. A memo of May 16, 1942 written by White for Morgenthau to send to President Roosevelt, contained a tentative proposal for an international monetary conference lasting 22 days, which turned out to be the length of the Bretton Woods conference. See Harry Dexter White papers, Box 7, Folder 2; also Morgenthau Diaries (v. 526: 111-153).

[23] Letter, Morgenthau to Cordell Hull (U.S. Secretary of State), April 5, 1944, in Morgenthau Diaries (v. 717: 185).

[24] Telegram no. 2651, Morgenthau to Anderson via Cordell Hull (U.S. Secretary of State) and John Winant (U.S. ambassador in London), April 5, 1944, in U.S. Department of State (1967: Document 77). The standard procedure was for communications from the U.S. Treasury to the British Treasury to go through the U.S. Department of State to the U.S. embassy in London, and for communications from the British Treasury to the U.S. Treasury to go through the British Foreign Office to the British embassy in Washington. Messages between cabinet officials were almost always written by and often intended mainly for lower-level officials working most directly with the issues discussed. So, a message from Morgenthau to Anderson would have been written by White or one of his subordinates for Keynes or someone in effect working for Keynes.

[25] Telegram no. 3175, Morgenthau to Anderson via Hull and Winant, April 20, 1944, in U.S. Department of State (1967: Document 91). A British message of the same day from Anderson for Morgenthau made the same suggestion (referred to in telegram no. 3821, Anderson to Washington [British embassy], May 2, 1944, UK National Archives, T 231/359. For the 1943 mention of a drafting committee, see Keynes (1980a: 374).

proposed International Clearing Union would have been about three times as big as the IMF initially was. Its scale and scope of functions would have made a Reconstruction Bank-type organization superfluous. The United States had published a Bank proposal on November 24, 1943 (chapter 3). Like the proposal for the Fund, it was the work of Harry Dexter White. The Chinese government had commented on it privately.[26] There seems to have been no other foreign commentary until April 13, 1944, when British experts had sent their comments on it to the British embassy in Washington for transmission to American experts. Because it was sent by "snail mail" rather by telegram, it did not reach the embassy until April 20.[27] Meanwhile, the Americans had prepared a draft statement on the Bank — not a proposed draft agreement, but a less detailed statement of some important points — that Morgenthau had sent to Anderson by telegram on April 17, 1944.[28] Keynes's reaction to the draft statement and to a document sent with it "Questions and Answers on the Bank" (which would undergo further revisions before the Atlantic City conference) was that

> A serious attempt has been made, without actually altering the text of the Scripture, to give it a slant in the direction we desire. In the aggregate the glosses of the Talmudist bring the proposal within striking distance of what we want.[29]

In a telegram of April 26, Morgenthau proposed to Anderson that on May 1 the U.S. government as host should send formal invitations to a

---

[26] Helleiner (2014: 196-198).

[27] Note from Redvers Opie (counselor, British embassy in Washington) to Harry Dexter White, April 20, 1944, in U.S. Department of State (1967: Document 88). Keep in mind how much costlier and slower communications were then. Transatlantic telephone calls were very expensive, hence rare. Diplomatic telegrams had to be written by the sender, delivered by hand to a transmitting office, encoded, transmitted after possibly waiting in a queue, decoded at the receiving end, and delivered by hand to the recipient. The process might take from a couple of hours to a couple of days depending on the volume of telegraph traffic and the urgency of the message. "Snail mail" might be carried by air or by ship.

[28] Telegram no. 3076, Morgenthau to Anderson via Hull and Winant, April 17, 1944, in U.S. Department of State (1967: Document 86).

[29] Memo from Keynes to Sir (Sigisimund) David Waley and Sir Wilfrid Eady (two of Keynes's nominal superiors), May 30, 1944, T 247/32.

conference on "the establishment of a monetary fund, and I hope a bank as well"; that a drafting committee of eight to ten countries meet in Washington about May 10 to prepare a conference agenda and drafts; and that the conference begin about May 26.[30]

The proposed schedule was too tight for the British given their need to achieve support for the Joint Statement in Parliament; to consult with the British Dominions; and to arrange transportation, including for European governments in exile they hoped to bring with them. Transatlantic passenger transportation at the time was by ship, and involved logistical and security considerations that were considerably more complex than in peacetime. Transport into and out of Britain remained far riskier than for other free Allied countries because of Britain's location on the front line of the war. Moreover, especially on such short notice, it was unlikely that Anderson himself would be able to attend the conference, as the Americans wished. On May 2, Anderson sent a telegram to the British embassy in Washington explaining these objections. He did say that a conference might be possible in early June. The tone of the message was one of concern that the Americans were racing ahead to reach an agreement without adequate time for Britain and other countries to voice objections or propose amendments.[31]

Further telegrams and conversations about the conference schedule and organization followed. The back-and-forth provoked one of Keynes's most biting private outbursts. Keynes was critical of American plans that would assure attendance at the full conference by many countries whose role in the prewar international financial system had been minor, while seeming more casual about attendance by a number of European governments in exile. He remarked to senior British Treasury officials,

> 21 countries have been invited which clearly have nothing to contribute and will merely encumber the ground, namely Columbia, Costa Rica, Dominica [Dominican Republic], Ecuador, [El] Salvador, Guatemala, Haiti, Honduras, Liberia, Nicaragua, Panama, Paraguay, Philippines, Venezuela, Peru, Uruguay, Ethiopia

---

[30] Telegram no. 3288, Morgenthau to Anderson via Hull and Winant, April 25, 1944, in Morgenthau Diaries (v. 724: 142-143).
[31] Telegram no. 3821, Anderson to Washington, May 2, 1944, UK National Archives, T 231/359. On April 28, Winant had already sent Morgenthau a telegram anticipating the British objections. Telegram no. 3507, Winant to Morgenthau, April 28, 1944, paraphrased in Morgenthau Diaries (v. 725: 47-49).

Iceland, Iran, Iraq, Luxemburg. The most monstrous monkey-house assembled for years.[32]

Keynes preferred a less multilateral style of negotiation, preferably with himself as one of the negotiators. (His second draft for the International Clearing Union proposed that it be founded, and by implication dominated, by the United States and the United Kingdom.[33]) On May 13, apparently, he expressed hope to a U.S. embassy official in London that Anglo-American talks on the Bank in parallel with the monetary conference might make sufficient progress that the Bank might be included as a subject at the conference before it ended.[34]

We omit a detailed review of Anglo-American wrangling about the conference schedule.[35] The conclusion was that on May 26, about five weeks after the Joint Statement had been issued, the U.S. government issued an invitation to "a conference of the United Nations and the nations associated with them, for the purpose of formulating definite proposals for an International Monetary Fund and possibly a Bank for Reconstruction and Development." This invitation was to what would be the Bretton Woods conference, though the location was not yet set.[36] The United States invited 43 countries; all accepted. Several were under German or Japanese occupation; the invitation was to their governments in exile rather than the governments established by the occupation powers.[37]

---

[32] Memo from Keynes to Sir David Waley and Sir Wilfrid Eady, May 30, 1944, p. 2, T 247/35, in Keynes (1980b: 42).

[33] Keynes (1980a: 61).

[34] Telegram from Howard Bucknell, Jr. (U.S. embassy, London) to Hull, May 13, 1944, in U.S. Department of State (1967: Document 32).

[35] For details, see U.S. Department of State (1967: Documents 91, 96-98); Morgenthau Diaries (v. 727: 143-146); UK National Archives, T 231/359.

[36] Circular telegram from Hull, May 25, 1944, in U.S. Department of State (1967: Document 99); see also UNMFC (1948, v. 1: 3-5). A circular telegram of June 3 gave Bretton Woods as the conference location and contained detailed information on arrangements.

[37] Australia, Belgium, Bolivia, Brazil, Canada, Chile, China, Colombia, Costa Rica, Cuba, Czechoslovakia, Dominican Republic, Ecuador, Egypt, El Salvador, Ethiopia, France, Greece, Guatemala, Haiti, Honduras, Iceland, India, Iran, Iraq, Liberia, Luxembourg, Mexico, Netherlands, New Zealand, Nicaragua, Norway, Panama, Paraguay, Peru, Philippine Commonwealth, Poland, Union of South Africa, Union of Soviet Socialist Republics, United Kingdom, Uruguay, Venezuela, Yugoslavia. Observers sympathetic to the Allies attended from

Two days before, Redvers Opie, the economic counselor in Washington at the British embassy in Washington, had met with Harry Dexter White and representatives of the Soviet Union to discuss the composition of the drafting committee and how to disclose its existence to countries not represented.[38] On June 1, Opie reported that White had telephoned him that morning to say that he was thinking of June 15 as the starting date for the drafting committee.[39] During late May and early June there was further Anglo-American wrangling, now about the composition of the drafting committee. The British, for instance, got India (then still a British colony) and Greece included in the invitation list; the United States got the Philippines (then still an American colony). On June 6, Edward Wood, Viscount Halifax, the British ambassador in Washington, reported that Morgenthau and White now wanted to have preliminary informal conversations with foreign representatives from June 19 and formal meetings of the drafting committee, which the Americans were now calling the Agenda Committee, starting June 24.[40]

Initially, the plan was for both the drafting committee "preconference" and the full conference to meet at Bretton Woods.[41] The Mount Washington Hotel, the site of the Bretton Woods conference, was being prepared for reopening after having being closed since 1942, and repairs would turn out to be not quite complete even by July 1, when the full

---

Denmark, which was occupied but had no government in exile. The United States was of course present as the host. The French delegation at Atlantic City and Bretton Woods was that of the Comité français de la Libération nationale (French Committee of National Liberation), or Free France. By late 1943 it controlled Corsica and all French overseas possessions except Indochina. The Free French government declared itself the provisional government of mainland France on June 3, 1944, but the other major Allies continued to recognize the rival, German-aligned Vichy government until October 1944.

[38] Telegram no. 391 Remac, Opie via Viscount Halifax to Foreign Office, May 27, 1944, UK National Archives, T 231/359.

[39] Telegram no. 410 Remac, Opie via Viscount Halifax to Foreign Office, June 1, 1944, T 231/359.

[40] As an example of the wrangling, see telegram no. 414 Remac, Opie via Viscount Halifax to Foreign Office, June 1, 1944, T 231/359. On India, see telegram no. 3048, Viscount Halifax to Foreign Office, June 6, 1944, T 231/359. The Indian delegation, though mainly Britons, showed surprising independence at Atlantic City and Bretton Woods. On dates, see telegram no. 394 Remac, Opie via Viscount Halifax to Foreign Office, May 24, 1944, T 231/359.

[41] Telegram no. 3048, Viscount Halifax to Foreign Office, June 6, 1944, T 231/359.

conference began. The disrepair of the Mount Washington Hotel made another location imperative for the drafting committee. The first mention we have seen that the drafting committee meeting would be at Atlantic City dates from June 6.[42]

Besides the availability of rooms, Atlantic City had other important advantages. Because of its location on the ocean, it was cooler than Washington, where the American delegation worked, or New York, where travelers from London arrived. Keynes suffered from an infection in his heart valves, which in those days before antibiotics was incurable and would to the heart attack that would kill him in 1946. Great heat would have taxed Keynes's health. On May 24, he wrote to Harry Dexter White, "For God's sake do not take us to Washington in July, which would surely be a most unfriendly act."[43] Atlantic City was far better suited to Keynes's health: in a letter he dictated on his last day there, he described the weather during his stay as "most comfortable and endurable." Keynes's wife, Lydia Lopokova, accompanied him to Atlantic City and Bretton Woods to tend to his health.[44]

Also, Atlantic City was accessible from Washington and New York but, in those days long before e-mail, distant enough to enable the American delegates to put their other work aside and concentrate on the conference.[45] White was able to operate with minimal oversight from Secretary of the Treasury Henry Morgenthau, Jr. and from the

---

[42] "Pre-Conference Plans," transcript of U.S. Treasury internal meeting, June 6, 1944, in Morgenthau Diaries (v. 740: 84-85).

[43] Keynes (1980: 27). President Roosevelt, who was quite familiar with Washington summers, suggested Portsmouth, New Hampshire as a possible location for what would become the Bretton Woods conference. Harry Dexter White, "Memorandum of a Conference at the White House, May 18, 1944, 12:30 P.M.," in Morgenthau Presidential Diaries (v. 5: 1369); see also "Date of Monetary Conference," U.S. Treasury internal meeting, May 18, 1944, in Morgenthau Diaries (v. 733: 25).

[44] Letter, Keynes to Sir Richard Hopkins ("Hoppy"; Permanent Secretary of the UK Treasury), June 30, 1944, T 231/365, in Keynes (1980b: 70); letter from H.E. Brooks (UK Treasury) to Lauren Casaday (U.S. Treasury attaché in London), June 8, 1944, T 231/365. Telegram no. 435 Remac, Viscount Halifax to Foreign Office (marked "Special (Treasury)," probably from Opie) indicates that "I understand it is particularly to suit Keynes that the Agenda Committee should meet in Atlantic City and not in Washington."

[45] The first two points came up in "Arrangements for Monetary Conference," transcript of a meeting of U.S. Treasury and State Department officials, June 1, 1944, Morgenthau Diaries (v. 738: 52-56).

Department of State — a point of contention, as we will see.

Finally, the Claridge Hotel, the site of the conference, had recently hosted another international conference, so the U.S. government could be confident that it could handle the meetings. The United Nations Relief and Rehabilitation Administration (UNRRA) had held its inaugural conference at the hotel in November 1943. The 44 countries that signed the UNRRA agreement in Washington, D.C. just before UNRRA's Atlantic City conference were the same countries that sent delegations to Bretton Woods. The first time that group of countries had met was the United Nations Conference on Food and Agriculture at Hot Springs, Virginia conference in June 1943; the culmination of their efforts would be the United Nations Conference on International Organization in San Francisco from April to June 1945 to establish the United Nations.

Atlantic City and the Claridge Hotel were accustomed to hosting conferences for a wide variety of groups. During the monetary conference the Claridge also hosted a conference for practitioners of homeopathic medicine. The monetary conference meetings were at the Claridge, and most of the attendees roomed there, but the conference directories show that some stayed at the nearby Shelburne Hotel, Hotel Brighton, Madison Hotel, and Marlborough-Blenheim Hotel.[46]

On June 10 the U.S. government sent a telegram officially inviting to Atlantic City most of the countries that would attend. It was merely a formality, since they had already been notified informally. The telegram read:

> In connection with the United Nations Monetary and Financial Conference to be held in the United States beginning July 1, the American technical experts in consultation with those of the United Kingdom, the U.S.S.R. and China are inviting the technical experts of a number of other countries to cooperate with them in the preparation of a draft agenda which will be submitted to the United Nations Monetary and Financial Conference for its consideration.

---

[46] "Homeopaths Meet Here," *Atlantic City Press,* June 26, 1944; Beyen (1949: 169); room directory of foreign delegates as of June 20, U.S. National Archives RG 56, Box 1, Folder A-3; room directory of U.S. delegates as of June 24, RG 82, Box 42, Folder "Atlantic City Drafting Committee"; room directory of foreign delegates as of June 26, same folder; and "List of Those Present at the Meeting of the Pre-Conference Agenda Committee at Atlantic City, June 24-June 30, 1944," RG 82, Box 1, Folder A-9.

The countries invited are the following:
Australia, Belgium, Brazil, Canada, Cuba, Czechoslovakia, India, Mexico, Netherlands, the Philippines, and the French Committee of National Liberation.[47]

The Philippines did not attend the Atlantic City conference, while Chile, Greece, and Norway, not mentioned in the telegram, did. The conference thus had 17 countries.

Some readers may wonder at this point why it took thousands of hours of work over three and a half years and multiple meetings, including at Atlantic City, to produce the Bretton Woods agreements, which are only the length of a couple of average book chapters. The answer is that achieving international agreement on important matters requires much thinking, writing, discussing, arguing, and amending to satisfy everybody. One of us has been on the periphery of international economic negotiations for some years in his job in Harry Dexter White's old haunts, and has seen that it is still the case that delegates to an international gathering will agonize for hours over a sentence or even a single word that they consider important. Even after the agreements were signed at Bretton Woods, questions about their interpretation persisted.[48]

American goals and preparations

Historians have often emphasized the differences between American and British goals leading up to the Bretton Woods agreements — particularly, American determination to displace Britain as the world's leading financial power. We think it at least as important to emphasize the goals the two countries had in common. Both wanted to steer a middle course between what they saw as the defects of pre-World War I laissez faire and those of interwar policies that had fragmented the world economy into sometimes hostile blocs. We also think it is important to remember that although the United States and Britain played the largest roles in establishing the Bretton Woods institutions, they were not the only parties involved. The Bretton Woods institutions would not have had legitimacy had they been simply an Anglo-American or, even more narrowly, a purely American arrangement dictated to other countries.

---

[47] U.S. Department of State, outgoing circular telegram, June 10, 1944, in Morgenthau Diaries (v. 742: 108).
[48] See for instance Keynes (1980b: 140-195).

China and the Soviet Union were proud enough that they would have refused to sign agreements that failed to give them what they considered a proper degree of influence, and the Soviet Union wound up not ratifying the agreements after it had signed them at Bretton Woods. Latin American countries suffered no wartime attacks and therefore had no need to supplicate for funds for postwar reconstruction, though they did want loans for economic development. And, as we will discuss later, it is evident from the minute that delegates besides those of the United States and Britain also made important contributions to the Atlantic City conference.

The American Technical Group (or Committee), as the American delegation called itself, was an assemblage of experts spanning a number of departments and agencies. It first met on May 28, 1942.[49] As the Atlantic City conference approached, it met with Secretary of the Treasury Henry J. Morgenthau, Jr. in Washington on June 8, 1944 for what seems to have been a perfunctory initial meeting (chapter 4). The group arrived in Atlantic City on June 14.[50] Because the Atlantic City conference would make no final proposals, most countries that attended, including the United States, refrained from sending high-level political figures, reserving them for Bretton Woods.

The American Technical Group was 27 members strong at Atlantic City. It core was staff from the Treasury's Division of Monetary Research, which Harry Dexter White directed. The division covered domestic and international monetary matters, which the war had fused to an unusual degree. White was also the chairman of the American Technical Group. He took with him so many key Treasury staff on international affairs that back in Washington, Morgenthau on June 22 asked White's deputy Harold Glasser, only half in jest, "You are staying here, aren't you? You are not going to this Conference, are you?....Because we have to have someone here."[51] The American Technical Group also included representatives of the Federal Reserve System, both the Board of Governors in Washington and the regional Federal Reserve Banks; the Department of State; Department of Commerce; Securities and Exchange Commission; Export-Import Bank; the Foreign Economic

---

[49] Young (1950: 779).
[50] "To Map Monetary Parley Agenda," *New York Times*, June 15, 1944: 28; memorandum for the Secretary from Harry Dexter White, June 22, 1944, in Morgenthau Diaries (v. 746: 139b).
[51] Meeting in Morgenthau's office, June 22, 1944, in Morgenthau Diaries (v. 746: 97).

Administration, which ceased operations soon after the war ended; and the private sector, in the form of a prominent Chicago banker who belonged to a Federal Reserve advisory council. A number of the American delegation were lawyers — a profession that Keynes disliked for what he saw as its narrow spirit. At Bretton Woods he grumbled that the United States was "a lawyer-ridden land."[52]

For White, Atlantic City was the opportunity to forge the American technicians into a close-knit team. White stressed to Morgenthau, "What we are doing is whipping the draft into shape."[53] Atlantic City functioned as a two-week training camp. Even though the Americans had the first days of the conference to themselves, their meetings were dense and arduous, usually spanning roughly fourteen hours and consisting largely of drafting sessions. The understanding was that once the negotiations at Bretton Woods began, opportunities would be scarce for the Americans to consult with one another. Therefore, unless drilled in precisely what they — or more realistically, White — wanted at Bretton Woods, the Americans faced being thrown off course by other delegations. Nevertheless, despite their taxing schedule, the Americans were able to enjoy some pleasure in spending two weeks of the summer on the Jersey Shore — even if only briefly. With the Claridge Hotel sitting just a block away from the boardwalk, members of the American secretariat had the inspiration to insist that White host the first meeting outdoors on the beach. After initial hesitations White ultimately relented.[54]

The Americans used their time away from the office routine of Washington to work intensively on many details of the draft IMF agreement and on the American proposal for the Bank. (The Bank at this stage was called the Bank for Reconstruction and Development; the Bretton Woods conference attached "International" to the front of its name; the moniker "World Bank" was used privately even before the Bank came into existence and was used publicly as early as 1946.[55]) The

---

[52] UNMFC (1948, v. 1: 1109); Acheson (1969: 83-84).

[53] Telephone conversation between Morgenthau and White, June 22, 1944, in Morgenthau Diaries (v. 746: 134).

[54] Conway (2014: 183).

[55] A memo of May 16, 1942 written by White for Morgenthau to send to President Roosevelt, contains the first use we have seen of the term World Bank, calling the organization "a World Bank for Reconstruction and Development." See Harry Dexter White papers, Box 7, Folder 2. From the inaugural meeting of the Bank and the Fund at Savannah, Georgia in March 1946, there is a photo of Keynes holding a document headed "World Fund and Bank" (Skidelsky 2001:

American Technical Group divided itself into working groups to prepare material for the consideration of other delegations when they arrived or for internal use as position papers. Only days before arriving in Atlantic City, the group had completed two long background documents that it later distributed to the other delegations, *Questions and Answers on the International Monetary Fund* and *Questions and Answers on the Bank for Reconstruction and Development*.[56]

The paper blizzard that the Americans generated was in the service of certain goals. One was to do considerable work on the drafts for the Fund and possibly the Bank, but to avoid reaching any final agreement, which required the approval of at least Morgenthau and possibly even Roosevelt. Another goal was to beat away British attempts to use the British Commonwealth or alliances with like-minded European countries to outmaneuver the United States on questions of governance. Although the Atlantic City conference did not discuss quotas (capital subscriptions to the IMF), the United States wanted a quota larger than the combined Commonwealth quota. Such a large quota would also give the United States greater voting power than the Commonwealth, since voting power was to depend mainly on quotas.[57] Finally, as the only major participant in the war that had not suffered extensive damage to its productive capacity, the United States was going to be the major net lender to other countries through the Bank and the Fund. To the Americans it was vital to ensure that the Bank and the Fund did not have blank checks on the U.S. Treasury.

Morgenthau relinquished to White the responsibility for planning the Atlantic City and Bretton Woods conferences. Morgenthau had no technical expertise in international monetary matters. Morgenthau could thereby spend the weeks of Atlantic City in Washington, where he was focused on an entirely different matter of importance: helping President Roosevelt prepare for the upcoming re-election campaign.[58] The only real

---

second illustration following 392; the caption for the photo, placing it at Atlantic City, is in error).

[56] U.S. Department of the Treasury (1944a, b). These documents should not be confused with two memos that circulated only to American officials, "Questions at Issue on the Fund" and "Questions at Issue on the Bank," for which see Morgenthau Diaries (v. 747: 232-249).

[57] The British had accepted that Commonwealth votes should not exceed American votes. Telegram, Treasury to Opie via Foreign Office and British embassy Washington, Camer no. 304, April 15, 1944, T 247/29.

[58] Connway (2014: 197).

oversight that White received during the final planning stages and early days of Atlantic City was from the State Department. It insisted on participating in draft plans, negotiating independently with other countries, and constantly demanding updates from the Treasury — all within its rights, but an annoyance for White, who desired full control over the conference. White successfully kept Dean Acheson, assistant secretary of state, away from Atlantic City, but Acheson sent the economist John Parke Young to monitor the conference.[59] Ultimately, however, White was in control of the proceedings at Atlantic City. Therefore, in addition to developing a clear American position, White had the position to push his vision of the Fund without resistance from other high American officials.

Since no real negotiations were being concluded at Atlantic City, White did not see the urgency of frequent contact with Morgenthau.[60] He gave Morgenthau no updates the whole first week that the American Technical Group was in Atlantic City. On June 22, the same day Morgenthau griped to Harold Glasser about the absence of key Treasury international staff in Washington, he chided White by telephone:

Morgenthau: I don't know what's going on other than I hear when you're short or bath towels or something like that…

White: (Laughs) Well, I didn't know we were.

Morgenthau: But other than that, I don't — I haven't the faintest idea. I don't know…

White: Well, I can tell you very briefly.

Morgenthau: Well, now, I mean — at any time, am I going to be informed between now and the first [of July, when the Bretton Woods conference starts] of what's going on and what I'm supposed to…

White: I'll send you a memorandum.

…

Morgenthau: Yeah, but look; Harry, you're leaving me completely high and dry and all the rest of the American delegates, and then you expect us to come up there and sign on the dotted line, and it won't work. It just won't…"

---

[59] Conway (2014: 185). Acheson (1969: 82), who had briefly been under secretary of the Treasury, remarked of White years later that "I have often differed, sometimes violently, with his policies."

[60] Conway (2014: 187).

White: "Well, I was going to suggest that...."
Morgenthau: "I mean it just won't work. It's very nice, I mean, I know you are working your head off, but you're leaving all the rest of us completely high and dry."[61]

White sent a long memo that very day to mollify Morgenthau.[62] It worked: Morgenthau did not go to Atlantic City or send anyone in his place. White sent further memos to Morgenthau on June 25, 26, and 27. He also returned to Washington so as to be present at a meeting in Morgenthau's office at 9:30 a.m. on June 30, the last day of the conference.[63]

British goals and preparations

The Americans were puzzled by what they saw as British delays in the months leading up to the release of the Joint Statement. The U.S. ambassador in London, John Winant, offered an explanation: "a majority of the directors of the Bank of England [the British central bank] are opposed to the program" because they were afraid that it would result in the pound sterling losing its international prominence. The directors were members of leading British financial firms and hence represented one of Britain's most powerful interest groups. On the other side, Sir John Anderson (to repeat, the Chancellor of the Exchequer), Keynes, and Thomas Catto, the new governor of the Bank of England, all favored the proposal.[64]

Under the rules of the British political system, release of the Joint Statement as an official government pronouncement made it subject to debate in Parliament. The British War Cabinet on May 5, 1944 discussed what line to take both in response to the American invitation to a conference and to a motion in the House of Commons scheduled for

---

[61] Telephone call between Morgenthau and White, June 22, in Morgenthau Diaries (v. 746: 133-134).

[62] Memorandum for the Secretary from Harry Dexter White, June 22, 1944, in Morgenthau Diaries (v. 746: 139b-139gg).

[63] Memorandum for the Secretary from Harry Dexter White, June 25, 1944, in Morgenthau Diaries (v. 747: 60a-60hh); Morgenthau (v. 747, 100a-100qqq, 141a-141v; v. 748: 226).

[64] Telegram no. 2990, Winant to Morgenthau via Hull, April 12, 1944, in U.S. Department of State (1967: Document 81); see also Moggridge (1992: 734).

May 10 that the Joint Statement provided a suitable foundation for further international consultation. The Cabinet concluded that the Parliamentary motion was sufficiently vague that the government could accept it and that Britain would be willing to send delegates to a conference but that they would not have the power to commit the government.[65]

The motion the House of Commons debated on May 10 was, "That this House considers that the Statement of Principles contained in CMD. 6519 provides a suitable foundation for further international consultation with a view to improved monetary co-operation after the war." Members expressed concern about possible curtailment of British monetary sovereignty, but approved the motion.[66] There was also a parallel but less important debate in the House of Lords on May 23, in which Keynes participated.[67]

In a telegram the next day summarizing the debate, Anderson told Morgenthau that if the Americans issued an invitation to the conference, Britain would gladly follow at the earliest date that security concerns permitted.[68] Those "security concerns" included preparations for D-Day, the Allied landings in Normandy to begin the liberation of mainland France, which would occur on June 6.

For the British government, the IMF and the Bank were important, but not urgent. The urgent thing was to secure sufficient financing during the last phase of the war to avoid the kind of financial collapse that so many belligerents had suffered in World War I. Victory was within sight, but achieving it would still be costly. The British government was already heavily indebted to governments and subjects within its empire and sphere of influence, notably India and Egypt. The United States was the only plausible source of further large-scale finance. Britain had already

---

[65] "Conclusions of a Meeting of the War Cabinet held at 10 Downing St., S.W.1, on Friday, 5th May, 1944, at 3 p.m.," UK National Archives, CAB 65/42/20; W.M. (44), 62nd Conclusions, Minute 1, Confidential Annex, CAB 65/46.

[66] The proposer of the motion was Walter Elliott of the Unionist Party. The British government at the time was a coalition that included all parties. *Hansard*, House of Commons, 5th series, v. 399, columns 1935-2046. Cmd. (Command paper) 6519 was a publication by the government for Parliament containing the Joint Statement and a preface explaining its major differences with the Keynes plan. Horsefield (1969, v. 3: 128-135) reprints it.

[67] *Hansard*, House of Lords, 5th series, v. 131, columns 834-883.

[68] Message from the Chancellor of the Exchequer [Anderson] to Mr. Morgenthau, May 11, 1944, UK National Archives, T 231/359.

lost the contest between the Keynes and the White plans because of its weak financial position. It was willing to sacrifice influence in the IMF and the Bank if necessary to have access to continued financing from the United States, which was occurring through the provisions of the Lend-Lease so-called program. The Atlantic City and Bretton Woods conferences would however give Britain an opportunity to bend the framework of the IMF more to its liking, and advance an alternative to the American proposal on the Bank.

Keynes identified the benefits of developing European solidarity as a strategy for conference negotiations. The British thus began planning to make collaboration a possibility as early as possible. On May 12, Keynes suggested a shared transport to the conference:

> If the Washington party comes off, I suggest that on this occasion we might go out of our way to facilitate the travelling arrangements of the Allies, making all the necessary facilities for them so far as they are made on this side and it depends on us. I believe that this would be much appreciated and there might be some further useful discussion on the ship.[69]

Once Keynes had proposed joint travel, other officials moved quickly to implement the suggestion. Transatlantic commercial airplane flights had begun shortly before World War II but were suspended during the war. Transatlantic passenger travel other than for very important individual persons who could hitch rides on military aircraft was therefore by ship. Civilian passengers had to compete with military needs for space, and scheduling was at the mercy of the vagaries of war, so securing transport would take some weeks.

On June 8, Sir John Anderson had a meeting with key members of the British delegation to Atlantic City and Bretton Woods to give them instructions on important points. Uppermost in the participants' minds was to secure for Britain and other member countries the ability to devalue without the IMF's approval when necessary. Article IV, Section 4 of the Joint Statement made devaluations beyond the first 10 percentage points from the original parity (exchange rate) when a member joined the IMF valid only with the IMF's approval. Lord Catto of the Bank of

---

[69] Memo from Keynes to Sir (Sigisimund) David Waley (Principal Assistant Secretary of the Treasury), May 12, 1944, T 231/359. Keynes was assuming that the conference would be in Washington.

England had been particularly emphatic that national governments should retain sovereignty in exchange rate matters.[70] The participants in the meeting also wanted to the IMF agreement to include an ample transition period before members would be obliged to remove restrictions on current transactions. The British delegates agreed to press for a transition period of five years from the end of the war in Europe rather than three years from the inauguration of the IMF. The delegates also agreed to push to revise certain language in the Joint Statement that might imply a British obligation to allow countries that had acquired assets in pounds sterling ("sterling balances") to convert those assets into U.S. dollars on demand. Britain's financial position was too weak to allow mass conversion at the existing official exchange rate of $4.03 per pound sterling.

The participants in the meeting agreed that the IMF should begin operations no earlier than August 1, 1945. They also stressed that the British delegates would if necessary remind the American delegation that they were not negotiating with power to bind the British government, and that the Fund and Bank agreements would be subject to approval by the British Parliament.[71]

Also on June 8, the British government announced that Keynes would lead the British delegation to the international monetary conference. As we have said, security concerns prevented Anderson from attending. In the delegation, Sir Wilfrid Eady held the second-highest career position in the Treasury and outranked Keynes, but he allowed Keynes to lead.[72]

For some months there had been Anglo-American discussion about the Bank, but neither the British government nor any other government had issued a rival proposal on the Bank to the American proposal of November 1943 comparable to the rival proposals on the IMF. On June 9, however, Keynes sent a memo to Anderson, presumably circulated to other British Treasury officials, proposing principles for British negotiations with the Americans on the Bank. The memo stressed that the "essential features" it proposed were to limit the amount of capital

---

[70] International Monetary Fund, memorandum by Lord Catto, May 3, 1944, T 247/28. The memo reiterated a position Catto had staked out in February.

[71] "Conference on International Monetary Fund, Meeting in the Chancellor's Room on Thursday, 8th June," T 231/359.

[72] Note from Sir Richard Hopkins (Permanent Secretary to the Treasury) to Anderson, apparently June 5, 1944, T 231/365, that "Sir Wilfrid Eady is perfectly happy that Lord Keynes should be the Head of the Delegation"; *Hansard,* 5th series, v. 400, column 1517, June 8, 1944.

countries would need to pay in (as opposed to pledge); to give the Bank wide freedom in making loans; and to give creditor countries a substantial vote, in effect limiting American power, although Keynes did not explicitly say so. Despite these differences with the American position, Keynes expressed optimism to a U.S. embassy official in London that Britain and the United States could find common ground on the Bank, which could then serve as the basis for agreement by other countries. On June 16, Anderson approved that the British delegation should proceed along the lines Keynes had proposed for the Bank.[73]

The same day, British delegates and delegates from other countries traveling with them left London to begin their trip to Atlantic City. The party was given the code name "Snakebite party." They took a train from Liverpool Street Station to Scotland, where they joined the *Queen Mary* at Gourock, which is downstream from Glasgow.[74] The *Queen Mary* had been the world's grandest ocean liner when she first sailed in 1936. After World War II began in 1939 she had been converted into a troop transport, painted gray for camouflage and stripped of her luxurious amenities. She often carried more than 10,000 passengers, versus around 2,000 in peacetime. She sailed from Gourock rather than from her prewar port of Southampton, England because Gourock was less exposed to German air attack. Her departure on this voyage, which occurred on June 17, had been delayed by "regulations imposed by the highest military authorities."[75] D-Day had been only ten days earlier. The passengers included thousands of German prisoners of war who had been captured in the Allied landings in Normandy and were being sent to America to keep them far from the battlefield.[76]

Besides the British delegation, the *Queen Mary* also carried delegates from Belgium, China, Czechoslovakia, Greece, India, Norway, the Netherlands, and Poland, as well as the U.S. Treasury attaché in London (see the list facing the first page of chapter 20). The two Indian delegates

---

[73] Telegram from Winant to Hull, June 15, 1944, in U.S. Department of State (1967: Document 35); Keynes (1980b: 49-54). The embassy official Keynes spoke to was perhaps Lauren Casaday, the U.S. Treasury attaché in London, who would travel with British delegates to Atlantic City.

[74] "Delegation Arrangements," note signed by "JACR," June 16, 1944, T 231/365; letter, General Secretary, Snakebite Party, to Officer in Charge, Police Duty Room, Home Office, June 12, 1944, T 231/365; Beyen (1949: 168); Harding (1982: 79).

[75] Harding (1982: 76-81); Conway 2015: 197).

[76] Beyen (1949: 169). Reinertsen (2017) has details of the *Queen Mary*'s trip.

and their secretary were in fact British subjects. Poland participated in the shipboard meetings even though it had had been invited only to Bretton Woods and not Atlantic City. The European ally notably absent aboard ship was France, whose government in exile had by then moved from London to Algiers. All the delegations onboard except Norway also already had delegates in the United States who could attend the Atlantic City conference before the *Queen Mary* arrived.

As the largest and most respected delegation onboard, Britain was in a position of major negotiating power in developing firm arguments and alliances to counter the Americans where there was disagreement. The British delegation met privately — often more than once a day — to discuss grievances concerning clauses of the Joint Statement. Afterwards, all allied delegations on board would meet and consider proposed British amendments to the draft. In similar vein, the British and other delegations onboard the *Queen Mary* had the opportunity to develop a detailed response on the Bank of Reconstruction and Development. The Bank was a higher priority for the Europeans than for the United States because their countries had been ravaged by the war and it had not.

At 10:30 a.m. on Monday June 19, the British onboard the *Queen Mary* had their first formal meeting, followed by a meeting of all the Allied delegations at noon.[77] Many of the meetings were in Cabin 10, which before the war had been part of the first-class deck. Gathered with the other delegations, Keynes explained that since the time at Atlantic City and Bretton Woods would be short, it would be useful to get as far ahead as possible in discussions and negotiations in advance to the larger meetings. The sequence of meetings was usually that the British delegation would meet privately to discuss amendments to the Fund and drafts on the Bank of Reconstruction. After preliminary redrafting among Keynes and his colleagues, the British would host a meeting with the other delegations at which they would distribute their suggested amendments for general review and discussion.

Below we will discuss in more detail the two major products of the voyage: British documents on the Fund and the Bank that presented counterpoints to the American drafts. For now, suffice it to say that the minutes of the meetings onboard the *Queen Mary* reveal that the most prominently discussed topic was Article IV of the Joint Statement, "Par Values of Member Currencies," particularly the extent to which member

---

[77] See chapters 20 and 31. There had been an informal meeting of the British delegates on June 17, recorded by George Bolton (Reinertsen 2017: Lørdag).

Table. Atlantic City Daily Highlights, June 1944

8	American Technical Group (ATG) meets in Washington, D.C.
10	American *Questions and Answers* documents on the Fund and Bank
14	ATG arrives in Atlantic City
15	ATG: Subcommittee assignments
16	ATG: Scarce currencies; Fund and Bank legal matters
	British, other European delegations leave London for *Queen Mary*
17	ATG: Assignments; capital movements; Bank guarantees
18	ATG: Bank guarantees; withdrawal from Bank
19	ATG: Foreign delegates; Fund quotas; Fund gold depositories
	Agenda Committee: Welcome to foreign delegations
	Queen Mary (UK): Views on Fund Article IV and Bank; convertibility
	Queen Mary (Allies): Organization of shipboard meetings
20	Agenda Committee: Depositories; repurchases; governance
	Queen Mary (UK): Sterling rate; transition period; IMF withdrawal
	Queen Mary (Allies): Exchange variations; convertibility
21	Agenda Committee: Member obligations; voting; scarce currencies
	Queen Mary (UK): IMF directors; Keynes on the Bank
	Queen Mary (Allies): Transition period; Fund management
22	Agenda Committee: Fund: purchase of currencies; obligations
	Queen Mary (UK): Proposed new clauses on the IMF
	Queen Mary (Allies): Keynes's view on the Bank
23	Agenda Committee: Fund immunities and voting for directors
	Queen Mary docks in New York City; delegates arrive in Atlantic City
24	Formal Agenda Committee begins; election of top officers
25	Sunday; no formal conference meetings
26	IMF: Articles I-III
27	IMF: Article III continued
28	IMF: Articles III-VII (morning); Articles VII-X (end) (afternoon)
29	IMF: Subcommittee reports; par values (morning)
	Bank: British proposal, Articles I-IV (afternoon)
30	Bank: British proposal, Articles IV-V (end)
	Delegates leave for Bretton Woods

Notes: Numbers are days in June 1944; ATG = American Technical Group; (UK) = British delegation meetings; (Allies) = Allied meetings; Agenda Committee = Atlantic City meetings before all foreign delegates arrived; Formal Agenda Committee = meetings with all delegates present.

countries of the IMF would have the right to change par values and how much power the IMF would have to refuse or sanction them. At the first Allied meeting, Keynes requested that given the short length of the journey, discussions regarding the Bank begin within two days.[78] The meetings onboard the *Queen Mary* were undeniably productive and boosted Keynes' optimism. He remarked, "we got down on paper every point we wanted to raise with White, and discussed nearly all of them with our Allied friends."[79]

The *Queen Mary* arrived in New York City in the morning on Friday, June 23. The passage had taken six days, about two days longer than fast prewar passenger service because of the need to follow a zig-zag course to avoid detection by German submarines. After disembarking, the British delegates met with Robert Brand, a British Treasury representative in the United States. The delegations then proceeded to Atlantic City, arriving there at about 6 p.m. the same day.[80]

Conference organization and schedule

The Atlantic City conference was sometimes called the preconference, to emphasize that it was a prelude to the Bretton Woods conference. The whole group of delegates at the conference was called the Agenda Committee before the delegates onboard the *Queen Mary* arrived, then then Formal Agenda Committee. The name indicated that its job was to set the agenda for Bretton Woods.

The Steering Committee, a small group of the leading countries at Atlantic City, determined certain matters connected with managing that conference. Four numbered subcommittees handled aspects of the IMF agreement: 1. Purposes, Policies and Subscriptions of the Fund; 2. Operations of the Fund; 3. Organization and Management of the Fund; and 4. Establishment of the Fund. They were the nearly the same as the committees of Commission I at the Bretton Woods conference, which dealt with the IMF. There were also several other ad hoc subcommittees on other aspects of the IMF agreement, not envisioned when the Atlantic

---

[78] See chapter 31.
[79] Letter from Keynes to Sir Richard Hopkins, June 25, 1944, T 231/365, in Keynes (1980: 59).
[80] Robbins and Meade (1981: 157); letter from Alice Bourneuf to Burke Knapp, June 24, 1944, p. 1, U.S. National Archives, RG 82, Box 42, Atlantic City 2nd folder, "Drafting Committee."

City conference began but established as perceived needs arose. They covered management; the provision of information to the IMF; immunities of the IMF; and certain technical matters. There was also an agenda subcommittee. We have only found records for some meetings of the ad hoc subcommittees. The conference often called all these groups committees, but we refer to most as subcommittees to make clear their place within the conference structure.

The United States and United Kingdom were represented on all committees; the other major Allied powers (the Soviet Union, China, and France), as well as Canada, were represented on most committees; and other countries were only represented on some committees. At Bretton Woods, the committees corresponding to subcommittees 1-4 at Atlantic City were open to all delegations. We surmise that the practice at Atlantic City was different because all delegations would have chances to discuss matters in the Agenda Committee and then at Bretton Woods along with the countries that had not been invited to Atlantic City.

Appendix B shows the schedule of meetings at the conference, insofar as we found records or could make solid inferences from conference minutes. Before the delegates onboard the *Queen Mary* arrived, subcommittees typically met in the morning and the Agenda Committee met in the afternoon. Once all delegates had arrived, the numbered subcommittees ceased meeting. Instead, the Formal Agenda Committee typically met in the morning and again in the afternoon.

All the secretariat staff at Atlantic City and at Bretton Woods were American. Hosting the conference gave the Americans the tactical benefit of having the greatest influence over the agenda.

Meetings of the partial conference

On June 19, delegates arrived at Atlantic City representing all countries except Greece, and Norway. However, Belgium, Czechoslovakia, India, the Netherlands, and the United Kingdom were lacking their most important members, who were on the *Queen Mary*.

While waiting for those delegates to arrive, the delegations present conducted some preliminary work. The Agenda Committee met five times, and each of the four subcommittees on aspects of the IMF agreement met four times. (There was no discussion of the Bank.) To emphasize that at this stage they were not presuming to speak for all 17 countries that would attend the conference, the committee of the whole called itself the Agenda Committee before the arrival of all delegates, whereas afterwards it called itself the Formal Agenda Committee.

We consider four points that the Agenda Committee and the subcommittees discussed to be major, substantially affecting how the IMF or the international financial system would operate. (1) The United States proposed a procedure for choosing Executive Directors such that the biggest economies, which would be the largest contributors, would appoint their own directors and smaller economies would form coalitions to elect the remaining directors. Though complex, the proposal adroitly balanced the interests of larger and smaller economies. (2) For the elected directors, whose alternates might be from a different country, Subcommittee 3 recommended that the alternates not vote unless the directors were absent; doing so prevented splits within directorships. The Agenda Committee touched on but did not really discuss the contentious issue of the voting power allocated to various countries. (3) The Agenda Committee debated the length of the transition period for retaining controls on current-account transactions but did not come to a firm conclusion about it. The Bretton Woods conference would allow the transition period to be indefinite. A few IMF members have retained controls on current-account transactions for decades, and the IMF agreement was designed to allow member countries to maintain permanent controls on capital movements if they wished. (4) The Agenda Committee also accepted Subcommittee 2's conclusion that the IMF agreement did not override previously existing treaties among members.

We consider the other points that the Agenda Committee and the subcommittees discussed before the delegations on the *Queen Mary* arrived to be less important. They included which national agency should be the counterpart for financial transactions with the IMF; rules for a country repurchasing its currency from the IMF with gold; certain legal considerations in establishing the IMF; calling special meetings of the Executive Directors; reductions in financial obligations for heavily war damaged countries; where the IMF should hold its gold; exempting the IMF from taxation by members; and protecting the value of the IMF's assets from depreciations of members' currencies.

In the days before the other delegations arrived, the Americans had prepared a substantial elaboration of the Joint Statement. By June 22, they had presented to the other delegations a detailed though not quite comprehensive draft agreement for the IMF.[81] If they were trying to present the British with a *fait accompli*, though, they failed. The British, the only delegation that could challenge the Americans in number of good

---

[81] In Morgenthau Diaries (v. 746: 139e-139gg).

brains, was about to do so.

Meetings of the full conference

As we noted, the delegations on board the *Queen Mary* arrived in Atlantic City at about 6 p.m. on Friday, June 23. Saturday there was brief meeting of the Formal Agenda Committee to select its officers. Keynes nominated White as chairman and White selected Keynes as one of the vice chairmen. The conference now officially had the power to arrive at the drafts that would be the foundation for Bretton Woods.

More substantively, there was also a meeting on Saturday between the American and British delegations to discuss the Bank. The British emphasized the points they had developed on the voyage.[82] They wanted to allow guarantees up to the amount of subscribed capital, rather than just paid-in capital (the November 1943 American proposal was silent on this point — the effect of the British proposal was to allow the Bank to begin with much lower paid-in capital than the Americans had envisioned); to charge uniform rates to members even though they would not all be of equal creditworthiness; to allow for loans for general economic stabilization rather than only, as the American proposal envisioned, for particular projects; and to allow the Bank into the gray area where the private sector was willing to lend but charged high interest rates. The American response was generally conciliatory.

Sunday was a day of rest, without formal meetings of the conference. Keynes and White apparently met one-on-one, though, because in the late afternoon Keynes gave a summary of their meeting to the British Commonwealth delegations. Most of the points would be covered at the meeting between the American and British delegations the next day, but two other matters are worth mentioning. One is that White did not want the Atlantic City conference to discuss quotas, presumably because it was a contentious issue that would consume time but could not be settled without the presence of the remaining countries that would sign the final IMF agreement. Also interesting are a few lines about conference procedure at Bretton Woods. White favored formal voting; Keynes was afraid that it would lead to deadlocks and wanted the chairman to resolve problems. The procedure the Bretton Woods conference ended up following was that the chairmen would shepherd commissions or committees to consensus, avoiding formal votes listing country names.

---

[82] See chapter 80.

Hectic activity followed from Monday, June 26 to up to final morning of the conference, Friday, June 30. The Formal Agenda Committee met each morning and the afternoon. In between were meetings of certain subcommittees. The four numbered subcommittees on the IMF ceased meeting because the Formal Agenda Committee was covering that ground, but there were subcommittees on IMF management, furnishing information to the IMF, and the organization of the Atlantic City or Bretton Woods conferences. On Monday there was a second meeting between the American and British delegations, this time on the IMF. As with the meeting on the Bank, the British worked from a document they had developed on the voyage to New York.[83] The British favored more latitude than the Americans for changes in par values (exchange rate parities); a transition period of five years rather than three; easier ability for members to draw on the IMF's resources up to certain limits; probation rather than immediate expulsion for countries that had breached their obligations to the IMF; and language clarifying that the IMF agreement did not supersede existing arrangements, such as certain preferential exchange controls in place in the British Commonwealth. As we have mentioned, the exchange rate clause was a priority for the British. They were also critical the American concept of a gold convertible currency, saying that as they understood the term, no such currency existed at the moment. (The United States remained on the gold standard during World War II officially, but wartime trading regulations and the dangers of ocean shipping in wartime meant that in practice, foreigners could not freely convert U.S. dollars for gold and ship the gold abroad as they had been able to do before the war.)

The second meeting of the Formal Agenda Committee was to distribute the draft of the IMF agreement adding alternatives by the United States and some other countries to the Joint Statement. Many of the alternatives incorporated language from subcommittees 1-4. The committee then had six meetings at which it covered the draft IMF agreement from start to finish.

John Maynard Keynes took over from White in the chair for the last two meetings of the Formal Agenda Committee, covering the Bank. In the five days since the Anglo-American meeting on the Bank, the British delegation had devised a document that showed where its proposals differed from the American proposals. It became Document B-1 of the conference. The British counterproposal was detailed, except that it had

---

[83] See chapter 82.

nothing to say about the management of the bank. The "Proposal for a Bank for Reconstruction and Development" that was the starting document of the Bretton Woods conference on the Bank (chapter 83) melded the American and British ideas where they were close and left the British proposals as alternatives where the American delegation had strong reservations about them. These were provisions proposing to allow stabilization loans; giving the Bank more leeway to shift expenditures that would drain foreign exchange reserves from countries where they were low; allowing countries with low foreign exchange reserves; and allowing countries that had ceased to be members of the IMF to continue to be members of the World Bank with the approval of other members, rather than dropping them automatically. The final Bank agreement signed at Bretton Woods had compromise provisions on all those points that were between the original American and British provision. For example, the agreement allowed the Bank some room to make stabilization loans, though the language was not as expansive as in the British proposal.[84]

The final week of the conference also saw meetings by two ad hoc subcommittees. The Steering Committee appointed a Special Committee on Furnishing Information to develop a list of the kinds of economic data that members would submit to the IMF. Keynes was among those who thought that better statistics would deepen understanding of the world economy. The Soviet Union, however, treated many statistics on its centrally planned economy as state secrets. To placate the Soviet Union, one of its delegates was appointed chairman of the subcommittee. The subcommittee seems to have met only once. Its report to the Formal Agenda Committee contained a recommendation that the IMF agreement include a clause that "In requesting information the Fund shall, however, take into consideration the ability of individual countries to furnish the data asked for" (see chapter 81).

The Subcommittee on Management held five meetings. It largely accepted American ideas about a three-tier management structure for the IMF, consisting of a Board of Governors including all countries to make constitutional-type changes, a small number of Executive Directors to supervise operations, and a General Manager and staff to execute policies. The British preferred for Executive Directors to be persons acting as international civil servants rather than for the governments that would

---

[84] UNMFC (1948, v. 1: 984-1014), Article I; Article III, Section IV, Subsection (vii); Article IV, Section 2; Article VI, Section 3.

choose them and thought that the Executive Directors should not be in continuous session, instead acting more like a typical corporation board of directors that meets, say, quarterly. The report that the Subcommittee on Management submitted to the Formal Agenda Committee did not try to resolve those matters, but the British were in the minority and were unable to carry their preferences into the final IMF agreement.

On the afternoon of June 30 most of the delegates left to meet a special train from Washington to Bretton Woods, which stopped in Philadelphia to pick them up and in New York City to pick up other delegates.[85] The Bretton Woods conference would begin the next day.

What the conference accomplished

In our view, the major accomplishment of the Atlantic City conference was arriving at a draft agreement for the Bank for Reconstruction and Development (chapter 83). When Harry Dexter White started work on the Fund and the Bank in December 1941 he conceived them as coordinate institutions, but in international discussions the Fund took priority. As we have seen, the invitation the United States extended for the Bretton Woods conference stated that its purpose was to formulate definite proposals for the Fund "and possibly" the Bank. A World Bank staff member who interviewed participants in Bretton Woods some years later summarized their composite view as considering the Fund spinach and the Bank dessert.[86] The Fund involved potentially difficult adherence to pegged exchange rates, while the Bank for most countries was a prospective source of loans. The requirement that members of the Bank be members of the Fund made them eat the spinach first. Atlantic City closed most of the gap between the Fund and the Bank proposals regarding their suitability to be considered at Bretton Woods. Before Atlantic City there was an international agreement on the principles for the Fund, the Joint Statement, whereas for the Bank there was only an American proposal that lacked any other country's assent. By the end of the Atlantic City conference there was a draft agreement on the Bank to go with the draft agreement on the Fund. The draft agreement on the Bank was less detailed, but it provided what turned out to be a successful

---

[85] Telegram no. 433 Remac, Viscount Halifax to Foreign Office, June 7, 1944, T 231/359.
[86] Rees (1973: 137-138); Boskey (1957: 2). See also World Bank Archives Oral History Program (1961: 6-8).

basis for the Bretton Woods conference to develop a final agreement.

John Maynard Keynes's role in establishing the Bank is, we think, underappreciated because it must vie for attention with his many other achievements. Keynes took the lead in developing the British draft on the Bank and in gaining support for it from the other delegations aboard the *Queen Mary*. Except for the portion of the document on management, where the British had developed no comments, it offered a complete alternative to the American proposal, although incorporating portions of the American proposal unchanged where they agreed with British views. At Atlantic City, Keynes chaired the sessions of the conference that discussed the Bank and enabled the melding of the American and British proposals in to a draft acceptable to a wider group of countries. At Bretton Woods, he was the chairman of Commission II, which developed the draft Bank agreement into a final agreement. There were some complaints about his methods, but he got results.[87] It is easy to conceive of the Fund agreement occurring even without Keynes; less so for the Bank agreement.

At Atlantic City, the British and the Allied delegations that agreed with them got some concessions from the Americans, but the Americans preserved their most important positions. On both the Fund and the Bank, the United States would have primacy, holding voting power such that the British Commonwealth would be unable to outvote it, although the precise numbers of votes would not be determined until the Bretton Woods conference. Also for both institutions, the combination of the legal framework and the high voting power of the United States went far to ensure that they would limit their demands on American resources to levels that would be politically acceptable to the U.S. government. And despite British objections that according to their understanding, no currency was gold convertible at the moment, at Bretton Woods the British would agree to put the dollar on a nearly equal footing with gold — a consequential decision that would make the Bretton Woods version of the gold standard to a large extent a U.S. dollar standard, causing problems when the United States failed to pursue policies to ensure that the dollar would remain as good as gold.

For the British, the most important concession they received from the Americans on the Fund was making the IMF much less of a supervisor and more of just an adviser on exchange rates. On the Bank, the most important concession the British and the Allied delegations that agreed

---

[87] Bittermann (1971: 69).

with them received was to reduce the amount of paid-in capital the Bank could operate with. Doing so reduced the Bank's demand on the resources of the war-torn countries, but also reduced its capacity to lend to them. To partly offset the reduction in lending capacity, the British proposed, and the Americans agreed to, a number of measures to expand the field for the Bank's loans and guarantees beyond what the Americans had originally envisioned.

Anglo-American relations at the conference were sometimes testy, as usually happens when countries disagree on important points. In a letter of June 25 after an Anglo-American meeting, Keynes wrote, "Harry White…seems extremely fit and happy, and inclined to agree with almost anything, which is said to him. Heaven grant that it continues but it seems too much to hope for."[88] It was of course too much to hope for. The Americans found the British suggestions "extremely complicated. They redefine most of the terms and revise so many of the provisions that it will take long and careful study to figure out what their suggestions amount to."[89] To the Americans, certain British proposals "make it appear that the main function of the Fund would be to provide countries with additional assets, whereas in American eyes stability was conceived to be the main objective."[90] Keynes considered the American position a misunderstanding: if their primary concern was stabilization, Keynes believed that access to additional assets was a way to promote it. His efforts to persuade White, however, were to no avail. Later in the week the British delegate George Bolton remarked,

> White, in a raging heat, has bluntly refused to accept any change whatsoever in the exchange and convertibility clauses in which the question of sovereignty arises [in other words, precisely the aspect the UK Treasury and Bank of England were most adamant about]. As expected, he says that the political position makes it impossible for him to retract any further.

Keynes threatened to walk out of the meeting.[91]

---

[88] Letter from Keynes to Hopkins, June 25, 1944, T 231/365, in Keynes (1980b: 64).
[89] Letter from Alice Bourneuf to J. Burke Knapp, June 24, 1944, U.S. National Archives, RG 56, Box 59.
[90] See chapter 29.
[91] Conway (2014: 191).

The Anglo-American relationship was the most important at Atlantic City because the United States and Britain were the world's two leading financial powers. Only Britain had the depth of talent to challenge the United States across the board in the negotiations on the Fund and the Bank. It would be a mistake, though, to depict Atlantic City as simply an Anglo-American deal. Other countries had, and used, opportunities to debate the provisions of the Joint Statement on the Fund and to propose alternatives that the Bretton Woods conference would consider. On the Bank, as we said, the discussions aboard the *Queen Mary* gave the delegations there the opportunity to influence the British draft. As Keynes acknowledged, they persuaded him on the importance of the Bank to them,[92] which perhaps he had not fully appreciated before because Britain did not expect to borrow from the Bank.

As would also be the case at Bretton Woods, a number of delegates from other countries exercised influence because of the importance of their countries or the force of their intellect. Antonio Espinosa de los Monteros (Mexico), Ervin Hexner (Czechoslovakia), André Istel (France) Louis Rasminsky (Canada), and Tingfu Tsiang (China) were chairmen or reporter of committees. Several other delegates, including Wim Beyen (Netherlands), Wilhelm Keilhau (Norway), and Felipe Pazos (Cuba) raised important issues that the conference had to acknowledge.

Atlantic City was the first gathering of a group fairly representative of the global economy to address what postwar global economic order would be. Before the conference, fact-to-face collaboration had taken place only across small groups of countries, such as Anglo-American discussions (sometimes also with Russian and Chinese participation) in Washington and British Commonwealth meetings in London. The Atlantic City conference was in a way a predecessor of today's Group of 20 (G20) nations, including economies both sufficiently important and sufficiently diverse that it had a plausible claim to set an agenda for other countries to consider.

The Atlantic City conference accomplished all these things while keeping a low profile. Short items about the conference did appear in local and big-city newspapers, but contained little of substance. In the Atlantic City papers, the conference of homeopaths at the Claridge Hotel received about as much attention as the monetary conference. We have seen only one newspaper article that was prominently placed, fairly long, and perceptive. In its June 29 issue, the *Commercial and Financial Chronicle*, a

---

[92] See chapter 28, appendix.

weekly New York newspaper with a small though influential readership, published an article that asked, "Has the Bretton Woods Conference Begun?" During the conference, the *New York Times* published a series of editorials criticizing the Joint Statement, but said next to nothing about the doings in Atlantic City.[93]

The documents

So much, then, concerning analysis of the conference. Now for a brief description of the provenance of the documents in this book.

The U.S. Department of the Treasury was the host of the Atlantic City conference.[94] Harry Dexter White noted that some of the delegates wanted no minutes to be kept of the conference, to preserve confidentiality.[95] Even so, the Treasury did keep minutes, as did the British delegation for some meetings. Henry Bittermann, a member of the American delegation who was one of the note takers, remarked years later, perhaps when the files were being prepared to be sent to the U.S. National Archives, that the American minutes were "not official and were not affirmed by any one as far as I remember."[96] The minutes were never intended to be public, but after 75 years, all the participants are dead, and the minutes contain nothing discreditable. Secretaries appointed by committees or members of the American Technical Group took handwritten minutes, which were later typed up. The British delegation also took minutes of some meetings. The original handwritten notes do note seems to have survived.

Besides the minutes that the U.S. Treasury and British delegation took, staff of the Board of Governors of the Federal Reserve System, especially Alice Bourneuf, took notes. They were written as aids to memory rather than as easily readable narratives, so we have not reproduced them here

---

[93] "Delegates Here for Money Study," *Atlantic City Press,* June 16, 1944: 1; "Homeopaths Meet Here," *Atlantic City Press,* June 26, 1944; Bratter (1944). The New York Times editorials were anonymous but later revealed to have been by Henry Hazlitt (1984), now best known for his book *Economics in One Lesson.*

[94] At Bretton Woods, the Department of State was the co-host, supplying for instance the secretary-general of the conference. At Atlantic City, we assume that it was nominally the co-host, although we have found no official mention. Whatever the case, Treasury staff filled all the most important roles.

[95] See chapter 39.

[96] Notes from Henry J. Bittermann to H. Patricia Scott, September 11, 1969 and July 16, 1970, U.S. National Archives, RG 56, Box 1, Folder A-9.

except in chapter 15, for which no other source was available. Sometimes they have useful additional details, though, and scholars doing original research related to the Atlantic City conference will want to consult them. They are included in the online companion files described below.[97]

The most comprehensive version of the conference minutes and other documents exists at the U.S. National Archives in College Park, Maryland. The UK National Archives in Kew (a neighborhood of London) contain documents of the British delegation and minutes of some meetings at Atlantic City. Where differing American and British versions of minutes exist, we have reproduced them both. For some meetings there were multiple versions of minutes by U.S. Treasury staff, and we have likewise reproduced them. The IMF Archives contain many of the conference documents, including a bit of material not found elsewhere. The IMF Archives documents have been available online for several years, but as is typical for archival documents, they contain a number of duplicate documents and are not organized to tell a coherent story as this book does. Consequently, they have been little used.

In the transcripts, delegates often make remarks that assume knowledge of the conference's system for organizing documents. Each document had a combination number and letter code. Documents F-1 to F-6 concerned the Fund (IMF), while document B-1 concerned the Bank for Reconstruction and Development. Document F-1 was the most scrutinized document, the preliminary draft for the IMF. It contained the Joint Statement plus "alternatives" (amendments) proposed by various delegations. It, and the draft Bank agreement, were divided into articles (the British often called them "clauses"), denoted by roman numerals; sections, denoted by Arabic numerals; and in some cases subsections, usually denoted by lower-case letters. Alternatives were denoted by capital letters. The copies of alternatives distributed to delegates did not explicitly identify the proposing country. It is however usually possible to identify who proposed what from a document of the American delegation and from the minutes (see Appendix D). Almost always, the delegation proposing an alternative was the first to speak about it. Also, Alternative A was typically the American alternative and B was typically the British alternative. Subsequent letters were the alternatives proposed by other delegations, with no letter consistently associated with a particular delegation.

---

[97] The source is U.S. National Archives, RG 82, Box 42, Atlantic City 1st folder and 2nd folder, both labeled "Drafting Committee."

The page numbering of the preliminary draft for the IMF also had a particular order. Main page numbers contained an article or a section of the Joint Statement and sometimes an alternative, while page numbers that included letters, such as 12a, typically only contained alternatives.

Besides the conference minutes and important conference documents themselves, this book includes minutes of the meetings of the American Technical Group at Atlantic City; minutes of meetings of the British and Allied delegations aboard the *Queen Mary;* and some other documents relevant to the conference. The whole collection enables readers to see how the American and British delegations developed their negotiating positions and how the other delegations at Atlantic City reacted.

To avoid making a long book still longer, the text excludes certain documents that are already in print. Among them are two documents by the U.S. Treasury, *Questions and Answers on the International Monetary Fund* and *Questions and Answers on the Bank for Reconstruction and Development*, both dated June 10, 1944. They were issued to the delegates at Atlantic City and Bretton Woods and years later were published.[98] We also excluded the "flimsies" that the conference subcommittees considered because much of their content found its way into alternatives incorporated into the draft IMF agreement. The excluded material is available among the companion files or in links provided there.

Our editorial changes

In editing the documents reproduced in the book, we have tried to preserve all the important content but have made certain changes in formatting to make the documents easier to read.

Our general rule has been to make unimportant changes silently but to identify important changes by brackets or footnotes. We have corrected obvious errors of punctuation and spelling; changed punctuation from the original where necessary for clarity; written in full some words abbreviated in the original typescripts; and modernized capitalization and spelling slightly. We have also generally converted British spelling and punctuation to their American equivalents.

In some cases, we have inserted paragraph breaks to make a new speaker or new point more apparent. We have adopted a uniform style for identifying conference meetings, delegations, participants, documents, and parts of documents.

---

[98] U.S. Department of the Treasury (1944a, b).

We have added several kinds of text to the conference proceedings and documents:

(1) Chapter titles, which are often ours rather than those of the original documents.

(2) Headline summaries of chapter content, in bold italics.

(3) Short narrative summaries of many meetings, identifying the key issues and speakers, in italics at the start of chapters.

(4) Material in single square brackets, indicating places where we have made insertions to clarify the text.

(5) Material in double square brackets, indicating insertions to clarify the text where we are less certain of our additions. In particular, for easier reference to the Joint Statement on the IMF and to the American and British draft proposals for the Bank, we have inserted names of our own invention to identify articles and sections only identified by number in the original.

(6) Footnotes. On the first pages of many chapters where the original text begins with a list of attendees, we have relegated the list to the footnotes for more efficient reading. Other footnotes contain our remarks to clarify the original text.

Online companion files, <www.centerforfinancialstability.org>

The Web site of the Center for Financial Stability contains PDF files containing photographs of or links to the original versions of all of the documents printed in this book. It also includes many documents not reproduced in the book, such as telegrams and memoranda. The documents are from the UK National Archives, the U.S. National Archives, and the U.S. Library of Congress, and are in the public domain.[99]

The IMF Archives contain many files that duplicate what we have, plus a bit of different content. They are available for free online.

As an aid to other researchers, we have compiled an extensive index to archival files and posted it among the online companion files. The index has item-by-item listings of the contents of the folders from these

---

[99] United Kingdom, Open Government License v3.0 for public sector information under section 163 of the Copyright, Designs and Patents Act 1988; United States Code, Title 17, Section 105; U.S. Library of Congress, Leo Pasvolsky Papers, online Finding Aid > Using This Collection > Access and Use > Copyright Status; all as of July 2019.

sources: U.S. National Archives; UK National Archives; IMF Archives; other archives we used in our research; and archives that we consulted but that turned out to have no material we used. The degree of detail in the index is far beyond what was previously available from online catalogs and should save researchers time in deciding whether to consult the material we list and in locating it.

Although the source documents for this book are not copyrighted, our edited version of the documents *is* copyrighted, as are our photographs in the electronic companion files just described. Persons who wish to make copies of the content in the electronic companion files may lawfully do so by seeking out and photographing the original documents, as we did, but may not copy our files without our permission.

To ensure that the material in the book will be free of the copyright problems that keep some important scholarly books out of print for decades before they pass into the public domain, we have limited our claim of copyright for the electronic edition to ten years.

Acknowledgments

For help obtaining archival documents of or related to the conference, we thank Selwyn Cornish, Julia Costet, Sam Kanson-Benanav, Noah Naparst, and Dylan Schuler. Gabrielle Canning thanks Prof. Michael Butler for advising her on a senior year research paper at the College of William and Mary that provided part of the material for this chapter. James Boughton, Eric Helleiner, Gail Makinen, and Robert Yee made helpful comments on a draft. For assistance with bringing the book to publication and with the online companion files to the book, we thank Rosa Tibau and, at the Center for Financial Stability, Jeff van den Noort, Lawrence Goodman, and Marshall Wilen.

References

For references focusing on the Bretton Woods conference rather than on Atlantic City, see Schuler and Rosenberg (2012/2013). Hyperlinks below were valid as of July 2019.

A. Archival material

Reference numbers of files are those in the archives, but the short titles that follow are ours. For item-by-item descriptions of the files below and of files that we ended up not using in our research, see the index in the companion files to this book at <www.centerforfinancialstability.org>. A source that apparently would have been useful but that we have not seen is the diary of George Bolton.

Diaries of George Bolton, Bank of England Archive, London, OV 38/8-10.

Alice Bourneuf papers. Letters and notes in the Bretton Woods Conference Collection, Ref. 8391, and in the U.S. National Archives, RG 82, Box 42.

Bretton Woods Conference Collection, International Monetary Fund Archives, Washington, D.C. and online, <archivescatalog.imf.org> ("Ref." = reference number) (Search electronically for "Atlantic City")

Bretton Woods Conference files, Ref. 8391, especially those headed "Atlantic City Conference."

Ansel F. Luxford Papers, Ref. 2563

Edward M. Bernstein Papers, Ref. 2121

Richard B. Brenner Papers, Ref. 8394

Diaries of Henry Morgenthau, Jr., April 27, 1933-July 27, 1945, Franklin D. Roosevelt Presidential Library and Museum, Hyde Park, New York, and online, <http://www.fdrlibrary.org> (While he was Secretary of the U.S. Treasury, Morgenthau was a compulsive keeper of records. He had many of his conversations tape recorded or stenographed, and later typed. The conversations plus the memos and other documents he kept have been a mine of detail for historians. These are the full records; three published volumes called *From the Morgenthau Diaries* contain a small selection.)

Morgenthau Diaries, 1933-1945, 864 vols.

Presidential Diaries, 1938-1945, 7 vols.

Leo Pasvolsky Papers, 1937-1953, U.S. Library of Congress

Box 1, Folder "International Economic Relations, 1944"

United Kingdom National Archives (formerly Public Record Office), Kew, London

Some material is online at <http://www.nationalarchives.gov.uk>. In the folder numbers below, CAB stands for Cabinet, FO for Foreign Office, and T for Treasury.

CAB 65/42/20, War Cabinet conclusions, May 5, 1944

CAB 65/46, Confidential annex to War Cabinet conclusions, May 5, 1944

FO 371/40916, Bretton Woods, July-August 1944.pdf

FO 371/40948, Article VII talks, July-September 1944.pdf

T 231/359, Conference related, May-June 1944

T 231/360, International Monetary Fund, June 1944

T 231/361, *Queen Mary* and Atlantic City, June 1944

T 231/362, Preconference papers for Atlantic City and Bretton Woods, June 1944

T 231/363, Preconference papers for Atlantic City and Bretton Woods circulated to Allied delegations, June 1944

T 231/364, Shipboard and Atlantic City minutes, June 1944

T 231/365, Atlantic City and Bretton Woods instructions and comments June/August 1944

T 247/21 Article VII, Bank, March-June 1944

T 247/22, Keynes, Bank for Reconstruction and Development, March 1944

T 247/28, Keynes, March-June 1944

T 247/29, Keynes, March-August 1944

T 247/32, Keynes, Bank for Reconstruction and Development, May/June 1944

T 247/32, Keynes, Bank for Reconstruction and Development, October 1943/July 1944

T 247/35, Keynes, International Monetary Fund, March/June 1944

T 247/55, Keynes, UK external finance in the transition to peace, May/June 1944

T 247/64, Keynes, correspondence including Atlantic City, June/August 1944

T 247/65, Keynes, external finance including Atlantic City, May/November 1944

United States National Archives, College Park, Maryland

In the identification system of the U.S. National Archives, RG means Record Group. RG 43 is records of international conferences; RG 56 is the general records of the Department of the Treasury, RG 59 is the general records of the Department of State; and RG 82 is the records of the Federal Reserve System.

RG 43, Box 1, Atlantic City and Bretton Woods conference arrangements, jacket 2

RG 43, Box 2, contains Mexican preconference silver promotion
RG 56, Boxes 1-2, Atlantic City documents
RG 56, Box 11, Harry Dexter White Atlantic City material
RG 56, Box 20, Atlantic City documents and Harry Dexter White correspondence
RG 56, Box 59, Atlantic City minutes of meetings and other material
RG 59.800.515, material on Bretton Woods agreements[100]
RG 82, Box 42, Atlantic City American and general meetings
Harry Dexter White Papers, Seeley G. Mudd Manuscript Library, Princeton University
  Box 4, Folder 13, Administrative files
  Box 7, Folder 2, Proposal for International Stabilization Fund
  Box 7, Folder 4, Expert analysis
  Box 7, Folder 5, Expert analysis and revised drafts of proposal for International Stabilization Fund
  Box 8, Folders 1-2, Foreign comments on International Stabilization Fund
  Box 8, Folders 3-4, Bank for Reconstruction and Development
  Box 8, Folder 6, British comments on International Stabilization Fund
  Box 8, Folder 1, Chinese comments on International Stabilization Fund

B. Other sources

Acheson, Dean. 1969. *Present at the Creation: My Years in the State Department.* New York: W.W. Norton and Company.
Atlantic City Daily Press.
Atlantic City Evening Union.
Baker, Ray Stannard. 1922. *Woodrow Wilson and World Settlement: Written from His Unpublished and Personal Material. Original Documents of the Peace Conference,* v. 3. Garden City, New York: Doubleday, Page and Company.
Bank of England. 1968. "The Exchange Equalisation Account: Its Origins and Development." *Bank of England Quarterly Bulletin,* December: 377-390.
Bank for International Settlements. 1937. *Seventh Annual Report, 1st April*

---

[100] Eckes (1975: 298-199 nn. 31, 36, 38, 29) and Van Dormael (1978: 314 n. 314) cite RG 59.800.515—BWA-6—2444 and RG 59.800.515/6—2844, which we were unable to find even with the help of an archivist. The numbers after the decimals refer to the Department of State classification system of material rather than to box numbers, the typical second-level specification for the location of records at the U.S. National Archives.

1936-31st March 1937. Basle: Bank for International Settlements.

Bao, Cecilia, Justin Chen, Nicholas Fries, Andrew Gibson, Emma Paine, and Kurt Schuler. 2018. "The Federal Reserve System's Weekly Balance Sheet since 1914." Johns Hopkins University Institute for Applied Economics, Global Health, and the Study of Business Enterprise, Studies in Applied Economics (working paper series), no. 115, July. At <https://sites.krieger.jhu.edu/iae/working-papers/studies-in-applied-economics/>.

Beyen, Johan W[illem]. 1949. *Money in a Maelstrom.* New York: Macmillan.

BIS. 1942. Bank for International Settlements. *Twelfth Annual Report, 1st April 1941-31st March 1942.* Basle: Bank for International Settlements.

Bisset, James. 1962. *Commodore: War, Peace and Big Ships.* With P. R. Stephensen. New York: Criterion Books.

Bittermann, Henry J. 1971. "Negotiation of the Articles of Agreement of the International Bank for Reconstruction and Development." *International Lawyer,* v. 5, no. 1: 59-88.

Black, Stanley W. 1991. *A Levite Among the Priests: Edward Bernstein and the Origins of the Bretton Woods System.* Boulder, Colorado: Westview Press. (Interviews with Bernstein.)

Bordo, Michael, Barry Eichengreen, Daniela Klingebiel, Maria Soledad Martinez-Peria, and Andrew K. Rose. 2001. "Is the Crisis Problem Growing More Severe?" *Economic Policy,* v. 16, no. 32, April: 53-82.

Bratter, Herbert M. 1944. "Has the Bretton Woods Conference Begun?" *Commercial and Financial Chronicle* (New York), June 29, Section 2: 2713 (front page), 2718.

Boskey, Shirley. 1957. "Bretton Woods Recalled." *International Bank Notes* (World Bank), July.

Boughton, James, and Roger J. Sandilands. 2003. "Politics and the Attack on FDR's Economists: From the Grand Alliance to the Cold War," *Intelligence and National Security,* v. 18, no. 3, Autumn: 73-99.

Bratter, Herbert M. 1944. "Has the Bretton Woods Conference Begun?" *Commercial and Financial Chronicle,* June 29: 2713, 2718.

Center for Financial Stability. Historical Financial Statistics (data set). <http://www.centerforfinancialstability.org/hfs.php>.

Conway, Edmund. 2014. *The Summit : Bretton Woods, 1944 : J. M. Keynes and the Reshaping of the Global Economy.* New York: Pegasus Books.

Cornish, Selwyn, and Kurt Schuler. 2019. "Australia's Full-Employment Proposals at Bretton Woods: A Road Only Partly Taken." In Naomi Lamoreaux and Ian Shapiro, editors, *The Bretton Woods Agreements: Together with Scholarly Commentaries and Essential Historical Documents:* 173-194. New Haven: Yale University Press.

Craig, R. Bruce. 2004. *Treasonable Doubt: The Harry Dexter White Spy Case.*

Lawrence, Kansas: University Press of Kansas.

Dormael, Armand van. 1978. *Bretton Woods: Birth of a Monetary System.* London: Macmillan.

Eckes, Alfred E. 1975. *A Search for Solvency: Bretton Woods and the International Monetary System.* Austin: University of Texas Press.

Eichengreen, Barry. 1992. *Golden Fetters: The Gold Standard and the Great Depression, 1919-1939.* New York: Oxford University Press.

Federal Reserve. 1943. United States. Board of Governors of the Federal Reserve System. "Postwar International Monetary Stabilization," *Federal Reserve Bulletin,* v. 29, no. 6, June: 501-521.

Funk, Walther. 1940. "Die wirtschaftliche Neuordnung Europas." July 25.

Harding, Stephen. 1982. *Gray Ghost: The R.M.S. Queen Mary at War.* Missoula, Montana: Pictorial Histories Publishing Company.

Harrod, Roy [Forbes]. 1951. *The Life of John Maynard Keynes.* New York: Harcourt, Brace and Company.

Haynes, John Earl, and Harvey Klehr. 1999. *Venona: Decoding Soviet Espionage in America.* New Haven: Yale University Press.

Haynes, John Earl, Harvey Klehr, and Alexander Vassiliev. 2009. *Spies: The Rise and Fall of the KGB in America.* New Haven: Yale University Press.

Hazlitt, Henry. 1984. *From Bretton Woods to World Inflation: A Study of Causes and Consequences.* Chicago: Regnery Gateway.

Helleiner, Eric. 2014. *Forgotten Foundations of Bretton Woods: International Development and the Making of the Postwar Order.* Ithaca, New York: Cornell University Press.

Horsefield, J[ohn] Keith. 1969. *The International Monetary Fund 1945-1965: Twenty Years of International Monetary Cooperation,* 3 v. *Volume I: Chronicle; Volume II: Analysis,* by Margaret G[arritsen] de Vries and J[ohn] Keith Horsefield; *Volume III: Documents.* Washington, D.C.: International Monetary Fund.

Irwin, Douglas A. 2012. "The French Gold Sink and the Great Deflation of 1929–32." *Cato Papers on Public Policy,* v. 2: 1-41.

Jin, Zhongxia. 2015. "The Chinese Delegation at the 1944 Bretton Woods Conference: Reflections for 2015." Official Monetary and Financial Institutions Forum, July. <https://www.omfif.org/analysis/reports/reports/the-chinese-delegation-at-the-1944-bretton-woods-conference-reflections-for-2015/>

Howson, Susan. 2011. *Lionel Robbins.* Cambridge: Cambridge University Press.

Keynes, John Maynard. 1919. *The Economic Consequences of the Peace.* London: Macmillan.

Keynes, John Maynard. 1930. *Treatise on Money,* 2 v. London: Macmillan.

Keynes, John Maynard. 1980a. *Activities 1940-1944: Shaping the Post-War World:*

The Clearing Union. The Collected Writings of John Maynard Keynes, v. 25. Edited by Donald Moggridge. London: Macmillan / New York: Cambridge University Press.

Keynes, John Maynard. 1980b. *Activities 1941-1946: Shaping the Post-War World: Bretton Woods and Reparations. The Collected Writings of John Maynard Keynes*, v. 26. Edited by Donald Moggridge. London: Macmillan / New York: Cambridge University Press.

Mason, Edward S[agendorph], and Robert E. Asher. 1973. *The World Bank Since Bretton Woods*. Washington, D.C.: Brookings Institution.

Mikesell, Raymond F[rench]. 1994. *The Bretton Woods Debates: A Memoir*. Essays in International Finance No. 192, March. Princeton, New Jersey: International Finance Section, Department of Economics, Princeton University.

Mikesell, Raymond F[rench]. 2000. *Foreign Adventures of an Economist*. Eugene, Oregon: University of Oregon Press.

Oliver, Robert W[arner]. 1975, 1996. *International Economic Co-Operation and the World Bank*, original edition, revised edition. London: Macmillan.

Rees, David. 1973. *Harry Dexter White: A Study in Paradox*. New York: Coward, McCann and Geoghegan.

Reinertsen, Maria Berg. 2017. *Reisen til Bretton Woods*. Oslo: Cappelen Damm.

Robbins, Lionel, and James [Edward] Meade. 1981. *The Wartime Diaries of Lionel Robbins and James Meade, 1943-45*. Edited by Susan Howson and Donald Moggridge. New York: St. Martin's Press.

Schuler, Kurt. 1992. "The World History of Free Banking." In Kevin Dowd, editor, *The Experience of Free Banking*: 7-47. London: Routledge.

Schuler, Kurt, and Mark Bernkopf. 2014. "Who Was at Bretton Woods?" Center for Financial Stability, Paper in Financial History, July 1.

Schuler, Kurt, and Andrew Rosenberg. 2012/2013. *The Bretton Woods Transcripts*, electronic edition / print edition. New York: Center for Financial Stability.

Selgin, George A., and Lawrence H. White. 1994. "How Would the Invisible Hand Handle Money?" *Journal of Economic Literature*, v. 32, no. 4: 1718-1749.

Skidelsky, Robert [Jacob Alexander]. 2001. *John Maynard Keynes. Volume 3: Fighting for Freedom, 1937-1946*. New York: Viking Penguin.

Steil, Benn. 2013. *The Battle of Bretton Woods: John Maynard Keynes, Harry Dexter White, and the Making of a New World Order*. Princeton, New Jersey: Princeton University Press.

United States. Department of State. 1967. *Foreign Relations of the United States: Diplomatic Papers, 1944, General: Economic and Social Matters, Volume II*. Edited by E. Ralph Perkins, S. Everett Gleason, and Fredrick Aandahl. Washington, D.C.: Government Printing Office.

United States. Department of the Treasury. 1939. *Annual Report of the Secretary of the Treasury on the State of the Finances for the Fiscal Year Ended June 30, 1938*. Washington, D.C.: Government Printing Office.

United States. Department of the Treasury. 1943. "Preliminary Draft Outline of a Proposal for an International Stabilization Fund of the United and Associated Nations," June 10. Washington, D.C.: U.S. Treasury.

United States. Department of the Treasury. 1944a. "Questions and Answers on the International Monetary Fund," June 10. Available in Horsefield 1969, v. 3: 136-182.

United States. Department of the Treasury. 1944b. "Questions and Answers on the Bank for Reconstruction and Development," June 10. For an easily readable version see Kurt Schuler and Dylan Schuler, editors, Center for Financial Stability Paper in Financial History, August 14, 1973. <http://www.centerforfinancialstability.org/bw/Q_A_08142013.pdf>.

UNMFC. 1948. United Nations Monetary and Financial Conference (1944: Bretton Woods, New Hampshire). *Proceedings and Documents of the United Nations Monetary and Financial Conference, Bretton Woods, New Hampshire, July 1-22, 1944*, 2 v. United States, Department of State, Office of Public Affairs, Division of Publications, publication no. 2866, International Organization and Conference Series I, 3. Washington, D.C.: Government Printing Office. (Page numbers in volumes are consecutive.) Also on FRASER (Federal Reserve Archival System for Economic Research, Federal Reserve Bank of St. Louis), <http://fraser.stlouisfed.org/publication/?pid=430>.

van Dormael. *See* Dormael.

Wintour, Timothy W. 2013. "The Buck Starts Here: The Federal Reserve and Monetary Politics from World War to Cold War, 1941-1951." Ph.D. dissertation, Kent State University, <https://etd.ohiolink.edu/rws_etd/document/get/kent1383927017/inline>.

World Bank Archives. Oral History Program. 1961. "Transcript of Interview with Ansel F. Luxford." July 13. <http://siteresources.worldbank.org/EXTARCHIVES/Resources/Ansel_Luxford_Oral_History_Transcript_44_01.pdf>.

Young, John Parke. 1950. "Developing Plans for an International Monetary Fund and a World Bank." *Department of State Bulletin*, November 13: 778-790.

Sources of chapters

Here is a list of the original sources for each chapter. Many of the documents also appear in other files, because multiple copies exist.

Source codes: RG = record group in U.S. National Archives in College Park, Maryland; T = Treasury files in UK National Archives in Kew (London); I.M.C. = British records of the 1944 International Monetary Conference, also at Kew.

The secretary here means the person who took the source notes, who may not be the same as the secretary appointed the Atlantic City conference to be an official of a committee.

Chapter	Source	Secretary
1	Not applicable	Not applicable
2-3	Published by U.S. Treasury	Not applicable
4	RG 56, Box 1, Folder A-9	Edward M. Bernstein
5-13	RG 56, Box 1, Folder A-9	Janet R. Sundelson
14	RG 56, Box 59	Dorothy F. Richardson
15	RG 82, Box 42, Atlantic City, first folder	Alice Bourneuf
16-19	RG 56, Box 1, Folder A-9	Dorothy F. Richardson
20-24	T 231/361, I.M.C. (44) (DEL) 1st-5th Meetings	H.E. Brooks & A.W. Snelling
25-26	T 231/361, I.M.C. (44) (DEL) 6th-7th Meetings	H.E. Brooks
27	T 231/361, I.M.C. (44) (DEL) 8th Meeting	H.E. Brooks & A.W. Snelling
28	RG 56, Box 1, Folder A-9 Pasvolsky Papers, Box 1	Dorothy F. Richardson Leo Pasvolsky
29	RG 56, Box 59, Folder "Minutes of Meetings"	Dorothy F. Richardson
	RG 56, Box 1, Folder A-9	No attribution
	T 231/361, I.M.C. (44) (DEL) 9th Meeting	A.W. Snelling
30	T 231/364, I.M.C. (44) (Com.) 2nd meeting	H.E. Brooks & A.W. Snelling
31	T 231/364, I.M.C. (44) (General) 1st-2nd Meetings	H.E. Brooks & A.W. Snelling

Chapter	Source	Secretary
33-37	T 231/364, I.M.C. (44) (General) 3rd-6th Meetings and 5th Meeting Corrigendum	H.E. Brooks & A W. Snelling
38-40	RG 56, Box 1, Folder A-9	Janet R. Sundelson
41	RG 56, Box 1, Folder A-9	Henry J. Bittermann Dorothy F. Richardson
42	RG 56, Box 1, Folder A-9	Janet R. Sundelson
43	RG 56, Box 1, Folder A-9	Dorothy F. Richardson
44	RG 56, Box 1, Folder A-9 T 231/364, I.M.C. (Prelim.) 2nd Meeting	Dorothy F. Richardson H.E. Brooks
45	RG 56, Box 1, Folder A-9 RG 56, Box 1, Folder A-9 T 231/364, I.M.C. (Prelim.) 3rd Meeting	Dorothy F. Richardson Janet R. Sundelson No attribution
46-47	RG 56, Box 1, Folder A-9	Raymond F. Mikesell
48-49	RG 56, Box 1, Folder A-9	Henry J. Bittermann Dorothy F. Richardson
50	RG 56, Box 1, Folder A-9	Dorothy F. Richardson Henry J. Bittermann
51	RG 56, Box 1, Folder A-9	Henry J. Bittermann
52	RG 56, Box 1, Folder A-9	Dorothy F. Richardson
53-56	RG 56, Box 1, Folder A-9	Emanuel E. Minskoff
57-60	RG 56, Box 1, Folder A-9	Raymond F. Mikesell
61-64	RG 56, Box 1, Folder A-9	Karl R. Bopp
65-68	RG 56, Box 1, Folder A-9	Richard H. Brenner
69	RG 56, Box 1, Folder A-9	H.E. Brooks
70	RG 56, Box 1, Folder A-9 T 231/364, I.M.C. (Prelim) 4th meeting	Richard H. Brenner No attribution
71	RG 56, Box 1, Folder A-9	Richard H. Brenner
72	RG 56, Box 1, Folder A-9	August W. Maffry
73	Not applicable	Not applicable
74	RG 56, Box 1, Folder A-3 UNMFC (1948, v. 1: 21-60)	No attribution Not applicable

Chapter	Source	Secretary
75-78	RG 56, Box 1, Folder A-3	No attribution
79	RG 56, Box 20, Folder A-11	Sir Wilfrid Eady
80	RG 56, Box 20, Folder A-11, I.M.C. (44) (B) 5	No attribution
81	RG 56, Box 59 UNMFC (1948, v. 1: 141-143)	August W. Maffry
82	RG 56, Box 1, Folder A-4, I.M.C. (44) (F) 11	H.E. Brooks [& A W. Snelling?]
83	UNMFC (1948, v. 1: 191-215)	Not applicable
Appendices		
A	RG 56, Box 1, Folder A-3	No attribution
	RG 82, Box 1, Folder A-9	No attribution
	RG 82, Box 42, 2nd Folder "Atlantic City Drafting Committee"	No attribution
B	Various	Data collected by editors
C	Not applicable	Not applicable
D	RG 56, Box 20, Folder A-11	No attribution

PART I

PRECONFERENCE DOCUMENTS

2

Joint Statement by Experts on the Establishment of an International Monetary Fund
April 21, 1944

I. Purposes and Policies of the Fund • II. Subscription to the Fund • III. Transactions with the Fund • IV. Par Values of Member Currencies • V. Capital Transactions • VI. Apportionment of Scarce Currencies • VII. Management of the Fund • VIII. Withdrawal from the Fund • IX. Obligations of Member Countries • X. Transitional Arrangements

The Joint Statement was published simultaneously in the United States, United Kingdom, and several other countries. The preliminary paragraph of the statement mentions the United and Associated Nations. The United Nations were the World War II Allies. On January 1-2, 1942, 27 countries signed the Declaration of United Nations on January 1-2, 1942 in Washington, D.C. Still more countries signed later. Associated nations were those had severed diplomatic relations with the Axis powers but had not declared war on them, or such other countries as the Allies might wish to participate.[101]

The Joint Statement has names for articles, but not for sections. We have inserted our own section names in double brackets, [[ ]]. We use the section names in later chapters to help readers understand more easily what topics the delegates to the Atlantic City conference are discussing.

The version of this statement published in the United States contained a foreword

---

[101] The original signatories were the United States, United Kingdom, the Union of Soviet Socialist Republics, and China on January 1, 1942; and Australia, Belgium, Canada, Costa Rica, Cuba, Czechoslovakia, Dominican Republic, El Salvador, Greece, Guatemala, Haiti, Honduras, India, Luxembourg, Netherlands, New Zealand, Nicaragua, Norway, Panama, Poland, South Africa, and Yugoslavia the next day. Subsequent signatories, in order of signature, were Mexico, Philippines, Ethiopia, Iraq, Brazil, Bolivia, Iran, Colombia, Liberia, France, Ecuador, Peru, Chile, Paraguay, Venezuela, Uruguay, Turkey, Egypt, Saudi Arabia, Syria, and Lebanon.

*by Secretary of the Treasury Henry Morgenthau, Jr., which we omit.
At Atlantic City the U.S. Department of the Treasury distributed to delegates a
long accompanying document, "Questions and Answers on the International Monetary
Fund." It is available elsewhere, so we omit it here; see the references in the previous
chapter.*

Sufficient discussion of the problems of international monetary cooperation has taken place at the technical level to justify a statement of principles. It is the consensus of opinion of the experts of the United and Associated Nations who have participated in these discussions that the most practical method of assuring international monetary cooperation is through the establishment of an International Monetary Fund. The principles set forth below are designed to constitute the basis for this Fund. Governments are not asked to give final approval to these principles until they have been embodied in the form of definite proposals by the delegates of the United and Associated Nations meeting in a formal conference.

I. Purposes and Policies of the Fund

The Fund will be guided in all its decisions by the purposes and policies set forth below:

1. *[[Promote International Monetary Cooperation.]]*[102] To promote international monetary cooperation through a permanent institution which provides the machinery for consultation on international monetary problems.

2. *[[Balanced Trade, High Employment and Real Income.]]* To facilitate the expansion and balanced growth of international trade and to contribute in this way to the maintenance of a high level of employment and real income, which must be a primary objective of economic policy.

3. *[[Lend to Members.]]* To give confidence to member countries by making the Fund's resources available to them under adequate safeguards, thus giving members time to correct maladjustments in their balance of payments without resorting to measures destructive of national or international prosperity.

4. *[[Promote Exchange Stability.]]* To promote exchange stability, to maintain orderly exchange arrangements among member countries, and

---

[102] Double brackets indicate section titles of our invention that we have added for ease of reference.

to avoid competitive exchange depreciation.

5. *[[Assist with Multilateral Payments Facilities.]]* To assist in the establishment of multilateral payments facilities on current transactions among member countries and in the elimination of foreign exchange restrictions which hamper the growth of world trade.

6. *[[Shorten Balance of Payments Disequilibrium.]]* To shorten the periods and lessen the degree of disequilibrium in the international balance of payments of member countries.

II. Subscription to the Fund

1. *[[Total Amount.]]* Member countries shall subscribe in gold and in their local funds amounts (quotas) to be agreed, which will amount altogether to about $8 billion if all the United and Associated Nations subscribe to the Fund (corresponding to about $10 billion for the world as a whole).

2. *[[Revisions to Quotas.]]* The quotas may be revised from time to time but changes shall require a four-fifths vote and no member's quota may be changed without its assent.

3. *[[Gold Subscriptions.]]* The obligatory gold subscription of a member country shall be fixed at 25 percent of its subscription (quota) or 10 percent of its holdings of gold and gold convertible exchange, whichever is the smaller.

III. Transactions with the Fund

1. *[[National Agency Dealing with Fund.]]* Member countries shall deal with the Fund only through their Treasury, Central Bank, Stabilization Fund, or other fiscal agencies. The Fund's account in a member currency shall be kept at the Central Bank of the member country.

2. *[[Purchases of Another Member's Currency.]]* A member shall be entitled to buy another member's currency from the Fund in exchange for its own currency on the following conditions:

(a) The member represents that the currency demanded is presently needed for making payments in that currency which are consistent with the purposes of the Fund.

(b) The Fund has not given notice that its holding of the currency demanded have become scare in which case the provisions of VI, below, come into force.

(c) The Fund's total holdings of the currency offered (after having been restored, if below that figure, to 75 percent of the member's quota) have not been increased by more than 25 percent of the member's quota during the previous 12 months and do not exceed 200 percent of the quota.

(d) The Fund has not previously given appropriate notice that the member is suspended from making further use of the Fund's resources on the ground that it is using them in a manner contrary to the purposes and policies of the Fund; but the Fund shall not give such notice until it has presented to the member concerned a report setting forth its views and has allowed a suitable time for reply.

The Fund may in its discretion and on terms which safeguard its interests waive any of the conditions above.

3. *[[Limitation on Purchases.]]* The operations on the Fund's account will be limited to transactions for the purpose of supplying a member country on the member's initiative with another member's currency in exchange for its own currency or for gold. Transactions provided for under 4 and 7, below, are not subject to this limitation

4. *[[Scarce Currency.]]* The Fund will be entitled at its option, with a view to preventing a particular member's currency from becoming scarce:

(a) To borrow its currency from a member country.

(b) To offer gold to a member country in exchange for its currency.

5. *[[Obligations of a Purchasing Country.]]* So long as a member country is entitled to buy another member's currency from the Fund in exchange for its own currency, it shall be prepared to buy its own currency from that member with that member's currency or with gold. This requirement does not apply to currency subject to restrictions in conformity with IX, 3 below or to holdings of currency which have accumulated as a result of transactions of a current account nature effected before the removal by the member country of restrictions on multilateral clearing maintained or imposed under X, 2 below.

6. *[[Purchase of Another Member's Currency with Gold.]]* A member country desiring to obtain, directly or indirectly, the currency of another member country for gold is expected, provided that it can do so with equal advantage, to acquire the currency by the sale of gold to the Fund. This shall not preclude the sale of newly-mined gold by a gold-producing country on any market.

7. *[[Fund's Acquisition of Gold.]]* The Fund may also acquire gold from member countries in accordance with the following provisions:

(a) A member country may repurchase from the Fund for gold any part of the latter's holdings of its currency.

(b) So long as a member's holdings of gold and gold convertible exchange exceed its quota, the Fund in selling foreign exchange to that country shall require that one-half of the net sales of such exchange during the Fund's financial year be paid for with gold.

(c) If at the end of the Fund's financial year a member's holdings of gold and gold convertible exchange have increased, the Fund may require up to one-half of the increase to be used to repurchase part of the Fund's holdings of its currency so long as this does not reduce the Fund's holdings of a country's currency below 75 percent of its quota or the member's holdings of gold and gold convertible exchange below its quota.

IV. Par Values of Member Currencies

1. *[[Establishing Par Value.]]* The par value of a member's currency shall be agreed with the Fund when it is admitted to membership, and shall be expressed in terms of gold. All transactions between the Fund and members shall be at par, subject to a fixed charge payable by the member making application to the Fund, and all transactions in member currencies shall be at rates within an agreed percentage of parity.

2. *[[Changes in Par Value.]]* Subject to 5, below, no change in the par value of a member's currency shall be made by the Fund without the country's approval. Member countries agree not to propose a change in the parity of their currency unless they consider it appropriate to the correction of a fundamental disequilibrium. Changes shall be made only with the approval of the Fund, subject to the provisions below.

3. *[[Fund's Approval of Changes in Par Value.]]* The Fund shall approve a requested change in the par value of a member's currency, if it essential to the correction of a fundamental disequilibrium. In particular, the Fund shall not reject a requested change, necessary to restore equilibrium, because of the domestic social or political policies of the country applying for a change. In considering a requested change, the Fund shall take into consideration the extreme uncertainties prevailing at the time the parities of the currencies of the member countries were initially agreed upon.

4. *[[Latitude for Change in Par Value.]]* After consulting the Fund, a member country may change the established parity of its currency, provided the proposed change, inclusive of any previous change since the establishment of the Fund, does not exceed 10 percent. In the case of application for a further change, not covered by the above and not exceeding 10 percent, the Fund shall give its decision within 2 days of receiving the application, if the applicant so requests.

5. *[[Uniform Changes in Par Values.]]* An agreed uniform change may be

made in the gold value of member currencies, provided every member country having 10 percent or more of the aggregate quotas approves.

V. Capital Transactions

1. *[[Use of Fund to Finance Capital Outflows.]]* A member country may not use the Fund's resources to meet a large or sustained outflow of capital, and the Fund may require a member country to exercise controls to prevent such use of the resources of the Fund. This provision is not intended to prevent the use of the Fund's resources for capital transactions of reasonable amount required for the expansion of exports or in the ordinary course of trade, banking, or other business. Nor is it intended to prevent capital movements which are met out of a member country's own resources of gold and foreign exchange, provided such capital movements are in accordance with the purposes of the Fund.

2. *[[Capital and Current Controls.]]* Subject to VI below, a member country may not use its control of capital movements to restrict payments for current transactions or to delay unduly the transfer of funds in settlement of commitments.

VI. Apportionment of Scarce Currencies

1. *[[Fund Warning of Scarcity.]]* When it becomes evident to the Fund that the demand for a member country's currency may soon exhaust the Fund's holdings of that currency, the Fund shall so inform member countries and propose an equitable method of apportioning the scarce currency. When a currency is thus declared scarce, the Fund shall issue a report embodying the causes of the scarcity and containing recommendations designed to bring it to an end.

2. *[[Rationing of Scarce Currencies.]]* A decision by the Fund to apportion a scarce currency shall operate as an authorization to a member country, after consultation with the Fund, temporarily to restrict the freedom of exchange operations in the affected currency, and in determining the manner of restricting the demand and rationing the limited supply among its nationals, the member country shall have complete jurisdiction.

VII. Management of the Fund

1. *[[Board and Executive Committee.]]* The Fund shall be governed by a board on which each member will be represented and by an executive

committee. The executive committee shall consist of at least nine members including the representatives of the five countries with the largest quotas.

2. *[[Voting Power.]]* The distribution of voting power on the board and the executive committee shall be closely related to the quotas.

3. *[[Voting Procedures.]]* Subject to II, 2 and IV, 5, all matters shall be settled by a majority of the votes.

4. *[[Publication of Financial Position.]]* The Fund shall publish at short intervals a statement of its position showing the extent of its holdings of member currencies and of gold and its transactions in gold.

VIII. Withdrawal from the Fund

1. *[[Procedure for Withdrawal.]]* A member country may withdraw from the Fund by giving notice in writing.

2. *[[Liquidation of Obligations.]]* The reciprocal obligations of the Fund and the country are to be liquidated within a reasonable time.

3. *[[Disposal of Withdrawing Member's Currency.]]* After a member country has given notice in writing of its withdrawal from the Fund, the Fund may not dispose of its holdings of the country's currency except in accordance with the arrangements made under 2, above. After a country has given notice of withdrawal, its use of the resources of the Fund is subject to the approval of the Fund.

IX. Obligations of Member Countries

1. *[[Gold Price.]]* Not to buy gold at a price which exceeds the agreed parity of its currency by more than a prescribed margin and not to sell gold at a price which falls below the agreed parity by more than a prescribed margin.

2. *[[Foreign Exchange Dealings.]]* Not to allow exchange transactions in its market in currencies of other members at rates outside a prescribed range based on the agreed parities.

3. *[[Current Transactions.]]* Not to impose restrictions on payments for current international transactions with other member countries (other than those involving capital transfers or in accordance with VI, above) or to engage in any discriminatory currency arrangements or multiple currency practices without the approval of the Fund.

X. Transitional Arrangements

1. *[[Entry into Force.]]* Since the Fund is not intended to provide facilities for relief or reconstruction or to deal with international indebtedness arising out of the war, the agreement of a member country to provisions III, 5 and IX, 3 above, shall not become operative until it is satisfied as to the arrangements at its disposal to facilitate the settlement of the balance of payments differences during the early post-war transition period by means which will not unduly encumber its facilities with the Fund.

2. *[[Transition Period.]]* During this transition period member countries may maintain and adapt to changing circumstances exchange regulations of the character which have been in operation during the war, but they shall undertake to withdraw as soon as possible by progressive stages any restrictions which impede multilateral clearing on current account. In their exchange policy they shall pay continuous regard to the principles and objectives of the Fund; and they shall take all possible measures to develop commercial and financial relations with other member countries which will facilitate international payments and the maintenance of exchange stability.

3. *[[Restrictions on Exchange.]]* The Fund may make representations to any member that conditions are favorable to withdrawal of particular restrictions or for the general abandonment of the restrictions inconsistent with IX, 3 above. Not later than three years after coming into force of the Fund any member still retaining any restrictions inconsistent with IX, 3 shall consult with the Fund as to their further retention.

4. *[[Adjustments during Transition Period.]]* In its relation with member countries, the Fund shall recognize that the transition period is one of change and adjustment, and in deciding on its attitude to any proposals presented by members it shall give the member country the benefit of any reasonable doubt.

3

[American] Preliminary Draft Outline of a Proposal for a Bank for Reconstruction and Development of the United and Associated Nations
November 24, 1943

Preamble • I. The Purposes of the Bank • II. Capital Structure of the Bank • III. The International Monetary Unit • IV. Powers and Operations • V. Management

Before the Atlantic City conference there was no internationally agreed statement on a bank for postwar reconstruction comparable to the Joint Statement on the IMF. The United States published the proposal below in 1943. We reproduce it because it was the most detailed proposal circulated before the conference. On the voyage to the United States aboard the Queen Mary, *the British delegation drafted a counterproposal that retained many aspects of the American proposal. The Atlantic City conference considered the British counterproposal as Document B-1, reproduced in chapter 80.*

The American proposal has names for articles, but not for sections. We have inserted our own section names in double brackets, [[ ]]. We use the section names in later chapters to help readers understand more easily what topics the delegates to the Atlantic City conference are discussing.

The original version of this statement contains a foreword by Secretary of the Treasury Henry Morgenthau, Jr., which we omit.

At Atlantic City the U.S. Department of the Treasury distributed to delegates a long accompanying document, "Questions and Answers on the Bank for Reconstruction and Development." It is available elsewhere, so we omit it here; see the references in the previous chapter.

Preamble

1. The provision of foreign capital will be one of the important international economic and financial problems of the postwar period. Many countries will require capital for reconstruction, for the conversion of their industries to peacetime needs, and for the development of their

productive resources. Others will find that foreign investment provides a growing market for their goods. Sound international investment will be of immense benefit to the lending as well as to the borrowing countries.

2. Even in the early postwar years it may be hoped that a considerable part of the capital for international investment will be provided through private investment channels. It will undoubtedly be necessary, however, to encourage private investment by assuming some of the risks that will be especially large immediately after the war and to supplement private investment with capital provided through international cooperation. The United Nations Bank for Reconstruction and Development is proposed as a permanent institution to encourage and facilitate international investment for sound and productive purposes.

3. The Bank is intended to cooperate with private financial agencies in making available long-term capital for reconstruction and development and to supplement such investment where private agencies are unable to meet fully the legitimate needs for capital for productive purposes. The Bank would make no loans or investments that could be secured from private investors on reasonable terms. The principal function of the Bank would be to guarantee and to participate in loans made by private investment agencies and to lend directly from its own resources whatever additional capital may be needed. The facilities of the Bank would be available only for approved governmental and business projects which have been guaranteed by national governments. Operating under these principles, the Bank should be a powerful factor in encouraging the provision of private capital for international investment.

4. By making certain that capital is available for productive uses on reasonable terms, the Bank can make an important contribution to enduring peace and prosperity. With adequate capital, countries affected by the war can move steadily toward reconstruction, and the newer countries can undertake the economic development of which they are capable. International investment for these purposes can be a significant factor in expanding trade and in helping to maintain a high level of business activity throughout the world.

I. The Purposes of the Bank

1. *[[Cooperate with Private Agencies in Reconstruction and Development.]]* To assist in the reconstruction and development of member countries by cooperating with private financial agencies in the provision of capital for sound and constructive international investment.

2. *[[Provide Capital when Private Agencies Do Not.]]* To provide capital for

reconstruction and development, under conditions which will amply safeguard the Bank's funds, when private financial agencies are unable to supply the capital needed for such purposes on reasonable terms consistent with the borrowing policies of member countries.

3. *[[Assist in Transition to Peacetime.]]* To facilitate a rapid and smooth transition from a wartime economy to a peacetime economy by increasing the flow of international investment, and thus to help avoid serious disruption of the economic life of member countries.

4. *[[Raise Productivity.]]* To assist in raising the productivity of member countries by helping to make available through international collaboration long-term capital for the sound development of productive resources.

5. *[[Promote Trade.]]* To promote the long-range balanced growth of international trade among member countries.

II. Capital Structure of the Bank

1. *[[Capital.]]* The authorized capital shall be equivalent to about $10 billion consisting of shares having a par value equal to $100,000.

2. *[[Shares.]]* The shares of the Bank shall be nontransferable, nonassessable, and nontaxable. The liability on shares shall be limited to the unpaid portion of the subscription price.

3. *[[Distribution of Shares.]]* Each government which is a member of the International Stabilization Fund shall subscribe to a minimum number of shares to be determined by formula to be agreed upon. The formula shall take into account such relevant data as the national income and the international trade of the member country. Such a formula would make the subscription of the United States approximately one-third of the total.

4. *[[Payments on Subscriptions.]]* Payments on subscriptions to the shares of the Bank shall be made as follows:

(a) The initial payment of each member country shall be 20 per cent of its subscription, some portion of which (not to exceed 20 per cent) shall be in gold and the remainder in local currency. The proportions to be paid in gold and local currency shall be graduated according to a schedule to be agreed upon which shall take into account the adequacy of the gold and free foreign exchange holdings of each member country.

(b) The member countries shall make the initial payment within 60 days after the date set for the operations of the Bank to begin. The remainder of their respective subscriptions shall be paid in such amounts and at such times as the Board of Directors may determine, but not more than 20 percent of the subscription may be called in any one year.

(c) Calls for further payment on subscriptions shall be made uniform on all shares, and no calls shall be made unless shares are needed for the operations of the Bank. The proportion of subsequent payments to be made in gold shall be determined by the schedule in II-4(a) as it applies to each member country at the time of each call.

5. *[[Unpaid Subscriptions.]]* A substantial part of the subscribed capital of the Bank shall be reserved in the form of unpaid subscriptions as a surety fund for securities guaranteed by the Bank or issued by the Bank.

6. *[[Excess Subscriptions.]]* When the cash resources of the Bank are substantially in excess of prospective needs, the Board may return, subject to future call, uniform proportions of the subscriptions. When the local currency holdings of the Bank exceed 20 percent of the subscription of any member country, the Board may arrange to repurchase with local currency some of the shares held by such a country.

7. *[[Repurchase of Local Currency.]]* Each member country agrees to repurchase each year its local currency held by the Bank amounting to not more than 2 percent of its paid subscription, paying for it with gold; *provided, however,* that:

(a) This requirement may be generally suspended for any year by a three-fourths vote of the Board.

(b) No country shall be required to repurchase local currency in any given year in excess of one-half of the addition to its official holdings of gold during the preceding year.

(c) The obligation of a member country to repurchase its local currency shall be limited to the amount of the local currency paid on its subscription.

8. *[[Exchange Restrictions.]]* All member countries agree that all of the local currency holdings and other assets of the Bank located in their countries shall be free from any special restrictions as to their use, except such restrictions as are consented to by the Bank, and subject to IV-3, below.

9. *[[Use of Resources.]]* The resources and facilities of the Bank shall be used exclusively for the benefit of member countries.

III. The International Monetary Unit

1. *[[Monetary Unit.]]* The monetary unit of the Bank shall be the unit of the International Stabilization Fund (137-1/7 grains of fine gold, that is, equivalent to $10 U.S.).

2. *[[Guarantee against Depreciation.]]* The Bank shall keep its accounts in

terms of this unit. The local currency assets of the Bank are to be guaranteed against any depreciation in their value in terms of gold.

IV. Powers and Operations

1. *[[Loans.]]* To achieve the purposes stated in Section I, the Bank may guarantee, participate in, or make loans to any member country and through the government of such country to any of its political subdivisions or to business or industrial enterprises therein under conditions provided below.

(a) The payment of interest and principal is fully guaranteed by the national government.

(b) The borrower is otherwise unable to secure the funds from other sources, even with the national government's guarantee of repayment, under conditions which in the opinion of the Bank are reasonable.

(c) A competent committee has made a careful study of the merits of the project or the program and, in a written report, concludes that the loan would serve directly or indirectly to raise the productivity of the borrowing country and that the prospects are favorable to the servicing of the loan. The majority of the committee making the report shall consist of members of the technical staff of the Bank. The committee shall include an expert selected by the country requesting the loan, who may or may not be a member of the technical staff of the Bank.

(d) The Bank shall make arrangements to assure the use of the proceeds of any loan which it guarantees, participates in, or makes for the purposes for which the loan was approved.

(e) The Bank shall guarantee, participate in, or make loans only at reasonable rates of interest with a schedule of repayment appropriate to the character of the project and the balance of payments prospects of the country of the borrower.

2. *[[Guarantees.]]* In accordance with the provisions in IV-1, above, the Bank may guarantee, in whole or in part, loans made by private investors; *provided, further:*

(a) The rate of interest and other conditions of the loan are reasonable.

(b) The Bank is compensated for its risk in guaranteeing the loan.

3. *[[Loan Participations.]]* The Bank may participate in loans placed through the usual investment channels, provided that all the conditions listed under IV-1 above are met except that the rate of interest may be higher than if the loans were guaranteed by the Bank.

4. *[[Equity Investment.]]* The Bank may encourage and facilitate

international investment in equity securities by securing the guarantee by governments of conversion into foreign exchange of the current earnings of such foreign held investments. In promoting this objective the Bank may also participate in such investments, but its aggregate participation in such equity securities shall not exceed 10 percent of its paid-in capital.

5. *[[Dealing in Securities.]]* The Bank may publicly offer any securities it has previously acquired. To facilitate the sale of such securities, the Bank may, in its discretion, guarantee them.

6. *[[Noncompetition with Private Investment.]]* The Bank shall make no loans or investments that can be placed through the usual private investment channels on reasonable terms. The Bank shall by regulation prescribe procedure for its operations that will assure the application of this principle.

7. *[[Spending of Proceeds of Loans.]]* The Bank shall impose no condition upon a loan as to the particular member country in which the proceeds of the loan must be spent; *provided, however,* that the proceeds of a loan may not be spent in any country which is not a member country without the approval of the Bank.

8. *[[Currency of Loans.]]* The Bank in making loans shall provide that:

(a) The foreign exchange in connection with the project or program shall be provided by the Bank in the currencies of the countries in which the proceeds of the loan will be spent, and only with the approval of such countries.

(b) The local currency needs in connection with the project shall be largely financed locally without the assistance of the Bank.

(c) In special circumstances, where the Bank considers that the local part of any project cannot be financed at home except on very unreasonable terms, it can lend that portion to the borrower in local currency.

(d) Where the developmental program will give rise to an increased need for foreign exchange for purposes not directly needed for that program, yet resulting from the program, the Bank will provide an appropriate part of the loan in gold or desired foreign exchange.

9. *[[Accounting.]]* When a loan is made by the Bank, it shall credit the account of the borrower with the amount of the loan. Payment shall be made from this account to meet drafts covering audited expenses.

10. *[[Payment Provisions.]]* Loans participated in or made by the Bank shall contain the following payment provisions:

(a) Payment of interest on loans shall be made in currencies acceptable to the Bank or in gold. Interest will be payable only on amounts withdrawn.

(b) Payment on account of principal of a loan shall be in currencies acceptable to the Bank or in gold. If the Bank and the borrower should so agree at the time a loan is made, payment on principal may be in gold, or at the option of the borrower, in the currency actually borrowed.

(c) In the event of an acute exchange stringency the Bank may accept local currency in payment of interest and principal for periods not exceeding three years. The Bank shall arrange with the borrowing country for the repurchase of such local currency over a period of years under appropriate terms that safeguard the value of the Bank's holdings of such currency.

(d) Payments of interest and principal, whether made in member currencies or in gold, must be equivalent to the gold value of the loan and of the contractual interest thereon.

11. *[[Charges.]]* The Bank may levy a charge against the borrower for its expenses in investigating any loan placed, guaranteed, participated in, or made in whole or in part by the Bank.

12. *[[Loans to International Agencies.]]* The Bank may guarantee, participate in, or make loans to international governmental agencies for objectives consonant with the purposes of the Bank, provided that at least one-half of the participants in the international agencies are members of the Bank.

13. *[[Effect of Loans.]]* In considering any application to guarantee, participate in, or make a loan to a member country, the Bank shall give due regard to the effect of such a loan on business and financial conditions in the country in which the loan is to be spent and shall, accordingly, obtain the consent of the country affected.

14. *[[Repurchase of Local Currency Proceeds.]]* At the request of the countries in which portions of the loan are spent, the Bank will repurchase for gold or needed foreign exchange a part of the local currency proceeds of the loan expended by the borrower in those countries.

15. *[[Other Powers.]]* With the approval of the representatives of the governments of the member countries involved, the Bank may engage in the following operations:

(a) It may issue, buy or sell, pledge, or discount any of its own securities and obligations, or securities and obligations taken from its portfolio, or securities which it has guaranteed.

(b) It may borrow from member governments, fiscal agencies, central banks, stabilization funds, private financial institutions in member countries, or from international financial agencies.

(c) It may buy or sell foreign exchange, after consultation with the

International Stabilization Fund, where such transactions are necessary in connection with its operations.

16. *[[Agency Powers.]]* The Bank may act as agent or correspondent for the governments of member countries, their central banks, stabilization funds and fiscal agencies, and for international financial institutions.

The Bank may act as trustee, registrar, or agent in connection with loans guaranteed, participated in, made, or placed through the Bank.

17. *[[Agencies Dealing with Bank.]]* Except as otherwise indicated, the Bank shall deal only with or through:

(a) The governments of member countries, their central banks, stabilization funds, and fiscal agencies.

(b) The International Stabilization Fund and any other international financial agencies owned predominantly by member governments.

The Bank may, nevertheless, with the approval of the member of the Board representing the government of the country concerned, deal with the public or institutions of member countries in the Bank's own securities or securities which it has guaranteed.

18. *[[No Assistance to Suspended Members.]]* If the Bank shall declare any country as suspended from membership, the member governments and their agencies agree not to extend financial assistance to that country without approval of the Bank until the country has been restored to membership.

19. *[[Political Neutrality.]]* The Bank and its officers shall scrupulously avoid interference in the political affairs of any member country. This provision shall not limit the right of an officer of the Bank to participate in the political life of his own country.

The Bank shall not be influenced in its decisions with respect to applications for loans by the political character of the government of the country requesting a loan.

V. Management

1. *[[Board of Directors.]]* The administration of the Bank shall be vested in a Board of Directors composed of one director and one alternate appointed by each member government in a manner to be determined by it.

The director and alternate shall serve for a period of 3 years, subject to the pleasure of their government. Directors and alternates may be reappointed.

2. *[[Board Voting.]]* Voting by the Board shall be as follows:

(a) The director or alternate of each member country shall be entitled to cast 1,000 votes plus one vote for each share of stock held. Thus, a government owning one share will cast 1,001 votes, while a government owning 1,000 shares will cast 2,000 votes.

(b) No country shall cast more than 25 per cent of the aggregate votes.

(c) Except where otherwise provided, decisions of the Board of Directors shall be by simple majority of the votes cast, each member of the Board casting the votes allotted to his government. When deemed to be in the best interests of the Bank, decisions of the Board may be made, without a meeting, by polling the directors on specific questions submitted to them in such manner as the Board shall by regulation provide.

3. *[[President.]]* The Board of Directors shall select a President of the Bank, who shall be the chief of the operating staff of the Bank and *ex-officio* a member of the Board, and one or more vice presidents. The President and vice presidents of the Bank shall hold office for 4 years, shall be eligible for reelection, and may be removed for cause at any time by the Board. The staff of the Bank shall be selected in accordance with regulations established by the Board of Directors.

4. *[[Executive Committee.]]* The Board of Directors shall appoint from among its members, an Executive Committee of not more than nine members. The President of the Bank shall be an *ex-officio* member of the Executive Committee.

The Executive Committee shall be continuously available at the head office of the Bank and shall exercise the authority delegated to it by the Board. In the absence of any member of the Executive Committee his alternate on the Board shall act in his place. Members of the Executive Committee shall receive appropriate remuneration.

5. *[[Advisory Council.]]* The Board of Directors shall select an Advisory Council of seven members. The Council shall advise with the Board and the officers of the Bank on matters of general policy. The Council shall meet annually and on such other occasions as the Board may request.

The members of the Advisory Council shall be selected from men of outstanding ability, but not more than one member shall be selected from the same country. They shall serve for 2 years, and the term of any member may be renewed. Members of the Council shall be paid their expenses and a remuneration to be fixed by the Board.

6. *[[Other Committees.]]* The Board of Directors may appoint such other committees as it finds necessary for the work of the Bank. It may also appoint advisory committees chosen wholly or partially from persons not regularly employed by the Bank.

7. *[[Delegation of Powers.]]* The Board of Directors may authorize any officers or committees of the Bank to exercise any specified powers of the Board except the powers to guarantee, participate in, or make loans. Delegated powers shall be exercised in a manner consistent with the general policies and practices of the Board.

The Board may by a three-fourths vote delegate to the Executive Committee the power to guarantee, participate in, or make loans in such amounts as may be fixed by the Board. In passing upon applications for loans, the Executive Committee shall act in accordance with the requirements specified for each type of loan.

8. *[[Suspension of Membership.]]* A member country failing to meet its financial obligations to the Bank may be declared in default and may be suspended from membership during the period of its default, provided that a majority of the member countries so decide.

While under suspension, the country shall be denied the privileges of membership but shall be subject to the obligations of membership. At the end of 1 year the country shall be dropped automatically from membership in the Bank unless it has been restored to good standing by a majority of the member countries.

If a member country elects to withdraw or is dropped from the Bank, its shares of stock shall, if the Bank has a surplus, be repurchased at the price paid. If the Bank's books show a loss, such country shall bear a proportionate share of the loss. The Bank shall have 5 years in which to liquidate its obligations to a member country withdrawing or dropped from the Bank.

Any member country that withdraws or is dropped from the International Stabilization Fund shall lose its membership in the Bank unless three-fourths of the member votes favor its remaining as a member.

9. *[[Distribution of Net Profits.]]* The yearly net profits shall be applied as follows:

(a) All profits shall be distributed in proportion to shares held, except that one-fourth of the profits shall be applied to surplus until the surplus equals 20 per cent of the subscribed capital.

(b) Profits shall be payable in a country's local currency or in gold at the option of the Bank.

10. *[[Collection of Information.]]* The Bank shall collect and make available to member countries and to the International Stabilization Fund financial and economic information and reports relating to the operations of the Bank. Member countries shall furnish the Bank with all information and data that would facilitate the operations of the Bank.

PART II

AMERICAN MEETINGS

Members of the American Technical Group[103]

Harry Dexter White, Department of the Treasury, Chairman
Hawthorne Arey, Export-Import Bank
Elting Arnold, Department of the Treasury
Edward Bernstein, Department of the Treasury
Henry Bittermann, Department of the Treasury
Karl Bopp, Federal Reserve Bank of Philadelphia
Alice Bourneuf, Board of Governors of the Federal Reserve System
Richard Brenner, Department of the Treasury
Edward E. "Ned" Brown, First National Bank of Chicago[104]
William Adams Brown, Jr., Department of State
Lauren Casaday, Department of the Treasury[105]
Frank Coe, Foreign Economic Administration
Emilio "Peter" Collado, Department of State
Joseph Dreibelbis, Board of Governors of the Federal Reserve System
Henry Edmiston, Federal Reserve Bank of St. Louis
Walter Gardner, Board of Governors of the Federal Reserve System
Emanuel Goldenweiser, Board of Governors of the Federal Reserve System
Alvin Hansen, Federal Reserve Board of Governors
Frederick Livesey, Department of State
Walter Louchheim, Securities and Exchange Commission
Ansel Luxford, Department of the Treasury
August Maffry, Department of Commerce
Raymond Mikesell, Department of the Treasury
Emanuel E. "Duke" Minskoff, Department of the Treasury
Leo Pasvolsky, Department of State
Dorothy Richardson, Department of the Treasury
Janet Sundelson, Department of the Treasury
John Parke Young, Department of State

---

[103] Source: Minutes of meetings. The list excludes some secretaries. For their names and for more biographical details on group members, see Appendix A.

[104] Edward E. Brown was also president of the Federal Advisory Council, a group of bankers that advised the Federal Reserve Board of Governors.

[105] Lauren Casaday was the Treasury attaché in London. He traveled aboard the *Queen Mary*, and so was not present for the early meetings of the group.

4

American Technical Group
First meeting
[Washington, D.C.]
June 8, 1944 at 3 p.m.

Treasury Secretary Morgenthau welcomes U.S. delegation • Overview by Harry Dexter White • U.S. policy concerning international conferences • Editors' appendix: List of American Technical Group flimsies and other documents

The American Technical Group (or Committee) was an assemblage of experts spanning a number of departments and agencies. It first met on May 28, 1942. The meeting numbers in the chapter headings only refer to meetings published in this book. The core of the group was staff from the U.S. Treasury Department's Division of Monetary Research, which Harry Dexter White directed. White was also the chairman of the group. The Americans at Atlantic City were technicians who were in many cases near but not at the top of their organizations. At Bretton Woods, they would be joined by their politically appointed superiors, most notably Marriner C. Eccles, Chairman of the Board of Governors of the Federal Reserve System, and Henry J. Morgenthau, Jr., Secretary of the Treasury.

The minutes do not record the place of this meeting, but it was apparently the Department of the Treasury. Dean Acheson, a top State Department official and former undersecretary of the Treasury who speaks at this meeting, attended the Bretton Woods conference but not the Atlantic City conference, so this is his only appearance in the book.

Secretary [of the Treasury Henry] Morgenthau presided.

Secretary Morgenthau welcomed United States delegates to the United Nations Monetary and Financial Conference. He expressed confidence that the delegates would work together to achieve the purposes of the conference. Secretary Morgenthau said it was expected to take up the Fund proposal, and if possible the Bank. He added that the facilities of the Treasury would be at the disposal of the delegates to help them prepare for the conference.

At the Secretary's request, **Mr. [Harry Dexter] White** explained briefly the work that has been done by the technical advisors, the discussions with the experts of the other United Nations, and the agreement on the principles in the Joint Statement. The Treasury staff has prepared material on the Fund and the Bank that will be sent to the delegates shortly.[106] Mr. White added that the technical staff would be available to discuss any questions of interest to the delegates [to the Bretton Woods conference].

Mr. [Dean] Acheson [Assistant Secretary, Department of State] spoke briefly of the policy of the United States in connection with international conferences. Secretary Morgenthau, as head of the delegation, would be instructed by the President to seek agreement on the Fund and the Bank on the basis of the principles made public. The other delegates are bound by the same instructions. If it becomes necessary, in order to reach agreement, to depart from the accepted principles, the Secretary is authorized to do so after considering the matter with the delegates.

The **Secretary** asked Mr. White to be sure to send the material to the delegates. He added that there would be regular meetings of the delegates at Bretton Woods and he hoped that additional meetings would be held in Washington. The Secretary explained that he would be busy with the War Bond drive, but that another meeting would be called soon, even if he could not attend.

Editors' appendix: List of American Technical Group flimsies and other documents

The American Technical Group called its discussion documents "flimsies." The list below reproduces that from the U.S. National Archives, RG 56, Box 2, Folder "(Bretton Woods) (Atlantic City Conf.) Flimsies," in the document "Flimsies Discussed by the American Technical Committee." The online companion files to this book contain photographs of the flimsies themselves, especially in RG 56, Box 2 and RG 82, Box 42.

1. Quotas

---

[106] Mainly, we presume, the "Questions and Answers on the International Monetary Fund" and the "Questions and Answers on the Bank for Reconstruction and Development."

2. Par values
3. Setting up the Fund and beginning operations
4. Payment of subscriptions
5. Depositories and form of currency holdings
6. Fund's power to acquire needed foreign exchange
7. Acquisition of gold by the Fund
8. Protection of the assets of the Fund
9. Charges by the Fund
10. Capital movements
11. Scarce currencies
12. Multilateral clearing
13. Governing Board and Executive Committee
14. Withdrawal, suspension and liquidation
15. Distribution of profits of the Fund
16. Taxation and immunity provisions
17. Relationship to other organizations
18. Transitional arrangements

The next page of the document contains a second list, "Flimsies not discussed by the American Technical Committee."

1. Method of presentation to Government
2. Definitions
3. Distribution of profits of the Fund
4. Additional undertakings on the part of member countries
5. Protection of the assets of the Fund
6. Transferability and guarantee of the currency holding of the Fund
7. Obtaining information, publication of reports, and consideration of recommendations of the Fund

Other documents

RG 82, Box 42, first folder, contains two other documents of the American Technical Group not listed above. The "Report of Subcommittee on Government Guarantees and Equity Investments" concerns the Bank and handwritten notes date it June 18 and mention Walter Louchheim, who was presumably the subcommittee chairman. The other document is the "Report of Subcommittee on Commercial Policy Aspects of Monetary Fund Proposal."

5

American Technical Group
Second meeting
Atlantic City
June 15, 1944 at 10:30 a.m.[107]

Group work • Subcommittees

The American Technical Group divides itself into subcommittees to address many details about the Bank and the Fund.

In opening the meeting, **Mr. White** called attention to the importance of giving the delegates and the press the fullest assistance in understanding the provisions of the Fund in the Bank. The discussion which followed

---

[107] *Editors' note:* The original minutes of the meetings of the American Technical Group at Atlantic City list the members present at the top of each meeting. We move the list to the footnotes. Apparently this first meeting was on the beach near the Claridge Hotel, the conference site; see the oblique reference to beach towels in the Morgenthau Diaries (v. 746: 133). Subsequent meetings were held inside the hotel. Memorandum for the Secretary from Harry Dexter White, June 22, 1944, in Morgenthau Diaries (v. 746: 139b) states that "the group began its meetings on June 14, 1944," but have found no record of a June 14 meeting.

Present: Mr. E[dward] E. ["Ned"] Brown of the First National Bank of Chicago; Messrs. [Emilio] Collado, [William Adams] Brown, [Frederick] Livesey, [and John Parke] Young of the State Department; Messrs. [Emanuel] Goldenweiser, [Joseph] Dreibelbis, [Walter] Gardner and Miss [Alice] Bourneuf of the Board of Governors [of the Federal Reserve System]; Mr. [Karl] Bopp of the Federal Reserve Bank of Philadelphia; Mr. [Henry] Edmiston of the Federal Reserve Bank of St. Louis; Mr. [August] Maffry of the Department of Commerce; Mr. [Walter] Louchheim of the Securities and Exchange Commission; Mr. [Hawthorne] Arey of the Export-Import Bank; Messrs. [Harry Dexter] White, [Edward] Bernstein, [Ansel] Luxford, [Richard] Brenner, [Elting] Arnold, [Emanuel E. "Duke"] Minskoff, [Henry] Bittermann, and Miss [Dorothy] Richardson and Mrs. [Janet] Sundelson of the Treasury.

also emphasized the importance of attaining maximum teamwork from the Technical Committee as a whole. It was requested that suggestions for changes be submitted to Mr. [Edward] Bernstein, who will present them to the entire group for discussion. It is also agreed that each member attempt to draft specific provisions embodying the recommendations.

It was decided to divide the American Technical Group into subcommittees to consider and draft the provisions on the following problems:[108]

1. The relationship between the provisions dealing with the rationing of scarce currencies in the prohibition of exchange restrictions.
   Chairman: Mr. [Emilio] Collado
   Committee: Messrs. [August] Maffry, Brown[109] and [Raymond] Mikesell

2. Charges and penalties levied by the Fund.
   Chairman: Mr. [Emanuel] Goldenweiser
   Committee: Messrs. [Walter] Gardner, [Karl] Bopp, [Elting] Arnold, Miss [Alice] Bourneuf and Mrs. [Janet] Sundelson

3. Taxation and immunity provisions for the Fund.
   Chairman: Mr. [Joseph] Dreibelbis
   Committee: Messrs. [Frederick] Livesey and [Richard] Brenner

4. Allocation of the income of the Bank and provisions for meeting the obligations of the Bank.
   Chairman: Mr. [Hawthorne] Arey
   Committee: Messrs. [John Parke] Young, [Walter] Louchheim, [Emanuel "Duke"] Minskoff and [Henry] Bittermann

5. Exemption of the Bank's operations from the security regulations of

---

[108] In subsequent chapters we assign shortened names of our own devising to the subcommittees as an aid to the reader.
[109] The American Technical Group had two Browns: Edward E. "Ned" Brown of the First National Bank of Chicago and William Adams Brown, Jr. of the Department of State. The minutes sometimes fail to list the first name of which Brown is involved. Where we have no clue we hazard no guess.

member countries.

Chairman: Mr. [Walter] Louchheim

Committee: Messrs. [Hawthorne] Arey, [John Parke] Young, [Emanuel "Duke"] Minskoff and [Henry] Bittermann

The meeting adjourned to permit the meeting of the subcommittees.

6

American Technical Group
Third meeting
Atlantic City
June 16, 1944 at 10 a.m.[110]

IMF charges and fees • Scarce currencies • Taxation and immunities of the Fund and Bank • Income of the Bank

The group considers reports from four of the five committees that it created at its previous meeting. We have not reproduced the "flimsies" in this book, though they are available in the online companion files. We do however reproduce reports that appear as attachments to minutes.

The group accepts with only minor changes the report of what we have dubbed the Committee on Charges and Penalties Levied by the Fund. Chairman Harry Dexter White asks committee member Walter Gardner to prepare a memorandum on the IMF's fees and charges for the delegates of other countries when they arrive at Atlantic City. The United States, as by far the largest prospective net lender to the IMF, was keen to make fees and charges sufficiently high that borrowing would not be nearly free.

The Committee on Scarce Currencies addresses a potential problem to which much thought was given in the design of the IMF, but that never arose in practice. It was expected that for at least a few years after World War II, many IMF members would have inconvertible currencies, as they continued with exchange controls to avoid devaluing to market-clearing levels and incurring the inflation that would result. The IMF's effectively usable resources would be limited to its holdings of gold and fully

---

[110] Present: Mr. Brown of the First National Bank of Chicago; Messrs. Collado, Brown, Livesey and Young of the State Department; Messrs. Goldenweiser, Dreibelbis, Gardner and Miss Bourneuf of the Board of Governors; Mr. Bopp of the Federal Reserve Bank of Philadelphia; Mr. Edmiston of the Federal Reserve Bank of St. Louis; Mr. Maffry of the Department of Commerce; Mr. Louchheim of the Securities and Exchange Commission; Mr. Arey of the Export-Import Bank; Messrs. White, Bernstein, Luxford, Brenner, Arnold, Minskoff, Bittermann, and Miss Richardson and Mrs. Sundelson of the Treasury.

convertible currencies — in practice, overwhelmingly U.S. dollars. If each member drew (borrowed) convertible currency up to the amount of its quota (contribution), there would not be enough for all. Harry Dexter White first introduced a clause to deal with the problem in his December 1942 draft proposal for the International Stabilization Fund, as he then called it. In practice, the IMF never had to invoke the scarce currency clause because drawings were smaller than gold and U.S. dollar holdings until after other major currencies became convertible.

The Committee on Taxation and Immunity of the Fund proposes that the IMF be completely exempt from taxation. The group accepts.

The Committee on Income of the Bank evidently proposes a solution for payment of the expenses of the Bank for Reconstruction and Development that the group finds unsatisfactory. The group specifies its preference on the issue. The underlying problem that the committee and the group are trying to address is to ensure that the Bank has sufficient capital and reserves to absorb losses, expenses, and dividend payments.

The meeting opened with a report by **Mr. [Emanuel] Goldenweiser** [[Committee on Charges and Penalties Levied by the Fund]] on the proposed charges and fees of the Fund.[111] After extensive discussion, it was agreed that the committee's report should be accepted with the following minor revisions:

(1) Add "small" and "uniform" to provision (a) to read as follows: "Any member country buying the currency of any other member country in exchange for its own currency shall be subject to a small uniform charge in addition to the exchange spread."

(2) Add "gold convertible currency" to provision (b) as follows: "The Fund may levy a reasonable handling charge on any member country buying gold from the Fund or selling gold or gold convertible currency to the Fund."

(3) Add "gold convertible exchange" to provision (e) as follows: "All changes shall be paid in gold and gold convertible currency."

(4) Omit the provision dealing with the apportionment of the excess of the operating expense over income.

Mr. White asked Mr. [Walter] Gardner [[Committee on Charges and Penalties Levied by the Fund]] to prepare a memorandum on fees and charges to be used by the delegates when they arrive. It was agreed that a strong statement of the purpose of the charges and a table showing the

---

[111] No. 9 on the list of flimsies discussed by the American Technical Group that is reproduced in the editors' appendix to chapter 4.

increments levied as the amount and duration of the borrowing incurred should be included in the memorandum.

Mr. [Emilio] Collado presented the report of his committee [[Committee on Scarce Currencies]] on the relationship between the rationing of scarce currencies and the prohibition against exchange restrictions.[112] He pointed out that this report broadened the terminology of provision VI of the Joint Statement, "Apportionment of Scarce Currencies,"[113] and avoided the use of the words "exhaust the Fund's holdings." After extended discussion, it was agreed to recommit the report for the following changes:

(1) To add a sentence requiring that a representative of the country whose currency was becoming scarce be included on the committee making the report:

(2) To strike out the words "despite all remedial measures" in [the] provision on scarce currencies;

(3) To select another word instead of "shortly" in the same provision;

(4) To add "subject to the provision regarding exchange rates" to the sentence "that a member country shall have complete jurisdiction over the allocation of a scarce currency among its nationals";

(5) To include a statement to the effect that the Fund will apportion the available and accruing supply of the scarce currency.

Mr. Collado was asked to embody the discussion on scarce currencies in a memorandum to be used by the foreign delegates.[114]

Mr. [Joseph] Dreibelbis reported on the work of the committee considering the taxation and immunity provisions as relating to the Fund. The committee's recommendation that the Fund be given complete immunity from taxation was accepted.[115] **Mr. [Ansel] Luxford** informed the meeting that this measure had been discussed tentatively with the Tax Division of the [U.S.] Treasury.

Extended discussion followed on the desirability of preventing the Bank from being sued. It was decided to permit the Bank to be sued with

---

[112] No. 11 on the list of flimsies discussed by the American Technical Group.

[113] Roman numerals indicate articles of the Joint Statement. Article headings in brackets are in the original. Roman plus Arabic numerals, such as VI-1, indicate sections of the Joint Statement. Section headings are not in the original; they are our invention for the convenience of readers and are in double brackets.

[114] Presumably no. 3 in the list of conference flimsies in the editors' appendix to chapter 38.

[115] No. 16 on the list of flimsies discussed by the American Technical Group.

its consent, although any conflict between the Fund and a member country would be settled by recourse to an international arbitration convention or to an international arbitration court, should one be established.

Mr. [Hawthorne] Arey remarked on the work of the committee on the allocation of income of the Bank. After considerable discussion of the problem involved, it was agreed to recommit the report[116] to the committee for a redraft along the following lines:

Expenses should be paid from both the guarantee and general loan accounts which would be set up. The next charges against both accounts would be reserves against the Bank's obligations. The balance in both accounts would then be placed in a single general account, from which the member countries would receive an amount equal to 2 percent of that part of their paid-in capital which had been employed in the loans made by the Fund [Bank]. The remainder would be used for surplus and dividends.

---

[116] No. 15 on the list of flimsies discussed by the American Technical Group.

7

American Technical Group
Fourth meeting
Atlantic City
June 16, 1944 at 4 p.m.[117]

*Bank's exemption from securities regulation • Income of the Bank •
Scarce currencies in the IMF*

Mr. [Walter] Louchheim [[Committee on Exemption of the Bank's
Operations from the Security Regulations of Member Countries]]
reported on the possibility of exempting the Bank's operations from the
security regulations of member countries. The committee had agreed that
the securities issued by the Bank should be subject to the security
regulations in each member country and, therefore, that only a provision
prohibiting the imposition of any discriminatory regulations need be
included. After discussion, it was agreed to accept the report of the
committee.[118]

The meeting then considered the redrafts of the earlier committee
reports. **Mr. [Henry] Bittermann** reported for Mr. Arey's committee on
the allocation of the income of the Bank.[119] After considerable discussion
of the revised draft, it was agreed that further revision was still necessary
along lines which would emphasize that, after both expenses and reserves

---

[117] Present: Mr. Brown of the First National Bank of Chicago; Messrs. Collado,
Brown, Livesey and Young of the State Department; Messrs. Goldenweiser,
Dreibelbis, Gardner and Miss Bourneuf of the Board of Governors; Mr. Bopp of
the Federal Reserve Bank of Philadelphia; Mr. Edmiston of the Federal Reserve
Bank of St. Louis; Mr. Maffry of the Department of Commerce; Mr. Louchheim
of the Securities and Exchange Commission; Mr. Arey of the Export-Import
Bank; Messrs. White, Bernstein, Luxford, Brenner, Arnold, Minskoff,
Bittermann, and Miss Richardson and Mrs. Sundelson of the Treasury.

[118] No. 16 on the list of flimsies discussed by the American Technical Group.

[119] No. 15 on the list of flimsies discussed by the American Technical Group.

have been paid out of the Guarantee Fee Account and the General Loan Account, the balance of all accounts would be put into a general account, from which the first payment would be a specific charge to be paid to member governments equal to 2 percent of the amount of its paid-in capital employed in loans. The report was recommitted to Mr. Arey for revision.

Mr. [Emilio] Collado presented a redraft prepared by his committee on the relationship between the rationing of scarce currencies and the prohibition of exchange restrictions.[120] The report was accepted. It was suggested, however, that a section be added, emphasizing that the equitable method of apportioning the scarce currency will follow the lines laid down in paragraph 3 of provision V-5 of the July 10 [1943] draft of the International Stabilization Fund.[121]

---

[120] No. 11 on the list of flimsies discussed by the American Technical Group.

[121] The paragraph cited says, "To facilitate appropriate adjustment in the balance of payments position of member countries, and to help correct the distortions in the pattern of trade balances, the Fund shall apportion its sales of such scarce currency. In such apportionment, it shall be guided by the principle of satisfying the most urgent needs from the point of view of the general international economic situation. It shall also consider the special needs and resources of the particular countries making the request for the scarce currency." U.S. Department of the Treasury (1943: 12).

8

American Technical Group
Fifth meeting
Atlantic City
June 17, 1944 at 10:30 a.m.[122]

Appointment of standing subcommittees • Price of Bank shares • Capital transactions and speculative capital movements • Withdrawal and suspension from the Fund • Liquidation of the Fund • Attachment A: Team assignments • Attachment B: Issue price of Bank shares • Attachment C: Payment of Bank subscriptions • Attachment D: Obligation of IMF members to buy gold • Attachment E: Withdrawal and suspension from the IMF • Attachment F: Liquidation of the Fund • Attachment G: Relation of the Fund and Bank to other international organizations • Attachment H: Proposed language on exchange controls

The group reshuffles itself into four parts corresponding to the four main subcommittees that will exist when foreign delegates arrive at Atlantic City, rather than the five committees it established at its second meeting. It then considers reports from the old committees. It instructs the Committee on the Income of the Bank to reduce the period for payment of initial subscriptions and to increase their amount, so as to give the Bank for Reconstruction and Development more capital faster. In response to the report of the Committee on Charges and Penalties Levied by the Fund, the group spends considerable time discussing capital transactions and speculative capital movements, a

---

[122] Present: Mr. E.E. Brown, First National Bank of Chicago; Messrs. Collado, Brown, Livesey and Young of the State Department; Messrs. Goldenweiser, Dreibelbis, Gardner and Miss Bourneuf of the Board of Governors; Mr. Bopp of the Federal Reserve Bank of Philadelphia; Mr. Edmiston of the Federal Reserve Bank of St. Louis; Mr. Maffry of the Department of Commerce; Mr. Louchheim of the Securities and Exchange Commission; Mr. Arey of the Export-Import Bank; Messrs. White, Bernstein, Luxford, Brenner, Arnold, Minskoff, Bittermann, and Miss Richardson and Mrs. Sundelson of the Treasury.

subject that over the decades has become increasingly important. Emanuel Goldenweiser, chief economist of the Federal Reserve System and the chairman of the committee, proposes additional provisions to the IMF agreement to put the agreement into effect and to limit government holdings of what we would now call eurocurrency reserves. He promises to draft language on the provisions for a future meeting.

Walter Gardner, a subordinate of Goldenweiser at the Federal Reserve, has evidently been appointed head of a new committee, on withdrawal from and liquidation of the Fund. The group accepts the committee's report on withdrawal and suspension of members with several clarifying changes and recommits the report on suspension of the Fund for further changes (see the appendices to this chapter). The group also accepts a report from Emilio Collado, chief of the State Department's Division of Monetary Affairs, on provisions concerning relations of the Fund and the Bank with other international organizations. Collado is the chairman of the Committee on Scarce Currencies that the second meeting of the group had established, so either the committee broadened its scope of work or Collado is reporting for a committee established since.

In order to facilitate the future work of the subcommittees [of the whole Atlantic City conference], it was decided that the following standing subcommittees [of the American Technical Group] should be established:

Committee 1: [Hawthorne] Arey, [Walter] Louchheim, [Henry] Bittermann, [John Parke] Young, [Walter] Dreibelbis

Committee 2: [Emanuel] Goldenweiser, [Alice] Bourneuf, [Frederick] Livesey, [Janet] Sundelson, [Emanuel "Duke"] Minskoff

Committee 3: [Emilio] Collado, [August] Maffry, [Raymond] Mikesell, [Elting] Arnold, [Dorothy] Richardson

Committee 4: [Walter] Gardner, [Karl] Bopp, [William] Brown, [Richard] Brenner.

The assignments to the standing committees are contained in Attachment A.

The meeting then considered the reports of the [old and new] subcommittees:

Mr. [Hawthorne] Arey reported on the issue price of shares for the Bank. The attached report of the committee [[Committee on the Income of the Bank]] (Attachment A [B]) was recommitted for the following changes:

(a) The shares of stock included in the initial subscription shall be issued at par if the subscription is received not later than one year after the date of operations, rather than the three years proposed by the committee.

(b) Other shares shall be issued at par or such other price as is fixed by the Board of Directors.

Mr. Arey then reported on the problem of the payment of subscriptions to the Bank. This report (Attachment C) was accepted subject to the following revisions:

(a) Not more than 10 percent of the subscriptions may be called in in one year;

(b) 25 percent of the par value of shares shall be paid in on the initial payment; and

(c) The second sentence in the second paragraph shall read "each such country shall pay as an initial payment the same *amount* of its initial subscription as is due, etc."

Mr. Arey stated that his committee had not yet had time to consider the other problem assigned to it.

Mr. [Emanuel] Goldenweiser reported on the discussion of his committee on gold and capital transactions of the Fund [[Committee on Charges and Penalties Levied by the Fund]]. Attachment D, the report of this committee, was accepted, but after considerable discussion it was agreed that the words "directly or indirectly" in the following sentence shall not be included in our own draft, but shall be raised again in the discussion with the British: "A member country may not use the Fund's resources directly or indirectly to meet a large or sustained outflow of capital and the Fund may require a member to exercise controls to prevent such use of the resources of the Fund."

Considerable discussion followed on capital transactions and speculative capital movements. It was decided that since each country would be able to handle the problem of speculative capital flowing to it, no provision on this subject need be inserted. **Mr. White** stated that he would arrange to have a memorandum prepared which would define capital transactions and transactions on current account. The borderline cases between them would be left for definition by the Fund.

Mr. Goldenweiser suggested that it would be desirable to include a provision to the effect that all member nations have agreed to the provisions of the Fund and will attempt to put them into effect. Mr. Goldenweiser stated that he would draft a provision to this effect and would submit it to a future meeting.

Mr. Goldenweiser then called the attention of the meeting to the fact that the Board of Governors wished to propose an additional provision as follows: official balances of member countries which are held in other countries shall be kept on deposit with the central banks of such countries unless authorized by the central bank to be held elsewhere. After lengthy discussion, it was the consensus of the meeting that this problem should be handled by each nation individually and not by an international fund. It was agreed, however, that Mr. Goldenweiser would attempt to draft language incorporating this suggestion for further consideration by the American Technical Group.

Mr. [Walter] Gardner reported on the withdrawal and suspension provisions of the Fund [Article VIII] (Attachment E). The report was accepted with the following changes:

(a) The word "previously" shall be added to the second sentence of Section 2 to read as follows: "At the end of one year from the date of suspension, the country shall automatically cease to be a member of the Fund unless a majority of the member countries voting in the same manner as for suspension had previously restored the country to good standing."

(b) The second sentence of Section 1, to the effect that "after a member country has served notice of its withdrawal, it may use the resources of the Fund only with the approval of the Fund," should be inserted in the latter part of the provision dealing with withdrawal and suspension.

(c) The following idea shall be added to the provision on the "Settlement of Accounts with Countries Ceasing to Be Members": When a country withdraws, if it should be unable to repurchase its local currency in excess of its quota with gold or free foreign exchange, the Fund may offer that currency in the open market.

(d) It shall be provided that when a country withdraws six months prior to liquidation, the settlement of that country's account with the Fund shall be part of the liquidation procedure.

It was agreed that Mr. [Ansel] Luxford and Mr. Gardner should meet together to consider the problem of appropriate time lags in the withdrawal arrangements.

The report (Attachment F) of Mr. Gardner's committee on the liquidation of the Fund was recommitted for the following changes:

(a) The Fund will freeze its operations and holdings at the date that the decision to liquidate is made;

(b) The second sentence in paragraph 2, beginning "if this is insufficient to complete the payment," shall be kept open for further discussion; and

(c) The Fund, rather than [the] Board of Directors, shall be given the power to liquidate.

Mr. [Emilio] Collado reported on the committee considering the relations of the Fund and Bank with international organizations, and a new provision, Article IX-4 [["Relation to Other Commitments"]]. Both were accepted and are at attached as Attachment H.

Attachment A   June 17, 1944

Team 1 – Mr. Arey, Mr. Louchheim, Mr. Bittermann, Mr. Young, Mr. Dreibelbis
Assignments
1. Limitation on the amount of guarantees and loans which Bank may make.
2. The extent to which the member countries' guarantees of the gold value of local currencies extends to (a) the Bank's holdings of securities issued in those currencies, (b) to securities sold from the bank's portfolio to the public and (c) Bank-guaranteed securities purchase from private investors.
3. Conditions for guarantees and direct loans, including guarantee fees and interest rates.

Team 2 – Mr. Goldenweiser, Miss Bourneuf, Mr. Livesey, Mrs. Sundelson, Mr. Minskoff
Assignments
1. Provision of currency for loans, including the extent to which the Bank shall provide local currencies.
2. Acquisitions of gold by the Fund.
3. Fund's power to require needed foreign exchange.

Team 3 – Mr. Collado, Mr. Maffry, Mr. Mikesell, Mr. Arnold, Miss Richardson
Assignments
1. Multilateral international clearing.
2. Quotas: formula and table.

Team 4 – Mr. Gardner, Mr. Bopp, Mr. W.A. Brown, Mr. Brenner
Assignments
1. Changes in par values.
2. Composition of Fund's depositories and form of currency holdings.
3. Distribution of profits.

Attachment B

Bank for Reconstruction

1. *Issue Price of Shares.*
Shares of stock included in the initial subscription of a country represented at the United Nations Monetary and Financial Conference shall be issued at par if the subscription is received not later than one year after the date set for operations of the Bank to begin. Other shares shall be issued at a price not below par fixed by the Bank with due regard to the surplus and reserves existing at the time of the subscription.

Attachment C

Bank for Reconstruction

2. *Payment of Subscriptions.*
The initial payment on the shares subscribed by the original member countries shall be 20 percent of the par value of the shares and shall be made on the date fixed by the Board.

Each country which becomes a member after the date so fixed shall make its initial payment at such time as may be determined by the Bank. Each such country shall pay as an initial payment the same proportion of its subscription as is due and payable on previously issued shares plus the amount, if any, by which the cost of the shares exceeds the aggregate par value thereof.

The remainder of the subscriptions of member countries shall be paid in such amounts and at such times as the Bank may determine, but not more than 10 percent of the subscriptions may be called in any one year unless required to pay obligations of the Bank. Calls shall be uniform on all shares and shall be made only when funds are needed for the operations of the Bank.

Attachment D

1. The committee [new Committee or Team 2] discussed whether or not to make an explicit provision in the Joint Statement that a member country shall be obligated to buy all the gold offered to it at a fixed price. It was agreed that it was a question of judgment about the psychological reaction to such a statement and that it should be left for decision by the United States delegation. However, it was realized that if foreign countries should request such a provision, it would be impossible for the United States to object to it vigorously.

2. The committee decided to recommend that the first sentence in Section V-1 [["Use of Fund to Finance Capital Outflows"]] be revised to read "A member country may not use the Fund's resources *directly or indirectly* to meet a large or sustained outflow of capital and the Fund may require a member to exercise controls to prevent such use of the resources of the Fund." The committee also recommends that the following sentence be inserted immediately after the sentence just quoted: "For failure to exercise appropriate controls the Fund may suspend a member country from making further use of the resources of the Fund." The committee considered dropping the last sentence in V-1 on the grounds partly that it is inconsistent with the first sentence in V-1 and partly that it is out of order, but decided that it was inadvisable, since this particular sentence has been negotiated at great length and since the reference to capital movements being "in accordance with the purposes of the Fund" is on the whole useful.

3. The committee discussed at great length the three provisions which aim at eliminating restrictions on payments on current transactions but allowing restrictions on capital transactions, i.e., III-5 [["Obligations of a Purchasing Country"]], V-2 [["Capital and Current Controls"]], and IX-3 [["Current Transactions"]]. The committee decided, on the basis of **Mr. [Edward] Bernstein's** interpretation of these provisions, to recommend no change in substance but to try to draft language which will be more nearly self-explanatory.

The committee reconsidered the possibility of including a general provision obligating member countries to control substantial exports of capital of a speculative or disturbing nature. The committee decided against such an inclusion, partly because the United States does not want to be forced to control an export of capital by its nationals, and partly because it was felt that under the terms of the Joint Statement adequate controls of capital inflow can be instituted by the receiving country.

Attachment E   June 17, 1944

International Monetary Fund
Withdrawal and Suspension of Member Countries

1. *Right of Member Countries to Withdraw.*
Any member country may withdraw from membership in the Fund at any time by serving written notice on the Fund at its principal office. Withdrawal shall become effective on the date such notice is received.

2. *Suspension of Membership.*
A member country failing to meet any of its obligations under this Agreement may be suspended from membership by decision of a majority of the member countries, each of which for this purpose shall have one vote, to be cast by its director or alternate. At the end of one year from the date of suspension, the country shall automatically cease to be a member of the Fund unless a majority of the member countries, voting in the same manner as for suspension, has restored the country to good standing.

While under suspension, a country shall be denied all of the privileges of membership except that of withdrawal, but shall be subject to all its obligations.

3. *Settlement of Accounts with Countries Ceasing to Be Members.*
When a country ceases to be a member, settlement of reciprocal accounts between the Fund and such country shall be made with reasonable dispatch, not to exceed three years from the date the country ceases to be a member. The Fund shall be obligated to pay to such country the amount of its quota plus any other amounts due at from the Fund. Such payments shall be made first in the currency of the country held in the Fund and, in the event that the Fund cannot make the entire payment in the country's currency, the remainder shall be paid in gold or in such other manner as may be agreed. Currency of the country in the Fund at the time its membership ceases shall be set aside to the extent necessary to meet the Fund's obligations to it; but no payment shall be made until the Fund's holdings of its currency in excess of the Fund's obligations to the country are redeemed. The country shall be obligated to redeem such excess currency in gold or in gold convertible exchange. The Fund may extend the period in which such redemption shall be completed.

Attachment F   Morning draft, June 17, 1944

International Monetary Fund
Liquidation of the Fund

The Board of Directors, after giving notice of at least three months to the member countries, may liquidate the Fund.

The obligations of the Fund, other than the repayment of quotas, shall be a prior claim on all the assets of the Fund. In meeting such obligations the Fund shall first use its holdings of the currency in which the obligation is due. If these holdings are insufficient, it shall then use its gold. If this is insufficient to complete the payment, the remainder shall be covered by drawing on the currencies held by the Fund of countries whose holdings of gold and gold convertible exchange exceed their quotas. Such currencies shall be utilized in proportion to the quotas of these countries.

The net assets of the Fund shall be distributed as follows:

(a) The Fund shall determine the percentage for each country by dividing its holdings of the currency of such country by the quota of such country.

(b) All countries shall have returned to them in their own currencies a proportion of their quotas equal to the smallest percentage determined in (a).

(c) The country having the next lowest percentage under (a) above shall then have returned to it the remainder of its holdings held by the Fund and the country whose currency holdings have been exhausted shall have returned to it an equivalent proportion of its quota in gold. If there is not sufficient gold, then the currency of the country having the second lowest percentage shall be divided between the two countries in such manner that each will have been repaid the same proportion of its quota. All other countries shall have paid to them amounts in their respective currencies which represent the same proportion of their quotas.

(d) Further distribution shall be made in the manner provided for in (c) above until the currencies of all countries have been exhausted.

Each member country shall redeem in gold or gold convertible exchange its currency held by another member country as a result of liquidation. Such redemption shall be made with reasonable dispatch, but in any event within three years.

Attachment G

International Monetary Fund
Relation of International Monetary Fund and Bank for Reconstruction and Development to Other International Organizations

The Fund may by a four-fifths majority of the aggregate votes of the member countries enter into working relationships with any general or specialized public international organizations, provided that no such arrangements involve a modification of the rights, privileges or obligations of any member country as set forth in this agreement without the consent of that member country.

Attachment H

International Monetary Fund
[[Article IX. Obligations of Member Countries. New Section.]]

IX-4. Not to prejudice through the use of such exchange controls as may be authorized or required by the Fund any existing or future international commitments regarding the nondiscretionary application of exchange restrictions or international undertakings for the progressive relaxation of barriers to trade.

9

American Technical Group
Sixth meeting
Atlantic City
June 18, 1944 at 9:30 p.m. [123]

Protection of Bank's assets against currency depreciation • Limit on guarantees to members • Withdrawal and suspension from the Bank • Reports on liquidation and multilateral clearing • Attachment A: Gold value of Bank's transactions • Attachment B: Withdrawal and suspension from Bank • Attachment C: Liquidation of Bank • Attachment D: IMF provisions concerning multilateral clearing

The group devotes most of this meeting to the Bank for Reconstruction and Development. It discusses how to protect the Bank's assets when members devalue their currencies and how much the Bank may guarantee in loans for a member; how to handle members who do not follow the Bank's rules; and how to liquidate the Bank if necessary. Discussion about the IMF is confined to a provision on multilateral clearing. Some years later, from 1950 to 1958, Western European countries participated in a multilateral clearing arrangement, the European Payments Union (EPU), with American help. The United States provided a nucleus of dollar that members used to settle accounts at the end of each month. The EPU was successful in allowing member

---

[123] The minutes note that the location for the meeting was Harry Dexter White's office at the conference. Present: Mr. E.E. Brown, First National Bank of Chicago; Messrs. Collado, Brown, Livesey and Young of the State Department; Messrs. Goldenweiser, Dreibelbis, Gardner and Miss Bourneuf of the Board of Governors; Mr. Bopp of the Federal Reserve Bank of Philadelphia; Mr. Edmiston of the Federal Reserve Bank of St. Louis; Mr. Maffry of the Department of Commerce; Mr. Louchheim of the Securities and Exchange Commission; Mr. Arey of the Export-Import Bank; Messrs. White, Bernstein, Luxford, Brenner, Arnold, Minskoff, Bittermann, and Miss Richardson and Mrs. Sundelson of the Treasury.

countries to reduce exchange controls as economic growth increased demand for their currencies, reducing the degree of overvaluation in their pegged official exchange rates. The EPU's members dissolved it in 1958 because they no longer need it as a support. They agreed to maintain convertibility of their currencies for current transactions, one of the key goals the IMF was established to encourage for members.

Mr. [John Parke] Young [Team 1] reported on the problems of protecting the Bank's assets against currency depreciation. After considerable discussion, it was agreed that the obligation to restore the gold value of the bonds falls on the borrower, no matter what the currency in which the bond is expressed. It was also agreed that the last sentence of provision 1 [of Attachment A below], to the effect that "the gold parity shall be that established by the International Monetary Fund so long as the Fund is in existence," shall be omitted.

The report (Attachment A) was resubmitted to Mr. Young's committee to consider ways of giving a member country the benefit of any appreciation on that part of its currency which has been borrowed by the Bank.

Mr. [Walter] Louchheim's [Team 1] report recommending a 300 percent limitation on the total amount of guarantees, participation in loans, and other investments made by the Bank, was accepted.[124]

Mr. [Hawthorne] Arey [Team 1] reported on the provisions concerning the withdrawal and suspension of member countries from the Bank. The report of the committee (Attachment B) was recommitted with the following suggestions [all concerning Attachment B, below]:

(1) Add to provision 3 the fact that this provision does not hold if either the Fund or the Bank does not come into existence;

(2) Add to provision 4(b)(1) the words "or its nationals" after "a former member country";

(3) Drop "to the Bank" in provision 4(b)(1) after the words, the "former member country";

(4) Recheck provision 5 of the flimsy.

Considerable discussion followed on the appropriate way of protecting the holders of bonds guaranteed by the Bank. This problem was to be considered again by the committee, which would then report back to the

---

[124] We have not found a written report on this recommendation. The proposed limitation was evidently that the Bank's total commitments to borrower should not exceed 300 percent of the Bank's capital and surplus. Capital was apparently subscribed capital, not paid-in capital, which would be far smaller.

full committee.

Mr. [Joseph] Dreibelbis reported on the discussion of his committee on liquidation.[125] The attached report (Attachment C) was accepted tentatively, and Mr. [Richard] Brenner and Mr. [Edward] Bernstein were requested to consider it further.

Mr. [Emilio] Collado's [Team 3] report (Attachment D) on the provision dealing with multilateral clearing was accepted tentatively, with the recommendation that a provision dealing with definitions, which would include a definition of capital transfers, should be developed.

---

[125] The committee considering liquidation may have been Team 3, or it may have been a new team created after the teams in the fifth meeting of the group.

Attachment A

Bank for Reconstruction and Development
Gold Value of Bank's Transactions

1. All payments of interest and principal to the Bank, whether made in currency or in gold, shall be equivalent to the gold value of such payments on the basis of the gold parity of the currency in which the loan was contracted at the time the loan was made. The gold parity shall be that established by the International Monetary Fund so long as the Fund is in existence.

2. Any loss realized by the Bank as a result of the depreciation of its local currency holdings in terms of gold shall be reimbursed to the Bank in such a local currency by the member country whose currency has depreciated.

Any gain realized by the Bank as a result of the appreciation of its local currency holdings in terms of gold shall be paid by the Bank in such currency to the member country whose currency has appreciated.

Payments for gains or losses in accordance with the provisions of this section shall be made not more than 60 days after such loss or gain is entered on the books of the Bank.

3. The value of all obligations, other than currency, held by the Bank shall be guaranteed to the Bank by the obligor and by the member government which has guaranteed such asset, in terms of the gold parity of the currency in which the obligation is expressed at the time such obligation was acquired by the Bank. Any gain realized by the Bank on any obligation other than cash as a result of appreciation of the currency in which the asset is expressed shall be paid by the Bank to the obligor of such asset.

Payments for gains or losses in accordance with the provisions of this section shall be in currency acceptable to the Bank and shall be made not more than 60 days after such loss or gain is entered on the books of the Bank.

Attachment B

**Bank for Reconstruction
Withdrawal and Suspension of Member Countries**

1. *Right of Member Countries to Withdraw.*

A member country may withdraw from membership in the Bank at any time by serving written notice on the Bank at its principal office. Withdrawal shall become effective on the date such notice is received.

2. *Suspension of Membership.*

A member country failing to meet any of its obligations to the Bank may be suspended from membership by decision of a majority of the member countries, each of which for this purpose shall have one vote, to be cast by its director or alternate. At the end of one year from the date of suspension, the country shall automatically cease to be a member of the Bank unless a majority of the member countries, voting in the same manner as for suspension, restores the country to good standing.

While under suspension, a country shall be denied all of the privileges of membership except the right to withdraw but shall be subject to all of its obligations.

3. *Cessation of Membership in International Monetary Fund.*

Any member country which ceases to be a member of the International Monetary Fund shall immediately cease to be a member of the Bank.

4. *Settlement of Accounts with Countries Ceasing to Be Members of the Bank.*

(a) When a country ceases to be a member, the Bank shall arrange to repurchase its shares as a part of the settlement of accounts with such country. The repurchase price of the shares shall be the amount actually paid thereon plus a pro rata share of any surplus existing on the date the country ceases to be a member of the Bank or minus a pro rata share of any impairment of capital existing on such date.

(b) The payment for shares repurchased by the Bank under this section shall be governed by the following conditions:

(1) The shares in any amount accruing thereon shall constitute collateral for the total outstanding obligations of the former member country or its nationals on loans for such country or its nationals guaranteed, participated in or made by the Bank. Such shares shall be

repurchased from time to time to the extent by which the amount due on the total shares exceeds the obligations until the former member has received the full repurchase price of the shares.

(2) Payments shall be made in the currency of the country receiving payment and any deficiency shall be paid in gold or gold convertible exchange at the option of the Bank.

(c) In the event the Bank goes into liquidation within six months of the date upon which any country ceases to be a member the Bank, all rights of such member shall be determined by the provisions governing liquidation instead of the provisions governing settlement of accounts with countries ceasing to be members of the Bank.

5. *Assessments to Meet Losses.*

(a) The Bank may levy upon any country from which it has repurchased shares, assessments totaling not more than the subscription price of the shares resold, to meet losses on loans and guarantees outstanding on the date the country ceased to be a member of the Bank, and the amount of such assessment shall be determined by ascertaining the proportion of the total paid-in capital on that date represented by such shares, allocating the appropriate portion of the loss to such shares, and reducing the amount of the assessment by that portion of the reserve for losses on guarantees or the reserve for losses on loans, as the case may be, which accumulated prior to cessation of membership and was attributable to such shares; and

(b) Assessments shall be paid to the Bank in gold and currency in the same proportion as prior payments were made on the shares.

6. *Protection of Assets.*

No change in the value of the currency of any former member country shall alter the gold value of the holdings of the Bank of the currency and appropriate payments to the Bank by the country or by the Bank to the country shall be made to compensate for any change.

Attachment C

Bank for Reconstruction
Liquidation

1. The Executive Committee, in an emergency, may suspend the operations of the Bank, pending an opportunity for the Board to consider and take appropriate action.

2. The Board may vote the Bank into liquidation by majority vote.

3. After liquidation, the Bank shall cease forthwith all activities except those incident to the orderly liquidation, conservation and preservation of its assets and the settlement of its obligations including outstanding commitments.

4. Upon liquidation all claims of creditors, including all contingent claims, shall be treated as if all such claims matured on the date the Bank went into liquidation.

5. The liability of all member countries for uncalled subscriptions to the capital stock of the Bank and their guarantee with respect to the depreciations of their own currencies shall continue until all claims of creditors including all contingent claims have been discharged.

6. Upon liquidation the Executive Committee shall set aside assets of the Bank sufficient in the judgment of the Committee, to ensure a distribution to holders of guaranty obligations, ratably with creditors holding direct claims.

7. No distribution shall be made to a member country on account of its capital contribution until all claims of creditors, including all contingent claims, have been discharged or have been provided for by the Executive Committee having set aside assets sufficient in its judgments to a compass that purpose.

8. The distribution to shareholders shall be governed and made according to the same principles and upon the same terms and conditions as those provided for liquidating the International Monetary Fund.

Attachment D

**International Monetary Fund
Provisions Concerning Multilateral Clearing**

III-5. *[[Obligations of a Purchasing Country.]]*
So long as a member country is entitled to buy a currency of another country from the Fund in exchange for its own currency under the provisions of III-2 [["Purchases of Another Member's Currency"]] above, it shall, upon the request of such other country, buy its own currency from such other country with the currency of that country or with gold. This requirement shall be without prejudice to exchange restrictions which are authorized or required under this agreement and shall not apply to holdings of currencies of member countries which have accumulated as a result of transactions of a current account nature effected before the removal by the member country of restrictions on payments or transfers maintained or imposed during the early postwar transition.

V-2. *[[Capital and Current Controls.]]*
Subject to VI [["Apportionment of Scarce Currencies"]] and X-2 [["Transition Period"]], below, a member country may not use its control of capital movements to restrict payments arising out of current transactions in goods and services or to delay unduly transfers of earnings, interest, and amortization.

IX-3. *[[Current Transactions.]]*
Not to impose restrictions on transfer payments arising out of current transactions and goods and services or to delay unduly transfers of earnings, interest, and amortization, except as provided in X-2 [["Transition Period"]], or to engage in any discriminatory currency arrangements or multiple currency practices without the approval of the Fund.

10

American Technical Group
Seventh meeting
Atlantic City
June 19, 1944 at 9 p.m.[126]

Meetings with foreign delegates • Formula for IMF quotas •
Gold held in depositories • Attachment: IMF par values

*The Americans would begin meetings with some foreign delegates the next day,
although the full delegations of Britain and several other European countries would not
be present until June 23, after the* Queen Mary *had arrived in New York City.*

Mr. White asked for suggestions for the procedure to be followed in the
meetings with the foreign delegates, which would commence on the
following day. After some discussion, it was agreed that four committees
on the Fund should be organized and that the members of the American
Technical Group would be assigned to specific committees.

Mr. White informed the meeting that it would be necessary to limit
American participation at the preconference meetings because of the very
large number in our own delegations and the danger of overwhelming the
smaller foreign delegations. He stated that the meeting could be arranged
in such a fashion that any technical members who were unable to sit on
the main tables would be able to participate as observers.

The desirability of publishing the formula [for determining IMF

---

[126] Present: Mr. E.E. Brown, First National Bank of Chicago; Messrs. Collado,
Brown, Livesey and Young of the State Department; Messrs. Goldenweiser,
Dreibelbis, Gardner and Miss Bourneuf of the Board of Governors; Mr. Bopp of
the Federal Reserve Bank of Philadelphia; Mr. Edmiston of the Federal Reserve
Bank of St. Louis; Mr. Maffry of the Department of Commerce; Mr. Louchheim
of the Securities and Exchange Commission; Mr. Arey of the Export-Import
Bank; Messrs. White, Bernstein, Luxford, Brenner, Arnold, Minskoff,
Bittermann, and Miss Richardson and Mrs. Sundelson of the Treasury.

quotas] was then considered. After extended discussion, it was agreed that although the formula could be given to the foreign delegates requesting such information, only the final figures should be made public. The basic data to be used in the computation of quotas will be submitted by the various foreign governments.

Mr. [August] Maffry was requested to make an array which would be progressive in spread and which would permit the rounding off of the quota figures. Only these rounded figures would be published.

The meeting considered the flimsy prepared on par values. It was accepted with certain minor changes which have been incorporated in the mimeographed flimsy, which is attached.[127]

The question of the amount of gold to be held in the various depositories of the Fund was discussed. It was the consensus of the meeting that the gold assets of the Fund should be held in the three or four largest countries, and that the question of holding one-half of the gold in the U.S. should await a decision by the American delegation.

---

[127] The attachment, which follows just below, is dated June 21. The original typescript in the U.S. National Archives is stapled to the minutes of the June 19 meeting, from which we conclude that it is the final version of the flimsy whose draft version this meeting reviewed.

[[Attachment]] June 21, 1944

International Monetary Fund
Par Values

1. The par value of the currency of each member country shall be agreed with the Fund and shall be expressed in terms of gold.

2. All transactions in the currencies of member countries shall be at rates of exchange within a stated percentage of parity fixed by the Fund.

All computations relating to currencies of member countries for the purpose of applying the provisions of this agreement shall be on the basis of their par values.

3. No change in the par value of the currency of any member country shall be made by the Fund without approval of the country.

Each member country agrees not to propose a change in the par value of its currency which affects its international transactions unless it considers such action appropriate to the correction of a fundamental disequilibrium.

4. Changes in the par values of the currencies of member countries shall be made only with the approval of the Fund, subject to the provisions below:

(a) The Fund shall approve a proposed change in the par value of the currency of a member country if in the judgment of the Fund the change is essential to the correction of a fundamental disequilibrium. In particular, the Fund shall not reject a proposed change, necessary to restore equilibrium, because of the domestic social or political policies of the member country or because of its economic policies in so far as those are designed to contribute to the maintenance of a high level of employment and real income.

(b) In considering proposed changes in the par values of the currencies of member countries, the Fund shall take into consideration the extreme uncertainties prevailing at the time the par values of the currencies of the member countries were initially agreed upon;

(c) After consultation with the Fund, any member country may change the par value of its currency, provided the proposed change, plus all previous changes, whether increases or decreases, since the par value of such currency was initially agreed with the Fund, do not exceed 10 percent of the initial par value of such currency; and

(d) Upon the request of a member country proposing a change in the par value of its currency, the Fund shall approve or reject the proposed change within two business days of receiving the request, provided the proposed change, plus all previous changes, whether increases or decreases, made under this paragraph, do not exceed 10 percent of the initial par value of that currency, or, in the case of a country which changed the par value of its currency under (c) above, 10 percent of the initial par value of the currency plus the percentage of change made under (c) above.

5. Notwithstanding the provision of 1 above, the Fund by majority vote may make uniform proportionate changes in the par values of the currencies of all the member countries, provided each change is approved by every country which has 10 percent or more of the aggregate quotas. Such uniform changes shall not apply against maximum changes under 2(c) and 2(d) above.

11

American Technical Group
Eighth meeting
Atlantic City
June 20, 1944 at 3:30 p.m. [128]

Changes in committee assignments

The following changes were made in subcommittee assignments:[129]

Mr. [Walter] Gardner is to join Subcommittee 3 and Mr. [Emilio] Collado to participate with Subcommittee 4 on questions of organization.

The secretaries of the committees reported that they anticipated difficulties on the following questions:

Subcommittee 1: [Purposes, Policies and Subscriptions of the Fund]

The distribution of gold in depositories according to quotas, raised by [Robert] Mossé [France].

French pressure for more than four depositories.

Subcommittee 2: [Operations of the Fund]

The question of whether or not countries are obligated to sell their currencies for gold.

---

[128] Present: Mr. E.E. Brown, First National Bank of Chicago; Messrs. Collado, Brown, Livesey and Young of the State Department; Messrs. Goldenweiser, Dreibelbis, Gardner and Miss Bourneuf of the Board of Governors; Mr. Bopp of the Federal Reserve Bank of Philadelphia; Mr. Edmiston of the Federal Reserve Bank of St. Louis; Mr. Maffry of the Department of Commerce; Mr. Louchheim of the Securities and Exchange Commission; Mr. Arey of the Export-Import Bank; Messrs. White, Bernstein, Luxford, Brenner, Arnold, Minskoff, Bittermann, and Miss Richardson and Mrs. Sundelson of the Treasury.

[129] The sentence refers to subcommittees of the whole Atlantic City conference, not committees of the American Technical Group.

Subcommittee 3: [Organization and Management of the Fund]
Preference for a unit of value expressed in terms other than U.S. dollars.

The reason for the shift from 100 votes to 25 votes for each country without regard to quotas.[130]

Subcommittee 4: [Establishment of the Fund]
[Daniël] Crena de Iongh's [Netherlands] suggestion for a separate committee to consider the relationship between the Fund and nonmember countries.[131]

Mr. [Walter] Gardner requested that an effort be made to give the American Technical Group the flimsies as early as possible, and **Mr. [Emilio] Collado** suggested that as much printed material as possible be made available to the foreign delegates.

---

[130] See the next chapter for discussion of this point.
[131] Subcommittee 4, first meeting, June 20; see chapter 65.

12

American Technical Group
Ninth meeting
Atlantic City
June 21, 1944 at 9:15 a.m. [132]

Initial exchange rates • Legal form of IMF agreement • IMF charges • Minimum number of votes • Voting procedures in the Executive Committee

Harry Dexter White notes that the IMF's charges to members who borrow, which will be on a graduated scale to discouraged large, long-term borrowing, are "not a technique for the restoration of equilibrium." He is implicitly contrasting the IMF's charges with the charges in John Maynard Keynes's plan for an International Clearing Union, which would have been aimed at restoring international equilibrium in the balance of payments and would have applied to countries with large balance of payments surpluses as well as those with large balance of payments deficits. The committee also discusses IMF voting power. To give smaller countries a voice in the IMF, each country will receive a certain number of base votes. Countries will receive further votes based on their quotas (capital subscriptions), which depend largely on the size of their economies.

The meeting considered certain specific problems on which difficulties were expected to rise. After considerable discussion, agreement was reached on the following points:

    1. A special committee of [August] Maffry, [Edward?] Brown, [Walter]

---

[132] Present: Mr. E.E. Brown, First National Bank of Chicago; Messrs. Collado, Brown, Livesey and Young of the State Department; Messrs. Goldenweiser, Dreibelbis, Gardner and Miss Bourneuf of the Board of Governors; Mr. Bopp of the Federal Reserve Bank of Philadelphia; Mr. Edmiston of the Federal Reserve Bank of St. Louis; Mr. Maffry of the Department of Commerce; Mr. Louchheim of the Securities and Exchange Commission; Mr. Arey of the Export-Import Bank; Messrs. White, Bernstein, Luxford, Brenner, Arnold, Minskoff, Bittermann, and Miss Richardson and Mrs. Sundelson of the Treasury.

Gardner and [Elting] Arnold will prepare a flimsy on the establishment of the initial exchange rates. It is our tentative understanding that the initial exchange rates will be those existing on July 1, 1943, or perhaps July 1, 1944.

2. The problem of the form in which the monetary proposal is to be expressed (whether a treaty, agreement, or undertaking) will be submitted to Mr. [Emilio] Collado's committee [Subcommittee 4, "Establishment of the Fund"], which will also consider a memorandum on the subject prepared by Mr. [Ansel] Luxford. Mr. Collado is to report back to the American Technical Group.

Mr. White questioned the desirability of discussing the problem of deterrent charges in the Preliminary Agenda Conference. After considerable discussion, it was agreed that the subject should be put before the Agenda Conference in the normal course of events, and that the American Technical Group should stress the fact that the deterrent charge is not a technique for the restoration of equilibrium, but is intended to restore the strength of the Stabilization Fund. It is also designed to prevent the weakening of the Fund which would result if the Fund were to be used as a source of long-term credits. The charge is to be an inducement to countries to shorten the time during which they hold other currencies, and thus to make them available to other countries as rapidly as possible. It was emphasized that the American Technical Group should criticize the argument that charges are equally appropriate for the creditor and debtor nations, since it is the borrower who takes the initiative in decreasing the Fund's assets.

The reason for the change from 100 to 25 votes allotted each country irrespective of quotas was discussed. It was believed desirable that the small countries have a larger number of votes than would be allotted to them on the base of quotas. However, while 100 votes had been appropriate when the Fund was expected to consist of 15 to 20 countries, the larger number of countries and increased quotas now anticipated necessitating a smaller basic vote to protect the voting power of the countries making the largest contributions. It is expected that the American Technical Group will also call attention to the fact that it would be impossible for the U.S.to accept a quota smaller than that allotted to the British Empire.

It was the consensus of the meeting that the desire of the smaller countries for 100 votes could be met by allotting each country 100 votes and making it one vote for every $250,000 of the quota.[133]

The voting provisions relating to the Executive Committee were considered. It was agreed:

a. That it was to our interest to make certain that voting in the Executive Committee would be on a one-to-one basis;[134]

b. There should be the possibility of rapid action on as many questions as possible;

c. That in the discussion of the election of the representatives of the smaller nations, the desirability of representation in the broader sense ought to be stressed in view of the objectivity of the Board and its actions;

d. That countries not represented on the Executive Committee should be able to call a Board meeting; and

e. That whenever any problem is considered by the Executive Committee which affects a particular country, that country shall be permitted to sit with the Executive Committee.

---

[133] We understand this paragraph to mean 25 base votes plus one additional vote for every $250,000 of the quota rather than one additional vote for every $1 million.

[134] That is, although Executive Directors will be elected by weighted voting, in the Executive Committee each director will have only one vote regardless of the size of his constituency.

13

American Technical Group
Tenth meeting
Atlantic City
June 22, 1944 at 9:15 p.m.[135]

*Steering committee • Distribution of U.S. proposal on IMF •
Treatment of press • Legal form of IMF agreement*

The preparatory work that the American delegation has been doing shows up in the existence of a full-fledged American draft of the IMF Articles of Agreement elaborating on the Joint Statement. The American draft will become the basic document considered by the full Atlantic City conference, which is awaiting the arrival of the British and other delegations traveling on the Queen Mary. *Although, as Harry Dexter White says, the alternatives of foreign delegates will be added without country identification, we have been able to identify almost all of the proposers through records that the American delegation kept.*

Emanuel Goldenweiser, the chief economist of the Federal Reserve System, proposes to share the American draft with the press under the promise that the press will keep it confidential, rather than have the document be leaked to the press and published. His suggestion worked.

Mr. White stated that the meeting had been called to consider the appropriate procedure for meetings of the full Preconference Agenda

---

[135] Present: Mr. E.E. Brown, First National Bank of Chicago; Messrs. Collado, Brown, Livesey and Young of the State Department; Messrs. Goldenweiser, Dreibelbis, Gardner and Miss Bourneuf of the Board of Governors; Mr. Bopp of the Federal Reserve Bank of Philadelphia; Mr. Edmiston of the Federal Reserve Bank of St. Louis; Mr. Maffry of the Department of Commerce; Mr. Louchheim of the Securities and Exchange Commission; Mr. Arey of the Export-Import Bank; Messrs. White, Bernstein, Luxford, Brenner, Arnold, Minskoff, Bittermann, and Miss Richardson and Mrs. Sundelson of the Treasury.

Committee.[136]

It was decided that the chairmen of the British, Chinese, Russian and American delegations should act as an informal steering committee.

After considerable discussion, it was also agreed to present to the foreign delegates an American draft of the Fund proposal incorporating the material prepared in the flimsies.[137] The draft would be used merely as a basis for discussion, and to it would be added, without country identification, the recommendations of the foreign delegates.

The approach to be adopted by the American Technical Group in the preconference meetings was considered. It was agreed that emphasis should be placed on those provisions on which there is clear agreement. In cases where disagreement exists, the American Technical Group was to work only to clarify the issues, which would be decided at Bretton Woods by the American delegates. **Mr. White** pointed out that the American technical members must be careful not to go beyond the technical functions by committing the American delegation.

Mr. White asked the American delegation for their judgment on the way in which we ought to handle the American draft of the agreement as far as the press is concerned. **Mr. [Emanuel] Goldenweiser** suggested that the only way of keeping such a document confidential would be to give it to the press directly and to put them on their honor. After extended discussion, the suggestion was accepted.[138]

The meeting checked the following flimsies prepared by the American Secretariat for distribution at the subcommittee meetings of the following day:

1. Protection of assets and transferability,
2. Obtaining information, and
3. Additional undertakings.[139]

Mr. [Emilio] Collado reported that the State Department believes that the final document of the conference should be the Articles of

---

[136] The "preconference" is the Atlantic City conference, and the full or Formal Agenda Committee is all its delegates, including those aboard the *Queen Mary*.

[137] In U.S. National Archives, RG 56, Box 1, Folder A-2, which is labeled "(Bretton Woods) (Atlantic City Conf.) Secret Treasury Draft (6/23/44)."

[138] This had been the procedure of the United Nations Relief and Rehabilitation Administration (UNRRA) conference in Atlantic City in November 1943; see "Meeting at the White House, May 25, 1944, 12:45 P.M.," Morgenthau Diaries (v. 735: 154).

[139] See the editors' appendix to chapter 5 for a list of all the flimsies.

Agreement, which would go into effect when accepted by X number of countries. Enabling legislation, in the form of a statute to be presented to Congress and the President, would be necessary in this country, but other nations would be able to present the Articles of Agreement to their own legislative bodies in whatever form was most acceptable. He also stated that the status of the Fund would not be that of an incorporated entity, but would be a creature of agreement. Mr. [Dean] Acheson [assistant secretary of the Department of State] is preparing a draft on the form and status of the agreement.

14

American Technical Group
Eleventh meeting
Atlantic City
June 23, 1944 at 2:15 p.m.[140]

Method of procedure for remaining meetings • Subcommittee 2:
Mexico's proposals regarding silver • Liquidation of blocked
balances • Subcommittee 1: Purposes and policies of the IMF •
Provision of information to the Fund • Furnishing of reports •
Subcommittee 3: Voting on the liquidation of the Fund •
Subcommittee 4: Gold value of Fund's assets • Multilateral clearing
during the transition period • Distribution of the Fund's profits

American delegates report on the doings of the subcommittees of the conference. The
original text calls them committees, but the meaning is clear enough that we have not
changed the wording. In Subcommittee 2, on the operations of the IMF, Mexico, a
large silver producer, is pressing for consideration of a role for silver in the international
monetary system. Also, questions related to exchange controls and multiple exchange
rates have arisen. Subcommittee 1, on the purposes and policies of the IMF, has
discussed the preamble to the IMF Articles of Agreement. Subcommittee 3, on the
organization and management of the IMF, has discussed the allocation of votes during
liquidation of the IMF. Subcommittee 4, on establishing the IMF, has discussed
whether the IMF should recognize the depreciation of black market exchange rates,

---

[140] Present: Mr. E.E. Brown, First National Bank of Chicago; Messrs.
Collado, Brown, Livesey, Young, and Brown of the State Department; Messrs.
Goldenweiser, Dreibelbis, Gardner and Miss Bourneuf of the Board of
Governors; Mr. Bopp of the Federal Reserve Bank of Philadelphia; Mr. Coe of
the Foreign Economic Administration; Mr. Maffry of the Department of
Commerce; Mr. Louchheim of the Securities and Exchange Commission; Mr.
Arey of the Export-Import Bank; Messrs. White, Bernstein, Luxford, Mikesell,
Brenner, Arnold, Minskoff, Bittermann, and Miss Richardson and Mrs.
Sundelson of the Treasury.

multilateral clearing, and the distribution of profits.

The meeting opened with a brief discussion of the press comments on the International Monetary Fund and the International Monetary Conference [at Bretton Woods]. There followed a discussion of the best method of procedure to be followed at the remaining meetings at Atlantic City. It was decided to undertake an examination of the complete draft of the Fund proposal rather than to continue discussion of isolated parts of the proposal set forth in flimsies. It was also decided that we would not hold a large group meeting with the United Kingdom.[141]

Mr. [Raymond] Mikesell reported on the discussions in Committee 2 [Operations of the Fund].[142] Mr. [Antonio Espinosa de los] Monteros (Mexico) wishes certain proposals regarding silver included on the agenda for the [Bretton Woods] Conference but does not want these proposal discussed in the committee meetings now going on. These proposals are:

1. The International Monetary Fund shall determine the proper role of silver in the international sphere.

2. The International Monetary Fund shall be authorized to follow whatever policy it deems desirable in regard to silver.

3. The member countries of the International Monetary Fund shall agree to abide by the decisions of the International Monetary Fund shall in regard to silver.

It was suggested that the question of silver might be referred to the Special Committee for the Increased Monetary Use of Silver.[143]

Mr. Mikesell reported that Mr. [Louis] Rasminsky (Canada) had raised a question as to the precision of the present wording of the provision on the maintenance of exchange rates [X-2, ["Transition Period"]]. Mr. Rasminsky inquired whether a country would meet the requirements of this provision by requiring its exporters to make all payments in a currency other than its local currency. He also inquired whether it would be permissible for a country to liquidate blocked balances by use of an exchange rate below the official rate. **Mr. White** felt that although there might be some advantage in allowing liquidation of blocked balances at a

---

[141] Despite this statement, there were large group meetings with British delegates on June 24 and June 26; see chapters 28 and 29.

[142] See chapter 60.

[143] There was no such subcommittee at Atlantic City, but at Bretton Woods, Committee 1 of Commission III discussed the international monetary use of silver.

rate below the official rate if the use of these balances were confined to such types of transactions as tourist expenditures and investment, we should be opposed to such practices by a member country without the approval of the Fund, since it will clearly result in multiple currency practices.

Mr. [Emanuel] Goldenweiser reported on the discussion of Committee 1 [Purposes, Policies and Subscriptions of the Fund].[144] The proposed provision "The purposes and policies of the International Monetary Fund shall be the purposes and policies of the member countries" was discussed at length. The chairman, Mr. [Tingfu] Tsiang (China) alternatively proposed that the article "Purposes and Policies" [Article I] should be begun with this sentence: "The purposes and policies of the member countries in establishing the International Monetary Fund are as follows:" Mr. White suggested the addition of the phrase "and the Fund shall be guided accordingly." There was a short discussion concerning the relative strength of the several suggested formulations.

The provision on the furnishing of information to the Fund [proposed new III-11, "Furnishing Information," Alternative A, U.S.] was also discussed in this Committee. Mr. [Wynne] Plumptre (Canada) did not like the suggested revision of the language of this provision. Professor [Fyodor] Bystrov (USSR) also commented on this provision. Mr. Goldenweiser reported that the committee had decided not to adopt the suggested revision of this provision but to report their discussion.

The revised provision on the furnishing of reports was accepted by the committee. The suggested revision of the wording of the provision that member countries shall give consideration to the views of the Fund was opposed by Professor Bystrov, who suggested the addition of the sentence "Such recommendations shall not deal with the fundamental economic structure of a member country." The committee decided to report this suggestion but not to support it.

Mr. [Karl] Bopp reported the discussion in Committee 3 [Organization and Management of the Fund].[145] Mr. Monteros (Mexico) suggested that in voting on the liquidation of the Fund, each member country should have only one vote. Mr. Bopp felt that the committee's attitude towards this suggestion was noncommittal.

Mr. [Walter] Louchheim reported the discussion in Committee 4

---

[144] See chapter 56.
[145] See chapter 64.

[Establishment of the Fund].[146] The French delegates expressed the opinion that the working of the provision on the maintenance of the gold value of the Fund's assets [IV, proposed additional article, Alternative A. U.S.] was too general and that this provision should not apply in all cases, but should be limited to cases where the depreciation of a country's currency is one undertaken by that country's government. If was felt that a depreciation on the black market should not be recognized.

A question was raised in this committee as to how the provision for multilateral clearing would apply during the transition period [X-2, ["Transition Period"]]. **Mr. White** stated that we had thought that this provision was to be applicable at all times.

The distribution of profits of the Fund was also discussed by **Committee 4** [Establishment of the Fund],[147] and a question was raised as to the justice of distribution on the basis of the use of a member's currency contribution to the Fund. It was felt among the American technical experts that we should maintain our position on this point.[148]

---

[146] See chapter 68.
[147] See chapter 68.
[148] Specified in VII, proposed additional section, Alternative A (U.S.).

15

American Technical Group
Twelfth meeting
Atlantic City
June 24, 1944, evening

IMF draft agreement

Alice Bourneuf, an economist at the Board of Governors of the Federal Reserve System, took the fragmentary notes below. The usual more detailed minutes by staff of the Treasury Department notes are absent, so these are the only notes of the meeting.

First full American draft discussed in detail — called Document No. 1 [F-1] — copies taken back by the Treasury. **White** explained desire to get up joint draft with suggestions of various countries listed as alternatives.

16

American Technical Group
Thirteenth meeting
Atlantic City
June 25, 1944 at 10 a.m.[149]

British comments on the IMF and U.S. reaction

Aboard the Queen Mary, *the British delegation wrote a document of commentary on the American proposal for the IMF. Upon reaching Atlantic City, the British gave the document to the Americans. The document is reproduced in chapter 82.*

The British are concerned that the IMF will act as more of a prescriber and less of an adviser than they desire. In particular, they want members to have more flexibility over changes to exchange rates than the American draft allows and to make it clear that national governments, not the IMF, are the ultimate authorities over exchange rates. They propose that the IMF automatically approve changes of exchange rates as long as they do not exceed 10 percent from the original parity, whereas the American draft requires IMF approval for all changes. The British also criticize the American definition of a gold convertible currency. The difference arises because the British have a stricter definition of the term than the Americans do.

The British document I.M.C. (44) (F) 11, June 21, 1944 [proposed British

---

[149] The minutes note that the location for the meeting was Harry Dexter White's office at the conference. Present: Mr. E.E. Brown, First National Bank of Chicago; Messrs. Pasvolsky, Livesey, Young and Brown of the State Department; Messrs. Goldenweiser, Gardner, Hansen and Dreibelbis and Miss Bourneuf of the Board of Governors; Mr. Bopp of the Federal Reserve Bank of Philadelphia; Mr. Edmiston of the Federal Reserve Bank of St. Louis; Mr. Coe of the Foreign Economic Administration; Mr. Maffry of the Department of Commerce; Mr. Louchheim of the Securities [and] Exchange Commission; Messrs. White, Bernstein, Luxford, Casaday, Mikesell, Bittermann, Brenner, Arnold, and Minskoff, [and] Mrs. Sundelson and Miss Richardson of the Treasury.

amendments to the IMF agreement] was discussed.[150] Paragraphs 2 and 3 in Annex B ["Amended Version of Clause [Article] IV"] were considered first. The following comments were made: The sentence in paragraph 2 "At present if the Fund and the member country ultimately disagree and exchange policy, the member can leave the Fund without notice, and, in effect, without penalty" is not a fair statement of the case. The provision of suspension rather than withdrawal as the penalty for a member country's failing to comply with the Fund's decision upon matters pertaining to alterations of its exchange rate will encourage members to resort to the expediency of exchange depreciation. Furthermore, this suggestion denies the principle that a member country must come to the Fund and work out the solution of its exchange rate problem with the Fund. It also, by implication, reintroduces the principle that member countries have a "right" of access to the resources of the Fund.

It was agreed that the first sentence of Annex B, 2 and the last sentence of Annex B, 3 embody large and objectionable changes of emphasis.[151]

Paragraph 5, on the definition of a "gold convertible" currency, was then discussed. It was pointed out that the definition suggested here means that no currency used in a capital transaction will be convertible. The American Technical Group then discussed our interpretation of the term "gold convertible." By a gold convertible currency, we mean a currency which is freely convertible into gold subject to any specifically stated exceptions.[152]

Paragraph 6 [on the definition of "holdings of convertible exchange"] was then discussed. It is generally felt that paragraph 6(a) was acceptable to the American Technical Group.

The paragraph dealing with the repurchase provisions were discussed. It was pointed out that there are several errors in paragraph 8 [on III-7,

---

[150] See chapter 82.

[151] The first sentence of Section 2 reads, "Subsequent changes in the par value of a member's currency shall not be made except at its own proposal." The last sentence of Section 3 reads, "For a change larger than 20 per cent the Fund will expect reasonable notice."

[152] The British contend that according to their experts, no gold convertible currency as they understand the phrase currently exists. The United States remained on the gold standard during World War II in principle, but wartime trading regulations and the dangers of ocean shipping in wartime meant that in practice, foreigners could not freely convert U.S. dollars for gold and ship the gold abroad as they had been able to do before the war.

["Fund's Acquisition of Gold"]. The example set forth in this paragraph rests upon the assumption that a member country may acquire more resources from the Fund than it needs currently and may hold these resources idle. This is not the case. It was felt that the formulation of the repurchase provisions set forth in paragraph 9 [suggesting alternative language] merits further consideration.

Paragraph 11 reintroduces a question which we have already settled with the British, i.e., that member countries must pay for half of the exchange which they acquire from the Fund in gold.

With regard to the suggestion in paragraph 14 that the phrase "provisions of the Fund" be substituted for "purposes of the Fund" in III-2 of the Joint Statement [["Purchases of Another Member's Currency"]], it was felt that this phraseology is not as desirable from our point of view, and that the argument given in justification is equivocal. **Mr. White** remarked that the use of the word "provisions" rather than "purposes" in provision III-2(a) destroys the qualitative element which we have tried to introduce here. There followed a short discussion as to whether the meaning of provision III-2(a) was the same with and without the first four words, "The member represents that." **Mr. White** remarked that it should be possible for the Fund to say that a country was mistaken in saying that its reason for requesting exchange from the Fund was consistent with the purposes of the Fund. However, since we have already stated that a country has a right to notice before being suspended for making for the use of the Fund's resources, it was decided that any limitation of III-2(a) must be introduced in III-2(d), which provides for suspension.

Paragraph 17, which deals with the transitional provision [X-2, ["Transition Period"]], was then discussed. It was felt by the American Technical Group that the phraseology of these provisions in the Joint Statement was weak, and that considerable revision would be required.

17

American Technical Group
Fourteenth meeting
Atlantic City
June 26, 1944 at 10:30 a.m.[153]

Subcommittee on Management • Preliminary American reaction to British suggestions on IMF • Conference schedule • Lauren Casaday's report on the voyage aboard the Queen Mary

Harry Dexter White describes some matters of conference organization. He then recounts the preliminary American reaction to British comments on the U.S. draft of the IMF Articles of Agreement. The United Kingdom, as a possible debtor of the IMF, favors more lenient provisions in certain matters than the United States, which is sure to be the biggest creditor for years to come. Lauren Casaday, the U.S. Treasury attaché in London, offers his impressions of the discussions among the Allied delegations traveling onboard the Queen Mary. *He relates the view that many of the European countries feel that the proposed organization of the Bretton Woods conference is too elaborate, because they will not have enough delegates to attend all the meetings that will likely be happening simultaneously.*

Mr. White reported that the Steering Committee had decided that the Subcommittee on Management should include one delegate and one

---

[153] The minutes note that the location for the meeting was Harry Dexter White's office at the conference. Present: Mr. E.E. Brown, First National Bank of Chicago; Messrs. Pasvolsky, Livesey, Young and Brown of the State Department; Messrs. Goldenweiser, Gardner, Hansen and Dreibelbis and Miss Bourneuf of the Board of Governors; Mr. Bopp of the Federal Reserve Bank of Philadelphia; Mr. Edmiston of the Federal Reserve Bank of St. Louis; Mr. Coe of the Foreign Economic Administration; Mr. Maffry of the Department of Commerce; Mr. Louchheim of the Securities [and] Exchange Commission; Messrs. White, Bernstein, Luxford, Casaday, Mikesell, Bittermann, Brenner, Arnold, and Minskoff, [and] Mrs. Sundelson and Miss Richardson of the Treasury.

technician from the UK delegation]; Mr. [Ansel] Luxford and one other technician from the American delegation; and one member [each] from the delegations of Mexico, USSR, China, and the Netherlands. The Agenda Subcommittee will include the members of the Steering Committee plus one member from the French [delegation] and one member from the Netherlands.

Mr. White then reported that in his conversation with Lord [John Maynard] Keynes [UK] yesterday morning he informed Lord Keynes at the American technicians have not yet had an opportunity to examine the suggestions of United Kingdom delegation carefully, but that there were three points in their draft which we would oppose. These are:

1. The provision for greater flexibility in the provisions on the alteration of exchange rates.

2. The fact that their draft of the provisions on the alteration of exchange rates implies that member countries have a "right" of access to the resources of the Fund.

3. The proposed provisions relating to the transitional period.

Lord Keynes felt that to avoid submitting provisions and then withdrawing them the UK delegations would like to discuss these questions with the American technicians before submitting them to the Agenda Conference [Committee]. The UK alternatives on these questions will be omitted from Document F-1 [the IMF Articles of Agreement] for the present.

Mr. White also reported that it had been agreed that meetings of the Agenda Conference will be held each day from 10:30 a.m. to 12:30 [p.m.] and from 4:30 p.m. to 6:30 p.m.; that we should conclude discussions of the major points of the Fund before proceeding to the Bank discussion; and that the question of quotas would be postponed until the representatives of all countries have arrived.[154] Meetings of members of the American delegation will be held regularly at 3:30 p.m.

Mr. White then stated that Lord Keynes had expressed interest in the proposed "commercial policy" revision.[155] He suggested that we discuss this provision with them, although we must wait until our delegation

---

[154] It is unclear whether this means at Atlantic City or at Bretton Woods.

[155] Proposed new section IX-4, [["Relation to Other Commitments,"]] significant in relation to Article VII of the Anglo-American Mutual Aid Agreement of February 28, 1942, which included a commitment "to the elimination of all forms of discriminatory treatment in international commerce, and to the reduction of tariffs and other trade barriers."

arrives before we can proceed further on this provision, since we have no instructions on this provision. **Mr. [Leo] Pasvolsky** felt that it was necessary that we make it clear that the proposed Fund will not solve all foreign trade problems, and that this provision cannot solve commercial policy problems.

Mr. [Lauren] Casaday reported upon the trip over. Only five group meetings [of all the Allied delegates] were held on shipboard and there were no subcommittee meetings. The first four of these were on the Monetary Fund, one of which was devoted exclusively to the discussion [and] definition of the term "gold convertible." The last meeting was on the Bank.[156] The principal suggested change in the Bank draft is the emphasis upon the guaranteeing of loans. Mr. Casaday felt that interest in the Bank proposal is much greater among the European countries than among the UK delegation.

Mr. Casaday also stated that a detailed formula has been worked out for quotas and voting power, and that the only significant difference of opinion was on the question of management. India made a strong bid for a permanent position on the Board of Directors. This was opposed by the European countries, who felt that only five memberships should be assigned, and who agreed that France should have one of the assigned memberships.

On the whole, Mr. Casaday felt that there was no friction between the UK delegation and the delegations of the European countries except on minor points. Dr. [Wilhelm] Keilhau [Norway], for example, attempted to reintroduce the concept of a monetary unit.[157]

In regard to the question the procedure of the conference, many of the European countries felt that in view of the fact that their delegations are small, the proposed committee organization is too elaborate.

---

[156] Actually, aboard the *Queen Mary* there were six meetings of the Allied delegations and the last two meetings were on the Bank.

[157] That is, an international monetary unit specific to the IMF and distinct from existing national currency units.

18

American Technical Group
Fifteenth meeting
Atlantic City
June 27, 1944 at 3:30 p.m.[158]

Exchange rates and stability • Definition of "gold convertible" •
Fund jurisdiction over member country's use of own resources •
Scarce currencies and commercial policy provision

This session is devoted to further American reaction to British suggestions about the IMF. The Americans consider some concessions to British views.

Mr. [Alvin] Hansen suggested, in regard to the British suggestions on the provisions concerning exchange rates, that we include in the draft a statement embodying the idea that internal stability must be the basis for international stability. He suggested the following wording: "[M]ember countries should be encouraged to maintain internal stability and a high level of employment and measures taken to promote these ends should be encouraged. Therefore changes in exchange rates which are necessary to achieve these goals should be granted by the International Monetary Fund." The problem of wording, Mr. Hansen pointed out, is that it must be full employment that the Fund is sanctioning and not inflation. Mr.

---

[158] The minutes note that the location for the meeting was Harry Dexter White's office at the conference. Present: Mr. E.E. Brown, First National Bank of Chicago; Messrs. Pasvolsky, Livesey, Young and Brown of the State Department; Messrs. Goldenweiser, Gardner, Hansen and Dreibelbis and Miss Bourneuf of the Board of Governors; Mr. Bopp of the Federal Reserve Bank of Philadelphia; Mr. Edmiston of the Federal Reserve Bank of St. Louis; Mr. Coe of the Foreign Economic Administration; Mr. Maffry of the Department of Commerce; Mr. Louchheim of the Securities [and] Exchange Commission; Messrs. White, Bernstein, Luxford, Casaday, Mikesell, Bittermann, Brenner, Arnold, and Minskoff, [and] Mrs. Sundelson and Miss Richardson of the Treasury.

Hansen felt that that the provisions of the Joint Statement as they now stand are fairly satisfactory in this connection, but agreed to attempt a revision.

It was decided to make one member of the American Technical Group responsible for explaining each provision of Document F-1 [the IMF Articles of Agreement] at the meetings of the Agenda Conference which are now going on. The remainder of this meeting was devoted to assigning the provisions which will be discussed this afternoon.

The alternative definition of "gold convertible" submitted by the United Kingdom delegation [in Document F-5, "Note on Certain Definitions"] was discussed briefly. It was decided to request the British to give us estimates of the effect of their definition of "gold convertible" currency upon various member countries' obligatory gold contributions to the Fund. It was also felt that in order to be eligible to be tendered to the Fund in place of gold, a "convertible currency" should at least be a currency desired by the Fund.

In regard to the provisions on capital transactions [X-2, ["Transition Period"]?], the question was raised as to whether the Fund had any jurisdiction over a member country's prior use of its own resources. **Mr. White** replied that our only position on this matter is that a country which has come to the Fund for foreign exchange last week and will come again next week is "coming to the Fund," and is therefore subject to these provisions.

In regard to the "commercial policy" provision [in proposed new Section IX-4, ["Relation to Other Commitments"]], **Mr. [Leo] Pasvolsky** remarked that the UK delegation had made it clear that the scarce currency provisions should be operative before this came into effect. He also stated that he had cleared the wording of this provision with the State Department.

19

American Technical Group
Sixteenth meeting
Atlantic City
June 28, 1944 at 3:30 p.m.[159]

Suggested British redraft on par values • Subcommittee on Management • Postponement of commercial policy provision

At this final meeting of American delegates at Atlantic City, the American delegation continues to consider British suggestions on the IMF, focusing on the alteration of par values. One of the delegates notes the disagreements among members of the Subcommittee on Management about various details of managing the IMF.

The suggested redraft of Article IV, "Par Values of Member Currencies," submitted by the United Kingdom delegation was discussed.[160]

The following rewordings of the second sentence of paragraph 1 [["Establishing Par Value"]] of this document were suggested:

a. "If an alteration in the par value of a member country's currency becomes necessary it shall be made only on the proposal of the member country. Member countries agree not to propose a change in the par value of their currencies unless:

---

[159] The minutes note that the location for the meeting was Harry Dexter White's office at the conference. Present: Mr. E.E. Brown, First National Bank of Chicago; Messrs. Pasvolsky, Livesey, Young and Brown of the State Department; Messrs. Goldenweiser, Gardner, Hansen and Dreibelbis and Miss Bourneuf of the Board of Governors; Mr. Bopp of the Federal Reserve Bank of Philadelphia; Mr. Edmiston of the Federal Reserve Bank of St. Louis; Mr. Coe of the Foreign Economic Administration; Mr. Maffry of the Department of Commerce; Mr. Louchheim of the Securities Exchange Commission; Messrs. White, Bernstein, Luxford, Casaday, Mikesell, Bittermann, Brenner, Arnold, and Minskoff, [and] Mrs. Sundelson and Miss Richardson of the Treasury.

[160] I.M.C. (44) (F) 11, June 21, 1944, Annex B; see chapter 82.

(a) Such changes required to correct a fundamental disequilibrium.

(b) Such proposal is dealt with by the Fund in accordance with the provisions set forth below.

(c) There is consultation with the Fund.

b. "Member countries agreed not to propose a change in the par value of their currencies unless it is required to correct a fundamental disequilibrium. An alteration of the par value of a member country's currency necessary to correct a fundamental disequilibrium shall be made only on the proposal of the member country and only after consultation with the Fund."

The inclusion of the phrase "and only [after] consultation with the Fund" was suggested by the lawyers, who pointed out that provision for consultation is omitted in paragraph 2(a) of the UK draft.[161]

It was agreed among the group that the wording used in the Joint Statement, "In the case of an application for a further change not covered by the above and not exceeding 10 percent" (second sentence of provision IV-4) was preferable to that of the first part of paragraph 2(b) of the UK draft. The following wording was suggested for the second part of Section 2(b) of the UK draft: "The Fund shall concur or object within 72 hours. A failure to reply shall be deemed a concurrence."

Mr. [Edward] Bernstein suggested that paragraph 2(c) of the UK draft might be included in paragraph 2(b). The following rewording of this provision was suggested: "on changes beyond 10 percent the Fund shall give a reply within a reasonable time."

It was pointed out in regard to paragraph 2(d) that there should be no comma after the word "domestic."

Consideration of paragraph 2(f) was postponed until after consideration of paragraph 3.

The following rewordings of [paragraph] (3) [["Fund's Approval of Changes in Par Value"]] were suggested:

"If the member country fails to conform in any of the above requirements, the Fund is authorized to suspend the member from the privileges of the Fund."

"If a member country fails to conform to any of the above requirements it may be suspended from the privileges of the Fund, but shall remain subject to its other obligations. At any time thereafter a

---

[161] Paragraph 2 is [["Changes in Par Value."]] The original British document does not subdivide paragraph 2 into letters. The Americans are referring to the first sentence in the paragraph as (a), the second as (b), and so on.

member country may be required to withdraw from the Fund."

Messrs. [Ansel] Luxford, Bernstein and [Walter] Gardner were designated as a committee to consider the question of suspension.[162]

It was announced that the Subcommittee on Management would meet at 9:30 p.m.[163] **Mr. Luxford** reported the following pointed disagreements among the members of this committee:

1. Whether the Executive Committee shall be in continuous session. A member of the Chinese delegation on this committee agreed with the members of the U.S. delegation that the Executive Committee must be in continuous session, at least during the first five years of the Fund's existence.

2. The method of electing the six members of the Executive Committee not assigned to the five countries with the largest quotas. Some members felt that the proposed system of voting would mean that little countries would never have a representative on the Executive Committee, and that this would lead to bloc voting.

3. Which matters the Board of Directors [Governors] should be empowered to delegate to the Executive Committee. In particular, there is disagreement as to whether they should be empowered to delegate decisions on the purchase of exchange by member countries.

Mr. [Leo] Pasvolsky requested that further consideration of the "commercial policy" provision [in proposed new Section IX-4, ["Relation to Other Commitments"]] be postponed.

The remainder of the meeting was devoted to assigning various members of the U.S. delegation to speak for various provisions of Document F-1 [the IMF Articles of Agreement] in the meeting of the Agenda Conference [Committee].

---

[162] Presumably Article VIII, proposed additional section, "Suspension of Membership or Compulsory Withdrawal," Alternative A (U.S.).
[163] We have found no record of this meeting.

PART III

BRITISH AND ALLIED INTERNAL MEETINGS

Passengers aboard the *Queen Mary* [164]

United Kingdom

Lord John Maynard Keynes, Treasury, Chairman
Lydia Lopokova (Lady Keynes)
W. Eric Beckett, Foreign Office
George Bolton, Bank of England
Sir Wilfrid Eady, Treasury
Dennis Robertson, Treasury
Lionel Robbins, War Cabinet Office
Nigel Ronald, Foreign Office
H.E. Brooks, Treasury, Secretary
A.W. "Peter" Snelling, Dominions Office, Secretary
Arthur S. Gambling, Treasury
Secretarial assistants
Florence Fadzzen
Jean C. Gregory
Miss M.F. Houlden
Miss Peek
Miss I. Storey
Miss L.D. Simpson
Miss F.N. Macey
Miss Page

United States

Lauren Casaday

Belgium

Baron René Boël

China

Ping-Wen Kuo
Mrs. Kuo
Helen Chin

Czechoslovakia

Ladislav Feierabend, Chairman
Jan Mládek

Greece

Kyriakos Varvaressos

India

Sir Jeremy Raisman, Chairman
Sir David Meek
Mrs. A.A. Henderson

Norway

Wilhelm Keilhau

Netherlands

Johan Willem "Wim" Beyen

Poland

Ludwik Grosfeld, Chairman
Leon Baránski
Gustaw Gottesman
Stanisław Kirkor
Mrs. Kirkor

---

[164] Sources: I.M.C. (44) (F) 11, Annex A, UK National Archives T 231-363; "U.K. Party" and "Allied Party," June 13?, 1944, T 231-365; Atlantic City room directory of foreign delegates as of June 26, U.S. National Archives RG 82, Box 42, Folder "Atlantic City Drafting Committee." Nigel Ronald and the Polish delegation were not at Atlantic City but were at Bretton Woods. Lauren Casaday was the U.S. Treasury Department attaché in London. Only Reinertsen (2017: Passasjerliste) lists Mrs. Kirkor. For more biographical details, see Appendix A.

20

British delegation
First meeting
Aboard the *Queen Mary*
June 19, 1944 at 10:30 a.m.[165]

*British suggestions on IMF • British suggestions on Bank •
Conference procedures • Editors' appendix: List of British
delegation documents*

The British delegation held a number of meetings while aboard the Queen Mary *to
New York City on the way to Atlantic City. Some meetings were internal, though
often with the participation of Sir Jeremy Raisman, an Englishman who was India's
Finance Member (equivalent to minister of finance) and chairman of the Indian
delegation. Other meetings were with all the other delegations aboard, including the
U.S. Treasury attaché in London as an observer. All delegations aboard except
Norway's had representatives already in the United States who would attend the
Atlantic City conference beginning June 19. The most important members of the
delegations, though, were generally on the* Queen Mary, *and the British in particular
were concerned that the Atlantic City conference not decide important matters before the
full delegations were present.*

*The British had thought extensively about the IMF before their voyage to the
United States but less about the Bank for Reconstruction and Development, referred to
here as the United Nations Bank and today known as the World Bank. They used
their shipboard freedom from routine office work to devise a detailed proposal for the
Bank in response to the U.S. proposal of November 1943. This meeting notes the first
results of the British effort. Chapter 3 reproduces the U.S. proposal, while chapter 80*

---

[165] *Editors' note:* The original minutes of the meetings aboard the *Queen Mary* list
members present at the top of each meeting. We move the list to the footnotes.

Present: Lord [John Maynard] Keynes (in the Chair), Sir Wilfrid Eady, Prof.
D[ennis] H. Robertson, Prof. L[ionel] C. Robbins, Mr. N[igel] B. Ronald, Mr. W.
E[Eric] Beckett, Mr. G[eorge] L.F. Bolton, Sir Jeremy Raisman (India—by
invitation), Mr. H.E. Brooks [and] Mr. A.W. ["Peter"] Snelling, Secretaries.

reproduces the British counterproposal.
There was an informal meeting of the British delegation on June 17. No official record of it was made, so we have not included it here. However, George Bolton, an official of the Bank of England who kept a diary of events aboard the Queen Mary, *at Atlantic City, and at Bretton Woods, noted that from the time the delegations boarded ship, the other delegations were telling the British that they wanted to press for larger quotas, which would largely determine their voting power in the Fund and the Bank.[166]*
 An editors' appendix lists documents that the British delegation wrote. All the documents we found in our research are available in the online companion files.

International Monetary Fund

1. The paper I.M.C. (44) (DEL) (F) 2,[167] consisting of a note by Lord [John Maynard] Keynes with a suggested redraft of Clause IV[168] of the Statement of Principles (White Paper version) [on promoting exchange stability] was discussed in detail and approved as a basis for discussions with the Allies subject to verbal alterations. (The final text was circulated to all delegations on board as I.M.C. (44) (F) 1).

2. The following points came under particular notice:-

(a) Even in the circulated version there remain ambiguities and constructions which could and should be removed: but it was felt desirable at this stage not to depart more than was necessary from the form of the agreed statement.

(b) The revised version stresses the "sovereign" rights of members, though the adjective was deliberately deleted to avoid offense or provocation. At the same time, the invention of disciplinary powers open to the Fund short of immediate expulsion ought to appeal to Dr. [Harry Dexter] White [U.S.].

(c) **Mr. [George] Bolton** was not satisfied with the content of IV-1 [["Establishing Par Value"]] as revised, and the point was left for further consideration. He was anxious that it should always be more expensive to

---

[166] Reinertsen (2017: Lørdag).
[167] See the editors' appendix to this chapter for an explanation of these codes.
[168] The British often called articles in the IMF and World Bank agreements "clauses." We remind the reader that in the agreements, articles have Roman numerals, sections have Arabic numerals, and subsections have letters.

have recourse to the Fund.[169]

United Nations Bank

3. The paper I.M.C. (44) (DEL) (B) 1, comprising a note and memorandum by Lord Keynes, was briefly examined. **Lord Keynes** reported on the oral directions he had received from the Chancellor,[170] which qualify this paper for use as a directive, and give effect to certain comments and criticisms made by the Governor of the Bank of England. The points of substance are:-

(a)   The Bank must proceed on prudent lines, which are not necessarily wholly commercial. The reconstruction functions are indispensable, although they involve risks.

(b)   A clear and unequivocal text both of the proposals and of the summary is highly desirable, though complete clarity may embarrass Dr. White.

(c)   We must insist that tied loans are not guaranteed by the Bank.

(d)   The planning and coordinating functions of the Bank need to be stressed.

(e)   Although our own liabilities may prove to be greater than the amounts suggested in the memorandum, this should not prevent our participation.

(f)   In theory it could be urged that the Bank should only exercise guarantee functions, but it was not practical politics to insist on this. There was an arguable case for giving the Bank plenty of weapons.

(g)   The problem of existing defaulted obligations was awkward, but we should resist if possible any suggestion of prior security for the new guaranteed loans, which would only cause resentment.

---

[169] Bolton, an official of the Bank of England, was thinking of the IMF in terms of the canons of central bank practice at the time, according to which borrowers from the central bank should pay a higher interest rate than the prevailing market rate to discourage excessive borrowing. In practice, the IMF has often charged interest rates below market rates, but has discouraged excessive borrowing by the conditions it attaches to loans.

[170] Chancellor of the Exchequer, the minister who heads the British Treasury and is therefore the counterpart to the U.S. Secretary of the Treasury and the minister of finance in other countries.

(h) The "Bank" is a misnomer: some better title should be sought.[171]

Procedure

4. It was agreed to keep the Allies, including Mr. [Lauren] Casaday, as fully informed as possible, in the hope that Dr. White could be informed of agreed views on several points immediately we arrive.

5. Credentials will apparently be required. **Mr. [Nigel] Ronald** and **Mr. [W. Eric] Beckett** undertook to arrange for these.

6. It appeared that a three-stage program lay ahead, viz. (a) a Final Act at Bretton Woods containing recommendations by the delegates to Governments on an ad referendum basis; (b) a Convention in legal form between Governments for submission to their Parliament; (c) ratification by Parliaments which would bring the convention into operation.

Editors' appendix: List of British delegation documents

These documents are mainly in the UK National Archives at Kew in the Treasury (T) folders indicated in parentheses. In the document identification system, "I.M.C. (44)" stands for "International Monetary Conference, 1944"; "B" indicates documents relating to the Bank; and "F" indicates documents relating to the Fund. Documents marked "DEL" were for the British delegation only. Documents not marked "DEL" could be circulated to foreign delegations. What the British call clauses are the articles of the Fund and Bank agreements.

The online companion files to this book contain photographs of the documents we found, as well as photographs of the minutes of the meetings of the British and Allied delegations. We were unable to find some documents listed below.

I.M.C. (44) (General) 1, no date [June 19, 1944?]: United Nations Monetary and Financial Conference, Organization proposed by the United States (T 231/364)

I.M.C. (44) (General) 2, June 19: United Nations Monetary and Financial Conference, Personnel of delegations (as known to UK Delegation) (T

---

[171] In a 1943 memo to Sir Wilfrid Eady, Keynes (1980a: 368) had written, "Harry [White] has chosen to call his Bank a fund and his Fund a bank." That is, the Fund lends for shorter periods and tries to remain highly liquid, rather like a commercial bank, whereas the Bank, like an investment fund, lends for longer periods and does not emphasize liquidity. See also Harrod (1951: 540).

231/364)

I.M.C. (44) (DEL) (B) 1, June 12, 1944: Prints of all the documents about the Bank which have passed between the UK and U.S. Governments, including a note and memorandum by Lord Keynes (T 247/21)

I.M.C. (44) (DEL) (B) 2, date unknown: Bank, further memorandum by Lord Keynes (not found; see however I.M.C. (44) (B) 2, a later draft)

I.M.C. (44) (DEL) (B) 3: I.M.C. (44) (DEL) (F) 5, renumbered

I.M.C. (44) (DEL) (F) 1, date unknown: Convertibility for current transactions (not found)

I.M.C. (44) (DEL) (F) 2, June 18: A modification of the Exchange Adjustment Clause proposed by the British Delegates (T 231/362)

I.M.C. (44) (DEL) (F) 3, date unknown: The duration of the transitional period, memorandum by Lord Keynes (not found)

I.M.C. (44) (DEL) (F) 4, no date [June 19?]: The definition of "Gold and Gold Convertible Exchange," memorandum by Lord Keynes (T 231/362); reissued as I.M.C. (44) (F) 2

I.M.C. (44) (DEL) (F) 5, no date [June 21?]: Sterling and dollar bonds in complete or partial default as to interest, note by Mr. Bolton (T 231/362)

I.M.C. (44) (DEL) (F) 6, date unknown [June 19?]: Management and inauguration, paper by Sir Wilfrid Eady (not found)[172]

I.M.C. (44) (DEL) (F) 7, June 20: The instruments to be produced by the conference, memorandum by Mr. Beckett (T 231/362)

I.M.C. (44) (DEL) (F) 8, June 21: The Perplexity concerning III(7)(b) and (c), memorandum by Lord Keynes (T 231/362)

I.M.C. (44) (DEL) (F) 9, June 22: Further consideration of III(7)(b) and (c), memorandum by Lord Keynes (T 231/362)

I.M.C. (44) (DEL) (F) 10, June 25: Criticisms of Fund Proposals by the American Bankers Association (T 231/362)

I.M.C. (44) (B) 1, June 12: A United Nations Bank for Reconstruction and Development: Proposals and Comments Thereon (T 247/21)

I.M.C. (44) (B) 2, date of original version unknown; revised version June 24, 1944: Suggested modifications to American proposal on the Bank,

---

[172] Presumably the report of the Atlantic City Subcommittee on Management, in chapter 79, reflects some of the concerns this document raised.

memorandum by John Maynard Keynes (U.S. National Archives, RG 56, Box 01, Folder A-8)

I.M.C. (44) (B) 3, date unknown: Note by Dr. Baránski, topic unknown (not found)

I.M.C. (44) (B) 4, date unknown: Stabilization loans, note by Lord Keynes. (not found)

I.M.C. (44) (B) 5, June 25, 1944: Draft outline of a proposal for a Bank for Reconstruction and Development, U.S. draft of November 1943 incorporating suggestions made by U.K. Delegation (U.S. National Archives, RG 56, Box 20, Folder A-11)[173]

I.M.C. (44) (F) 1, June 19: International Monetary Fund, Proposed Redraft of Clause IV, Note by the UK Delegation (T 231/363)

I.M.C. (44) (F) 3 and annex, June 19: International Monetary Fund, A draft amendment proposed by the British Delegates relating to Clauses III(2)(a), III(5), IX(3), which, between them, ensure convertibility for current transactions, memorandum by Lord Keynes (T 231/363)

I.M.C. (44) (F) 4 and annex, June 20: International Monetary Fund, The duration of the transitional period, memorandum by Lord Keynes (T 231/363)

I.M.C. (44) (F) 5, June 20: International Monetary Fund, Clause VIII, Withdrawal, note by Lord Keynes (T 231/363)

I.M.C. (44) (F) 6, June 20: Note by Mr. Varvaressos on III(7)b and IV (T 231/363)

I.M.C. (44) (F) 7, June 20, and corrigendum, June 22: International Monetary Fund, The instruments to be produced by the conference, memorandum by Mr. Beckett (T 231/363)

I.M.C. (44) (F) 8, no date [June 20?, and] Revise, June 25: International Monetary Fund, I Management and II Inauguration of the Fund (T 231/363)

I.M.C. (44) (F) 9, June 20: International Monetary Fund, note by Dr. Mládek (T 231/363)

I.M.C. (44) (F) 10, June 20: International Monetary Fund, Amendments to Clause IV(1), note by Professor Keilhau (T 231/363)

I.M.C. (44) (F) 11, June 21: International Monetary Fund, Report by the United Kingdom Delegation on the preliminary conversations with other delegates, and suggestions for the amendment of the agreed

---

[173] Atlantic City Document B-1, in chapter 80.

Statement of Principles (T 231/363; U.S. National Archives, RG 56, Box 1, Folder A-4)[174]

Annexes to I.M.C. (44) (F) 11 (T 231/363)

A: List of Delegates, etc. participating in discussions during the voyage

B: Amended version of Clause IV, text as in Annex to I.M.C. (44) (F) 4

C: Amendments to Clause X(3), text as in Annex to I.M.C. (44) (F) 4

D: Instruments to be produced at Bretton Woods; text is Mr. Beckett's paper I.M.C. (44) (F) 7, as amended

E: Suggestions regarding Management; text is I.M.C. (44) (F) 8 as amended in discussion

I.M.C. (44) (F) 12, June 22: International Monetary Fund, memorandum by Lord Keynes [responding to I.M.C. (44) (F) 10] (T 231/363)

I.M.C. (44) (F) 13, June 25: International Monetary Fund, Quotas (T 231/363)

I.M.C. (44) (F) 14, June 29: International Monetary Fund, Quotas [revised] (T 231/363) (T 231/363)

---

[174] Reproduced in chapter 82 with appendices B-E.

21

British delegation
Second meeting
Aboard the *Queen Mary*
June 19, 1944 at 5 p.m.[175]

Gold and gold convertible exchange • Convertibility for current transactions • Machinery for settling disputed questions

The British are critical of phrasing in the Joint Statement about gold convertible exchange, because as they understand the phrase, no currency is gold convertible at present. They also examine ambiguities in the phrasing of the Joint Statement about convertibility for current transactions and the extent to which the IMF should be the final authority when differences arise between it and member countries.

International Monetary Fund: Gold and Gold Convertible Exchanges

1. A paper by **Lord Keynes** (I.M.C. (44) (DEL) (F) 4) ["The Definition of 'Gold and Gold Convertible Exchange'"] was considered in detail and it was agreed to circulate the amended version to all the Allied delegates (see I.M.C. (44) (F) 2). The following points emerged:-

(1) It appeared that there is no known currency which can be described correctly as gold convertible.[176] This may be unwelcome news

---

[175] Present: Lord Keynes (in the Chair), Sir Wilfrid Eady, Prof. D.H. Robertson, Prof. L.C. Robbins, Mr. N.B. Ronald, Mr. W.E. Beckett, Mr. G.L.F. Bolton, Sir Jeremy Raisman (India—by invitation), Mr. H.E. Brooks [and] Mr. A.W. Snelling, Secretaries.

[176] Article II, Section 3 of the Joint Statement [["Gold Subscriptions"]] specifies using gold convertible exchange as a factor in calculating the amount of initial gold subscriptions to the IMF. The United States remained on the gold standard during World War II in principle, but wartime trading regulations and the dangers of ocean shipping in wartime meant that in practice, foreigners could not

to the U.S. Treasury, but its implications for the text of the Statement of Principles etc. cannot be ignored.

(2) The proposed substitution of "convertible" for "gold convertible" involves certain risks, both for other countries whose holdings of the currency concerned suddenly become reckonable for the purposes of Clause III-7 [["Fund's Acquisition of Gold"]], and for the country accepting convertibility, since its own access to the Fund may be blocked by its releases to the Fund of its currency from the balances hitherto hold by its creditors. This might involve a degree of saturation of the Fund with sterling, if holders of sterling balances were suddenly able to honor their exchange or gold obligations to the Fund with sterling hitherto blocked. The second risk is however one that we need only run when we feel able to. The former would bear further consideration; but in principle the proposal was considered sound, especially as there would be considerable advantages for us (e.g. sterling balances would be deductible from our gross gold etc. holdings.)

(3) The proposed definition of "convertible exchange" to include Bank deposits and government obligations of an official category ("official" being defined) was provisionally agreed, on the basis that it was not practicable to define so closely and comprehensively that all risk of evasion was eliminated. On the contrary, there would be marginal cases about which Fund and member must argue. The conception of "net official holdings" was also agreed.

(4) It was agreed to put a revised version of III-7(b) [["Fund's Acquisition of Gold"]], somewhat amended from Lord Keynes' draft, to the Allies.

Convertibility for Current Transactions

2. I.M.C. (44) (DEL) (F) 1 was then considered, with a view to removing possible ambiguity between III-5 [["Obligations of a Purchasing Country"]] and III-2(a) [["Purchases of Another Member's Currency"]] and other minor drafting changes. The substance of the paper was agreed, and subject to certain amendments in the new draft [of] IX-3 [["Current Transactions"]] it was agreed to circulate the paper to the Allies (see I.M.C. (44) (F) 3) ["International Monetary Fund, Draft Amendment Proposed by the British Delegates Relating to Clauses

---

freely convert U.S. dollars for gold and ship the gold abroad as they had been able to do before the war.

III(2)(a), III(5), IX(3), Which, between Them, Ensure Convertibility for Current transactions," memorandum by Lord Keynes].

Machinery for Settling Disputed Questions

3. As noted in 1(3) above, and at many important points in the Fund proposals, there will be many opportunities for difference of view about policy and about interpretation. Disputes between members as to the interpretation of the documents implementing the Fund proposals would naturally be proper for decision by the Fund without appeal elsewhere. Many questions between Fund and member are reserved to the judgment of the Fund, and a legalistic interpretation is not called for. There may however be interpretation disputes between Fund and member, and the question was discussed whether these should be subject to the final arbitrament of the Fund (using the term in its widest sense and without reference to its organizational structure). It was generally felt that for the great majority of cases reference to a separate International Court would not be appropriate, but **Prof. [Lionel] Robbins** and **Mr. [W. Eric] Beckett** undertook to consider whether there were any special cases, e.g. rights on withdrawal or liquidation, for which some such provision should be made.

22

British delegation
Third meeting
Aboard the *Queen Mary*
June 20, 1944 at 10:30 a.m.[177]

Dollar-sterling rate • Duration of transition period •
Withdrawal from IMF

Dollar-Sterling Rate

1. **Sir Jeremy Raisman [India]** mentioned that many critics in India of the Fund had referred to uncertainty regarding the future dollar-sterling rate. Despite the arithmetical attractions of the 4.00 rate [$4 = £1], the balance of advantage seemed to the Delegation to lie with an early declaration that 4.03 would continue into the postwar period, thus avoiding even a 1 percent depreciation of sterling and the revaluation of registered sterling amounts.[178] It was decided to seek authority by telegram to purpose the 4.03 rate for postwar to Dr. White. It seemed unnecessary to consult the Dominions in advance, as no change in the present rate is involved.

---

[177] Present: Lord Keynes (in the Chair), Sir Wilfrid Eady, Prof. D.H. Robertson, Prof. L.C. Robbins, Mr. N.B. Ronald, Mr. W.E. Beckett, Mr. G.L.F. Bolton, Sir Jeremy Raisman (India—by invitation), Mr. H.E. Brooks [and] Mr. A.W. Snelling, Secretaries.

[178] The British government had allowed the pound sterling to float against gold on September 21, 1931. Sterling depreciated against the dollar from the former rate of $4.8665 =£1. The government established the Exchange Equalisation Account, which began operations on July 1, 1932, to manage the exchange rate. The rate was sometimes floating and other times pegged for up to months at a stretch. On August 24, 1939 the fund abandoned its recent pegged rate of $4.68. On January 8, 1940, the government set a new rate of $4.035, which lasted until September 19, 1949, when it devalued to $2.80 (Bank of England 1968: 378-384).

Duration of the Transitional Period

2. Paper I.M.C. (44) (DEL) (F) 3 ["The Duration of the Transitional Period," memorandum by Lord Keynes] was considered and some drafting changes made; the revised text to be circulated to the other Delegations as I.M.C. (44) (F) 4 [under the same title]. The addition of a five-year "line" to the existing three-year line seemed likely to remove misunderstandings, though it might be unwelcome to the U.S. and Canadian representatives.[179]

Withdrawal

3. Arising from the discussion on this paper[180] it was agreed that VIII ["Withdrawal from the Fund"] ought to be stiffened by giving the Fund specific powers to suspend facilities to or expel a member who flagrantly fails to accept the convertibility obligations when able to do so. The paper I.M.C. (44) (F) 5 ["International Monetary Fund, Clause VIII, Withdrawal," note by Lord Keynes] was subsequently prepared and circulated together with (F) 4.

---

[179] The British do not expect the pound sterling to be ready to become convertible for current transactions within three years after the IMF comes into force. Accordingly, they propose that countries be allowed to delay convertibility for current transactions indefinitely, but that after three years the IMF report on countries whose currencies are still not convertible and that those countries consult the IMF annually about restrictions on convertibility every starting five years after the IMF comes into force.

[180] It is unclear to us whether "this paper" refers to the paper mentioned in the previous paragraph, or to a new paper on withdrawal from the IMF.

23

British delegation
Fourth meeting
Aboard the *Queen Mary*
June 20, 1944 at 5:30 p.m.[181]

Withdrawal from IMF • Restrictions on current account payments •
Management • Documents to be produced at Bretton Woods

International Monetary Fund: Withdrawal from the Fund

1. The paper I.M.C. (44) (F) 5 ["International Monetary Fund, Clause VIII, Withdrawal," note by Lord Keynes] proposing a redraft of Clause VIII [["Withdrawal from the Fund"]] was discussed and slightly amended; to be circulated to the Allied Delegation forthwith.

Clause IX-3, 4 [["Current Transactions"; "Relation to Other Commitments"]]

2. A revised version of this Clause in the light of the discussion of the Second (Joint) Meeting was considered and after amendment passed for inclusion in the minutes of that Meeting.[182] A discussion followed with **Sir Jeremy Raisman [India]** on the significance of this clause in relation to Indian sterling balances. He pointed out that Indian critics would be likely to seize on the apparent blocking of current sterling balances accruing after the war as highly objectionable. **Lord Keynes** and **Sir Wilfrid Eady** said that it was essential for the United Kingdom that this problem should not be within the jurisdiction of an international body but should remain for the discussion and settlement between the United Kingdom and India. If this Clause was not so included, convertibility of

---

[181] Present: As at Third Meeting.
[182] For the minutes of the joint (Allied) meeting, see chapter 32.

sterling might be indefinitely delayed. The matter was left on the basis that further discussions with Sir Jeremy Raisman would take place shortly.

Clause [III-7] (b) and (c) [["Fund's Acquisition of Gold"]]

3. A brief note by **Professor [Dennis] Robertson** suggesting that both sections of the clause were necessary was considered and accepted. **Lord Keynes** thought, however, that it would be possible to improve the wording of these two sections and possibly to bring their substance into one section.

Management and Inauguration

4. It was agreed to circulate the paper I.M.C. (44) (DEL) (F) 6 by **Sir Wilfrid Eady** to the Allied delegations forthwith.

Future Procedure

5. A memorandum by **Mr. [W. Eric] Beckett** (I.M.C. (44) (DEL) (F) 7) on the instruments to be produced by the Bretton Woods conference was examined and slightly amended; to be circulated forthwith to the Allies.

24

British delegation
Fifth meeting
Aboard the *Queen Mary*
June 21, 1944 at 10:30 a.m.[183]

*Sterling and dollar bonds in default • Seats on IMF Directorate
(Executive Committee) • Keynes's comments on the Bank*

*The British consider sterling and dollar bonds in default apparently as a way of
gauging how big an issue it might be for the upcoming conferences or for the early days
of the IMF. They then discuss political problems with weighting schemes for votes of
Executive Directors, deciding to hear the views of other delegations on board before
proceeding. Finally, they discuss a paper by Keynes proposing revisions to the American
draft on the Bank for Reconstruction and Development.*

1. The Minutes of the 1st, 2nd and 3rd Meetings were approved as
circulated, with the addition to the last Minutes that paragraph 4 of I.M.C.
(44) (DEL) (F) 4 was withdrawn (see Minute 2 of I.M.C. (44)
(GENERAL) 2nd Meeting).[184]

Sterling and dollar bonds in default

2. A paper by **Mr. [George] Bolton** (I.M.C. (44) (DEL) (F) 5)
["Sterling and Dollar Bonds in Complete or Partial Default as to
Interest"], which should be renumbered I.M.C. (44) (DEL) (B) 3, was

---

[183] Present: Lord Keynes (in the Chair), Sir Wilfrid Eady, Prof. D.H. Robertson,
Prof. L.C. Robbins, Mr. N.B. Ronald, Mr. W.E. Beckett, Mr. G.L.F. Bolton, Sir
Jeremy Raisman (India—by invitation), Mr. H.E. Brooks [and] Mr. A.W.
Snelling, Secretaries.
[184] See chapter 21 for the minutes. Paragraph 4 in the document in question was
Keynes's query whether paragraphs (b) and (c) of III-7 [["Fund's Acquisition of
Gold"]] were both necessary.

considered and found reassuring. The dimensions of the problem of existing bonds in default are clearly not so large as was feared.

Management of the Fund

3. A brief and inconclusive discussion took place on I.M.C. (44) (F) 8 ["I. Management and II. Inauguration of the Fund"] in the light of criticisms by Dr. [Ladislav] Feierabend [Czechoslovakia]. Two points of substance are at issue:-

(a) The proposals in the paper give the United Kingdom plus Canada plus India four votes on the Directorate against three for the United States of America. The fact that the [British] Empire members are quite free, and indeed likely, to vote against the United Kingdom is never appreciated in the USA, where critics will certainly protest.

(b) Any proposal to correct this by excluding India while retaining China (purely on political grounds) will be a major difficulty for India, quite apart from the lack of economic justification. India attaches great importance to equality of quota with China.

Lord Keynes thought tentatively that the problem might be soluble by giving one vote for each 1,000 million dollars of quota or part thereof (exceeding the first 1,000), thus encouraging grouping, but doubt was felt as to the wisdom of proceeding on this basis. It was decided to await the views of the Allies.

United Nations Bank

4. An important paper by **Lord Keynes** (I.M.C. (44) (DEL) (B) 2), subsequently circulated to the Allies as I.M.C. (44) (B) 2, was considered in detail and approved, subject to the amendments incorporated in the second version. Among the points discussed were the following:

(a) IV-1(a) [The Bank may only lend where "The payment of interest and principal is fully guaranteed by the national government."] **Mr. [W. Eric] Beckett** confirmed that the wording "fully" guaranteed" could not reasonably be construed to include provision for specific hypothecation of particular assets;

(b) IV-6 ["The Bank shall make no loans or investments that can be placed through the usual private investment channels on reasonable terms."] The present wording seemed unnecessarily positive and to involve some risks of challenge to the Bank's activities. In particular there was ambiguity as to loans which could be placed privately on worse terms. Various redrafts were considered, but it was decided first to bring the point of substance to the attention of the United states representatives;

(c) **Professor [Lionel] Robbins** raised the question whether it would not be worthwhile to propose that countries with a substantially favorable balance of payments should be required to waive any right to tie their subscription in their own currency. **Lord Keynes** thought this might jeopardize the compromise with the Americans, and he was not sure that it would suit our own interests;

(d) The question of the currency in which a loan is made by the Bank was raised by **Mr. [George] Bolton,** and left for further consideration;

(e) Some doubts were expressed about the provision in the new IV-6(c)(iii) — page 6 of paper — for stabilization loans.[185] It was agreed to transfer this provision elsewhere and to express it in a more generalized form. The view was expressed that such loans should not be made without the concurrence or at least the observation of the IMF.

(f) The new IV-8 [["Limit on Guarantees"]] was passed after discussion on the grounds that on the whole it would be wise to exclude the lendable assets of the Fund from the cover for guarantees, which was large and specific.

---

[185] This paragraph provided that in in general, loans by the Bank were to be for specific projects, but in exceptional circumstances, the Bank could make or guarantee loans for broad purposes of economic stabilization.

25

British delegation
Sixth meeting
Aboard the *Queen Mary*
June 21, 1944 at 6:15 p.m.[186]

IMF unit of account • Seats on IMF Directorate (Executive Committee) • Maintenance of full employment • Nearly equal emphasis on Bank and Fund

The last item of the minutes says that the British delegation will try to reach agreement on the Bank with the United States behind the scenes at Atlantic City. Ultimately, this decision enabled the Bank for Reconstruction and Development to be born alongside the IMF. John Maynard Keynes would be the chairman of the Atlantic City and Bretton Woods sessions on the Bank.

1. The minutes of the 4th Meeting of the Delegation were approved.

International Monetary Fund

2. A brief discussion of Professor [Wilhelm] Keilhau's [Norway] paper on Clause IV ["Par Value of Member Currencies"] (I.M.C. (44) (F) (10) ["International Monetary Fund, Amendments to Clause IV(1)"] took place. It was agreed that nothing was possible on the Unitas point,[187] but as regards initial rates of founder members the text of IV-1 [["Establishing Par Value"]] needed amendment: Mr. [W. Eric] Beckett was asked to consider.

---

[186] Present: As at 5th Meeting except Mr. Snelling.

[187] The Unitas was the name of the international currency in Keynes's plan for an International Clearing Union. Keilhau proposes that the IMF use a unit of account specific to it, which could be called the Unitas, rather than denominate its accounts in any existing national currency. Today, the IMF uses the Special Drawing Right (SDR) in precisely such a capacity.

3. **Lord Keynes's** paper on Clause III-7(b) and (c) [["Fund's Acquisition of Gold"]] (I.M.C. (44) (DEL) (F) 8) ["The Perplexity Concerning III(7)(b) and (c)," memorandum by Lord Keynes] was discussed at some length, but no agreed conclusion was reached. Controversy focused on the question whether it was legitimate for a member to pile up gold and convertible exchange resources outside the Fund by having recourse to the Fund to get exchange for current transactions. Lord Keynes urged that an attempt should be made to get rid of both clauses. **Sir Wilfrid Eady** recalled that 7(c) had in fact been accepted as serving an unusual purpose, and its effect in strengthening the Fund's holdings of gold and dollars ought not to be lightly dismissed. **Mr. [George] Bolton** thought the operation of the sections would be a nightmare to the management, and that in any case a coach and horses would be driven through them. **Professor [Dennis] Robertson** remained provisionally of opinion that the substance of both sections should be retained. The point was left for further consideration.

4. There was general agreement on the concluding proposals of this paper as regards the exclusion of balances which suddenly become convertible from the reckoning of the increase in net official holdings of convertible exchange.

Management

5. **Professor [Lionel] Robbins** suggested for consideration that we should be prepared to abandon the concept of reserved seats on the Directorate, since we were bound to get one seat and could afford to risk the U.S. getting three.[188] This would probably entail transferable votes. No conclusion was reached.

Employment Policy

6. The desirability of including in the Final Act a Resolution on maintenance of employment was accepted: to be raised with the U.S. at an early opportunity. This topic might well fall to [Bretton Woods] Commission III.

---

[188] Robbins is referring to the idea, later abandoned, that the countries with the most votes might choose multiple Executive Directors rather than just one apiece.

United Nations Bank

7. It was decided to try to reach agreement with the U.S. on the Bank behind the scenes at Atlantic City, so that if possible Bank discussions at Bretton Woods could begin nearly level with Fund discussions.

26

British delegation
Seventh meeting
Aboard the *Queen Mary*
June 22, 1944 at 4:15 p.m.[189]

Proposed new clauses on the IMF

This is the last shipboard meeting. The Queen Mary *arrived in New York City the next morning. The British delegation met with officials from the British consulate in New York to exchange information before traveling by train to Atlantic City, which they reached in the early evening.*

1. The minutes of the 5th Meeting of the Delegation were approved.

International Monetary Fund

2. New Clauses XI, XII, and XIII as drafted in informal notes by **Mr. [Nigel] Ronald, Professor [Lionel] Robbins** and **Mr. [W. Eric] Beckett** were approved for inclusion in the Report on the voyage discussions.[190] It was decided not to include provision for appeal to an outside body in the case of any dispute.

3. **Mr. [George] Bolton's** note of his conversations with Baron [René] Boël [Belgium] about the gold holdings of the Fund was noted: no

---

[189] Present: As at 6th Meeting.
[190] I.M.C. (44) (F) 11, June 21: International Monetary Fund, Report by the United Kingdom Delegation on the preliminary conversations with other delegates, and suggestions for the amendment of the agreed Statement of Principles (reproduced in chapter 82). Clause XI concerned the Fund's giving advice to members; Clause XII provided that the Fund could make arrangements with other international organizations; and Clause XIII laid down rules for amendments of the IMF agreement.

action to be taken.[191]

4. A correction of I.M.C. (44) (F) 7 ["The Instruments to be Produced by the Conference," memorandum by Mr. Beckett] was approved.

5. **Lord Keynes's** comments on Mr. [Wilhelm] Keilhau's [Norway] paper [I.M.C. (44) (F) 10, "International Monetary Fund, Amendments to Clause IV(1)"] were agreed, and the text of IV-1 [["Establishing Par Value"]] is amended accordingly (see I.M.C. (44) (F) 12 ["International Monetary Fund," memorandum by Lord Keynes] — as amended in the minutes of the sixth joint meeting held later).

6. The paper I.M.C. (44) (DEL) (F) 9 ["Further Consideration of III(7)(b) and (c)," memorandum by Lord Keynes] containing further suggestions with regard to III-7(b), (c) [["Fund's Acquisition of Gold"]] was discussed in great detail, and it was eventually decided to incorporate the text in the report so that the argument could be brought fully to the notice of the U.S. representatives. **Professor [Dennis] Robertson** was not satisfied that the present clauses did not serve any useful purpose, though he accepted the first redraft rolling them into one section; but he thought the simplified second version had no chance whatever of acceptance. **Lord Keynes** thought it was wise to acquaint the U.S. representatives of the difficulties inherent in the present draft, and to press for elimination; the other versions were by way of compromise. The concluding suggestion of the paper with regard to balances which suddenly become convertible was however warmly approved.

---

[191] We have not found this note in the papers we examined, but apparently the note is in Bolton's diary in the Bank of England Archive (Reinertsen 2017: Noter, Søndag, n. 14).

27

British delegation
Eighth meeting
Atlantic City
June 25, 1944 at 4 p.m.[192]

*Keynes's meeting with White • Sterling-dollar rate • Documents at
Bretton Woods • Subcommittee on Management • IMF quotas*

*The final internal meeting of the British delegation for which minutes exist from this
period took place in Atlantic City. The most revealing statements concern Keynes's
report of the features the United States desired for IMF quotas. Although the proposed
quotas were roughly proportional to economic power, they also reflected political factors,
such as the U.S. wish that the combined quotas of the British Commonwealth not
exceed the U.S. quota. In defense of the U.S. position, one may note that World War
II made the economic statistics of many countries unreliable or unrepresentative of the
likely postwar reality, so initial quotas were going to result from a combination of
guesswork and negotiation rather than any simple formula.*

1. **Lord Keynes** gave a brief account of some of the points of
particular importance to the UK that he had discussed with Dr. [Harry
Dexter] White.

Sterling-Dollar Exchange Rate

2. Dr. White was going to propose at Bretton Woods that initial
exchanges rates for the purposes of the Fund should be those in force on
July 1, 1944, except where the Fund agreed otherwise. This meant that
the sterling-dollar rate would be $4.03½. It was agreed that a telegram
should be sent to London early on this point. **Lord Keynes** had pointed

---

[192] Present: Lord Keynes, Sir W. Eady, Prof. Robertson, Prof. Robbins, Mr.
Beckett, Mr. Bolton, Mr. Brooks, Mr. Snelling.

out to Dr. White that this solution left unsolved the problems of the exchange rates (a) for the occupied countries, and (b) for Latin American countries, some of which had a multiplicity of rates.

Procedure at Bretton Woods

3. **Lord Keynes** had put to Dr. White Mr. [W. Eric] Beckett's proposals for a "Final Act" and Dr. White had liked the idea.

Management

4. It was agreed that in order to save time, there ought to be appointed at an early date a separate subcommittee to consider management problems and that Sir W[ilfrid] Eady, Mr. [George] Bolton, and Mr. [W. Eric] Beckett should be the UK representatives.

Quotas

5. **Lord Keynes** had agreed with Dr. White that quotas should not be discussed at Atlantic City. Dr. White's desiderata were that:

(a) The U.S. quota should not be more than $2,750 million.

(b) The UK quota should be $1,300 million.

(c) The Russian quota should be 10 per cent of the total quotas.

(d) China should have the next largest quota.

(e) France should have the next largest quota.

(f) The total quotas should be not more than $8,000 million.

(g) The voting strength of the British Commonwealth should not be more than that of the U.S. (The Americans now showed some disposition to reduce voting strength from quotas plus 100 to quotas plus 25.)

The major snag in this list of conditions appeared to be the position of India. It was agreed that the Indian claim for a larger quota should be supported so far as was reasonably possible, but not to the point of jeopardizing the whole scheme on this account.

28

First Anglo-American meeting
Atlantic City
June 24, 1944 at 3 p.m.[193]

*Suggested British changes regarding Bank • Unpaid balance of
shares payable in gold • Uniform interest rates and charges •
Stabilization loans • Competition with private-sector lenders •
Appendix: Pasvolsky's memorandum of a conversation with Keynes*

*The British having arrived in Atlantic City the previous evening, they meet with the
American delegation to explain how their draft of the articles of agreement for the
Bank for Reconstruction and Development differed from the American draft. There are
a number of technical differences, and three big conceptual ones: the British want the
Bank to have 20 percent rather than 100 of its capital paid in; to be able to make
stabilization loans; and to have some ability to lend even where private-sector loans are
available. The British proposal for lower paid-in capital fits with the straitened
financial circumstances of Britain and many other countries that have been fighting
World War II. The desire that the Bank be able to make stabilization loans reflects
Britain's own possible need for them after the war. The proposal that the Bank have
some ability to compete with the private sector reflects the skepticism of Keynes and his
school that the private sector is better than the public sector at evaluating risks and
returns.*

 *The minutes here were taken by the American delegation. We found no minutes by
the British delegation. As an appendix we attach a memo of a conversation between
John Maynard Keynes and Leo Pasvolsky at an unspecified time the same day.
Pasvolsky was an economist and journalist who had become the supervisor of the*

---

[193] Present: Lord [John Maynard] Keynes, Sir Wilfrid Eady, Messrs. [Lionel]
Robbins, [Dennis] Robertson, [Redvers] Opie, [Eric] Beckett, [George] Bolton,
[Charles] Campbell, [H.E.] Brooks and [A.W. "Peter"] Snelling of United
Kingdom; Messrs. [Harry Dexter] White, [Edward] Bernstein, [Ansel] Luxford,
E[dward] E. Brown, [August] Maffry, [Walter] Louchheim, [Emanuel]
Goldenweiser, [Walter] Gardner, [Frederick] Livesey, [Leo] Pasvolsky, and Miss
[Dorothy] Richardson of United States.

Division of Political and Economic Studies at the U.S. Department of State, a counterpart to the Division of Monetary Research that Harry Dexter White headed at the U.S. Treasury Department. Keynes and Pasvolsky were well acquainted. The summary comes from Pasvolsky's personal papers, which are deposited at the U.S. Library of Congress.

The purpose of the meeting was to give **Lord Keynes** an opportunity to explain to some members of the American delegation the principal changes which the English suggest in the draft of the proposed Bank for Reconstruction and Development.[194] Lord Keynes explained that in drafting this document, the British used three documents: the [U.S.] November [24, 1943] draft, the "Questions and Answers [on the Bank for Reconstruction and Development]," and the American reply to the British memorandum of April 20, 1944.[195]

The first change suggested was that the 80 percent of member country shares not subscribed at the outset should be reserved permanently to implement guarantees given by the Bank and should be payable only in gold [II-4, ["Payment of Subscriptions,"] in both the American and British drafts]. Upon discussion, it appeared that it was intended, firstly, that this reserve should be in addition to regular reserves which would be accumulated out of profits and guarantee fees, and, secondly, that this 80 percent should serve as reserve for guaranteed loans only. In regard to the second point, **Mr. White** remarked that it might be possible to work out a provision by which it would be possible to avoid separating so completely the two functions of the Bank, the guaranteeing of loans and the granting of direct loans.

Since this 80 percent of member country shares would be payable only in gold, the British also suggested that there would be no need for gradual redemption in gold of member country currencies paid to the Bank in connection with the initial subscriptions of 20 percent of the shares.

Lord Keynes remarked that it appeared desirable that the rates of interest on guaranteed loans and the commission for guaranteeing charged by the Bank should be uniform among all countries, although some differences might be introduced in the rate of the commission charges by the local governments for their guarantees [["Payment Provisions,"] IV-10 in American draft and IV-6 in British draft]. The

---

[194] Document B-1 of the conference, reproduced in chapter 80.
[195] The U.S. November 24, 1943 draft is in chapter 3, while the other two documents are available in the online companion files to this book.

reason given for this suggestion was that the Bank should not discriminate among the various member countries. The specific rates he suggested for use at the outset were 3½ percent per year interest, and 1 percent per year guarantee commission. Lord Keynes also suggested that the rate of amortization might be 2 percent a year.

A question was raised in regard to Lord Keynes's explanation of the establishment of reserves as to whether it was intended that no profits should be distributed to member countries [["Distribution of Net Profits,"] V-9 in American draft and IV-12 in British draft]. **Lord Keynes** seemed to consider the distribution of profits unnecessary in connection with the proposed Bank.

The question of tied and untied loans as discussed briefly. The **British** suggested that guaranteed loans, and loans made from borrowed funds, should be untied. **Mr. White** stated the American position that a country may specify the currencies which it desires in connection with any loan, but that after credits in specific currencies are extended to a borrowing country in connection with a loan, the borrower is required to spend these credits in the country in whose currencies these credits have been made.[196]

Lord Keynes then explained that the British draft of the Bank proposal provides for a type of loan not included in the American proposal, i.e., stabilization loans [III-6 in British draft]. **Mr. White** remarked that this constituted a substantial change, and that it would be necessary to consider this suggestion very carefully.

Lord Keynes remarked that in the American draft proposal of November 24, 1943, considerable emphasis was placed upon the fact that the Bank should avoid making any loans which could be made through private investment channels [IV-6, ["Noncompetition with Private Investment"]]. **Mr. White** remarked that this had been our intention and that we consider this principle fundamental. **Lord Keynes** replied that the members of the British delegation agreed that the Bank should not make loans which could be made through private channels on reasonable terms. There followed a short discussion of the possible interpretation of the phrase "unreasonable terms." One of the members of the **American**

---

[196] At the time, and for some years afterwards, the existence of exchange controls on many currencies, the lack of eurocurrency markets (for lending or borrowing in a currency outside the country of issue), and the smallness of forward markets in foreign exchange made it much harder than today to spend the proceeds of a loan in a particular currency anywhere except in the country issuing the currency.

delegation pointed out that the service charges which Lord Keynes suggested for guaranteeing loans would act, in many cases, as a safeguard against the Bank's engaging in investments of this type which could be carried on through private investment channels.

It was pointed out that the members of the British delegation have not yet had an opportunity to consider the question of management. A number of copies of the British draft of suggestions were then supplied to the members of the American delegation to be held in confidence, after which the meeting was adjourned.

Appendix: Pasvolsky's memorandum of a conversation with Keynes

Keynes told me that the British have come to the conclusion that the establishment of a Bank is absolutely indispensable in order to meet the situation which is going to arise in the reconstruction field because of the obvious inadequacy of the UNRRA [United Nations Relief and Rehabilitation Administration] for that purpose. He said that on the way over, he and his colleagues had discussed the matter very thoroughly with the representatives of several governments-in-exile, especially the Czech, Belgian, Polish and Norwegian, and were very much impressed by the argument that these countries and other liberated countries in Europe are more anxious about their ability to secure foreign financing for the purpose of restoring their economic activity as rapidly as possible than they are about almost any other question. On the trip over the British discussed the ideas which they are now putting before us with these European representatives and believe that those governments would be most anxious to support the proposal.

Keynes also gave me a picture of some of the difficulties which he believed it is important for us to realize in connection with the British situation. When I said to him that his speech in the House of Lords has caused us considerable trouble here, he replied that the situation was so bad that he felt absolutely necessary to say the things he had said. In fact, he said that just before he delivered his speech, there was an almost universal conviction in the parliamentary circles that the opposition had won out and the proposal for the stabilization fund was dead as far as Britain was concerned. That situation, he said, was changed by his speech, but there is still much trouble ahead. We did not have a chance to discuss further the points which he raised in his letter to me but are planning to do so before I leave Atlantic City.

29

Second Anglo-American meeting
Atlantic City
June 26, 1944 at 11:30 a.m.

*Exchange rate adjustments • Suspension from the Fund •
Transition period • Effect on other international agreements*

This second Anglo-American meeting at Atlantic City discusses the IMF. The British desire an IMF with less power over member countries than the Joint Statement envisions, and use this meeting to propose that certain ambiguities in the Joint Statement be resolved favorably to British views. In particular, the British wish to assert national supremacy over the IMF on exchange rate matters; establish a probationary status allowing a member that does not meet its obligations time to change its behavior rather than expelling it immediately; lengthen the postwar transition period to current account convertibility; clarify the relationship of the IMF agreement to other international agreements; and restrict the IMF's ability to report on a member's policies without the member's consent.

We have, and reproduce here, two somewhat different accounts of the meeting by the American delegation and an account by the British delegation.

(American version by Dorothy F. Richardson)

Paragraph 4 of Annex B of the British document I.M.C. (44) (F) 11, June 21, 1944 was discussed at length.[197] **Lord Keynes** remarked that there are two points to be considered in connection with this paragraph: the fact that the wording emphasizes a country's sovereignty with regard to its exchange rate, and the introduction of the concept that it may be desirable to provide some solution other than withdrawal when there is disagreement between the Fund and a member country on questions relating to alterations of its rate of exchange, especially in view of the fact that difficulties on questions relating to the country's rate of exchange

---

[197] British criticisms of the Joint Statement, reproduced in chapter 82.

may be solved if more time is allowed.

Mr. White replied that he appreciated the political difficulties confronting the UK delegation on this matter, but that anything which would suggest that the basic aim of the proposed Fund is not exchange stability would immediately defeat it in this country.

Lord Keynes suggested that it might be possible to achieve a formulation which would be helpful to the understanding of the proposal in both the U.S. and UK. The UK is concerned about its ultimate sovereignty in regard to its domestic affairs, and considerations of sovereignty are important to the US, also; however, it is desirable that when a mere difference of opinion is involved, a country shall not be forced to resort to withdrawal.

Mr. [Alvin] Hansen [U.S.] pointed out that the Joint Statement recognizes that changes necessary for domestic social or political stability shall be permitted by defining the goals of internal stability.[198] **Mr. [Lionel] Robbins [UK]** replied that although a change of the exchange rate may not be the best method of achieving full employment, it might be the best method under the circumstances. In such a case it would be undesirable to freeze the situation by forbidding a country the right to alter its exchange. **Mr. Hansen** suggested that the Fund will depend upon the influence of the advice it gives to member countries. The members of the **United Kingdom** delegation expressed opposition to the Fund's interfering in any way any member country's domestic affairs. **Mr. [Walter] Gardner [U.S.]** inquired whether it would not be an aid to United Kingdom in its domestic policy to know that it was necessary not to alter its exchange rate except on specific conditions.

Mr. White remarked that the group to whom exchange stability is important is the group upon whom we must rely for support. **Lord Keynes** stated that he would like to attempt redrafting of these provisions.

Mr. White remarked that the British suggestion [in section IV of its paper] that failure to comply with the decisions of the Board of Directors of the Fund on questions relating to alteration of exchange rates shall be punished by deprivation of access to the resources of the Fund embodies an important change of substance, since it suggests that the purpose of the Fund is not stabilization of exchange rates, but provision of assets. We do not regard member countries as having any "right" of access to

---

[198] Perhaps a reference to I-2 [["Balanced Trade, High Employment and Real Income."]]

the resources of the Fund. We consider that the Fund provides resources to member countries to aid them in pursuing the goal of stabilization of exchange rates. We feel that alteration of the rate of exchange is a very important step, especially in the case of an important member country, and is therefore a member of sufficient seriousness to overrule questions of sovereignty. **Lord Keynes** felt, from the remarks of the members of the American delegation, that the United Kingdom's redrafting of these provisions must have been faulty, since their purpose in suggesting that a country be suspended from access to the resources of the Fund was to discourage a member from withdrawing the from the Fund, so that it would remain subject to the obligations of the Fund and would not be free to engage in such devices as multiple currency parities.

The paragraphs dealing with the provisions relating to the transitional period [Article X] were then discussed. **Lord Keynes** stated that the pace at which the transitional [period] was accomplished in the United Kingdom would depend not only on the actions of United Kingdom but also on the actions of other countries. **Mr. White** stated that we agree that there must be an adjustment period, and that the duration of that period is uncertain. However, we feel that it would be reassuring if this period were not too long. **Mr. [Leo] Pasvolsky [U.S.]** suggested that a five-year period would not be implausible. **Mr. Robbins [UK]** pointed out that the United Kingdom draft of these provisions does not leave the duration of the transition uncertain, but provides that after five years a member country must consult with the Fund each year concerning the desirability of retaining restrictions.

Mr. [Ansel] Luxford [U.S.] pointed out that the U.S. draft of this provision does not state that at the end of three years a member country must give up exchange restrictions, but that it must consult with the Fund, and the Fund will determine whether or not these restrictions shall be retained. **Mr. [Edward] Bernstein [U.S.]** pointed out the provision is now drafted also states that in case of a difference of opinion between the Fund and a member country on matters relating to the transition period, the country shall be given the benefit of every reasonable doubt.

Mr. White felt that after some period it must be compulsory that the member country obtain the Fund's approval in order to retain these restrictions. **Lord Keynes** felt that this would necessitate naming a very long period and that this was undesirable. It was decided in the light of the foregoing discussion to submit Annex C [of document I.M.C. (44) (F) 11] for consideration of the full group [the Formal Agenda Committee].

The inclusion of suggested provision IX-4 [["Relation to Other Commitments"]], the "commercial policy" provision, was then discussed.

Lord Keynes felt that publication of this provision would prejudice the Fund's reception in United Kingdom. He felt that it was acceptable as regards further agreements, i.e., with the deletion of the word "existing." He remarked that the United Kingdom's authority over her own affairs must be absolute during the transition period. The **American** technician pointed out that this provision did not mean that the Fund would supersede all existing commercial policy agreements. Therefore, the problem with which Lord Keynes is concerned is independent of the establishment of the International Monetary Fund. It was decided that Messrs. Luxford and Pasvolsky and several members of United Kingdom delegation should meet to discuss this question further.

Lord Keynes felt that the phrase "give consideration to" in [the] provision on "Consideration of the Recommendations of the Fund" [Article III, proposed additional section, Alternative A, U.S.] in Document F-1 [the IMF Articles of Agreement] implied that the Fund had authority with regard to member countries' internal affairs. **Mr. White** suggested that this matter be presented to the full group for discussion.

(American version, no attribution)

1. *Exchange rate adjustments:* **Keynes** points out that [the] British proposal permits [the] Fund to penalize [a] country which shifts its rate without Fund approval by either denying the country for the use of the Fund resources or, if the country persists in a policy which the Fund regards as flagrantly contrary to its purpose, to oust it. There is a general provision in the British proposal which permits the Fund to oust a member which persistently pursues policies contrary to the purposes of the Fund. Keynes emphasizes the House of Commons debate, and says new language is needed to satisfy the House.[199] **Harry [White]** says that, on account of our public and Congress, we can't budge an inch.

Keynes insists our objectives are essentially the same. **Hansen [U.S.]** proposes a criterion of internal stability. **Robbins [UK]** objects that nothing is gained by freezing a situation which has previously got out of hand if this means freezing also an overvalued currency. **Keynes** says any

---

[199] The British House of Commons debated the Joint Statement on May 10, 1944 (*Hansard,* 5th series, v. 399, columns 1935-2046).

kind of outside interference would make Bevin's job impossible.[200]
Gardner [U.S.] asked Keynes in what sense he regarded the Fund as
contributing to exchange stability. Merely that it was at liberty to pour its
resources into supporting a currency that was being forced out of line by
domestic policy? Or did the British recognize that in joining the Fund,
they were accepting some obligations to modify their domestic policy in
the light of its international effect on stability? **Keynes** said they would —
but at their own discretion. He finally seem to admit that it might be
helpful to have an obligation to the Fund to back up those who are
working for some modification of domestic policy, providing the Fund
did not issue orders on some specific phase of domestic policy such as
wages. **[Emanuel] Goldenweiser [U.S.]** pointed out the particular
advantage to a foreign trading country such as England of general stability
of world exchange rates. Why was that not a good selling point to the
British? **Keynes** agreed it might be, but that he did not settle in his mind
the question the Fund's authority versus the country. He did not wish a
country to have to leave the Fund entirely if it disagreed with it. **White**
pointed out the one-year suspension arrangement. **Keynes** was
impressed. The British will try their hands at a new draft taking full
account of the American position.

2. *Transition period:* **Keynes** says [the] implication of three years is too
strong in [the] present draft because England may find that because of
international, even more than domestic, developments it is impossible to
abandon exchange controls. Anything stronger on the three-year
provision would be quite hopeless. The Chancellor [of the Exchequer]
has assured Parliament that England retains her liberty of action in this
regard. The **American** position was briefly reasserted with no new
comments of interest.

Keynes asks if the three-year provision will be carried to Bretton
Woods. If it were to get out, it would create consternation in England and
prejudice the whole press reaction. Later abandonment of the point
would not repair the damage. The British, meanwhile, will release their
five-year consultative provision to the Atlantic City meeting.

3. *Alter existing treaties and agreements:* **Keynes** recalls that the British
have a commercial agreement with the U.S. which permits exchange
control only in time of war. Does that govern at the end of this war?
Pasvolsky [U.S.] states that there is an escape provision. **Keynes**

---

[200] Ernest Bevin, a Labour Party member of Parliament who was Minister of
Labor and National Service in the wartime British coalition government.

proposes a phrase in the Fund draft such as "notwithstanding *existing* agreements." He is prepared to accept *future* commercial agreements as overriding. The British will endeavor to clear the point with Pasvolsky and [Ansel] Luxford [U.S.].

4. *Right of the Fund to report on a country's policies:* **Keynes** opposes, and **White** appears to agree with him. What **Keynes** asked was whether the Fund could tell the U.S. that the New Deal was all wrong. **White** had meant only that the Fund could not criticize social and political policy.

(British Version by A.W. Snelling)

Exchange Adjustment Clause

1. **Lord Keynes** explained the difficulties arising out of the debate in the House of Commons and from other expressions of public opinion in the UK about the present draft of the Exchange Adjustment Clause (IV in the Joint Statement). He said that the Chancellor of the Exchequer wanted to be able to go to Parliament and say to them that their sovereignty in money matters had been assured. He agreed that the aim of both the UK and U.S. Delegations was to reach arrangements where exchange rates should be as stable as possible, but Parliament had very much in mind the experience of the early [nineteen-]thirties. He thought it possible that Congress might dislike, as much as Parliament, having its freedom of action in matters of exchange rates fettered by an international agreement.

2. **Dr. White** explained the serious difficulties to which the first sentence of the new UK draft of IV-4 [["Latitude for Changes in Par Value"]] gave rise. These difficulties were absolutely basic. The idea of the Fund had been put across in America as something conductive to exchange stability. Already, the United States had made major concessions to United Kingdom views in order to ensure a reasonable measure of flexibility. He was convinced that he could not retract any further on this point in view of the criticism to which he had already been exposed because the plan envisaged a right to depreciate by 10 percent at unilateral discretion and a further 10 percent at very short notice. Unfortunately, those people in the United States who stressed the sovereignty of Congress in monetary matters were also the strongest opponents of the plan who were prepared to block its progress on any pretext. His chief aim was to make sure of the support of the much larger group whose main desire was to see exchange stability. He thought,

therefore, that Lord Keynes' criticisms and proposals went right to the root of the plan, and that if he insisted upon them it would be impossible to reach agreement.

3. **Mr. W.R. Gardner [U.S.]** envisaged a situation in which a country had already depreciated its exchange by 20 percent, and wished to do so further. In this situation the consent of the Fund would be required and he thought that if a country did depreciate further in defiance of the wishes of the Fund, that would represent a grave step of such fundamental economic importance that the country ought not to do so except after the most careful deliberation. If that deliberation led to the conclusion that the step must be taken despite the views of the majority in the Fund, withdrawal from the Fund seemed to be the only possible consequence. **Mr. Goldenweiser [U.S.]** remarked that the international financial position of the United Kingdom had been built upon exchange stability and he hoped that the prospect of future stability would enable the idea of the Fund to be put across more easily in England.

4. **Mr. Alvin Hansen [U.S.]** remarked that American critics said that the Fund did nothing to prevent domestic inflations and suggested that some provision should be inserted about the necessity for the maintenance of internal stability. **Professor Robbins [UK]** thought that this would be dangerous because it would tend to encourage the Fund to intervene in domestic political issues. Those who were anxious to prevent inflationary tendencies would, he thought, find their hands weakened rather than strengthened if it could be represented that anti-inflationary steps were being taken at the dictation of an outside body of international financers.

5. **Lord Keynes** undertook to reconsider the UK draft and hoped to be able to prepare a redraft which would be of help to the U.S. authorities in securing acceptance for the plan in America whilst enabling the Chancellor to meet Parliamentary criticism.

Suspension from the Facilities of the Fund

6. **Lord Keynes** developed his arguments in favor of having a half-way house between full membership of the Fund and complete withdrawal from it, emphasizing in particular that differences of view between members of the Fund might be of a temporary nature and that it would not be desirable, except as a last resort, to take the drastic step of requiring a member to withdraw completely from the Fund. He therefore advocated an arrangement whereby a member might be suspended from the facilities of the Fund whilst at the same time retaining its obligations

to the Fund.

7. **Dr. White** criticized this proposal as making it appear that the main function of the Fund would be to provide countries with additional assets, whereas in American eyes stability was conceived to be the main objective. Access to additional assets was in fact intended to be a device that would aid stabilization. He referred to the new American redraft on page 25 of Doc. F-1 [Article VIII, proposed additional section, Alternative A, U.S.] about suspension of membership and the UK delegates undertook to consider this redraft.

Transitional Period

8. **Lord Keynes** pointed out that three years would probably prove an insufficient period, not only for the UK but also for many of the European Allies, to effect adjustments that had to be made before the obligation of multilateral convertibility could be accepted. He added that the speed with which the UK would be able to accept this obligation would depend a great deal on the policy of other countries and particularly of the United States. **Mr. Pasvolsky [U.S.]** hoped that the existence of the Fund would tend to shorten the transitional period; he thought that three years would be reasonable. **Mr. Luxford [U.S.]** and **Mr. Bernstein [U.S.]** pointed out that the present draft did not lay down that countries would have to accept the obligations of multilateral convertibility at the end of three years, but only required them at that stage to "consult" the Fund.

9. It was agreed that Annex C of I.M.C. (44) (F) 11 ["Amendments to Clause X(3)"] should be circulated to all the Delegations at Atlantic City.

Effect on Other International Agreements

10. **Lord Keynes** expressed some doubts about the new draft U.S. provision [IX-4, ["Relation to other Commitments"]] reading "Nothing in this agreement shall be deemed to affect in any way existing or future international commitments regarding the non-discriminatory application of exchange restrictions or international undertakings for the progressive relaxation of barriers to trade." He suggested that the effect of such a provision on existing agreements such as the UK-U.S. Trade Agreement of [November 17,] 1938 needed to be considered and **Mr. Pasvolsky [U.S.]** undertook to look into this matter.

30

British Commonwealth delegations
Second meeting
Atlantic City
June 25, 1944 at 4:45 p.m.[201]

Harry Dexter White's views in general on the IMF, according to Keynes • Exchange adjustment clause • Transitional period • Quotas • Conference procedure at Bretton Woods

On board the Queen Mary, *the British delegation had invited the chairman of the Indian delegation, Sir Jeremy Raisman, to sit in its meetings, and had met with the full Indian delegation in meetings with all delegations on board. At Atlantic City, delegations from two other British Commonwealth nations, Australia and Canada, were present, and the British delegation met with them twice.*

No official record was kept at the first meeting, which took place in the morning on June 24, the first full day that the British delegation was in Atlantic City. Lionel Robbins, head of the economic section of the British War Cabinet Office, did however write a paragraph on it in his diary. He reported that Keynes summarized the work that the delegations had done aboard the Queen Mary, *and the changes the British proposed to the IMF (chapter 82). Louis Rasminsky of Canada told the British that their proposal to assert national sovereignty bluntly with respect to exchange rates seemed almost designed to upset the Americans.[202]*

This second meeting is given over to Keynes's summary of Harry Dexter White's views on issues concerning the IMF and on what White claims to be the domestic U.S.

---

[201] The minutes for this meeting remark, "No record has been kept of the first meeting." Present: Lord Keynes (in the Chair) [UK]; United Kingdom: Sir W[ilfrid] Eady, Prof. D[ennis] H. Robertson, Mr. W. E[ric] Beckett, Mr. G[eorge] L.F. Bolton; Mr. H.E. Brooks [and] Mr. A.W. ["Peter"] Snelling, Secretaries; Canada: Mr. L[ouis] Rasminsky, Mr. A.F. W[ynne] Plumptre, Mr. J[ohn] J. Deutsch; Australia: Mr. L[eslie] G. Melville, Mr. J[ames] B. Brigden; Mr. A[rthur] N. Tange; Mr. F[rederick] H. Wheeler; India: Sir J[eremy] Raisman, Sir T[heodore] E. Gregory, Sir Chintaman Deshmukh.

[202] Robbins and Meade (1981: 158).

political constraints the IMF agreement faces.

1. The meeting was called in order to enable **Lord Keynes** to give an account of a discussion which he had with Dr. White.

Dr. White's Views in General

2. Dr. White's general reaction had been that, from a technical point of view, many of the UK suggestions were acceptable, but that some of them were likely to be politically unacceptable in the U.S. Among the questions on which Dr. White thought that there was a divergence of view between the UK and the U.S. were the following:

(i) How far the IMF proposals amounted to a return to the Gold Standard. On this point, the UK tended to emphasize the importance of elasticity of the exchanges, and the U.S., the importance of exchange stability.

(ii) As regards disciplinary powers, the UK stressed the rights of individual countries as against the Fund, whilst the U.S. emphasized the importance of the powers of the Fund as against the individual countries.

(iii) On the size of the Fund, the UK was suggesting larger figures, whilst in the U.S., the Fund had been criticized for being so big.

(iv) As regards to the transitional period, the U.S. wanted to make it as short and definite as possible, whilst the UK suggestions tended in the opposite direction.

Exchange Adjustment Clause

3. Dr. White had taken strong exception to the first sentence of the new IV-4 [["Latitude for Change in Par Value"]], which stressed the sovereignty of Governments in monetary matters. The question therefore arose whether the UK should withdraw this suggestion and if so, whether now or later. Dr. White's view was that this sentence would give rise to great political difficulties in the U.S., and **Mr. [Louis] Rasminsky [Canada]** said that, in his opinion, Dr. White was right on this point. **Sir T[heodore] Gregory [India]** and **Mr. [Leslie] Melville [Australia]** both shared the view of the UK that it was desirable to emphasize the sovereignty of Governments in monetary matters, but **Mr. [W. Eric] Beckett [UK]** pointed out that from the legal point of view, the sentence left much to be desired. The general conclusion was that it would be desirable to withdraw this sentence and replace it by something less

provocative before any documents reached the Press. **Lord Keynes** had also agreed with Dr. White that the UK proposals as regarding exchange adjustments (Annex B of I.M.C. (44) (F) 11) ["Amended Version of Clause [Article] IV"] should be reserved for the time being.

Transitional Period

4. The UK suggestions that five years should be substituted for three years, and that the duration of the transitional period should be made less rather than more definite gave rise to difficulties, because the thoughts of the Americans had been moving in the opposite direction. Dr. White appreciated the reasons for which the UK wanted these changes, but foresaw trouble with the rest of his Delegation. **Sir T. Gregory [UK]** thought that there ought to be room for compromise, but **Lord Keynes** pointed out that public opinion in the UK was strong on this matter. **Mr. Rasminsky [Canada]** wondered whether it would be possible to devise an objective test of the conditions in which countries should accept the obligation of multilateral convertibility. **Lord Keynes** thought that this would be impossible because of the existence of war debts to be paid off, and of the necessity for giving credit for current exports.

5. **Mr. [John] Deutsch [Canada]** drew attention to the new American suggestion that "no member country should prejudice through the use of exchange restrictions which are authorized under this Agreement or requested by the Fund any existing or future international commitments regarding the nondiscriminatory application of exchange restrictions or international undertakings for the progressive relaxation of barriers to trade." It was agreed that there was a danger that this new suggestion would make nonsense of the provisions as to scarce currencies, and that the position needed to be explored thoroughly with Dr. White. **Mr. Beckett [UK]** thought that unless the international monetary convention explicitly overrode the provisions of treaties such as the UK-U.S. Trade Agreement of 1938, relating to exchange restrictions, the latter would continue to be binding upon the UK. **Lord Keynes** thought that one solution might be to delete "existing or" in the new clause quoted above.

Quotas

6. Dr. White was anxious that the question of quotas should not be discussed at Atlantic City. **Lord Keynes** thought however that notwithstanding its unsatisfactory nature, discussions at Bretton Woods

would probably start on the basis of the U.S. formulas. He suggested, therefore, that the Dominion and Indian representatives should check the figures in the United States formula for each of their own countries.

Conference Procedure at Bretton Woods

7. Dr. White had it in mind to suggest that at Bretton Woods each country should have one vote. **Lord Keynes** pointed out that the UNRRA Conference[203] showed that this procedure was undesirable, and he had therefore suggested to Dr. White that it should be laid down that there would be no voting at Bretton Woods, but that the Chairman should get the sense of the meeting and be responsible for resolving any deadlocks.

---

[203] The conference that worked out the details of the United Nations Relief and Rehabilitation Administration, held in November 1943 in the same hotel as this conference.

31

Allied delegations
First meeting
Aboard the *Queen Mary*
June 19, 1944 at noon[204]

Purpose of onboard meetings • Circulation of documents • Schedule of meetings

The British delegation held several meetings on the Queen Mary *with delegates from other countries, who were mainly representing European governments-in-exile that the British were hosting in London. A delegate from China and the U.S. Treasury's attaché in London also attended. The British used the meetings to try to persuade the other delegations to support British positions. The British were, however, willing to modify their proposals to address criticisms by other delegations.*

1. **Lord Keynes** explained that as the time at Atlantic City and at Bretton Woods would be short it had seemed convenient to get ahead as far as possible in advance of the larger meetings. The UK delegation had a number of amendments to the Fund Statement of the Principles to suggest, which would be circulated, and also some suggestions covering

---

[204] *Editors' note:* The original minutes of the meetings aboard the *Queen Mary* list members present at the top of each meeting. We move the list to the footnotes.

Present: Lord [John Maynard] Keynes (United Kingdom) (in the Chair); United Kingdom: Sir Wilfrid Eady, Professor L[ionel] C. Robbins, Professor D[ennis] H. Robertson, Mr. N[igel] B. Ronald, Mr. W. E[ric] Beckett, Mr. G[eorge] L.F. Bolton; Belgium: Baron [René] Boël; China, Dr. P[ing-]W[en] Kuo; Czechoslovakia, Dr. [Ladislav] Feierabend, Dr. [Jan] Mládek; Greece, Mr. [Kyriakos] Varvaressos; India, Sir Jeremy Raisman, Sir David Meek, Mrs. [A.A.] Henderson; Netherlands, Mr. J[ohan] Willem "Wim"] Beyen; Norway, Professor W[ilhelm] Keilhau; Poland, Dr. [Ludwik] Grosfeld, Dr. [Leon] Baránski, Dr. [Stanisław] Kirkor, Mr. [Gustaw] Gottesman; USA, Mr. L[auren] W. Casaday; Secretariat, Mr. H.E. Brooks, Mr. A.W. ["Peter"] Snelling [both United Kingdom].

points not hitherto discussed in any detail, e.g. procedure on liquidation, coming into force, etc. As the journey would not be long he hoped that it would be possible to begin discussions of the Reconstruction Bank by Wednesday at the latest, since this was of particular interest though not in so advanced a state.

2. The following documents were circulated:

I.M.C. (B) (44) 1, containing prints of all the documents about the Bank which have passed between the UK and U.S. Governments.

I.M.C. (44) (General) 1, containing the U.S. proposals for the organization of the conference.

Some discussion followed on the second document, **Lord Keynes** explaining that it had been suggested to Dr. White that fusion of certain committees would be desirable, and that co-ordination was a function rather for the separate commissions that for a special committee to the whole conference. Nothing was yet known of the intended agenda for Commission III, and it appeared improbable that there would be time for it to do much. Several delegates expressed concern at the number of committees.

3. It was agreed to hold further meetings daily, the next at 11:30 a.m. on Tuesday, 20th June, at which it was hoped to have further proposals available together with a list of delegates to the Conference so far as these had been notified.

32

Allied delegations
Second meeting
Aboard the *Queen Mary*
June 20, 1944 at 11:30 a.m.[205]

Exchange variations • Gold and gold convertible exchange •
Convertibility for current transactions

The Allied delegates consider British criticisms of three parts of the Joint Statement.
The British propose redrafting of Article IV, "Par Values of Member Currencies," to
acknowledge the supremacy of national authorities over exchange rates and to provide
for suspension from the IMF as an intermediate step between full membership and
expulsion. The British criticize American language about "gold convertible currency"
on the grounds that no currency is currently convertible into gold. Finally, the British
propose to elaborate on the obligation of members not to impose restrictions on current
transactions. Britain has incurred large debts during the war to some countries
supplying it with materiel. The British wish for the settlement of these debts, known as
the sterling balances, to remain a matter for bilateral negotiation between Britain and
the creditor countries, not a matter involving the IMF. The other delegations on board
agree with the British on the Article IV and gold convertible exchange, but the minutes
do not record their reaction to the question of the sterling balances. At Bretton Woods,
the delegation of Egypt and India, two of Britain's largest creditors for wartime
materiel, would advocate for making the sterling balances a matter for IMF
involvement, but would be unsuccessful.

---

[205] Present: Lord Keynes (United Kingdom) (in the Chair); United Kingdom: Sir
Wilfrid Eady, Professor L.C. Robbins, Professor D.H. Robertson, Mr. N.B.
Ronald, Mr. W.E. Beckett, Mr. G.L.F. Bolton; Belgium: Baron Boël; China: Dr.
P.W. Kuo; Czechoslovakia: Dr. Feierabend, Dr. Mládek; Greece: Mr.
Varvaressos; India: Sir Jeremy Raisman, Sir David Meek, Mrs. Henderson;
Netherlands: Mr. J.W. Beyen; Norway: Professor W. Keilhau; Poland: Dr.
Grosfeld, Dr. Baránski, Dr. Kirkor, Mr. Gottesman; USA: Mr. L.W. Casaday;
Secretariat: Mr. H.E. Brooks, Mr. A.W. Snelling.

Exchange Variations [Article IV]

1. A paper by the UK Delegation (circulated as I.M.C. (44) (F) 1) ["International Monetary Fund, Proposed Redraft of Clause IV, Note by the UK Delegation"] was considered in detail, and found general approval subject to the following points:

(a) Clause IV-2 [["Changes in Par Value"]] should begin "Subject to (5) below [IV-5, ["Uniform Changes in Par Value"]], subsequent changes etc. ..."

(b) **Baron [René] Boël [Belgium]** was anxious that the revised wording of IV-2 should not be capable of the construction that a member could depreciate its currency on an unsupported plea of fundamental disequilibrium: he preferred wording which emphasized that the Fund must be satisfied of that fact. **Lord Keynes** said this was the intention of the revised clause, as indeed of the original, and he thought that the new (4) [i.e., IV-4] read with (2) [IV-2] gave the Fund an enhanced status in that respect. He was doubtful whether it was wise to be more specific in (2).

(c) At some stage it must be made clear that a member was required to make good to the Fund any fall in the international value of the Fund's holdings of its currency occasioned by depreciation.

(d) It was important that the Fund should not be precluded from giving informal advice. A new clause on interpretations and general powers was probably desirable.

(e) **Mr. [Jan Willem "Wim"] Beyen [Netherlands]** criticized the phrase "political policy" as mysterious.

(f) A consequential change on IX-1 [["Gold Price"]] (delete "agreed" in first line) was noted.

All delegates approved of the object of the amendment.

Gold and Gold Convertible Exchange [III-7, "Fund's Acquisition of Gold"]

2. The paper I.M.C. (44) (F) 2 ["International Monetary Fund, The Definition of 'Gold and Gold Convertible Exchange,'" Memorandum by Lord Keynes"] was considered in detail, in the light of the view (which **Mr. Beyen** supported) that the U.S. dollar is not gold convertible. Paragraph 4 of the paper was withdrawn by the UK Delegation for further consideration. Among the points mentioned in discussions were

the following:

(a) **Baron Boël** thought that gold required for restocking and rehabilitation ought to be excluded from the computation of "net official holdings." **Lord Keynes** thought this point arose rather on Clause II; he did not agree with the proposition as put but suggested that the point should be raised at the main Conference [at Bretton Woods].

(b) Similarly, **Professor [Wilhelm] Keilhau [Norway]** desired dollar resources held by the Norwegian Government against the ship replacement requirements of Norwegian nationals to be excluded from Norway's reckoning of convertible exchange. **Mr. Beyen** (and others) thought this would open the door to many other claims; there might be special categories of government holdings in trust for private citizens for which special provision would be appropriate, but in general it was impossible to define with more precision and the anomalies inescapable from a rough-and-ready rule would have to be tolerated. Those special cases which were specifically due to the war would probably have to be settled anyway before the end of the transitional period.

Convertibility for Current Transactions [IX-3, "Current Transactions"]

3. Paper I.M.C. (44) (F) 3 ["International Monetary Fund, A Draft amendment proposed by the British Delegates relating to Clauses III(2)(a), III(5), IX(3), Which, between Them, Ensure Convertibility for Current Transactions, Memorandum by Lord Keynes"] proposing the elimination of III-5 [["Limitation on Purchases"]] and the amendment of IX-3 [["Current Transactions"]] was considered, and a number of amendments were suggested. The revised text of IX-3 and [proposed new Section IX-]4 which results, is as follows:-

3. To buy balances held with it by another member with that member's currency or with gold, if that member represents either that the balances in question have been currently acquired or that their conversion is needed for making current payments which are consistent with the provisions of the Fund. This obligation shall not relate to transactions involving

(a) capital transfers:

(b) holdings of currency which have accumulated as a result of transactions of a current account nature effected before the removal by the member country of restrictions on multilateral clearing maintained or imposed under X-2 [["Transition

Period"]] below:

(c) the provision of a currency which has been declared scarce under VI [["Apportionment of Scarce Currencies"]] above; nor shall it apply to a member who has ceased to be entitled under III-2 [["Purchases of Another Member's Currency"]] or VIII [["Withdrawal from the Fund"]] above to buy other members' currencies from the Fund in exchange for its own currency.

4. Not to impose restrictions save as otherwise provided on payments for current international transactions with other member countries, or to engage in any discriminatory currency arrangements or multiple currency practices without the approval of the Fund.

33

Allied delegations
Third meeting
Aboard the *Queen Mary*
June 21, 1944 at 12:15 p.m.[206]

*Minutes of previous meetings • Note by Varvaressos • Note by
Mládek • Duration of the transitional period • Withdrawal from the
IMF • Management and inauguration of the IMF*

*The Allied delegations consider a variety of issues. The one that occasions the most
discussion is the composition of the IMF's Executive Directors. The Joint Statement
says that they will be at least nine strong. The delegates work with twelve as the
number. There are different ideas about how many of those seats should go to the
countries with the largest quotas and how many should be divided somehow among the
remaining countries. The question also arises to what extent the directors will be
representatives of their countries rather than international civil servants.*

Minutes of Previous Meetings

1. The minutes of the first meeting (held on 19th June) were approved.

2. The minutes of the second meeting (held on 20th June) should be
amended in the following respects:

(i) Add a new paragraph 1(g) as follows:

(g) **Dr. [Jan] Mládek [Czechoslovakia]** drew attention to
some of the consequences of the provision in the new IV-4
regarding suspension of facilities. First, the country suspended
would be free to have recourse to restrictive measures. Second,
the currency of that country would be bound to become scarce
in the Fund. **Lord Keynes** agreed that the second point merited
close examination, but his preliminary view was that the

---

[206] Present: As at previous Meetings. Mr. A.W. Snelling, Secretary.

possibility that its currency would become scarce might serve to doter a country from altering its exchange rate without the concurrence of the Fund.

(ii) Paragraph 2(b): amend the beginning of this paragraph to read as follows:

Similarly, **Professor Keilhau [Norway]** remarked that the insurance sums held by the Norwegian Government in trust for private ship-owners cannot be included in the reckoning of Norway's official convertible exchange. Mr. Beyen (and others), whilst sympathizing with the difficulty, thought that this would.....

(iii) Add a new paragraph 2(c) as follows:

(c) The words "Government obligation which can, at the option of the holder, be made available on demand within three months" in paragraph 2(ii) of I.M.C. (44) (F) 2, should be interpreted as meaning "Government obligations either whose maturity is less than 90 days or redeemable in not more than 90 days."

(iv) The new IX-3(a) [["Current Transactions"]] should be amended to read "(a) capital transfers as defined in V-1."

Note by Mr. Varvaressos, I.M.C. (44) (F) 6 [on III-7(b), ["Fund's Acquisition of Gold"]]

3. It was agreed to postpone consideration of III-7(b) [["Fund's Acquisition of Gold"]] until the United Kingdom Delegation had an opportunity of thinking further about the clause.

4. **Mr. [Kyriakos] Varvaressos's [Greece]** proposal for the addition of a sentence at the end of paragraph 2 of the revised version of IV [["Changes in Par Value"]] annexed to I.M.C. (44) (F) 1 was agreed.[207]

Note by Dr. Mládek, I.M.C. (44) (F) 9 [on various clauses]

5. It was agreed that **Dr. Mládek's** suggestions in connection with

---

[207] Varvaressos proposes that the IMF be allowed at its discretion to waive III-7(b). In effect, he would allow countries such as Greece to retain more of their gold reserves domestically rather than paying it to the IMF when they purchase foreign currency through it. The IMF would end up with less gold and more IOUs from members in its assets than otherwise.

VII-2 [["Voting Power"]] should be considered when the proposals for management and inauguration were discussed.

6. As regards IX-3 [["Current Transactions"]], **Lord Keynes** said that he understood that quantitative controls, import quotas, etc., would not be prohibited.

7. It was agreed that **Dr. Mládek's** question about X-3 [["Restrictions on Exchange"]] should be discussed on I.M.C. (44) (F) 5.

Duration of the Transitional Period, I.M.C. (44) (F) 4 [X-3, ["Restriction on Exchange"]]

8. The meeting agreed with the revised draft Annex to this paper, and agreed with the view that the words "the Fund shall report on the restrictions still in force...." should be constructed as meaning that the Fund should do more than merely produce a list of such restrictions.

Withdrawals, I.M.C. (44) (F) 5 [VIII-1, ["Procedure for Withdrawal"]]

9. It was agreed to amend the new VIII-1 [["Procedure for Withdrawal"]] to read as follows:

(1) If the Fund finds that a member persists, after having received a special notice from the Fund, in acting in a manner inconsistent with the purposes and policies of the Fund, the Fund may at its option either:
(a) give notice that the member is suspended from making further use of the Fund's resources without the approval of the Fund, or
(b) require that member to withdraw from the Fund.

10. It was agreed that the decision to require a member to withdraw from the Fund would be a matter of considerable importance which ought to require a large majority — say, two-thirds.

Management and Inauguration, I.M.C. (44) (F) 8 ["International Monetary Fund, I Management and II Inauguration of the Fund"][208]

11. The proposal that the management of the Fund should be in three tiers met with general agreement.

12. After some discussion (particularly in connection with the translation of the descriptions into French) it was also agreed that the nomenclature in paragraph 6 should be adopted.[209]

13. It was agreed to reserve for further consideration the question whether voting strength on the General Council should equal quotas or whether, as had been suggested, the quota plus 100 should determine the size of the vote.

14. It was agreed that the Directorate should consist of twelve Directors.

15. A lengthy discussion took place on the composition of the Directorate (see paragraph 6(b)).[210] Among the proposals discussed were the following:

(1) The United Kingdom suggestion that there should be seven permanent Directors from the members having the seven largest quotas, and that the remaining five seats should be filled from other countries.

(2) A suggestion by **Baron Boël [Belgium]** that the five countries with the largest quotas (U.S., UK Russia, China, France) should appoint permanent Directors; that the next six countries in order of quotas (India, Canada, Australia, South Africa, Belgium, Netherlands) should between them choose three Directors; and that the four remaining seats should be filled by Directors representing Member States on a geographical basis, e.g. two for Latin America and two for Europe.

(3) A suggestion by **Dr. [Ludwik] Grosfeld [Poland]** that there should be six permanent Directorships from the countries with the six

---

[208] For the shipboard version of this paper, see I.M.C. (44) (F) 11, Annex E, reproduced in chapter 82. The version of I.M.C. (44) (F) 8 in T 231/363 is a revised version dated June 25 with somewhat different numbering of paragraphs from the shipboard version, as a covering note to the June 25 version remarks.

[209] The paragraph uses the nomenclature Council, Directorate, and Chairman for what are now called the Board of Governors, Executive Directors, and Managing Director, respectively.

[210] The document presented to the delegates contains no detail on how directors are to be chosen.

largest quotas (i.e. including India) and that there should be elections every two years for the six remaining Directorships. Dr. Grosfeld also suggested that it should be publicly stated that the composition of the Directorate should not be taken as a precedent for other international organizations.

16. **Sir Wilfrid Eady [UK]** entered a plea that the Directors should be regarded not as representatives of countries, but as highly skilled individuals selected for their personal knowledge and experience. He hoped that they would then develop a sense of corporate responsibility to all the members of the Fund and would not regard themselves merely as representatives of the countries of which they were nationals. **Mr. Beyen [Netherlands]** thought that this would not be incompatible with representation on a geographical basis, and favored Baron Boël's suggestion. **Professor Keilhau** thought that the constitution of the Hague Court might be taken as a useful precedent,[211] and he, **Dr. [Ping-Wen] Kuo [China], Dr. [Ladislav] Feierabend [Czechoslovakia], Dr. Mládek, Dr. [Stanisław] Kirkor [Poland],** and **Dr. Varvaressos** were not in favor of Baron Boël's suggestion because it involved dividing countries into three categories.

17. **Lord Keynes,** summing up the discussion, said that he understood the view of the majority to be:

(1) that there should be six permanent and six non-permanent Directors;

(2) that the six non-permanent Directors should be appointed in the alternative manner proposed in the passage in square brackets in paragraph 2(b);[212]

(3) that the aim should be to foster a sense of responsibility on the part of the Directors towards all members of the Fund on the lines which Sir Wilfrid Eady [UK] had suggested.

18. As regards paragraph 2(c), it was thought desirable that the

---

[211] The Permanent Court of International Justice in The Hague, nicknamed the World Court. Article 2 of the statute of the court said, "The Permanent Court of International Justice shall be composed of a body of independent judges, elected regardless of their nationality from amongst persons of high moral character, who possess the qualifications required in their respective countries for appointment to the highest judicial offices, or are jurisconsults of recognized competence in international law." Article 9 said, "the whole body also should represent the main forms of civilization and the principal legal systems of the world."

[212] It is unclear to us what passage this refers to.

Chairman should be co-opted from outside rather than be appointed from among the directors.

34

Allied delegations
Fourth meeting
Aboard the *Queen Mary*
June 21, 1944 at 4:30 p.m.[213]

*Management of the IMF • Voting on the Board of Directors •
Function of the Council (Board of Governors) • Instruments
(documents) to be produced by the Bretton Woods conference*

*The discussions in this session mainly concern the Joint Statement's Article VII,
"Management of the Fund," as discussed in a British paper on the IMF.*

The Management of the International Monetary Fund

1. The consideration of the paper I.M.C. (44) (F) 8 ["International
Monetary Fund, I Management and II Inauguration of the Fund"] was
resumed at paragraph 6. At the suggestion of **Mr. Beyen [Netherlands]**
it was agreed to revise 6(e) in order to clarify two points:
   (i) the responsibility for appointing the Chief Assistants to the General
Manager;
   (ii) the terms of appointment of the General Manager, with the object
of securing that although his appointment should be intended to be of a
long term nature it should be terminable at six months' notice.

Paragraph 7(a), Voting on the Council [Board of Governors]

2. The last phrase of line 6 should be read "this means four-fifths of
the total voting power." **Lord Keynes** explained that the effect of this
sentence was that members absenting themselves from a meeting of the

---

[213] Present: Delegates and Advisers as at previous meetings. Secretariat: Mr. H.E.
Brooks.

Council when a special vote was to be taken would in fact be voting against the resolution.

3. It was agreed that it would be convenient to have a general clause enabling the Council to make rules and regulations as to its procedure save where it was bound by the relevant Statute.

Paragraph 7(b), Voting on the Directorate [Executive Directors]

4. In reply to **Dr. Feierabend [Czechoslovakia], Lord Keynes** said that the UK would have no objection to simple voting by heads, but he thought the United States delegates would wish their preponderant quota proportion to be reflected on the Directorate. **Dr. Grosfeld [Poland]** repeated that concurrence in these proposals should not be construed as a precedent for other international organizations. It was generally agreed that there was no good reason for prescribing that the Directors must be members of the Council, since in practice they would probably tend to be chosen for their technical ability, whereas Council members would be more likely to be political representatives. The relatively small quorum proposed for the Directorate was discussed and it was agreed that the proposal should be modified to provided that not less than one-half of the voting power and one-half of the number of Directors constituted a quorum. It was also agreed to insert provision for alternates both on the Council and on the Directorate but not to provide for voting by proxy.

Clause [paragraph] 8, Functions

5. It was agreed that the Council should have the functions in 8(a)(i), (iii), (v), (vi), (viii) and (ix). Some discussion took place on (iv), **Sir Wilfrid Eady [UK]** feeling that the apportionment of scarce currencies involved such drastic action against a country that the authority of the Council was desirable. The general view of the meeting was, however, that the necessary urgency of such a decision could not await an annual meeting of the Council and the responsibility must rest on the Directorate. It was agreed provisionally that two further functions needed to be ascribed to the Council:

(x) alteration of Statutes; and

(xi) co-operation with other bodies.

6. A discussion took place on the extent to which it would be proper to provide that the Council should delegate any of its functions to the Directorate. **Baron Boël [Belgium]** and others thought, on the one

hand, that this would be opening the door to a wholesale unloading of responsibility on to the shoulders of the Directorate which might have unfortunate results. **Lord Keynes,** on the other hand, was of opinion that it was wise to give the technical experts as much power as possible. No conclusion was reached and it was decided accordingly to omit and reference to this point from the proposed text.

7. **Sir Wilfrid Eady [UK]** added that it was intended that the Directorate should meet not less frequently than every three months, or at the instance of the Chairman, or at the request of three of the Directors.

8. In discussion of the functions of the Chairman it was noted that it would be necessary to provide for delegation also to the Deputy Chairman, but a suggestion that delegation to the General Manager might also be permitted was negatived. The allocation of the action under VI [i.e., paragraph 6] to the Directorate involves consequential changes in 8(c)(ii) of the paper, since this is a function which obviously ought not to be delegated by the Directorate to its Chairman.

9. The responsibilities and functions of the General Manager were discussed and differing points of view emerged. **Sir Wilfrid Eady** was anxious that the General Manager should be responsible for the staff and establishment of the Fund while the Chairman would exercise constant oversight of the operations of the Fund of which the routine aspects would naturally fall to the General Manager. **Mr. Beyen,** on the other hand, was uncertain whether this division of functions could be satisfactorily incorporated in legal provisions, though doubtless it would be the practical compromise between any two reasonable men.

10. Widely different views were expressed on the question whether the Chairman of the Directorate should be ex officio the Chairman of the Council. On the one hand several delegates thought that the Council would benefit greatly from the practical and intimate knowledge of the Chairman of the Directorate. On the other hand other members were of the opinion that the necessary impartiality of an acceptable Chairman would be in question if he were in fact defending his own actions for any substantial proportion of the time of the Council. It was agreed eventually that a general clause might be included saying that the Chairman of the Directorate had the right to attend Council meetings, to take part in them, and, if the Council so desired, to be its Chairman.

11. At this point **Dr. Grosfeld** pointed out that after the establishment of the Fund it was to be expected that further countries would be allowed to join at a later date, first perhaps the neutrals and later the ex-enemies. He thought in these circumstances there should be provision for

increasing the number of Directors. **Baron Boël** suggested that this pint would be met by the provision made for amendment of the Statutes etc., so that matter could be effectively discussed at the right time.

12. In deference to **Professor Keilhau [Norway],** it was agreed to delete paragraph 3 of the paper.

The Instruments to Be Produced by the [Bretton Woods] Conference

13. The paper I.M.C. (44) (F) (7) ["International Monetary Fund, The Instruments to be Produced by the Conference, Memorandum by Mr. Beckett"] by **Mr. Beckett [UK]** was expounded by him and found acceptable by all the Delegations present. The following points emerged in discussion:-

(a) Several delegates emphasized that it would be desirable to bring discussions on the Bank as far as possible towards the degree of readiness of the Fund proposals and to include Resolutions about the Bank in the Final Act.

(b) **Dr. Kuo [China]** pointed out that it would be necessary to make provision for the appointment, location, etc. of any temporary secretariat.

(c) **Professor Keilhau** suggested that the Resolutions might include advice from the Fund to prospective members as to steps which they might usefully take to bring their internal monetary systems into harmony with the prospective operations of the Fund. It was agreed to await Professor Keilhau's specific proposals on these points.

14. **Lord Keynes,** in conclusion, said that at the next meeting it was hoped to begin the consideration of the Bank proposals, and the loose ends still left in the Fund proposals must therefore be left for the time being. This would include such questions as the problem of location of the Fund, the thorny question of Clause III-7(b) and (c) [["Fund's Acquisition of Gold"]], and the paper just circulated by Professor Keilhau on Clause IV-1 [["Establishing Par Value"]]. The United Kingdom Delegation were also examining the difficult questions connected with the institution and the coming into operation of the Fund. They would return to the discussion of these points as and when time permitted.

35

Allied delegations
Fifth meeting
Aboard the *Queen Mary*
June 22, 1944 at 11 a.m.[214]

Outline of Keynes's proposals on the Bank • General views on Keynes's proposals • Detailed consideration of U.S. November 1943 draft as modified by Keynes's proposals

This session is devoted to reviewing the British proposal on the Bank, developed onboard ship as a response to the U.S. proposal of November 1943.

1. The meeting had before it the U.S. preliminary draft outline [on the Bank] dated November 1943 (printed in I.M.C. (44) (B) 1) ["Preliminary Draft Outline of a Proposal for a Bank for Reconstruction and Development of the United and Associated Nations"], a memorandum by **Lord Keynes** suggesting modifications of this U.S. Treasury draft (I.M.C. (44) (B) 2) ["Suggested Modifications to American proposal on the Bank, Memorandum by John Maynard Keynes"], a note by **Dr. [Leon] Baránski [Poland]** (I.M.C. (44) (B) 3) [title unknown], and a note by **Lord Keynes** about stabilization loans (I.M.C. (44) (B) 4) ["Stabilization Loans, Note by Lord Keynes"].

Outline of Lord Keynes's Proposals

2. **Lord Keynes** gave a brief outline of the reasons which had led him to suggest the modifications, contained in I.M.C. (44) (B) 2, of the U.S. Treasury draft. In the original U.S. draft before November 1943, the main function of the Bank had been to make loans out of its own capital. Lord Keynes had urged on Dr. [Harry Dexter] White [U.S.] the importance also

---

[214] Present: As at previous Meetings.

197

of the guarantee functions of such an institution; only countries with favorable balances of an payments would be in a position to undertake foreign investment, but these investments would benefit not only lenders and borrowers but many other countries also. The first change proposed by Lord Keynes was therefore that there should be a separation of the function of exporting capital from the function of guaranteeing loans. The November 1943 draft and the [American] "Questions and Answers [on the Bank for Reconstruction and Development]" went a long way to meet this point, but the result was not very clear. The modifications now suggested by Lord Keynes were intended by him to clarify what he understood to be implicit in the November 1943 draft. For direct loans, he accepted the U.S. proposals. In a separate watertight compartment should be the guarantee fund which, in his view, should absorb 80 percent of the subscribed capital of the Bank.

3. Another major change introduced in Lord Keynes' draft was the suggestion that loans and guarantees made by the Bank, though on a prudent scale, should not be conducted according to strict commercial criteria. Many investments, e.g. by the UK and the Netherlands in Far Eastern rubber, would have proved of immense benefit to mankind even if they had not been commercially successful.

4. A third modification introduced by Lord Keynes related to the treatment of borrowers who got into difficulties. He wanted to find a solution of this problem which would minimize the prospect of countries being forced into defaulting upon obligations to an international institution. The revised U.S. draft went some way to meet this point, but the Bank was only left with one method of lessening the burden upon debtors in times of crises. He thought therefore that the provisions for relaxation of service charges ought to be extended, and that some provision should be made for stabilization loans.

General Views on Lord Keynes's Proposals

5. In the course of a general discussion upon I.M.C. (44) (B) 2, the following points were made:-

(i) **Dr. Grosfeld [Poland]** and **Dr. Feierabend [Czechoslovakia]** stressed the need for the Bank to start operations as soon as possible after the cessation of hostilities, so that it would be in a position to assist, within say three months, countries at present occupied by the enemy.[215] **Lord Keynes** thought that at this early date there might be serious limitations upon the amount of capital goods that could be made available, and that the functions of the Bank would therefore have to be confined at first to the making of stabilization loans.

(ii) **Dr. Baránski [Poland]** and **Dr. Kirkor [Poland]** thought that it would be necessary to work out plans for the utilization not merely of foreign but also of domestic capital, because the amount of domestic investment affected the need for and the ability to pay service charges on overseas loans. **Baron Boël [Belgium]** and **Dr. Varvaressos [Greece],** on the other hand, saw difficulties in this proposal because of the interference in domestic issues which might result.

(iii) **Mr. Beyen [Netherlands]** pointed out that an international institution would probably accept losses less philosophically that would private inventors; he thought therefore that it would be desirable for the Bank to build up a strong reserve as quickly as possible. He also suggested that it should be made clear in the draft that the Bank would be able to make medium-term loans (of 5 to 10 years duration) as well as long-term loans.

(iv) **All the Delegates** expressed the view that Lord Keynes's proposals represented a real improvement upon the November 1943 draft and that they happily harmonized the legitimate interests of investors and borrowers with those of the rest of the world.

Detailed Consideration of U.S. November 1943 Draft as Modified by Lord Keynes's Proposals

Preamble

6. **Mr. Beyen** suggested that it might be desirable to transfer to the Preamble the new Section III-6 [["Stabilization Loans"]] of Lord Keynes about the acceptance of risks by the Bank. After some discussion, in the course of which **Sir Wilfrid Eady [UK]** emphasized the desirability of giving unquestionable authority to the Managers of the Bank to take risks, **Lord Keynes** suggested that reference to the point should be included both in the Preamble and in the main body of the text.

---

[215] As it turned out, the Bank officially began operations on June 25, 1946 and approved its first loan on May 7, 1947.

I. The Purposes of the Bank

7. No comments were made on this section.

II. Capital Structure of the Bank

8. **Lord Keynes** gave some arithmetical illustrations of the way in which his suggestions would work out. It had been understood that the United States would probably be willing to subscribe 33 percent, and the UK 10 percent of the capital of the Bank. The remaining 57 percent would be subscribed by at least 30 countries whose individual subscriptions would thus vary from 1 percent up to about 4 percent. If the standard rate of interest were to be 3½ percent, the standard amortization 2 percent, and the standard commission 1 percent, the commission would equal nearly one-fifth of the total service of the loans. Therefore 20 percent of the Bank's loans could be in default at any one time before it would be necessary to call upon the guarantors. Assuming the acceptance of the 20 percent / 80 percent division of the capital, the guarantee fund would amount to £2 billion. Service charges on this sum and 5½ percent would be £110 million, and the cost of implementing the guarantees — on the worst possible assumption that all loans went into default right from the start — would be £110 million per annum, of which the UK would be liable to find £11 million. On any reasonable hypothesis as to the frequency of default, the burden upon the UK would be smaller and that upon other countries would be correspondingly less.

9. **Mr. Beyen** raised the question whether Lord Keynes' draft effectively accomplished his stated intention of dividing the capital available for direct loans and for guarantees into watertight compartments. He thought that the new clause IV-8 [["Limit on Guarantees"]] (on page 7 of I.M.C. (44) (B) 2) did not make it clear whether guarantees were to be secured in part on paid up capital or not. His view was that the guarantee should be secured on the paid up capital as well as upon the uncalled capital. Lord Keynes thought otherwise, and after some discussion it was agreed, for purposes of clarification, to insert "only" after "secured" in the new IV-8.

10. **Dr. Kuo [China]** tentatively suggested that it might be desirable to increase about 20 percent the proportion of the subscribed capital of the Bank which would be available for direct loans by the Bank. **Dr. Mládek [Czechoslovakia]** also pointed out that, in the early post-war years when there would be severe shortages of capital goods available for export, it might not even be possible for the Bank to make direct loans to the

extent of 20 percent of the capital. **Lord Keynes** thought, however, that the guarantee of the Bank would prove attractive to U.S. investors, who would necessarily be the largest subscribers to loans in this early period and that later on, it would prove advantageous to everybody for the larger part of the capital of the Bank to be taken up in guarantees rather than direct loans.

11. The other charges proposed by Lord Keynes in II ["Capital Structure of the Bank"] were thought to be acceptable.

III. General Provisions for Loans to Member Countries

12. **Sir Wilfrid Eady** drew attention to IV-1(b) [["Loans"]] and IV-6 [["Noncompetition with Private Investment"]] of the November 1943 draft which attempted to ensure that recourse should not be had to the Bank in cases where loans could be secured on reasonable terms through private channels. **Lord Keynes** thought that it would be very difficult to establish satisfactory criteria on this point. Would it, for example, be permissible for the Bank to make or guarantee a loan to a member at 4½ percent if that member could obtain money outside the Bank at 5 percent? It was generally agreed that this section needed redrafting, particularly in view of the impossibility of ever bringing satisfactory negative proof. Lord Keynes mentioned, however, that Dr. White attached considerable political importance to this point, and did not therefore put forward any concrete proposals at the moment.

13. Some discussion took place on the new III-4(e) [["Conditions on which Bank May Guarantee or Make Loans"]], which should be read in connection with IV-1(d) [["Loans,"] paragraph on proceeds] and IV-7 [["Spending on Proceeds of Loans"]] in the November 1943 draft. **Baron Boël** thought that the words "without unduly encroaching on its discretion" in the new III-9(e)[216] were somewhat obscure and perhaps by implication derogated from the general principle that there should be non-interference by the Bank with the domestic affairs of particular countries. The question was raised whether complete discretion should be left to a borrower to spend the proceeds of Bank loans how he chose, or whether the Bank should retain powers to enable it to exercise some supervision as to how and where the money was spent. Baron Boël's suggestion, which met with general agreement, was that the draft should

---

[216] This reference is evidently a mistake or a reference to a version of the document that we were unable to find.

be amended to make clear, first that the borrower had discretion to make such arrangements as it deemed most satisfactory, and secondly, that the Bank had a right to intervene only in cases where the facilities of the Bank were gravely abused.

14. Considerable discussion took place on III-4(d) [["Currency of Loans"]] (formerly IV-(8)(d) in the November 1943 draft). **Lord Keynes** explained that this clause had been inserted to deal with cases in which a large part of the cost of an undertaking would necessarily be incurred for the maintenance of labor as distinct from the import of capital goods. Thus, if it were proposed to undertake large development works in the Yangtze Valley, a comparatively small part of the cost of the undertaking would be incurred in connection with the import of capital goods and most of the money with be required for the maintenance of the labor force employed. **Dr. Kirkor** pointed out that, even in such a case, the result might be to bring about an increase in imports of consumption goods. The same result would indeed follow from large-scale domestic investment. He asked how such secondary increases in imports would be financed. **Lord Keynes** admitted that there was no provision in the Plan for financing such imports and that this constituted a real gap in the proposals. He was, however, of the opinion that it would be unwise to formulate at the present stage suggestions for filling the gap, because such action might serve to raise the question of the service of loans that have been floated in the past, and because provisions to deal with the problem would serve to make the size of loans somewhat intermediate. The general view of the meeting was with Lord Keynes.

15. The new clause relating to stabilization loans (I.M.C. (44) (B) 4) ["Stabilization Loans, Note by Lord Keynes," referring to III-6 ["Stabilization Loans"] in the British proposal] was accepted by the meeting as highly desirable, but it was agreed that in the seventh line of the draft "consultation" should be deleted and "agreement" substituted.

16. The section now numbered III-5 [["Accounting"]] (formerly IV-9) was criticized by **Mr. Beyen** and **Dr. Varvaressos** as unnecessary in such a statement, and it was agreed to raise this point with Dr. White.

36

Allied delegations
Amendments to fifth meeting
Atlantic City
June 24, 1944

Amendments concerning minutes on the Bank

1. The following amendments should be made to the Minutes I.M.C. (44) (General) 5th meeting held on board ship on 22nd June, 1944.

2. Paragraph 5(i), delete lines 5-10 and substitute the following: "at present occupied by the enemy. **Lord Keynes** agreed that every effort should be made to expedite the operation of the Bank but thought that at this early date there might be serious limitations upon the amount of capital goods that could be made available."

3. In paragraph 8, line 7, insert "less than" between "from" and "1 percent."

4. Paragraph 14, delete lines 11 to the end and substitute the following:
"'employed.' **Dr. Kirkor [Poland]** pointed out that, whilst in such a case the result might be to bring about an increase in imports of consumption goods, the same result would follow from large-scale domestic investment. He asked how such secondary increases in imports would be financed. **Lord Keynes** admitted that there was no provision in the Plan for financing such imports and that this constituted a real gap in the proposals. He was, however, of the opinion that it would be unwise to formulate at the present stage suggestions for filling the gap, because similar loans that had been floated in the past had often led to abuses, and become the appropriate size of such loans would be somewhat indeterminate. The general view of the meeting was with Lord Keynes."

203

37

Allied delegations
Sixth meeting
Aboard the *Queen Mary*
June 22, 1944 at 5 p.m.[217]

Bank for Reconstruction and Development • Redraft on IMF • Procedure at Atlantic City

In their final shipboard meeting, the Allied delegations consider a variety of issues related both to the Bank and the Fund. The Queen Mary *would reach New York the next day.*

Bank for Reconstruction and Development

1. The meeting continued the detailed examination of the U.S. November 1943 draft as modified by Lord Keynes' proposals.

2. In paragraph 13 of I.M.C. (44) (B) (2) ["Suggested Modifications to American Proposal on the Bank, Memorandum by John Maynard Keynes"], it was agreed to substitute "lending" for "investment" in the second and fourth lines.

V. Miscellaneous Provisions

3. The proposals in paragraph 14 of I.M.C. (44) (B) 2 for a new Section [Article] V, entitled "Miscellaneous Provisions," were agreed.

III. Powers and Operations

4. It was agreed to amend the new IV-1(b) [["Loans"]] to read as follows:

---

[217] Present: As at previous Meetings.

(b) By direct loans out of funds raised by the Bank as a charge against its reserves and uncalled capital (see (8) below) in the market of a particular country;

5. On the new IV-2 [["Loan Participations"]] (IV-3 in November 1943 draft), **Mr. Beyen [Netherlands]** raised the question whether obligations to the Bank should have transfer priority over other obligations. Lord Keynes thought that it would be inadvisable to make such a suggestion.

6. In the new IV-4 [["Currency of Loans"]], it was agreed to amend "expenditures" in the penultimate line to "sum expended."

7. On the new IV-6 [["Payment Provisions"]], **Lord Keynes** asked whether there was general agreement (a) that the rate of interest and commission on loans through the Bank should be at a flat rate, i.e. that the rates should not vary in accordance with the assessment of the risk attached to each particular loan; and (b) whether any objection was seen to the proposal that the commission should be of a substantial size, e.g. 1 percent per annum. The general view was that the answer to both these questions should be in the affirmative but there was some difference of opinion whether the commission should be levied on the total amount of a loan or upon that part of it which was outstanding at any moment. On the latter point, Lord Keynes favored the making of service payments on an annuity basis.

8. It was agreed to amend IV-6(a)(i) [["Payment Provisions"]] to read as follows:

(i) a standard rate of interest fixed by the Bank and the same to all borrowers but modifiable from time to time for new loans;

9. It was agreed to amend IV-6(a)(iii) [["Payment Provisions"]] to read as follows:

(iii) an annual contribution to amortization either at a flat, or at a progressive, rate sufficient to repay the capital within a determined number of years, the length of which shall be fixed with regard not only to the character and purpose of the loan, but also (especially in the case of reconstruction loans) to the conditions in the borrowing country which may delay the time within which the country can repay the loan — not normally exceeding 30 years but extensible to 50 years in particular cases.

10. On IV-6(b) [["Payment Provisions"]], **Dr. Varvaressos [Greece]** raised the question whether service charges should be a gold obligation. In his view justice demanded that borrowers should be required to meet service charges in the currency in which they had borrowed. If this course were not adopted, he feared that gold clauses would spread from obligations to the Bank to all forms of private international investment

and so assume a universal character. He considered that this would be inequitable and undesirable. All loans would have to be made in some specified currency and there should therefore be no difficulty in ensuring that service charges were met in the same currency. A considerable measure of support was given to Dr. Varvaressos's suggestion and after some discussion it was suggested that IV-6(b) should be amended to read as follows:

(b) the loan and its annual service shall be fixed in whatever currency may be stipulated by the Bank in making the loan, and shall be paid, at the option of the borrowing country, in a convertible IMF currency or in gold or, at the discretion of the Bank, in any other currency acceptable to it at the prevailing rate of exchange of the currency in which the service has been fixed.

11. **Mr. Beyen** pointed out that IV-6(c) [["Payment Provisions"]] about defaults, as at present drafted, only applied to direct and not to guaranteed loans. It was agreed that further consideration should be given to the treatment of cases of default on obligations guaranteed by the Bank. IV-6(c)(iii) would be deleted as it was now being dealt with elsewhere.

12. On IV-10 [["Suspension of Membership"]], **Mr. Beyen** pointed out that in actual practice it would be unlikely that the Bank would take the drastic step of "declaring a country in default" and that, even if it did so, the political reactions in the defaulting country might not be what the draftsmen of the document evidently expected.

13. It was agreed that IV-8[218] about withdrawal from the Bank needed further examination.

[Redraft of provisions on the IMF; procedure at Atlantic City]

14. A short discussion then took place on I.M.C. (44) (F) 12, in which **Lord Keynes** had proposed a further redraft of IV-1 of the International Monetary Fund [["Establishing Par Value"]]. It was agreed that this section should be redrafted. For the text, see Annex B to I.M.C. (44) (F) 11 ["Amended Version of Clause [Article] IV"].

15. In conclusion, **Lord Keynes** explained the procedure which was contemplated on arrival at Atlantic City. He said that a Report was being

---

[218] This seems to be an error; the reference should be to IV-10 [["Suspension of Membership"]] or IV-11 [["Withdrawal or Expulsion from Bank"]] of the British proposal.

prepared summarizing the results of the discussions at sea on the International Monetary Fund. This Report would be presented at Atlantic City as a UK document.[219] None of the other representatives taking part in the present discussions would be committed by anything said in the Report, but it would, of course, be pointed out that the UK Delegation has had the benefit of hearing the views of the other representatives upon most of the points covered.

---

[219] See chapter 82.

PART IV

CONFERENCE MEETINGS: AGENDA COMMITTEE

38

Agenda Committee
First meeting
Atlantic City
June 19, 1944 at 6 p.m.[220]

*Chairman's welcoming remarks • Attachment on subcommittee
assignments • Editors' appendix: List of conference flimsies*

*The Agenda Committee, also called the Preconference Agenda Committee or the
Agenda Conference, was the committee of the whole at Atlantic City. Its name came
from its task of developing the agenda that the Bretton Woods conference would
consider. Remember that the Bretton Woods conference was scheduled to start on July
1, 1944, less than two weeks after the first meeting of the Agenda Committee.*

*Harry Dexter White was the committee chairman, though in the sessions on the
Bank for Reconstruction and Development (which at Bretton Woods became the
International Bank for Reconstruction and Development) he would turn over the chair*

---

[220] The original minutes of the meetings of the Agenda Committee have a list of
delegates present at the top of each meeting. We relegate it to the footnotes. The
list of delegates lists a Chinese delegates named Hoo. No such person appears in
the room directories for the conference; apparently it is a typographical error for
Yee-Chun Koo. Victor Chi-Tsai Hoo was at Bretton Woods with Koo.
Present: Messrs. [Leslie] Melville, [James] Brigden, [Arthur] Tange and
[Frederick] Wheeler of Australia; Baron [René] Boël of Belgium; Mr. [Octavio de]
Bulhões of Brazil; Messrs. [John] Deutsch, [Louis] Rasminsky, and [Wynne]
Plumptre of Canada; Mr. [Herman Max] Coers of Chile; Mr. [Felipe] Pazos of
Cuba; Messrs. [Tingfu] Tsiang, [Ts-Liang] Soong, [Yu-Chung] Hsi, [Ting-Sen]
Wei and Hoo [Yee-Chun Koo] of China; Messrs. [Antonín] Basch and [Ervin]
Hexner of Czechoslovakia; Sir Theodore Gregory of India; Messrs. [Rodrigo]
Gómez and [Antonio Espinosa de los] Monteros of Mexico; Messrs. [Daniël
Crena] de Iongh and [Jacques] Polak of the Netherlands; Mr. [Redvers] Opie of
United Kingdom; Messrs. [A.P.] Morozov, [Aleksei] Smirnov and [Fyodor]
Bystrov of the USSR; the Technical Committee and Mr. E.E. Brown of United
States.

to John Maynard Keynes. Members of the American Technical Group doubled as the conference secretariat. At Bretton Woods there would be a large, separate conference secretariat, again all Americans, working as translators, stenographers, typists, editors, logistics coordinators, etc.

The first five meetings of the Agenda Committee occur before the British and other delegations on board the Queen Mary *arrive at the conference. After all delegates arrive, the Agenda Committee will call itself the Formal Agenda Committee. The delegates present on June 19 establish four subcommittees, all dealing with the IMF. The Atlantic City conference documents sometimes call them committees; typically we retain the original term because the references are sufficiently clear. They are similar to the four subcommittees that would deal with the IMF at Bretton Woods. Delegates sometimes call the Atlantic City conference the "preconference" and the Bretton Woods conference the "formal conference." There are no subcommittees dealing with the Bank at Atlantic City because the most detailed plan for the Bank is an American draft that had not been negotiated with other countries, whereas for the IMF the Atlantic City conference start from a negotiated statement, the Joint Statement by Experts on the Establishment of an International Monetary Fund. No discussions on the Bank occur until the thirteenth meeting of the Agenda Committee, on June 29, the next to last day of the Atlantic City conference.*

Except as noted, minutes of all the Agenda Committee meetings are by American secretaries, hence occasional references to "our" views mean American views.

We have inserted as an appendix the list of "flimsies," the draft provisions distributed at the conference.

Dr. [Harry Dexter] White [U.S., Chairman] welcomed the delegates. He explained that the purpose of these informal plenary meetings was to obtain further discussion and exchange of views in advance of the conference and the work of drafting the agenda for the formal [Bretton Woods] conference would begin after the other delegates arrived on June 24.

After some discussion, it was agreed that the conference would split into four subcommittees. The general subjects, chairmen, reporters and secretaries for the subcommittees were announced, together with the topics which it was suggested should be taken up first. (See attachment.) The **Chairman** suggested that the subcommittees should start work in the mornings and carry on during such hours as they wished. The full committee would meet each day in the afternoon.

It was arranged that the subcommittees would meet June 20 at 10 o'clock [and] that the full committee would meet on June 20 at 4 o'clock. Mr. Frank Coe, USA, was designated as Secretary to the Full Committee.

[Attachment on Subcommittee Assignments]

Committee 1 – Purposes, Policies and Subscriptions
 Chairman – China
 Reporter – Brazil
 Secretary – Mr. [Emanuel 'Duke"] Minskoff [U.S.]

Committee 2 – Operations of the Fund
 Chairman – France
 Reporter – Canada
 Secretary – Mr. [Raymond] Mikesell [U.S.]

Committee 3 – Organization and Management
 Chairman – USSR
 Reporter – Mexico
 Secretary – Mr. [Karl] Bopp [U.S.]

Committee 4 – Establishment of the Fund
 Chairman – United Kingdom
 Reporter – Czechoslovakia
 Secretary – Mr. [Richard] Brenner [U.S.]

Topics to be assigned at first meeting:

Committee 1
 1. Form of subscription
 2. Fund depositories
 3. Statement of policies

Committee 2
 1. Gold transactions of the Fund
 2. Exchange controls
 3. Scarce currencies
 4. Capital movements

Committee 3
 1. Governing Board and Executive Committee
 2. Withdrawal and suspension of membership

3. Liquidation of the Fund

Committee 4
1. Setting up of Fund and beginning of operations
2. Transitional arrangements
3. Taxation and immunities

Editors' appendix: List of conference flimsies

The discussion documents of the conference were called "flimsies." The list below reproduces that from the U.S. National Archives, RG 56, Box 1, Folder A-5, in the document "Flimsies Distributed at Atlantic City Conference." The online companion files to this book contain photographs of the flimsies themselves, which are all elsewhere in the same folder.

Committee 1
1. Depositories and Form of Currency Holdings (dated June 19)
2. Payment of Subscriptions (dated June 19)
3. Obtaining Information (date June 21)
4. Additional Undertakings on the Part of Member Countries (dated June 21)
5. Relationship to Other International Organizations (June 21) (distributed?)

Committee 2
1. Capital Movements (dated June 18)
2. Fund's Power to Acquire Needed Foreign Exchange (dated June 19)
3. Scarce Currencies (dated June 18)
4. Provision Concerning Multilateral Clearing (dated June 19)
5. Acquisitions of Gold by the Fund (dated June 18)

Committee 3
1. Withdrawal and Suspension of Member Countries; Liquidation of the Fund (dated June 19)
2. Governing Board and Executive Committee (dated June 19)

Committee 4
1. Transitional Arrangements (dated June 19)

2. Setting up the Fund, Beginning Operations, etc. (dated June 19)
3. Distribution of Profits of the Fund (dated June 21)
4. Taxation and Immunities Provisions (dated June 21)
5. Protection of the Assets of the Fund [no date]

Flimsies not distributed
1. Method of Presentation to Government (dated June 21)
2. Definitions (dated June 21
3. Par Values (dated June 21)
4. Charges by the Fund (dated June 21)

39

Agenda Committee
Second meeting
Atlantic City
June 20, 1944 at 4 p.m.[221]

*Subcommittee minutes and schedules • Subcommittee 1:
Depositories • Subcommittee 2: Repurchases of currencies with
gold • Subcommittee 3: Board of Governors and Executive
Committee • Subcommittee 4: Various issues*

*Chairman Harry Dexter White notes the wish of many delegates not to keep minutes
of the subcommittee meetings. Minutes were kept, however, and we reproduce.*

*Subcommittee 1 (Purposes, Policies, and Subscriptions [of the Fund]) reports on
the question of designating depositories. The IMF will deal mainly through central
banks, but some countries, such as Cuba, did not have central banks at the time.
When queried by Cuba's delegate about the form of IMF holdings of local currency, an
American delegate replies that it envisions them as being in noninterest-bearing
government obligations payable on demand. That is still the form in which the IMF
holds quota contributions, but it also holds interest-bearing investments.*

*Subcommittee 2 (Operations of the Fund) reports on the obligation of a member to
redeem its currency in gold. The minutes report that the discussion emphasized that the
proposed postwar international monetary system will not be a revival of the old gold
standard because it will be more flexible. As it turned out, the postwar gold standard
would be not perhaps as flexible as envisioned here.*

---

[221] Present: Messrs. Melville, Brigden, Tange and Wheeler of Australia; Baron
Boël of Belgium; Mr. Bulhões of Brazil; Messrs. Deutsch, Rasminsky, and
Plumptre of Canada; Mr. Coers of Chile; Messrs. Tsiang, Soong, Hsi, Wei and
Hoo [Koo] of China; Mr. Pazos of Cuba; Messrs. Basch and Hexner of
Czechoslovakia; Sir Theodore Gregory of India; Messrs. Gómez and Monteros
of Mexico; Messrs. de Iongh and Polak of the Netherlands; Mr. Opie of United
Kingdom; Messrs. Morozov, Smirnov and Bystrov of the USSR; the Technical
Committee and Mr. E.E. Brown of United States.

Subcommittee 3 (Organization and Management [of the Fund]) reports that it thinks alternate executive directors should be able to vote unless executive directors are absent. A delegate from Czechoslovakia, a country small enough that does not expect to have one of its own nationals as an executive director, emphasizes that to protect the interests of the smaller countries, limits should exist on the powers that the Board of Governors can delegate to the Executive Directors.

Subcommittee 4 (Establishment of the Fund) reports its consideration in particular of problems in setting rules for establishing the IMF. A Chinese delegate calls attention to his country's probable need for a longer than usual grace period for complying with certain obligations. Doubtless he has in mind that China is one of the countries most damaged by the war.

In opening the meeting, **Dr. White** called attention to the belief of many delegates that minutes should not be kept for the subcommittee meetings in view of the informal and exploratory nature of the discussions. The question of staggering committee meetings was raised, but after discussion it was agreed that such staggering would delay their progress unduly, and that it would be preferable for the larger group to meet more often, if necessary.

Committee 1 [Purposes, Policies and Subscriptions] [222]

Mr. [Octavio de] Bulhões [Brazil], the reporter, stated that attention had been paid to the problem of the designation of depositories by the Fund [III-1, ["National Agency Dealing with the Fund"]]. He reported that his committee believed that in countries in which there is no central bank, the country shall recommend the depositary to be used by the Fund. Considerable discussion followed on the desirability of having the country designate a depository rather than merely recommend one.

Mr. [Felipe] Pazos [Cuba] stated that he wished to be put on record as believing that the designation of the depository was a sovereign right of the government concerned and that there can be no question of permitting the Fund to ignore the judgment of the country.

The appropriate form in which the currency holdings of the Fund in excess of working balances should be held was discussed in terms of the

---

[222] For the minutes of the meeting, see chapter 53. The flimsy the subcommittee discussed was "Depositories and Form of Currency Holdings." In the minutes of the Agenda Committee and the subcommittees, we list in brackets the related provisions of the draft IMF agreement.

following possibilities:

(a) Whether they should be confined to noninterest-bearing demand obligations;

(b) Whether investment should be permitted in interest-bearing securities, effects of such investment on the domestic money market of member countries, and the possible usefulness of such operations to the central banks of member countries;

(c) Whether such investments should be limited to the local currency paid in under the quota or whether it should also be permitted for future accretions of local currency.

In this connection, it was explained that the **American Technical Committee** had never considered that the Fund would hold its local currency assets in any form other than demand, noninterest-bearing government obligations.

As a partial solution of the problem, **Mr. [Redvers] Opie [UK]** [223] suggested the inclusion of a provision specifying that the Fund shall deal only through central banks. **Mr. White** explained that this has always been our [the American] interpretation of the Fund agreement.

Committee 2 [Operations of the Fund] [224]

Mr. [Louis] Rasminsky [Canada, Reporter] reported that the committee was agreed that any country should at any time be able to repurchase with gold any part of its currency held by the Fund.

In connection with the paragraph dealing with a country's obligations to pay for half of its net currency purchases of other currencies from the Fund with gold, if its official holdings of gold and gold convertible exchange exceeded its quota [III-7(b), ["Fund's Acquisition of Gold"]], Mr. Rasminsky stated that the timing of such settlements had been considered at length. The committee proposed that current payments with adjustments at the end of the quarter succeeding the end of the financial year be substituted for the quarterly adjustment suggested in the flimsy. In this connection, **Mr. [André] Istel [France]** called attention to the fact that the penalty which might result from the double transaction

---

[223] Opie was a counselor at the British Embassy in Washington, so he was able to attend the Atlantic City conference while other members of the British delegation were still aboard the *Queen Mary*.

[224] For the minutes of the meeting, see chapter 57. The flimsy the subcommittee discussed was "Fund's Power to Acquire Needed Foreign Exchange."

involving exchange spreads required for settlement under this provision is an additional reason for supporting the current settlement of such obligations.

The extent of a country's obligation to the Fund under the provision requiring payment in gold for 50 percent of total purchases from the Fund was then considered. **Mr. Istel** suggested that it would be desirable to provide a special adjustment in the repurchase provision for country substantially damaged by the enemy and therefore requiring gold reserves for reconstruction purposes. **Mr. White** pointed out that the gold provisions of the Fund, although they undoubtedly represented some sacrifice on the part of a member country, had been included for the greater good of all. He also emphasized that any adjustment allowed for countries damaged by the enemy should be made only once, and that such considerations were already taken care of in the small gold contributions and in the fact that countries with gold resources have access to the Fund.

Mr. Rasminsky mentioned the belief of the American Technical Group that there was an implied obligation on the part of member countries to buy gold in exchange for their national currencies. He added that he believed it was probably undesirable to make such an obligation explicit because it would appear to be a revival of the old gold standard. The discussion which followed emphasized the fact that, in view of the flexibility introduced into the international exchange rate picture by the Fund, this obligation could not be considered a revival of the gold standard.

Committee 3 [Organization and Management of the Fund][225]

Mr. [Antonio Espinosa de los] Monteros [Mexico, Reporter] reported that it was the belief of the subcommittee that alternates should not vote unless directors are not present [VII-1, ["Board and Executive Committee,"] Alternative A, U.S.].

He questioned the extent to which it was desirable to permit the Board of Governors to delegate the power to the Executive Committee and stated that it was the committee's belief that such powers as the suspension of membership, liquidation of the Fund, and power to change the price of gold should be considered powers which might not be

---

[225] For the minutes of the meeting, see chapter 61. The flimsy the subcommittee discussed was "Governing Board and Executive Committee."

delegated. **Mr. [Ervin] Hexner [Czechoslovakia]** emphasized the fact that the limitation on the power of the Board to delegate powers was necessary to protect the smaller countries not represented by the Executive Committee.

The other points considered by this committee were as follows:

(a) Should member countries have the right to call meetings of the Board?

(b) What would be an appropriate place for meetings of the Board?

(c) Why were the votes allotted to countries irrespective of quotas changed in the various drafts from 100 votes to 50 votes to 25 votes?

(d) The shifts in voting power which would result as a country becomes more or less indebted to the Fund.

Committee 4 [Establishment of the Fund][226]

Mr. Hexner [Reporter] reported that his committee had considered:

(1) The order in which new members become subject to the obligations of the Fund [proposed Article XIII, ["Putting the Fund into Operation"], Alternative A, U.S.];

(2) The problem of nonmember countries in relation to the Fund [proposed new Section IX-4, ["Relation to Other Commitments"]];

(3) The establishment of initial par values [IV-1, ["Establishing Par Value"]];

(4) The appropriate form in which a contribution for administrative expenses of 1/20th of 1 percent shall be paid [proposed new Section XIII-1, "Entry into Effect," Alternative A, U.S.]; and

(5) The disadvantages of the provision which specifies that an exchange transaction should not begin until three months after the cessation of hostilities.

Mr. Hexner stated that the committee believe that the interval of conditional or partial membership which would result immediately after the establishment of the Fund should be specifically limited. In this connection, **Dr. [Te-Mou] Hsi [China]** called attention to the need for a longer interval of time for China. **Mr. Rasminsky** pointed out the difficulty requesting parliaments to accept the Fund before such basic questions as exchange rates and quotas as had been established.

---

[226] For the minutes of the meeting, see chapter 65. The flimsy the subcommittee discussed was "Setting up the Fund, Beginning Operations, etc."

40

Agenda Committee
Third meeting
Atlantic City
June 21, 1944 at 4 p.m.[227]

American and other drafts • Schedule of meetings • Subcommittee 4: Order of obligations of membership • Transitional arrangements • Subcommittee 3: Power to call Board meetings • Votes irrespective of quotas • Subcommittee 2: Soviet suggestions • Scarce currencies

Harry Dexter White explains that the American draft of the IMF Articles of Agreement is intended to serve as a basis for discussion but not to limit it. Other countries will submit proposed alternatives (amendments), but no other country has a full-fledged draft, giving the United States an advantage at achieving its goals.

Subcommittee 4 reports on its discussions of the early period of the IMF. The most important result of the subcommittee's deliberations is its recognition that there will be a transition period after World War II when many countries will continue to impose exchange controls. When the proposal for a three-year limit on exchange controls without the IMF's approval comes up, a Canadian delegate suggests deferring further discussion of the transition period until the full British delegation arrives, given British interest in the subject.

Subcommittee 3 reports strong sentiment in favor of a provision to allow countries that are not on the Executive Board to call meetings of the Board of Governors — a

---

[227] Present: Messrs. Melville, Brigden, Tange and Wheeler of Australia; Baron Boël of Belgium; Mr. Bulhões of Brazil; Messrs. Deutsch, Rasminsky, and Plumptre of Canada; Mr. Coers of Chile; Messrs. Tsiang, Soong, Hsi, Wei and Hoo [Koo] of China; Mr. Pazos of Cuba; Messrs. Basch and Hexner of Czechoslovakia; Sir Theodore Gregory of India; Messrs. Gómez and Monteros of Mexico; Messrs. de Iongh and Polak of the Netherlands; Mr. Opie of United Kingdom; Messrs. Morozov, Smirnov and Bystrov of the USSR; the Technical Committee and Mr. E.E. Brown of United States.

safeguard for small countries to ensure that their interests are adequately represented.
Subcommittee 2 reports on a Soviet proposal concerning the retention of newly mined gold that would benefit the Soviet Union, and on discussion about scarce currencies, which, as we indicated in chapter 6, is not something the IMF has had to worry about in practice.

Mr. White explained that the flimsy submitted to the subcommittees[228] represented the attempt of the American delegation to implement the Joint Statement, which was to serve as a basis for the discussion of the conference but which is not to be considered a limitation upon it. He stated that it was our [the American] expectation that the foreign delegations would also submit drafts of suggested provisions for discussion. He suggested that they be turned over to Mr. [Frank] Coe [U.S.], the Technical Secretary of the conference, who would submit them to the proper committee.

It was agreed that the meeting of the subcommittees would take place each day from 9:30 [a.m.] to 12:00 [noon]. The possibility of staggering meetings was again considered. After some discussion, it was considered preferable that the committees meet at the same time and that further meetings be held of the full general committee, if necessary.

Committee 4 [Establishment of the Fund][229]

Mr. Hexner [Czechoslovakia, Reporter] reported on the committee's discussion of the order in which the obligations of membership would be assumed [proposed Article XIII, ["Putting the Fund into Operation,"] Alternative A, U.S.]. He also called attention to the difficulties involved in arranging agreement on par values for the original members of the Fund. After considerable discussion, it was recognized that any difficulty was apparent rather than real, since the rates of exchange accepted at the time of membership would probably be a pattern of rates prevailing at some previous date. Adjustments would be made for any countries whose exchange rates could not be arranged satisfactorily on this basis. A transitional period would be allowed for making the necessary adjustments.

---

[228] Possibly the American draft of the IMF Articles of Agreement in U.S. National Archives, RG 56 Box 01 Folder A-2.

[229] For the minutes of the meeting, see chapter 66. The flimsy the subcommittee discussed was "Transitional Arrangements."

Mr. [James] Brigden [Australia] then suggested that it might be possible to have a group of countries which, by accepting both the agreement and the exchange rates of the previously agreed-upon date, would constitute themselves the Fund for the purpose of working with other members on establishing appropriate rates for those not willing to accept the de facto pattern of a particular date.

In the course of this discussion, **Mr. Monteros [Mexico]** questioned the desirability of expressing currencies in terms of gold [IV-1, "Establishing Par Value"]]. He suggested that it might be more appropriate to express them in terms of exchange ratios. **Mr. [André] Istel [France]** pointed out that there is no difference in the two conceptions. **Mr. White** explained that since it was considered inappropriate to express member currencies in terms of any particular national currency, it had been decided to express them in terms of gold.

Mr. Hexner summarized the rest of the work of his committee as follows:

(a) They suggested that some indication be given of the form in which the 1/20 of 1 percent of the quota used for meeting administrative expenses should be paid [proposed new Section XIII-1, "Entry into Effect," Alternative A, U.S.].

(b) The committee recommended that the date for the beginning of exchange transactions should be left to the discretion of the Board [proposed new Section XIII-5, "Fixing Initial Par Values," Alternative A, U.S.].

(c) The committee recommended the deletion of the sentence which states that no exchange transaction shall be undertaken by the Fund in a particular currency until that country has assumed the obligations of Article III, Section 5 [["Obligations of a Purchasing Country"]].

Mr. [Antonín] Basch [Czechoslovakia] reported on the committee's work on transitional arrangements. The committee recommended that the provision permitting member countries to maintain and adapt exchange regulations to changing circumstances [X-2, ["Transition Period"]] be extended to permit the introduction of such exchange regulations in the case of countries occupied by the enemy. It was generally agreed that the point was well taken.

Mr. [Daniël Crena] de Iongh [Netherlands] suggested that, in relaxing exchange regulations, priority be granted nonresidents. Mr. de Iongh was requested to draft a provision which would incorporate his idea.

Mr. Basch called attention to the committee's discussion of the following points:

(a) The relationship of the discussion on the Fund to the overall agreements to be made under Article VII ["Management of the Fund"].

(b) The suggestion that three years after the date on which the obligations of the Fund commence, any member country maintaining restrictions shall retain them only with the approval of the Fund [X-3, ["Restrictions on Exchange"]]. The discussion that followed emphasized the fact that if a three-year transitional period is to be allowed, the Fund should have some control over the termination or continuation of such controls after that date. **Mr. Rasminsky [Canada]** suggested that, in view of the UK's special interest in the transitional arrangements, this discussion be deferred until a representative of the UK delegation be present.

(c) The belief of the committee that paragraph 3 of the "Transitional Arrangements" [[X-3, "Restrictions on Exchange"]] relates not only to Section 10 of the Joint Statement [i.e., Article X, "Transitional Arrangements"] but to the whole agreement.

Committee 3 [Organization and Management of the Fund][230]

Mr. Monteros [Mexico, Reporter] reported the following recommendations of the committee:

(a) Member countries not represented on the Executive Committee shall have the power to call meetings of the Board. In view of the considerable approval of this provision, **Mr. White** asked the secretary of the committee [Karl Bopp, U.S.] to draft a provision to this effect.

(b) The Board of Directors' place of meeting should be specified, as it had been in an earlier draft.

Mr. Monteros inquired why the votes allocated to countries irrespective of quotas had been reduced from 100 to 25. **Mr. White** explained that it was the belief of the American Technical Committee that each country should have a reasonable number of votes without regard to its quotas. The figure of 100 votes have been selected at a time when a Fund of only $5 billion in only a limited number of countries had been contemplated. However, as the quotas and the number of members had increased, it became necessary to re-examine the allocation of shares to the smaller countries. The figure of 25 is presented as only a tentative suggestion, which could undoubtedly be adjusted along lines which Mr.

---

[230] For the minutes of the meeting, see chapter 62. The flimsy the subcommittee discussed was "Governing Board and Executive Committee."

Monteros would consider reasonable. It was agreed that the determination of the exact amount must be deferred until after such time as a decision had been made on quotas.

Mr. Monteros questioned the desirability of expressing all numerical quantities in terms of dollars, as is the practice in the Joint Statement [e.g., II-1, ["Total Amount"]]. It was suggested that the question of a unit of account other than the dollar be examined in Committee 3.

Mr. Rasminsky inquired concerning the voting procedure of the Executive Committee [VII-2, ["Voting Power"]]. **Mr. Monteros** explained that this problem had been considered by his committee but that they were not ready to report.

Committee 2 [Operations of the Fund][231]

Mr. Rasminsky [Reporter] reported that the **Russian** delegation had made the following suggestions:

(a) That provision IV-7(b) of the Joint Statement [["Fund's Acquisition of Gold"]] should not be applied to countries substantially damaged by the enemy, and

(b) That provision IV-7(c) should not apply during the period of restoration [reconstruction] to increases in gold holdings resulting from newly mined gold, in the case of countries substantially damaged by enemy occupation.

The committee considered the desirability permitting the Fund to issue a report on an approaching scarcity before the technical condition of scarcity was declared and rationing introduced [VI-1, ["Fund Warning of Scarcity"]]. It was hoped that by a prior report, the need for declaration of scarcity and rationing might be avoided. Considerable discussion followed, in the course of which it was pointed out that the type of report envisaged might further injure the situation by inducing increased demand for the scarce currency, both inside the Fund and outside in the free market. It was the consensus of the meeting that the issuance of a report prior to the declaration of scarcity was optional, but that it was mandatory upon the Fund at the time the currency was declared to be scarce.

Mr. Rasminsky reported that his committee was entirely in sympathy with the provision which gave a country whose currency was in process

---

[231] For the minutes of the meeting, see chapter 58. The flimsies the subcommittee discussed were "Scarce Currencies," "Provisions Concerning Multilateral Clearing," and "Acquisitions of Gold by the Fund."

of becoming scarce the right to sit in on the committee making the report.

The attention of the meeting was called to the suggestion that in determining the manner of rationing the supply of a scarce currency among its nationals, the member country shall have complete jurisdiction subject to the provisions of Article X-2 [["Transition Period"]]. **Mr. Rasminsky** informed the delegates that this change would prevent a currency from being auctioned to the highest bidder.

Considerable discussion followed on the question of whether it was appropriate for the Fund to acquire scarce currency from another member country. In this connection, the question of the implications of the passivity of the Fund were also considered. It was agreed that under provision III-3 of the Joint Statement [["Limitation on Purchases"]], the Fund was undoubtedly prohibited from engaging in such practices.

Mr. Rasminsky stated that the committee felt that the redraft of provision III-4(a) [["Scarce Currencies"]], which stated that "no country was under obligation to lend the Fund," was an unnecessary addition. **Mr. White** pointed out that the provision had been included to reassure countries concerning their rights to refuse to lend to the Fund.

41

Agenda Committee
Fourth meeting
Atlantic City
June 22, 1944 at 4 p.m.[232]

Subcommittee 2: Purchase of currencies • Subcommittee 1: Gold deposits • Definitions regarding gold • Subcommittee 2: Obligations of member countries

Subcommittee 2 reports on its discussion of a section of the IMF draft articles requiring a country to purchase its own currency from other members with their currencies or with gold. The provision applies only to postwar current payments, not to capital transactions or to balances blocked before the agreement enters into force.

Subcommittee 1 reports on alternatives to the U.S. proposal that the IMF hold its gold deposits in four main countries (expected to be the United States, United Kingdom, Soviet Union, and France or possibly China). A discussion follows about how to define the terms "gold convertible exchange" and "official gold holdings."

Subcommittee 2 then resumes with a report on a potential conflict between provisions of certain existing commercial treaties and the IMF agreement insofar as the latter affects the rationing of currency in bilateral trade dealings. U.S. delegates state that the IMF agreement will not override other treaties. The session concludes with Subcommittee 2's relation of its discussion of whether the IMF should allow multiple exchange rates, a question the subcommittee did not resolve.

The American delegation took two sets of notes on this meeting; we show both.

---

[232] Present: Messrs. Melville, Brigden, Tange and Wheeler of Australia; Baron Boël of Belgium; Mr. Bulhões of Brazil; Messrs. Deutsch, Rasminsky, and Plumptre of Canada; Mr. Coers of Chile; Messrs. Tsiang, Soong, Hsi, Wei and Hoo [Koo] of China; Mr. Pazos of Cuba; Messrs. Basch and Hexner of Czechoslovakia; Sir Theodore Gregory of India; Messrs. Gómez and Monteros of Mexico; Messrs. de Iongh and Polak of the Netherlands; Mr. Opie of United Kingdom; Messrs. Morozov, Smirnov and Bystrov of the USSR; the Technical Committee and Mr. E.E. Brown of United States.

(Version by Henry J. Bittermann)

Mr. Rasminsky [Canada, Reporter], reporting for Committee 2 [Operations of the Fund], discussed the rewording of III-5 [["Obligations of a Purchasing Country"]].[233] He questioned the necessity for the clause in its entirety. In any event, the committee suggested the deletion of the words "on current account" on the grounds that blocked balances were blocked, irrespective of origin. Mr. White [U.S.] maintained that the Fund and the country were concerned with the question only insofar as there were large and sustained capital movements. Mr. [Daniël] Crena de Iongh [Netherlands], in turn, pointed out that the revised phrasing required a country to sell its currencies for gold, but that a country with gold could not be required to sell its currency when its quota is already exhausted.

Dr. [Octavio de] Bulhões [Brazil, Reporter], for Committee 1 [Purposes, Policies and Subscriptions], suggested alternatives to the Secretariat's phrasing for the clause requiring the Fund to maintain its gold deposits in four main countries [VII, proposed new section, "Depositories," Alterative A, U.S.].[234] The first alternative was to give the Fund complete discretion having regard to the quotas and the facilities for custody; the other was to allocate the deposits in proportion the gold holdings, quotas and needs for gold, leaving some gold on deposit in each country. Mr. White indicated that the Fund's need for gold would not be proportional to gold contributions. Mr. [Robert] Mossé [France] showed that the original proposal gave no protection either to the large or small countries. Mr. Bulhões objected to the use of merely four countries, but favors some apportionment according to quotas. To Mr. Rasminsky's objection that there was no reason for apportioning gold except convenience in use, Mr. White answered that it was not a purely economic question. He favored the deposit of some gold in each country, with a rough division in proportion to needs, and suggested the possibility of allocation by geographic areas. Mr. [Aleksei] Smirnov [USSR] insisted that the four-country allocation was adequate geographically.

Mr. Bulhões suggested the need of defining the terms "gold

---

[233] This is a continuation of the subcommittee's discussion of the previous day, for which see chapter 58.

[234] This is a continuation of the subcommittee's discussion of the previous day, for which see chapter 54.

convertible exchange" and "official gold holdings." He indicated that in his committee, some countries had favored a reduction of gold contributions from 50 to 75 percent of a standard contribution for those countries which have suffered from devastation and invasion [II-3, ["Gold Subscriptions,"] Alternative B, USSR]. **Mr. [Felipe] Pazos [Cuba]** could see no advantage of this to the countries concerned, and thought the Fund would be considerably weakened. **Sir Theodore Gregory [India]** likewise questioned the need for any such provision. **Mr. [André] Istel [France]** argued that the gold would be needed for reconstruction, to which **Mr. [Redvers] Opie [UK]** responded that in terms of XI-1 [["Entry into Force"]] the Fund was not to be used for reconstruction, but that was a function of the Bank. **Mr. Smirnov** answered with the argument that since the draft had recognized the necessity of reduction of gold contributions for the invaded countries, this provision should be retained. **Mr. [Tingfu] Tsiang [China]** pointed out that though China had been invaded, she asked for no special consideration. **Sir Theodore** proposed the elimination of this clause on the grounds that it would lend to continual difficulties in definition, and in any case would serve no useful purpose.

Mr. Bulhões also reported that there had been discussion about the proper wording of the statement of the purposes of the Fund [Article I].[235] **Messrs. Hexner [Czechoslovakia]** and **Opie** defined the word "consultation" as having a special significance diplomatically for the procedure of the Fund.

Mr. Rasminsky, for Committee 2, reported a consensus of the members on the importance of Article VII of the Mutual Aid Agreement.[236] He pointed out that the new provision IX-4 [["Relation to

---

[235] For the minutes of the meeting, see chapter 55.
[236] The Mutual Aid Agreements were a set of agreements among the Allies. The first of them, the Anglo-American agreement of February 28, 1942, contained this language in Article VII, which many of the subsequent agreements imitated:

> In the final determination of the benefits to be provided to the United States of America by the Government of the United Kingdom in return for aid furnished under the Act of Congress of March 11, 1941, the terms and conditions thereof shall be such as not to burden commerce between the two countries, but to promote mutually advantageous economic relations between them and the betterment of world-wide economic relations. To that end, they shall include provision for agreed action by the United States of America and the United Kingdom, open to participation by all other countries of like mind,

Other Commitments"]] involves conflicts in terms of trade treaties and the provisions for rationing scarce currencies. **Messrs. [Emilio] Collado and White [U.S.]** noted that a distinction must be made between rationing and discrimination in terms of the reasonableness of the regulations adopted. The jurisdiction of member countries under the Fund agreement must be taken concurrently with other previously assumed obligations. **Mr. [Antonio Espinosa de los] Monteros [Mexico]** argued that the Fund has no jurisdiction in matters of commercial policy, which must be treated by the appropriate methods provided in commercial treaties. **Mr. Rasminsky** completed his report with the suggestion that capital and current account transactions be more precisely defined for purposes of IX-3 [["Current Transactions"]].[237]

(Version by Dorothy F. Richardson)

Mr. Rasminsky (Canada, [Reporter]) continued the report of yesterday's discussion in Committee 2 [Operations of the Fund].[238]

The provision on multilateral clearing, III-5 [["Obligations of a Purchasing Country"]], has been redrafted as set forth in the attached memorandum.[239] This redrafting attempts to emphasize that the Fund's holdings of any member's currency should not be increased except as a result of the purchase of another member country's currency by that country or as the result of the Fund borrowing the currency of that country. This redrafting also takes into consideration a problem minimizing the effect on the money markets of the countries in question.

---

directed to the expansion, by appropriate international and domestic measures, of production, employment, and the exchange and consumption of goods, which are the material foundations of the liberty and welfare of all peoples; to the elimination of all forms of discriminatory treatment in international commerce, and to the reduction of tariffs and other trade barriers; and in general, to the attainment of all the economic objectives set forth in the Joint Declaration made on Aug. 12, 1941, by the President of the United States of America and the Prime Minister of the United Kingdom.

[237] For the minutes of the meeting, see chapter 59. The flimsy the subcommittee discussed was "Capital Movements."

[238] See chapter 58.

[239] U.S. National Archives, RG 56, Box 2, has multiple versions of documents on multilateral clearing, but we are uncertain which of them, if any, is meant here.

Mr. Rasminsky pointed out that the word "required" had been changed to "requested" and explained the reason for this change. He also pointed out that the clause "of a current account nature" should be deleted, and that the word "any" should be inserted before "transactions."

Dr. Bulhões [Brazil, Reporter] reported for Committee 1 [Purposes, Policies and Subscriptions].[240]

Three formulations of the provision as to where the Fund's gold should be held were proposed and discussed in this committee [proposed new Section VIII-6, "Depositories"; Alternative A, U.S.; B, UK; C, Netherlands]:

1. The Fund's gold holdings shall be distributed among depositories in the four countries with the largest quotas in such proportions as the Fund may determine.

2. The Fund may hold all of its assets, including gold, in such member countries as the Fund may select, with due regard to the quotas of the member countries and shipping facilities.

3. The Fund may hold all of its assets, including gold, in such member countries as the Fund may select.

The committee found the first formulation of this provision [Alternative A, U.S.], which is the one set forth in the flimsy, unsatisfactory, and felt that the second formulation [Alternative B, UK] involved technical disadvantages in that it sets up two different criteria.

In regard to the provision providing for a reduction of 25 percent in the obligatory gold contribution of member countries whose home areas have been substantially devastated through enemy action or occupation, the Russian member of the committee suggested that the percentage reduction should not be uniform among all countries, but could range from 50 to 75 percent [II-3, ["Gold Subscriptions,"] Alternative B, USSR].

Mr. Opie (UK) felt that provision X-1 [["Entry into Force"]] should rule out any appeal to reconstruction needs as a reason for special concessions, and suggested that the Bank was a more appropriate instrument for provision of aid for such purposes. **Sir Theodore Gregory (India)** also opposed this provision. **Mr. Istel (France)** felt that the important consideration was the amount of a country's gold holdings, which, so far as could be judged, would be used for immediate reconstruction. **Sir Theodore Gregory (India)** suggested that there

---

[240] This is a continuation of the subcommittee's discussion of the previous day, for which see chapter 54.

would be difficulties in defining "substantial" or "more" devastation. The reports of the discussions which took place in the various committees this morning were then submitted.

Mr. Bulhões ([Brazil, Reporter]) reported for Committee 1.[241] It was suggested that the purpose No. 6 [in Article I] should be changed to fourth place, that No. 4 should be put in fifth place, and No. 5 should become No. 6. **Mr. [Wynne] Plumptre [Canada]** explained that logically Nos. 1, 2, 3, and 6 should follow each other, since all relate to broad objectives, and that Nos. 4 and 5 should follow these, since they relate to the means of obtaining these objectives.

Mr. Bulhões stated that he had desired to include a provision relating the Fund to the Bank in the following manner: if the Fund has already studied a particular member's situation and feels that country is in need of long-term capital, the Bank shall give priority to the country's request for a loan — but that the committee had not agreed with him on this point. It was suggested that Mr. Bulhões should draft a provision to this effect.

Mr. Rasminsky (Canada, [Reporter]) reported for Committee 2.[242] Mr. Rasminsky reported that the committee had continued discussion of provisions III-5 [["Obligations of a Purchasing Country"]], IX-3 [["Current Transactions"]], and IV-4 [["Latitude for Change in Par Value"]]. Some of the members of the committee felt that rights of smaller countries as set forth in provisions VI-2 [["Rationing of Scarce Currencies"]] and X-2 [["Transition Period"]] should not be limited by provision IX-4 [["Relation to Other Commitments"]].

Mr. [Ansel] Luxford (U.S.) felt that adherence to the Fund by a member country did not constitute abrogation of all other treaties, and that provision IX-4 spelled this out. **Mr. Monteros (Mexico)** felt that the Fund's jurisdiction was limited to questions of exchange stability, and that the Fund had no jurisdiction over other types of agreements.

Mr. Luxford (U.S.) explained that IV-2 [["Changes in Par Value"]] meant that a member country had complete freedom in the method of rationing as far the Fund was concerned, but he felt that member countries remained subject to restrictions laid down in other agreements. **Mr. White (U.S.)** felt that it is only when rationing is unreasonably applied that it becomes discriminatory.

It was generally agreed that these provisions required further discussion.

---

[241] For the minutes of the meeting, see chapter 55.
[242] For the minutes, see chapter 59. The flimsy was "Capital Movements."

Mr. Rasminsky reported that a question had been raised, in regard to IV-4, as to whether it was wise to allow any multiple currency practices, and that the committee had discussed at length methods of exchange control. The chairman, **Mr. Istel (France),** had suggested setting out a list of the types of transactions over which a member country would not impose exchange control at the beginning of provision V-1 [["Use of Fund to Finance Capital Outflows"]].

42

Agenda Committee
Fifth meeting
Atlantic City
June 23, 1944 at 10 a.m.[243]

Arrival of other delegations • Subcommittee 4: Immunities of the Fund • Subcommittee 3: Voting procedures for Executive Directors

In this brief meeting, Harry Dexter White announces that the remaining delegations will arrive soon. The Agenda Committee will become the Formal Agenda Committee with their arrival.

Subcommittee 4 reports its opinion that the IMF and the Bank should be exempt from taxation. The Agenda Committee arrives at a consensus that the IMF's currency holdings should be protected from depreciations in par values unless all countries depreciate at once. Subcommittee 3 reports its favorable impression of the rather complex U.S. proposal for choosing Executive Directors.

Mr. White informed the meeting that the Formal Agenda Committee meetings would begin the following day, Saturday, June 24, with the arrival of the other delegations. **Mr. Opie [UK]** and **Sir Theodore Gregory [India]** requested that the Chairman make a statement at the opening meeting describing the procedure which had been followed during these plenary sessions and proposing the procedure to be followed by the Agenda Committee.

---

[243] Present: Messrs. Melville, Brigden, Tange and Wheeler of Australia; Baron Boël of Belgium; Mr. Bulhões of Brazil; Mr. Pazos of Cuba; Messrs. Deutsch, Rasminsky, and Plumptre of Canada; Mr. Coers of Chile; Messrs. Tsiang, Soong, Hsi, Wei and Hoo [Koo] of China; Mr. Pazos of Cuba; Messrs. Basch and Hexner of Czechoslovakia; Sir Theodore Gregory of India; Messrs. Gómez and Monteros of Mexico; Messrs. de Iongh and Polak of the Netherlands; Mr. Opie of United Kingdom; Messrs. Morozov, Smirnov and Bystrov of the USSR; the Technical Committee and Mr. E.E. Brown of United States.

Committee 4 [Establishment of the Fund][244]

Mr. Hexner [Czechoslovakia, Reporter] reported that, after extended discussion, Committee 4 had agreed that the broadest type of immunity from taxation would be appropriate for the Fund and the Bank.

The desirability of protecting the assets of the Fund was then considered. It was the consensus of the meeting that the Fund's currency holdings would always be the equivalent of [$]8 billion in gold unless a universal change in par values occurs and that the Fund should be protected against de facto as well as de jure currency depreciation.

The meeting turned its attention to the implications of provision III-5 [["Obligations of a Purchasing Country"]] and decided that this provision needed further attention and clarification. It would also be desirable to include in the final document definitions of transactions on current account and capital transfers. A discussion followed on [the] extent to which the Fund's resources will be freely convertible.

Committee 3 [Organization and Management of the Fund][245]

Mr. Monteros [Mexico, Reporter] reported on the discussion by Committee 3 of the proposed voting procedure for the Fund. The method, which was explained by **Mr. [Edward] Bernstein [U.S.]**, allowed for an Executive Committee of twelve members, five to be appointed by the countries with the largest quotas and six to be elected on the basis of proportional representation.[246] Each country would cast its voting power for a single member, and any director getting between 16 and 17 percent of the aggregate will be declared elected. Surplus votes would be turned over to the voting country's second choice. **Mr. Monteros** stated that in spite of the apparent complications of the method proposed it had very great merit and offered fundamental justice and equity.

---

[244] For the minutes of the meeting, see chapter 68. The flimsy the subcommittee discussed was "Protection of the Assets of the Fund."

[245] For the minutes of the meeting, see chapter 64. The flimsy the subcommittee discussed was "Governing Board and Executive Committee."

[246] Either the General Manager was envisioned as the remaining member of the Executive Committee, or "six" in the original text should be "seven."

43

Formal Agenda Committee
First meeting
Atlantic City
June 24, 1944 at 4 p.m.[247]

Election of chairman and vice chairmen •
Distribution of draft proposals

With the arrival of the British and other delegations that had traveled aboard the Queen Mary, *all the conference delegates are now present. The rump informal Agenda Committee now becomes the Formal Agenda Committee, with Harry Dexter White continuing as chairman and John Maynard Keynes elected as one of the vice chairmen.*

Mr. [Frank] Coe [U.S., Secretary] suggested that the group elect a Chairman with the power to appoint four Vice Chairmen.

Lord Keynes (UK) nominated Mr. Harry D. White (U.S.) for Chairman. **Prof. Smirnov (USSR)** seconded the nomination. Mr. White was unanimously elected.

After taking the chair, **Mr. White** announced he would appoint the following to serve as Vice Chairmen: Lord Keynes (UK), Prof. Smirnov (USSR), Mr. [Tingfu] Tsiang (China) and Mr. [Antonio Espinosa de los] Monteros (Mexico).

Mr. White explained that the members who arrived earlier had been considering a large number of provisions of the Monetary Fund which had been submitted by the Secretariat. He suggested that these provisions and others which the delegations would submit in the next few days be combined in a document setting forth the alternative provisions for the consideration of this group. Mr. White asked that the delegations give

---

[247] No list of those present was made for any of the meetings of the Formal Agenda Committee.

these proposed provisions to the Secretary.

Copies of the provisions (flimsies) which had been under discussion in Atlantic City were given to all members.[248]

It was decided that the full group would meet next at 10 a.m., Monday, July 26, 1944 in the Binnacle Room.[249]

---

[248] See the editors' appendix to chapter 38.

[249] A conference room at the Claridge Hotel, since renamed.

44

Formal Agenda Committee
Second meeting
Atlantic City
June 26, 1944 at 10 a.m.

Distribution of draft IMF articles • Subcommittee on Management

In this short meeting, the draft agreement for the IMF is circulated to delegates. John Maynard Keynes suggests appointing a subcommittee on management.
Minutes for this meeting exist in both American and British versions.

(American version by Dorothy F. Richardson)

Copies of Document F-1, "Preliminary Draft of Suggested Articles for the Establishment of an International Monetary Fund," were distributed, and the paging and notation were explained. [250] The confidential nature of this document was stressed.

Lord Keynes suggested that in order to save time it would be desirable to appoint a small committee to work on questions of management, which have hitherto been treated very sketchily.

It was also suggested that although no plan had been arranged for seating arrangements, it would be desirable for the remainder of the group take the same place as each day.

Since there was no other business, the meeting was adjourned until 3 p.m., at which meeting discussion on Document F-1 will be begun.

---

[250] Chapter 74 reproduces the form of Document F-1 at the end of the conference, giving the text of the Joint Statement and all alternatives (proposed amendments) submitted at the conference. Appendix D summarizes all alternatives. On the paging and notation, see chapter 1.

(British version by H.E. Brooks)

1. **Dr. White** explained the character of the Document F-1 which had been circulated to delegations, and said it was proposed to pass over purely drafting amendments at this stage which were indicated by an asterisk and to concentrate on the amendments of substance. He appreciated that delegations had not had time to study the papers and the meeting would therefore be short but would resume at 3 o'clock the same afternoon.

2. On the proposition of **Lord Keynes** it was agreed to appoint a small working committee on the management of the Fund, the members to be chosen by the Steering Committee.

3. In adjourning the meeting, **Dr. White** emphasized the confidentiality of the papers and proceedings and asked delegates to occupy the same seats at future meetings, so far as possible.

45

Formal Agenda Committee
Third meeting
Atlantic City
June 26, 1944 at 3 p.m.

Agenda Subcommittee • Subcommittee on Management • IMF
purposes and policies • Subscription to the Fund • Transactions
with the Fund • Ineligibility to use the Fund's resources •
Scarce currencies

This first long meeting of the Formal Agenda Committee starts by dispensing with some organizational matters, including appointing an Agenda Subcommittee. We have found no records of the subcommittee, whose purpose seems to have been to ensure that discussions at Atlantic City covered effectively the issues delegations wanted to raise and to propose the organizational structure for the Bretton Woods conference — or, more accurately, to ratify the structure the United States had already developed.

The committee then reviews proposals on the IMF draft agreement's Article I, "Purposes and Policies of the Fund"; Article II, "Subscription to the Fund"; and part of Article III, "Transactions with the Fund." India proposes amending Article I to promote greater focus on poor countries such as itself, while Australia proposes greater emphasis on full employment and on avoiding the ills associated with deflation, which Australia suffered acutely in the 1930s. As for Article II, a number of delegates note the probable uncertainties of the immediate postwar period and the great extent of war damage in many countries, reducing their ability to contribute to the IMF.

Concerning Article III, discussion centers on the conditions under which member countries may purchase currencies from other members through the IMF, or lose access to the ability to borrow from the IMF. The issue is the extent to which borrowing from the IMF is a guaranteed right versus the IMF's need for discretion to protect itself from members that borrow continuously in breach of their obligations. At the end, the group gets partway toward a consensus. A number of countries express support for Australia's concern that countries such as itself that are subject to wide swings in the balance of payments need flexibility to address the swings.

Minutes of this meeting exist in three American versions and a British version. We omit one of the American versions because it seems to be merely a draft of another.

(American version by Dorothy F. Richardson)

At the meeting of the Steering Committee this morning[251] it was decided that meetings of the full group, which is to be known as the Formal Agenda Conference, will be held every day at 10:30 a.m. and at 4:30 p.m.

It was also decided that there should be appointed an Agenda Subcommittee. The United Kingdom, the USSR, China, France, Mexico and the United States should each appoint a member to serve on this subcommittee.

The members who are to serve on the Management Subcommittee are as follows: [Ansel] Luxford (U.S.), Sir Wilfrid Eady (UK), Prof. [Fyodor] Bystrov (USSR), Dr. [Antonio Espinosa de los] Monteros (Mexico), Dr. [Jan Willem] Beyen (Netherlands), and Hsi Te-Mou (China).

Mr. [Frank] Coe [U.S., Secretary] announced that he had been informed that in one or two cases provisions submitted for consideration have not been included in the document distributed this morning. These provisions will be included as soon as possible.

The discussion of the Document F-1 ["Preliminary Draft of Suggested Articles for the Establishment of an International Monetary Fund"], which was distributed this morning, was begun.

[Article] I ["Purposes and Policies of the Fund"], [Alternative] A [U.S.]

Sir Jeremy Raisman (India) stated that he would like to amend I, [Alternative] A, [Section] (2) by adding the following phrase: "and to assist in the full utilization of the resources of the undeveloped countries." Since the suggestion had not been included in the document circulated this morning, consideration was deferred to a later meeting. The **Chairman [Harry Dexter White]** stated that provisions passed over would be included among the first items of the next meeting.

[I, Alternative B, Australia]

Mr. [Leslie] Melville (Australia) explained that this alternative is intended to reconcile the statement of the purposes and policies of the

---

[251] We have found no minutes of the meeting.

Fund with the provisions of the Fund. As an example Mr. Melville pointed out that in accordance with the provisions of the Joint Statement, alterations of exchange rates can be made for correction of a fundamental disequilibrium, whereas I-4 of the Joint Statement reads as follows: "To promote exchange stability, to maintain orderly exchange arrangements among member countries, and to avoid competitive exchange depreciation." Similarly, IV-3 [["Latitude for Change in Par Value"]] provides that the Fund shall not reject the requested change because of the domestic social or political policies of the country applying for a change, whereas I-6 [["Shorten Balance of Payments Disequilibrium"]] seems to indicate an opinion that the period of adjustment could be shortened by deflation.

The Australians have therefore suggested that the purposes and policies be altered to place more emphasis upon the maintenance and achievement of a high level of employment and upon the power of the Fund to permit alterations in exchange rates, and to make it clear that the Fund will not have discretionary powers to interfere in any member country's domestic monetary policies. Specifically, the phrase "in this way" in I-2 of the Joint Statement [["Balanced Trade, High Employment and Real Income"]] is either unnecessary or else restrictive, and the phrase "thus giving member countries time to correct maladjustment in a balance of payments without resorting to measures destructive of national or international prosperity" suggests that if member countries are not, within that time, able to correct the difficulties they will be forced to resort to destructive measures.

Lord Keynes (UK) suggested that the preamble is not the proper place for provisions relating to the creation of the Fund.

Prof. [Wilhelm] Keilhau (Norway) stated that he preferred the draft of Article I in the Joint Statement, since this draft emphasizes exchange stability is the fundamental purpose of the Monetary Fund, and unless exchange stability is thus emphasized, the layman may misunderstand the purposes and objectives of the Fund.

Baron [René] Boël (Belgium) remarked that there are two goals in regard to exchange rates: to promote exchange stability and to avoid competitive exchange depreciation; and that the method by which these goals were to be achieved was by maintaining orderly changes in exchange rates. He therefore suggested the addition [of] the following sentence: "by securing orderly changes in exchange rates among member countries where necessary to correct exchange disequilibrium," to I-4 of the Joint Statement [["Promote Exchange Stability"]]. **Mr. [Antonín] Basch (Czechoslovakia)** supported the suggestion.

Lord Keynes (UK) suggested that the opening sentence of I, [Alternative] A should be reserved for later consideration: the first purpose should be stated as in I-A; the second and third purposes should be stated in I, [Alternative] B; the fourth purpose should either be as in the Joint Statement or as requested by Baron Boël; the fifth purpose should be stated as in the Joint Statement; and the sixth purpose should be stated as in the Joint Statement with the addition of the Australian suggestion "in accordance with the above principles." **Mr. [Edward] Bernstein (U.S.)** felt that it was desirable to retain the working of the Joint Statement for the second purpose.

I, [Alternative] C [Brazil]

Lord Keynes (UK) remarked that there is in another place in this document a provision substantially similar to this provision. He therefore suggested that this provision be reserved for later discussion.

II-1 [["Total Amount"]]

Lord Keynes (UK) felt that matters relating to the inauguration of the Fund should be dealt with in a different place in the draft. **Baron Boël (Belgium)** suggested that there should be inserted in the second paragraph of II-1 some provision concerning neutral countries which join the Fund after its inauguration. **Mr. Luxford [U.S.]** explained that after the Fund is inaugurated, the question of any country's joining the Fund will be a matter for decision by the Board of Directors.

II-1, [Alternative] A [U.S.; proposed Section 3, "Time and Place of Payments"]

The section "Time and Place of Payments" was discussed. **Dr. [Ervin] Hexner (Czechoslovakia)** suggested that a period of nine months might be allotted to working out special arrangements between the Fund and countries whose currency systems have been disrupted, the Fund being guaranteed against losses from depreciation of such countries' currencies during this period. Dr. Hexner agreed to submit a written draft to the Secretariat.

Prof. Keilhau (Norway) pointed out that a number of countries would not be able to join the Fund without ratification of their parliament. If the parliaments of occupied countries have not been able to meet before the time of inauguration of the Fund, special arrangements will have to be made with these countries.

Mr. Melville (Australia) felt that this alternative draft seems to give the Fund power to examine the needs of member countries for revision of their quotas, but does not give it the power to make the necessary changes, except by implication. He also noted the difference between the time interval, which is "every five years" in this draft and "from time to time" in the Joint Statement.

Dr. [James] Brigden (Australia) felt that there are two types of quota revisions: (1) revision of the quota formula, and (2) revision of the quota figures by substitution of more recent data. The original International Stabilization Fund proposal was very clear on this point. Dr. Brigden therefore suggested that we keep provision II-2 of the Joint Statement [["Revisions to Quotas"]] and revive II-5 of the International Stabilization Fund proposal of July 10, 1943.[252] Dr. Brigden also suggested that the first revision be made after five years. **Lord Keynes (UK)** pointed out that Dr. Brigden's statement assumes that there will be a definite formula.

Mr. Rasminsky (Canada) felt that either July 1, 1944 or the December 31 preceding the inauguration of the Fund was a more desirable date for the determination of a country's gold holdings than January 1, 1944. **Mr. [Jan] Mládek (Czechoslovakia)** observed that countries which have been occupied will not know what the gold holdings are.

In regard to the section "Payments when Quotas Are Changed" [II-3, Alternative A, U.S., proposed new Section 6], **Mr. Melville (Australia)** pointed out that when a country's quota is raised, the country's obligatory gold contribution in connection with the increase in the quota is set at 25 percent of the quota regardless of the amount of its holdings of gold and gold convertible currencies. He suggested that consideration should be given to a country whose holdings of gold and gold convertible currencies are low at the time when a change in this quota is made. **Lord Keynes (UK)** supported the suggestion.

---

[252] II-5 of the July 1943 proposal read, "Quotas shall be adjusted on the basis of the most recent data 3 years after the establishment of the Fund, and at intervals of 5 years thereafter, in accordance with the agreed upon formula. In the period between adjustment of quotas, the Fund may increase the quota of a country, where it is clearly inequitable, out of the special allotment reserved for the equitable adjustment of quotas."

Mr. Luxford (U.S.) felt that the alternative method of determining the amount of the country's obligatory gold contribution which is provided for in connection with members' payment of their quota subscription at the time of the inauguration of the Fund is intended to be a concession to the peculiar and temporary circumstances which will exist in the early postwar period. In this connection, Mr. Luxford pointed out that a country is not obligated to accept an increase in its quota granted to it by the Fund. **Lord Keynes (UK)** replied that it is precisely at the time when a country's holdings of gold and gold convertible currency or low that an increase of its quota will be important to it. **Mr. Luxford (U.S.)** replied that a waiver of the limitations on the purchase of exchange on the Fund would accomplish the same purpose as an increase of a country's quota.

Mr. Rasminsky (Canada) felt it was open to question whether countries joining the Fund subsequent to its inauguration should be allowed the advantage of the alternative method of determining the amount of their obligatory gold contribution, and that he therefore supported Mr. Luxford's position. He suggested that a country which is granted an increase in its quota might be allowed to use part of that increase for the purpose of buying gold to meet its obligatory gold contribution to the Fund. **Ambassador [Kyriakos] Varvaressos (Greece)** felt that in case the Fund should find it equitable to increase the quota of any country, the conditions in regard to its obligatory gold contribution should be the same as in regard to its initial gold contribution.

II-3, [["Gold Subscriptions"], Alternative] B [USSR]

Baron Boël (Belgium) remarked that the difficulties in assessing the amount of damage would be great, and that he preferred that the obligatory gold subscription of countries which had been occupied by the enemy should be reduced uniformly. **Lord Keynes (UK)** agreed with the statement. **Prof. Smirnov (USSR)** stated the reason of the experts of the USSR in proposing this alternative provision. **Prof. Keilhau (Norway)** suggested the phrase "enemy action" in place of "hostilities." The reaction of the group seemed to be generally in favor of a flat reduction.

III-1, [["National Agency Dealing with Fund,"] Alternative] A, [U.S.]

This provision differs from the provision of the Joint Statement only in the addition of the phrase "and the Fund shall deal only through the same agencies." **Lord Keynes (UK)** felt this was an improvement. **Mr. Bernstein (U.S.)** pointed out that the second statement of the formulation of this provision in the Joint Statement had not been dropped but had been transferred to another place in the document.

III-2, [["Purchases of Another Member's Currency,"] Alternative] A [U.S.]

Lord Keynes (UK) stated that he preferred the wording of the Joint Statement. Firstly, the phrase "country is entitled to buy" has been changed to a "country may buy." Secondly, the verb in Subsection (1) has been changed from "represents" to "needs." It is thus not clear whether it is the Fund or the member country which decides whether the payments for which a country requests exchange from the Fund are consistent with the purposes and policies of the Fund. Thirdly, the meaning of Subsection (4) is not clear. Fourthly, the phrasing of the last sentence of provision II-2(a) implies that the Fund must require collateral or other securities before it can waive any the conditions regarding the purchase of exchange. Lord Keynes felt that the phrase "on terms would safeguard its interests" gives the Fund sufficient protection.

In answer to Lord Keynes's third point, **Mr. Luxford (U.S.)** pointed out that the phrase "under this Article" in Subsection (4) refers to the following subsection [section], "Declaring Member Countries Ineligible to Use the Resources of the Fund." **Dr. [Wim] Beyen (Netherlands)** stated that he would submit to the Secretary an amendment to meet Lord Keynes' fourth point.

Mr. Mládek (Czechoslovakia) felt that the phrase "purposes of and policies of the Fund" in Subsection (1) of provision III-2, [Alternative] A [U.S.] seemed to refer to Article I, whereas it is intended to refer to all provisions of the Fund's proposals. He suggested, that this condition might be transferred to the bylaws. **Mr. Luxford (U.S.)** felt that there was merit in Mr. Mládek's point.

In regard to Lord Keynes's (UK) first point, **Mr. Bernstein [U.S.]** stated that the Fund must be in a position to protect its assets from clear abuse. The fact that a country informs a Fund that it needs exchange for purposes and policies in accordance with the Fund constitutes doubtful protection. There must be some provision for the Fund to question a country's statement on this point. There followed considerable discussion among the group as to the differences in the implications of the term "may purchase exchange" in the phrase "is entitled the purchase exchange." **Lord Keynes (UK)** felt that a country has an unqualified right to purchase exchange, subject to the provisions of the Fund. **Mr. Bernstein (U.S.)** felt that a country's "right" is to approach the Fund to purchase exchange and pointed out that the verb "represents" had been changed to "needs" because it was necessary for the Fund to be able to invoke Subsection (4) if Subsection (1) was violated. **Dr. Beyen (Netherlands)** felt that this explanation was acceptable provided that a country's purchase of exchange could be limited or suspended only under Subsection (4).

The **Chairman** felt that the fact that the Executive Committee would be given authority, in borderline cases, to determine whether a request for exchange is consistent with the purposes of the Fund does not mean that the central bank of a country cannot count on obtaining exchange from the Fund, or that a request will initiate prolonged discussion between the central bank of that country and the Fund. **Dr. [Emanuel] Goldenweiser (U.S.)** suggested the addition of the phrase "in accordance with the provisions of the Fund" in the first [sub]section of III-2, [Alternative] A might aid in the understanding of this provision.

III-2, [Alternative] A [U.S., continued, proposed new Section], "Declaring Member Countries Ineligible to Use the Resources of the Fund"

Lord Keynes (UK) felt that this subsection [section] does not belong under Article III. He also suggested that the verb "determine" in the first sentence of the subsection should be changed, and that the second sentence be altered to read as follows: "If no reply is received within the stated time, or the reply receipt is unsatisfactory, the Fund may, after giving reasonable notice to the country, restrict that country's use of its quota, or declare it ineligible to use the resources of the Fund." **Dr. Monteros (Mexico)** also felt that this subsection did not belong in Article III. **Mr. Bernstein (U.S.)** felt that it would not be appropriate to include this subsection with the other provisions on suspension of a member country, since this provision involves only limitation of the use of the Fund's resources. He also suggested there was some psychological advantage to having all the provisions relative to the purchase of exchange together.

III-2, [Alternative] B [Canada]

Mr. Rasminsky (Canada) explained this provision. Provision V-1 of the Joint Statement [["Use of Fund to Finance Capital Outflows"]] places restrictions on the use of the Fund for capital transactions. A strict interpretation of III-2, [Alternative] A [U.S.] also imposes restrictions upon the use of the Fund for capital transactions since is refers to purposes of the Fund, and the fifth purpose [I-5] contains the phrase "on current account." Mr. Rasminsky felt that such restrictions should not be placed upon countries which are not making use of the Fund's resources. These will be capital-exporting countries and it will be advantageous if the exports of capital are carried out through the Fund.

In order to assure that the country is truly in a position to export capital, the proposed provision requires that the Fund's holdings of the currency of a member country which desires to use the Fund's resources for capital transactions must be below 75 percent of its quota for a period of not less than six months, and that the purchase of exchange for capital transactions must not raise the Fund's holdings of that country's quota above 75 percent.

Mr. Rasminsky explained further that in the absence of this provision a country's ability to export capital would not be limited, but that it might be possible to relieve the scarcity of that currency in the Fund by allowing that country to purchase exchange for capital transactions from the Fund rather than in the open market. In this connection, the **Chairman** posed the hypothetical problem of two countries, both of whose currencies were scarce in the Fund, one of which desired to purchase the currency of the other country for purposes of capital transactions. **Mr. Rasminsky** agreed that restrictions to meet this point would have to be introduced into this proposed provision.

Mr. Coe (U.S.) pointed out that under provision III-2 [["Purchases of Another Member's Currency"]] it would be possible for a country to use the resources of the Fund for capital transactions. **Mr. Bernstein (U.S.)** pointed out that Article V of the Joint Statement ["Capital Transactions"] was also pertinent. **Mr. Istel (France)** supported Mr. Rasminsky's provision but felt that it should be included in a separate article entitled "Scarce Currencies," the word "scarce" in this connection being used in a general sense and not as defined under the Fund's proposal. **Lord Keynes (UK)** also supported Mr. Rasminsky's proposal.

Mr. Melville (Australia) agreed with the purpose of Mr. Rasminsky's provision, but felt that it would[253] constitute a limitation upon the operations of a member country and of the Fund if the operations envisaged could be carried out under other provisions of the document. **Mr. [Dennis] Robertson (UK)** expressed the view that such operation could not be satisfactorily carried out under other provisions of the document, and pointed out that under Article V-1, special action by the Fund is required. The **Chairman** explained the reasons for and applications of provision V-1 [["Use of Fund to Finance Capital Outflows"]] and stated that the term "large" as used in this provision relates to the particular country in question. He agreed with Mr. Robertson (UK) that V-1 was not intended to cover the same transactions as are dealt with in Mr. Rasminsky's provision but stated that he was not sure that the provisions on waiver would not cover these transactions.

III-2, [Alternative] C [Australia]

Mr. Melville (Australia) explained that the purpose of this provision is to prevent countries whose resources at the time [of the] inauguration of the Fund are adequate, and which are subject to large fluctuations in their balance of payment, from having to rely on the discretionary powers of the Board in granting them use of the resources of the Fund to an extent greater than 25 percent per year. **Dr. Bulhões (Brazil)** pointed out that all agricultural countries are subject to wider fluctuations in their balance of payments and should be allowed the benefit of this provision. He also suggested that such countries might be required to contribute a larger proportion of their quota in gold. **Dr. Monteros (Mexico)** suggested that the benefit of this provision might be extended to all raw material producing countries. He stated that he did not think that this provision should be based on the ground that a country has little gold at the conclusion of the war. **Dr. Beyen (Netherlands)** supported this point but pointed out that it was important not to endanger the assets of the Fund.

The **Chairman** pointed out that there is flexibility in the provisions relating to members' purchases of foreign exchange. **Dr. Beyen (Netherlands)** replied that at the time of the inauguration of the Fund, cases in which there will be need for amounts of foreign-exchange in excess of 25 percent per year will be common, and will therefore be

---

[253] Shown as in the source text; perhaps the word "not" is missing.

difficult to handle under the general waiver provision. **Mr. Istel (France)** felt that it is the purpose of the Fund to supply funds for exceptional and not for ordinary needs.

The **Chairman** pointed out that the Fund was not designed to meet fully the needs of the transition period, although it could be assumed that it would be more lenient in granting credits during that period. He also pointed out that the remarks by various members of the group on this provision seemed to display a tendency to concentrate on members' needs for foreign exchange while ignoring the other side of the picture, i.e., the country's ability to repay. **Mr. [Walter] Gardner (U.S.)** felt that it would be difficult to designate the countries which would need greater resources from the Fund, especially in view of the fact that individual countries have different amounts of resources outside the Fund, and that it would be better to take care of these cases individually. **Mr. Melville (Australia)** reminded the group that the Fund would be able to restrict use of its resources when the purposes for which a country requests foreign exchange are not in accord with the purposes and policies of the Fund.

Mr. Istel (France) felt that as this provision is now worded, member countries will be tempted to attempt to use the full 25 percent of their quota allowed them during each year. **Mr. Gardner (U.S.)** pointed out that the 12 months' period referred to was not a calendar year but any continuous twelve months' period.

III-3 [["Limitation on Purchases"]]

Since this provision embodies no change in substance, it was reserved for later discussion.

III-4 [["Scarce Currencies"], Alternative A, U.S.]

Mr. Luxford (U.S.) pointed out that the change in this provision consists in allowing the Fund, with the approval of the member countries, to buy other members' currencies from any source whatsoever. **Lord Keynes (UK)** supported this provision.

*   *   *

The **Secretary [Frank Coe, U.S.]** announced that Sir Wilfrid Eady would call a meeting of the Management Subcommittee for later today.

He also announced that the secretaries of the various delegations should get copies of the following materials from him at the close of the meeting or at Mr. White's office.

1. Brazilian proposal [I, Alternative C?]
2. Index to the Document F-1
3. Additional pages to Document F-1
4. Explanatory material available:
   Questions and Answers on [the] Fund
   Questions and Answers on [the] Bank

(American version by Janet R. Sundelson)[254]

(Not present for the opening of the meeting.)

II-3 [["Gold Subscriptions"]], Alternative A [U.S.], "Payments when Quotas are Changed" [proposed Section 6]

Mr. Melville [Australia] suggested that the character of such payments should be determined at the time quotas are changed.

Lord Keynes stated that he saw no reason why the formula applied to subsequent quota payments should be different from the original formula used.

Mr. Luxford [U.S.] stated that the provision allowing gold payments equal to 10 percent of official gold holdings was appropriate only in terms of the unusual conditions prevailing at the end of the war.

Lord Keynes stated that he believed it might be most important to increase the quotas of those countries which did not have substantial supplies of gold and, therefore, that the retention of the 10 percent provision was desirable.

Mr. Rasminsky [Canada] supported Mr. Luxford's contention that the 10 percent reduction should not be permitted for countries other than the original participants in the Fund.

Mr. Varvaressos [Greece] expressed the belief that the conditions established for original members should also be applied to countries

---

[254] There is also another version of the minutes, also by Sundelson, which we have omitted because it is shorter and less detailed. It may have been a draft.

requesting membership at a later date.

II-3 [["Gold Subscriptions"]], Alternative B [USSR], "Reduction in Gold Payments for Countries Damaged by Hostilities"

Baron Boël [Belgium] stated that it would be extremely difficult to estimate the damage inflicted on different countries. He therefore recommended that the reduction in gold payments allowed for countries whose home areas have suffered from enemy occupation should be a flat reduction of 25 percent.

Lord Keynes agreed with Baron Boël and requested that the statement on this point included in the flimsy presented at an earlier date[255] also be included in Document F-1.

Mr. Smirnov [USSR] explained that the proposal submitted had attempted to differentiate among the various countries according to the extent of the damage suffered in order to apply different treatment. He believed it would be unfair to apply the same treatment to all countries without regard to the severity of the damage inflicted upon them. **Mr. Keilhau [Norway]** suggested that the reduction in gold payment be permitted for countries which have suffered from enemy "action," rather than enemy "occupation."

(Not in room.)

III-2, Alternative A [U.S.], "Conditions for Purchases of Currencies from the Fund"

Mr. Varvaressos feared that a delay might result if a country had to appear before the Fund and prove its need each time it wished to use the resources of the Fund. He believed it would be sufficient for a country merely to represent its need; if a country should represent falsely, the Fund will be able to declare it ineligible for further use of the resources of the Fund.

Mr. Beyen [Netherlands] supported Mr. Varvaressos but pointed out that since a declaration of ineligibility was a very drastic measure, there must be some halfway position between that and the complete acquiescence of the Fund to the use of its resources. He added that, while

---

[255] The flimsy "Payment of Subscription."

in general there would be no question of proof involved, the Fund should have the right to refuse some requests.

Lord Keynes proposed that the words of the Joint Statement, including "entitled" and "represents," both be reinserted.

Mr. Melville stated that he was in accord with Lord Keynes's proposal because he believed that a central bank must be certain that the resources it has counted upon will be available as required.

Mr. Bernstein [U.S.] objected to the idea that a mere statement of need is sufficient to draw upon the resources of the Fund.

Mr. Beyen stated that there can be no question of convincing the Fund on such matters and that the provision as it now stands in Alternative A is impossible.

Mr. White emphasized that when the granting of a request for foreign exchange would violate the purposes of the Fund, the Fund must be given sufficient flexibility to make its own decisions.

Lord Keynes stated of the Fund's power to refuse requests should relate only to future requests for funds.

Lord Keynes stated that he believed the second section on the bottom of page 6a [on the ineligibility of members to use the Fund] was a very desirable provision, but doubted that Article III was the appropriate place for it. He suggested two changes: (1) that the word "determined" in the first sentence of this provision should be changed, and (2) that the Fund, after giving reasonable notice to a country, be permitted either to restrict the amount of its quota which the country might use or declare it ineligible to use the resources of the Fund.

Mr. Monteros [Mexico] stated that since this provision dealt with the right of a country to use the resources of the Fund, it should be included in the section on withdrawal and suspension.

Mr. Bernstein stated that he believed it was unwise to assume that to limit a country's use of the Fund contained any implications of withdrawal or suspension.

III-2, Alternative B [Canada], "Use of the Fund for Capital Transactions"

Mr. Rasminsky [Canada] stated that although the restrictions on the use of the Fund for capital purposes were appropriate in the case of net users of the Fund's resources, they should not apply to capital exporters, which should be permitted to make their currencies available for purchasing foreign currencies from the Fund for capital transfers. The proposal, presented in Alternative B, would permit a country, so long as it has not been making net use of the resources of the Fund for six months, to use the resources of the Fund for any purpose whatever, including capital transactions.

Mr. White asked Mr. Rasminsky about the possibility of Canada's purchasing United States dollars, which might be equally scarce in the Fund.

Mr. Rasminsky stated that it would be necessary to draft the provision with due regard to the relative scarcities of particular currencies in the [Fund] and that, in particular, the country of the currency being bought must approve the transaction.

Mr. Coe [Secretary, U.S.] added that the general waiver provision and III-3 [["Limitation on Purchases"]][256] would permit this type of transaction if it were to the Fund's interests.

Mr. Bernstein pointed out that Article V also permitted the use of the Fund's resources for capital transactions of a reasonable amount.

Lord Keynes and **Mr. Istel [France]** expressed their approval of Mr. Rasminsky's proposal because it would enable a country to make certain that any capital export which it might wish to make would really be used in such a way as to replenish the resources of the Fund.

Mr. Melville called attention to the fact that if Mr. Rasminsky's proposal is already included in Provision [Article] V ["Capital Transactions"], to include the new amendment would have the effect of limiting the Fund's power in this connection, rather than expanding it.

Mr. Robertson [UK] stated that Article V is not intended to take care of Mr. Rasminsky's point.

Mr. White called attention to the fact that the words "large" and "sustained" had been used in Provision V so that neither the Fund or member countries would find it necessary to examine small transactions.

III-2, [Alternative] C, [Australia], "Limitation on the Use of the Fund's Resources"

Mr. Melville [Australia] explained that this provision, permitting a country to draw 33-1/3 percent of its quota during a twelve-month period, had been suggested to care for those countries having very small reserves outside the Fund because it was inappropriate that any country

---

[256] The original text says "III-3-2," an unclear reference.

should continually be forced to throw itself on the discretion of the Fund.

Mr. Beyen supported the provision and added that at the end of hostilities, it was likely that the ordinary credits used in commercial transactions would not be immediately available.

Mr. Bulhões [Brazil] suggested that he believed all agricultural countries would support the 33-1/3 percent provision because of the wide swings to which their economies are subject. He added that it might be desirable to require that the countries wishing to avail themselves of the 33-1/3 percent provision make larger gold contributions.

Mr. Monteros stated that countries producing raw materials were normally subject to these wide swings and that, therefore, this provision should be permitted to apply to countries without regard to the size of their resources outside the Fund.

Mr. [Felipe] Pazos [Cuba] presented an example of the problem being discussed. He said that if some of the formulas now being discussed were adopted, Cuba might have a quota of $[40 million], 25 percent of which would be $10 million. He compared with these figures the swings and she in Cuba's balance of payments, which he said ranged in the neighborhood of $100 million.

Mr. White pointed out that the ability of a country to purchase exchange is not limited to its quota. By a decision of the Executive Committee, the country may always exceed the quota.

Mr. Istel stated that the general purpose of the Fund was to supply funds for needs which were accidental and nonrecurrent, although for large amounts, and that it was not to be used for meeting regular capital requirements. He said there was a danger in Alternative C that countries would be induced to make the greatest possible use of their rights in the Fund.

Mr. White called attention to the fact of the Fund was not meant to handle the whole transactional problem, although it would facilitate the transaction adjustments required.

Mr. Melville agreed that the Fund should provide only working balances, but he felt that the present provision was not adequate for the swings likely to develop.

Mr. [Walter] Gardner [U.S.] pointed out that the 25 percent provision in the Joint Statement applies to any twelve months' period rather than to any calendar year. He also added that it would be difficult to take care of the volatile variations in the balance of payments of different countries.

Article III-4 [["Scarce Currencies"]], Alternative A [U.S.]

Mr. Luxford [U.S.] explained that the only change in substance in this provision was to give the Fund the right to borrow the currency of a member country with its approval from any source whatsoever

Lord Keynes expressed his approval of the provision.

(British version, no attribution)

Meetings

1. It was agreed that until further notice meetings should be held daily 10:30-12:30 and 4:30-6:30.

Agenda Subcommittee

2. The **Chairman [Harry Dexter White, U.S.]** announced that representatives of the UK, USSR, China, France, Mexico and the United States comprised the Agenda or Steering Subcommittee.

Management Subcommittee

3. The **Chairman** announced that the following countries had been invited to appoint representatives to the Committee on the management provisions of the Fund: China, Mexico, Netherlands. United States, USSR, under the chairmanship of Sir Wilfrid Eady (UK).

[Alternatives]

4. **Mr. Coe [Secretary, U.S.]** indicated that a few proposals had been omitted from the Document F-1 ["Preliminary Draft of Suggested Articles for the Establishment of an International Monetary Fund"], circulated that day. These would be circulated as soon as identified with the papers for the next day's meetings.

The **Chairman** explained that the various Alternatives which had been circulated would be examined and Delegates who desired to suggest further drafts should hand them to the Secretariat for distribution. The fact that a particular clause had been passed at any meeting did not commit any person present to accepting that as final. Any further proposal dealing with clauses already passed in discussion would constitute first business at the next morning.

International Monetary Fund: Constitution of Article I ["Purposes and Policies of the Fund"]

5. The alternative versions of the clause were discussed at some length, particularly as regards I-2, 3 and 4 [["Balanced Trade, High Employment and Real Income," "Lend to Members," "Promote Exchange Stability"]]. Apart from doubts whether all the points should be covered in this clause, the view was expressed that Alternative A [U.S.] would be acceptable for (1) and Alternative B [Australia] for (3). (2) remained unsettled, and (4) awaits a redraft designed to bring out the three elements in the original version. (5) is unchanged from the original text and (6) would be as in the B version. On Alternative C [Brazil], no discussion took place.

Article II-1 [["Total Amount"]]

6. On Section I, first new section (countries eligible for membership), there was a suggestion that this should be included in an article on Inauguration. On the content, it was explained that the adherence of e.g. the neutrals would be left to the charter members expressing their will through the organs of the Fund.

7. The section on quotas was left over as involving only drafting changes. As regards the amount, time and place of payment, it was suggested that disrupted countries would need special relief and also arrangements to deal with their legislative difficulties as regards to ratification.

Article II-2, "Adjustments of Quotas"

8. It was pointed out that the clause as drafted did not provide powers to change quotas, and it was not clear whether changes could take place at more frequent intervals than five years. **One delegate** pointed out that there were two sorts of quota changes possible: either (1) a change flowing from variations in the relevant statistics, or (2) in the formula for assessment. It was observed that the present Clause did not commit the Fund to a formula of any description.

Article II-3 [["Gold Subscriptions"]]

9. In the new section on initial payments (in Alternative A [U.S.]) the date January 1st, 1944 was challenged and it was suggested that either July 1st, 1944 or the end of the calendar year preceding the inauguration of the Fund would be more appropriate. It was also pointed out that occupied countries might not be at any selected date in a position to determine their monetary reserves with any precision.

10. In relation to the new section on changes of quota, the suggestion was made that the concessions as to gold subscription made on the initial institution of the Fund should be repeated when a quota was enlarged. It did not follow that because an increase in quota was justified the country was able to furnish 25 percent of the increase in gold; on the contrary, it might have no gold resources at all, that being one of the factors in its request for an increased quota. On the other hand, it was pointed out that certain powers of waiver existed and that as a long-term provision, the Fund was based on 25 percent gold subscription. As a compromise suggestion, the idea of allowing a country in such circumstances to purchase the necessary gold with its increased quota was put forward.

11. Alternative B [USSR] (which adds a new section to II-3 dealing with countries ravaged by the enemy) occasioned some controversy. On the one hand it was urged that measurement of degree of damage was exceptionally difficult and it was proposed accordingly that countries which satisfied a single simple criterion should be relieved of 25 percent of the gold subscription otherwise payable; on the other, the degrees of damage were considered to be significant and to require a varying degree of relief.

Article III-1 [["National Agency Dealing with Fund"]]

12. It was pointed out that Alternative A [U.S.] was in substitution of the first sentence only of the existing text. The second sentence was incorporated elsewhere.

Article III-2 [["Purchases of Another Members' Currency"]], Alternative A [U.S.; and other alternatives]

13. A long discussion took place on the conditions upon which member countries may purchase currencies of other member countries, or be deprived of their access to the facilities of the Fund. Two schools of

thought emerged. The first school stressed the importance of declaring in unequivocal terms the entitlement of a member country to buy currency from the Fund provided it could satisfy the conditions set out in III-2, and had not been given any notice of withdrawal in respect of future demands under the new section proposed (whereby the Fund may deprive a country of the use of its resources after due notice). The second urged that it was wrong for a country to be able to draw continuously from the Fund in breach of its obligations and the Fund must retain its discretion to deprive members of their access. In the result, the two groups did not seem to be so far apart as at the opening of the discussion. On the text of the new section, it was suggested that the second sentence should be strengthened by inserting after "country" in line 6 "(a) restricting the use of the quota or (b)." The word "last" in the next sentence should read "first." The word "determines" in line 1 was also criticized.

14. The inclusion of provision for collateral in the last sentence of Alternative A, first section, was challenged on the grounds that it might be impolite, and that the actual drafting seemed to mean that waiver always involved terms and terms always involved provision of collateral.

15. On III-2(1) [["Purchases of Another Member's Currency"]], the substitution of "provisions" for the existing "purposes and policies" met with general approval. It was felt that the suggestion that the new section on ineligibility should be associated with the article on Withdrawal would be bad psychology.

16. Alternative B [Canada]. The object of this amendment to sub-division (a), which is to promote the flow of a currency which might be becoming scarce into the Fund, where this can safely be done without causing a scarcity in another currency, found general support. It was felt, however, that the wording would have to be watched very carefully. There was also the effect of the prohibition on the use of the Fund to facilitate large and sustained capital movements to consider. It was pointed out that it is not practicable for the Fund to apply a ban on capital transfers extending to every conceivable type of exchange operation.

17. Several delegations commented on [Australia's] Alternative C to III-2 [["Purchases of Another Member's Currency"]], supporting the idea that countries which are subject to violent swings in the balance of payments, need a good deal of flexibility. Among the points mentioned were:

(1) Ordinary commercial credit would be limited during the initial period, until confidence had been restored;

(2) Provision for a higher annual drawing than 25 percent of quota might be made optional or contingent on a corresponding increase in the gold subscription.

(3) All raw material [producing] countries were subject to wide fluctuations, irrespective of their particular gold holdings.

(4) Some reliance must be placed on the waiver powers of the Fund.

(5) The purposes of the Fund would be defeated if all the emphasis was placed on use of its resources, and none on the necessary replenishment of its resources. While the Fund would be of assistance during the transitional period, it was not designed to deal fully with its problems.

(6) The year mentioned in III-2 is not a calendar year but a running 12 months.

(7) Member countries desiring special facilities from the Fund in excess of their quota might not enjoy sufficient voting strength to secure those facilities.

Article III-4 [["Scarce Currencies"]]

18. Alternative A, which amends the present text to make clear that purchases of scarce currency from another country are legitimate, if made with the first country's consent, support.

46

Formal Agenda Committee
Fourth meeting
Atlantic City
June 27, 1944 at 10:30 a.m.

Multilateral clearing • Acquisition of gold by the Fund

The Formal Agenda Committee continues its discussion of Article III of the IMF agreement with Section 5, which concerns the conditions on which IMF member countries may purchase the currencies of other members. The issue is central to the IMF, because most of its members will initially have currencies that are not fully convertible, so it is important to define the conditions neither so loosely as to invite abuse nor so strictly as to discourage postwar exchange. The committee then discusses provisions concerning acquisition of the currencies of members by other members for gold and the IMF's acquisition of gold. The United States, as the country with by far the largest gold reserves in the world at the time, is trying to avoid the IMF from acquiring gold disproportionately from U.S. reserves.

III-5, "Multilateral Clearing"

Mr. [Jan] Mládek [Czechoslovakia] suggested that a provision be added to III-5 [["Obligations of a Purchasing Country,"] Alternative C, Czechoslovakia] which would make it clear that currency which has found its way out of a country in violation of that country's currency laws should not be entitled to be repurchased under III-5.

Dr. [Tingfu] Tsiang [China] raised the question of holdings of currency by enemy countries and suggested that this problem be considered sometime in the course of the [Bretton Woods] international monetary conference. The **Chairman [Harry Dexter White, U.S.]** suggested that this question be considered by the Agenda Committee.

Sir Jeremy Raisman [India] stated that India wished to include a statement with regard to war balances in the section on purposes and policies of the Fund [Article I].

Mr. [Dennis] Robertson [UK] stated that in Alternative A [U.S.] for III-5 it should be made clear that if a member country offers the currency of a second member country to such member, the option of payment in its own currency or in gold should rest with the second member country.

Mr. [Ansel] Luxford [U.S.] suggested the following addition to Alternative A: "Nothing in this section shall be deemed to modify or effect the obligation of a member country under IX-2 [["Foreign Exchange Dealings"]] and IX-3 [["Current Transactions"]]."

Lord Keynes suggested that in Alternative A the word "early" should be deleted.

Mr. [Louis] Rasminsky [Canada] suggested the deletion of "a current account nature" in Alternative A.

Lord Keynes referred to the British alternative proposal on page 30 in which the substance of III-5 is placed under the section on obligations of the members.

Mr. Rasminsky raised the question as to what exactly was meant by the term "currently acquired" and under what conditions balances currently acquired may be converted.

Lord Keynes stated that balances currently acquired can be converted unless they have been used for making capital investments in the country. Lord Keynes stated further that he preferred not to have rigid definitions of capital and current transactions, but that rather the Fund should build up case law in respect to what transactions were to be considered as current transactions or capital transactions. In regards to this point, **Sir Theodore Gregory [India]** objected that balances are often built up in sterling over a period of two years and then withdrawn, and that unless such balances could be withdrawn at a later stage it would be disadvantageous to a raw material producing country. India's position was that the Fund plan must be explicit on this point.

Mr. Rasminsky raise the question as to whether a country which asked another country to repurchase its own currency would be asked for what purpose the balances were to be used. He further asked regarding the conditions under which countries would not be required to repurchase their own currencies under III-5.

Mr. [Edward] Bernstein [U.S.] pointed out that under the language proposed by the British in Alternative B for Article III-5 a member country would be required to repurchase its own currency if the member offering that country represents that the balances in question have been currently acquired or that their conversion is needed for making current payments.

262

III-6, "Acquisition by Member Countries of the Currency of Other Member Countries for Gold" [Alternative A, U.S.]

Mr. Rasminsky asked what was meant in III-6 by "with equal advantage." **Lord Keynes** replied that this phrase was purposely vague and not limited to questions of price.

Mr. White stated that the Fund would be able to raise questions as to the degree of equal advantage, although he admitted that the term "equal advantage" seriously weakened the provision.

III-7, "The Acquisition of Gold by the Fund"

It was agreed that 7(b) in Alternative A [U.S.] needed clarification and **Mr. Luxford** stated we would redraft this provision.

Baron Boël [Belgium] stated that in his view, accumulations of gold and gold convertible exchange under 7(c) should be related to the increase of such holdings above the amount held by the member country at the time of joining the Fund. Baron Boël agreed to put his amendment in writing.

Mr. [August] Maffry [U.S.] stated that 7(b) and 7(c) already represented a substantial concession to those countries which had been occupied or had suffered severe damage, since the ideal situation would be to require all countries with gold and gold convertible exchange in excess of their quotas to use their own resources for the purchase of foreign exchange rather than go through the Fund.

Mr. [Walter] Gardner [U.S.] pointed out that the requirement to pay gold will not diminish the resources of a member country if it included as a part of its resources the ability to draw on the Fund; to the extent that a country repurchases its currency with gold, it thereby increases its rights to draw on the Fund.

Lord Keynes acknowledged his agreement with Messrs. Gardner and Maffry. However, he stated that if it were decided to depart from the original statement, he suggests the addition of loss or damage to Alternative B [USSR].

Mr. Smirnov [USSR] took issue with Mr. Gardner, on the grounds that the Fund cannot grant credits for the purpose of making purchases for capital equipment for reconstruction, so that a member country would not be in the same position if it had additional rights to draw on the Fund rather than gold.

47

Formal Agenda Committee
Fifth meeting
Atlantic City
June 27, 1944 at 4:30 p.m.

Transfer of gold and guarantee of the assets of the Fund • Charges and commissions • Consideration of recommendations of the Fund Furnishing information • Par value of member currencies

The committee continues its review of Article III of the IMF agreement. Most of the discussion is about the IMF's proposed charges and commissions on loans to member countries. Most countries at Atlantic City expect to be net borrowers from the IMF, so it is understandable that they think the proposed charges, which increase as the ratio of borrowing to a member's quota rises, are too harsh. The United States, which will be the main net lender to the IMF, is on the other side of the debate.

Delegates also discuss the extent to which the IMF should be able to have information about and comment on the economic policies of members. It is a question of balance between the IMF's responsibilities as a steward of the international monetary order and the necessity of being responsive to the political sensitivities of its members. At the end of the meeting, John Maynard Keynes proposes that currencies be expressed in gold as a common denominator. Keynes's criticisms of the gold standard over more than thirty years are well known, and he does not intend for gold to have the leading role in the international monetary system that it did before World War II. The practical alternative to gold as the common denominator, however, would be the U.S. dollar, the only major currency that will be freely usable, without extensive exchange controls, after the war. For the British delegation, using the dollar would be an unwelcome acknowledgment of the inferiority of the pound sterling.

"Transfer of Gold and Guarantee of the Assets of the Fund" [proposed new Section III-9, Alternative A, U.S.]

Mr. [Edward] Bernstein [U.S.] explained the reason for the second sentence under Alternative A [U.S.] as being the need for assuring that the Fund's holdings of any member's currency could be used to purchase imports from that country.

Lord Keynes agreed to the second sentence of this provision, but objected to the first sentence on the grounds that it was both redundant and not sufficiently limited.

"Charges and Commissions" [proposed new Section III-10, Alternative A, U.S.]

Lord Keynes suggested that a commission be formed to deal with the following technical problems: charges and commissions; the range of exchange rate fluctuations the buying and selling prices of gold; and the location of the Fund's gold depositories. It was agreed that this commission would be appointed.[257] **Mr. Gardner [U.S.]** explained and justified section [paragraph] (c) of Alternative A [U.S.] under "Charges and Commissions."[258]

Mr. Beyen [Netherlands] was critical of the principle involved in section (c) on the grounds that the Fund should not attempt to prevent the misuse of its resources by means of penalties. He stated that it would only work a hardship on those countries which were in good faith, but that it would not deter those countries which were in bad faith.

Mr. Gardner pointed out that the charges were not intended to keep the resources of the Fund from those really in need.

Lord Keynes stated that he agreed with the principle of progressive charges but believed that the charges as presented in the table were too harsh. Lord Keynes suggested that there be no charge up to 125 percent [of quota], ½ percent up to 150 [percent], and after that the charges should be about one-half of our own [American] schedule. **Mr. Gardner** pointed out that these charges were only marginal charges, and it was shown that the average percentage charge would work out to be much lower.

Mr. Smirnov [USSR] supported the view that the schedule of payments as presented was prohibitive. He, however, did not object to the principle of increasing rates as a function of time and amount. He further pointed out that the rates should not be independent of prevailing market rates and that exact rates should not be stated in the agreement

---

[257] Apparently the Subcommittee for Consideration of Certain Technical Matters.
[258] Evidently the explanation involved the table of charges in conference Document F-4, reproduced in chapter 77.

but left to the discretion of the Fund. **Mr. Varvaressos [Greece]** agreed that the principle of penalties and deterrence on the use of the Fund's resources was not in accord with the spirit of the Fund proposal.

Mr. Melville [Australia] objected both to the scale of charges and to the principle, at least up to 200 percent of the quota. He also mentioned that charges might be put on creditors as well.[259]

Mr. White relinquished the Chairmanship to Lord Keynes and explained at length the need for the charges. He stated that treasuries and central banks, in deciding on alternative courses, should be confronted with the fact of higher costs in using the resources of the Fund over other means of securing an adjustment in the balance of payments position of a country. Mr. White also pointed out that it is the creditor country's currency which is used, and that they should be compensated for the cost of borrowing that currency in their own markets.

Lord Keynes suggested two lines of compromise: (1) a small flat charge for any use of the resources of the Fund; (2) start progressive charges only after the first or second year after the resources have been acquired.

Lord Keynes objected to section [paragraph] (d), which states that all charges and commissions shall be paid in gold, and suggested that this should be modified in the case of countries whose holdings of gold and gold convertible exchange were less than half their quota. In such cases he recommended that the charges be paid by reducing the quota of the country by the amount of the charges. **Mr. White** took the view that this would not be an adequate deterrent on borrowing countries.

Mr. [Antonín] Basch [Czechoslovakia] agreed with Lord Keynes.

"Furnishing Information" [proposed new III-11, Alternative A, U.S.]

Mr. Maffry [U.S.] explained the purpose of this provision and stated that a list of required information would be furnished later on. **Lord Keynes** stated that in his view the list should be comprehensive and that the greater the range of the better it would be for the Fund.

Mr. Beyen [Netherlands] thought that we should not attempt to delimit the information with the Fund might require, but make it as general as possible.

---

[259] As in Keynes's plan for an International Clearing Union.

Sir Theodore Gregory [India] took the view that there must be some limitation on the information which the Fund could require because of the limited statistical facilities of many of the member countries.

Mr. White stated that one of the important objectives of the Fund is to get countries to gradually improve their statistical data.

"Consideration of Recommendations of the Fund" [III, proposed additional new section following proposed new Section 12, Alternative A, U.S.]

Mr. Goldenweiser [U.S.] discussed this topic and stated that if countries were not meeting their obligations under the purposes and policies of the Fund, the Fund should make recommendations to such countries.

Lord Keynes called attention to an alternative draft on page 37 [Alternative B, UK], which in his estimation would prevent the Fund from making formal recommendations with regard to domestic policies of a member country.

Mr. Goldenweiser stated that he preferred Alternative A [U.S.] on the grounds that it limited the field of recommendations and provided for a formal report, which in his opinion would be more effective.

Mr. Varvaressos [Greece] considers that such a report would be dangerous and an intrusion on the sovereignty of the member countries.

Mr. Keilhau [Norway] suggested that instead of the term "policy" there either be substituted the term "conditions" or "developments."

Sir Theodore Gregory asked if the term "consideration" implies the obligation on the part of the country to make a reply.

Mr. Luxford [U.S.] suggested that in the preparation of a report on economic conditions that the representative of the member country concerned be included as a member of the committee making the report.

Mr. Smirnov [USSR] expressed objection to the provision on recommendations in Alternative A and argued for the substitution of Alternative C [USSR] on page 12b.

IV-1, "Par Values of Member Currencies"

Lord Keynes suggested that currencies be expressed in terms of gold as a common denominator.

48

Formal Agenda Committee
Sixth meeting
Atlantic City
June 28, 1944 at 10:30 a.m.

Note on definitions • Convertibility • Monetary reserves • IMF acquisition of gold from members • Fund's refusal of a change in parity • Metropolitan and colonial currencies • Scarce currency • Holdings of gold and currencies• Committee on supplying information • Committee on technical problems

The British delegation initiates a discussion of certain definitions that affect multiple articles of the IMF agreement. The definitions are important because, for instance, they will affect whether a country can count its holdings of another country's currency as convertible exchange.

The committee moves through various provisions of the agreement, from the portions of Article III not discussed at the previous meeting through Article VII. The issues that attract the most discussion concern scarce currencies and depositories. As we explained in chapter 6, it was expected that for at least a few years after World War II, the existence of exchange controls on the currencies of many IMF members would limit the IMF's effectively usable resources to its holdings of gold and fully convertible currencies — in practice, overwhelmingly U.S. dollars. If each member borrowed as much convertible currency as it was entitled to do, there would not be enough for all. As it turned out, the IMF never had to invoke the scarce currency clause. Concerning depositories, a Dutch delegate who is a former president of the Bank for International Settlements criticizes the American proposal that at least half the IMF's gold holdings be deposited in the country where the IMF has its headquarters (which will be the United States). He also asks whether the IMF might not generate revenue by holding interest-bearing securities issued by members as an alternative to charges and commissions.

Two versions exist of the minutes of this meeting, both by the American delegation.

(Version by Henry J. Bittermann)

(References to the text are to the Fund statement of April 21, 1944 [the Joint Statement], and to the "Preliminary Draft of Suggested Articles of Agreement for the Establishment of an International Monetary Fund," document F-1.)

The discussion opened with consideration of [the UK's] Document F-5, "A Note on Certain Definitions." **Lord Keynes** suggested that [paragraph 1 of] the original draft should be amended and the words "monetary reserves" be substituted for the original expression "gold and gold convertible exchange." Strictly speaking, he said, there is no gold convertible exchange.[260] In the original draft the intention was to include gold and U.S. dollars. His proposal was that member countries might accept the conditions of IX-3 [["Current Transactions"]] and, by so doing, their currency would become convertible for the purpose of the Fund. (Cf. [Document] F-4 ["Minimum Percentage Charges Payable by a Country on Fund's Holdings of Its Currency in Excess of Its Quota"], page 34a.) **Mr. [Alvin] Hansen [U.S.]** suggested "international monetary reserves" would be a preferable term in view of the pre-emption of the other term. To this **Lord Keynes** had no objection.

The **Chairman [Harry Dexter White, U.S.]** called the attention the committee to the fact that monetary reserves might be kept in banks other than the central bank. **Mr. Basch [Czechoslovakia]** raised the question of when the balances in banks other than the central bank were to be regarded as excessive and asked who was to determine the amount. **Mr. Bernstein [U.S.]** called attention to the Alternative A [U.S.] (page 37) referred to in Article XII, Section [2, "Definitions," paragraph] (b), which would include as convertible exchange any foreign currency which could be used directly or indirectly for the purchase of gold. **Mr. Rasminsky [Canada]** suggested the substitution of the foreign exchange holdings of the bank.[261] Lord Keynes insisted that the only basis of distinction of convertibility of currency was the legal acceptance of the obligation of convertibility under IX-3 [["Current Transactions"]]. **Mr.**

---

[260] The United States remained on the gold standard during World War II in principle, but wartime trading regulations and the dangers of ocean shipping in wartime meant that in practice, foreigners could not freely convert U.S. dollars for gold and ship the gold abroad as they had been able to do before the war.

[261] It is unclear whether this should say "the Fund," whether it instead means the central bank, or whether the phase should have been "the banks," which would have included commercial banks.

Rasminsky raised the issue whether nonmember currencies would be regarded as convertible in the sense. **Lord Keynes** wished to let the Fund decide in particular cases.

Mr. Bernstein defined "net official gold holdings" as equal to gold plus gold convertible currency minus gold liabilities. **Lord Keynes** regarded this definition as satisfactory for the subscription but argued that later it would be unacceptable for other purposes. The **Chairman** concluded the discussion by suggesting the preparation of a table which would show how the use of each definition would affect the situation of some three countries.[262]

With reference to Article III, Section 7 [["Fund's Acquisition of Gold"]], **Lord Keynes** called attention to [the UK's] Alternative C (page 11b). The objectives of the original draft, he said, could be evaded merely by increasing the turnover of exchange. The purpose of Alternative C is identical with that of the original draft. He pointed out that the introduction of "gold convertible exchange" in this clause might develop into a situation in which a country which has no increment of gold is nevertheless required to pay gold to the Fund as part of its increased holdings in gold and gold exchange. **Mr. Bernstein** suggested the reference of this question to the Committee on Definitions [at Bretton Woods]. **Mr. Varvaressos [Greece]** spoke in favor of Alternative E [Greece], which would permit the Fund to waive the conditions for currency repurchases in special cases.

Article IV ["Par Values of Member Currencies"] (page 13) was passed for later consideration when additional material would be supplied. No changes were made in Article IV, Section 5 [["Uniform Changes in Par Values"]] (page 15). With reference to the supplementary material added to Article IV (page 16), **Sir Wilfrid Eady [UK]** queried whether the clause applied to changes in parity or de facto depreciation without a change of parity. The **Chairman** said that the intention was to cover both cases. **Prof. Robertson [UK]** commented that actual depreciation could not occur under the terms of the Fund. The **Chairman** indicated that it should not, but provision should be made for the contingency of a country refusing to take proper measures at a time when the Fund refused a change in its parity. **Sir Wilfrid** suggested that a redrafting of this provision would make clear the precise implications for the two cases. This was satisfactory to the Committee.

Discussing Alternative B to Article IV, additional section (page 16)

---

[262] We have not found such a table.

proposed by the Netherlands delegation [on separate currencies used within a member country], **Mr. Crena de Iongh [Netherlands]** mentioned the specific case of the Netherlands and the Netherlands Indies, which had a common currency, and suggested that the provision of this article should be applied to each of these currencies.[263] **Prof. Robertson** asked for time to consider this question since the UK and its colonies have a single quota. In his opinion, changes in the relative values of the pound sterling and the colonial currencies are beyond the operation of the Fund.

Article V, Section 1 [["Use of Fund to Finance Capital Controls"]], Alternative B [Canada] was passed over without decision.

Referring to VI-1 [and] 2 [["Fund Warning of Scarcity" and "Rationing of Scarce Currencies"], Alternative A, U.S.] (page 19a), **Mr. Bernstein [U.S.]** made the distinction between the general scarcity of a currency and a scarcity in the Fund holdings of a currency. The new provisions permit the Fund to anticipate a scarcity in its holdings and permit the issue of a report in advance of the formal declaration of scarcity. He pointed out that under the provisions of VI-[2, ["Rationing of Scarce Currencies"]], the member country is entitled to ration any scarce currency but may not permit its appreciation on exchanges beyond the agreed range.

Sir Wilfrid Eady, as Chairman of the Special Committee on Management, reported that it would be ready to submit its findings in the afternoon meeting of June 29th.

Mr. Luxford [U.S.] gave an explanation of the additional section added to Article VII (page 23) [proposed Section 6, "Depositories," Alternative A, U.S.]. **Mr. Beyen [Netherlands]** offered the criticism that elaboration of these clauses was unnecessary and that the Fund should be given discretion in its disposition of gold according to circumstances and needs. **Dr. Keilhau [Norway]** suggested that a rigid allocation is undesirable, since unpredictable circumstances in the future might require a rapid transfer gold holdings from one place to another. **Prof. Smirnov [USSR]** asked for deferment of the question to a later date in view of a new draft being submitted. With reference to Alternative A (page 23), the **Chairman** indicated that it was his understanding that the Fund was to determine the amount of a local currency which would be needed for

---

[263] The Netherlands Indies (now Indonesia) had a separate note issue and coinage from the Netherlands, but the Netherlands Indies guilder was equal to the Dutch guilder, so in that sense they had a common currency.

current transactions and that the balance might be paid by the member countries in the noninterest-bearing demand note. **Mr. Beyen** favored the substitution of interest-bearing securities of the member countries for the special form of note proposed in the draft. He suggested that interest in local currency secured in this way would be preferable to the system of charges for the purchases of currency proposed in the meeting of June 27.[264] **Mr. Rasminsky [Canada]** emphasized that the distinction should be made [between] the local currency offered on subscription and currency acquired in the course of its business at a later time by the Fund.

The following committees were appointed:

A committee on the supplying of information by member countries. Mr. [A.P.] Morozov (USSR) was designated chairman and the other members were to be designated by the heads of the delegations of India, Netherlands, Brazil, Canada, and the U.S. Mr. [August] Maffry was designated as the U.S. member.

The ad hoc committee to consider certain technical problems was to be composed of representatives of the U.S., UK, Canada, the Netherlands, and Czechoslovakia. Mr. [Walter] Gardner was designated as chairman with Mr. [Raymond] Mikesell as additional U.S. representative. Special questions referred to this committee are page 12, [Alternatives] A [U.S.] and B [USSR] [III, additional section]; page 13a [IV-1, ["Establishing Par Value,"] Alternative B, UK]; page 20, Alternative A [U.S.], second paragraph [VII-1, ["Board and Executive Committee,"]]; page 23 [Article VII, proposed Section 6, "Depositories," Alternative A, U.S.]; and the definition of gold holdings [in relation to II-3, ["Gold Subscription"]].

(Version by Dorothy F. Richardson)

Document F-5, "Note on Additional Material" [UK], was discussed. **Lord Keynes (UK)** called attention to the use of the terms "monetary reserve," "net," "official," and "convertible."

In regards to the term "convertible," Lord Keynes remarked that at the present time there is no currency which is "gold convertible." It is therefore advantageous to have a definition which will include not only dollars at the present time but which will include other currencies in the future.

---

[264] See the previous chapter.

The term "monetary reserves" was discussed. **Mr. Rasminsky (Canada)** remarked that it would be necessary to determine the amount of a country's monetary reserves for purposes of determining its initial payments to the Fund before the country joined the Fund. However, the amount of its monetary reserves will depend upon what countries have accepted the obligations of convertibility under IX-3 [["Current Transactions"]]. **Lord Keynes** pointed out that X-3 [["Restrictions on Exchange"]] provides that member countries will indicate whether they accept the obligation of convertibility under IX-3 "after the establishment of a Fund but before it commences operations."

Mr. Bernstein (U.S.) felt that the appropriateness of the definition of the term "monetary reserves" would depend upon whether or not all currencies were convertible. **Lord Keynes** pointed out that liabilities in a currency would not be deductible until that currency became convertible.

Mr. Hansen (U.S.) suggested that the term "international monetary reserves" or "international reserves" would be preferable to the term "monetary reserves." The **Chairman** suggested that until further decision we should use the term "international monetary reserves."

The term "official" was discussed. In reply to a question by **Dr. Basch (Czechoslovakia), Lord Keynes (UK)** stated that it was expected that the determination of the amount of a country's holdings of gold and "convertible" currencies which are in excess of necessary working balances would be left to the decision of the Fund. The **Chairman** remarked that this point involved a substantial problem which the U.S. technical experts have tried to meet in an earlier draft, and asked **Mr. Bernstein (U.S.)** to read aloud section [paragraph] (c) of [proposed Section 2, Alternative A, U.S., for] Article XII, "Definitions."

Mr. Rasminsky (Canada) suggested that the British provision might be altered by substitution of the phrase, "but should include the holdings of institutions other than the Central Bank when resources of gold and convertible currency are customarily held by those institutions" for the phrase "in excess of working balances." The **Chairman** referred this point to the Special Committee for Consideration of Technical Matters.

The term "convertible" was then discussed. The **Chairman** stated that there are three types of currencies: (a) currencies which are freely convertible; (b) currencies which are freely convertible for the purposes of the proposed Fund; and (c) currencies on which the issuing country imposes special restrictions. He suggested that it would be possible to define the term "convertible" for practical purposes by reference to these three categories. **Lord Keynes (UK)** felt that the legal test of whether or not a country had accepted the convertibility provisions of this document [the IMF Articles of Agreement] was a preferable method of defining this term.

The **Chairman** pointed out that some holdings of currencies of countries which had accepted the convertible [i.e., convertibility] provision of the Fund would not be convertible, for example, holdings resulting from capital transactions. **Lord Keynes (UK)** replied that all balances accumulated by one country in any other country which had accepted the obligation of convertibility would have to be considered to be convertible, since it would be impossible to tell whether restrictions will be placed upon transfers under the provisions of the Fund until a request for transfer is made. **Mr. Bernstein (U.S.)** remarked that this definition of the term would lead to a variety of borderline cases which would have to be resolved by reference to the practice of the country. **Lord Keynes (UK)** expressed agreement with this view.

Mr. Rasminsky (Canada) inquired whether any thought had been given to the question of the convertibility of nonmember currencies. **Lord Keynes (UK)** stated that it had been assumed that all large countries would be members of this institution. However, if this should not be the case, it will be necessary to establish regulations governing the relations between member and nonmember countries. **Mr. Bernstein (U.S.)** suggested that the definition of gold convertible currencies in Section [2, paragraph] (b) of [proposed new] Article XII, "Definitions" [Alternative A, U.S.], might be applied to nonmember currencies. **Lord Keynes (UK)** felt that this definition would be acceptable for the initial period but would not be appropriate if the British definition of the term "convertible" was later used. The **Chairman** felt that in any de facto situation it would not be difficult to determine whether or not it was possible to obtain gold for any specified currency. **Lord Keynes (UK)** preferred giving the Fund broad powers to determine whether a nonmember currency was convertible to attempting to establish rules and regulations that in advance of knowing the actual situation.

The **Chairman** suggested that a table be prepared showing the amount of several countries' gold and convertible holdings as determined by the several definitions.[265]

---

[265] We have not found such a table.

Article III, Section 7 [["Fund's Acquisition of Gold"]], Alternative C [UK]

In regards to Part 1, **Dr. Mládek (Czechoslovakia)** inquired whether the decision as to whether contributions should be made in gold or in a convertible currency would be made by the member country or by the Fund. **Lord Keynes** answered that under Part 1 the member country would make this decision, but that under Part 2 there would be no option. **Mr. Gardner (U.S.)** felt that a country could escape the repurchase provisions of III-7, [Alternative] C by holding dollars instead of gold.

The **Chairman** suggested that this provision be referred to the subcommittee which will be appointed to set up the table referred to above.

Mr. Melville (Australia) inquired as to the effect on a country's "monetary reserves" when a currency which has previously been "nonconvertible" becomes "convertible." The **Chairman** suggested that this point would require special consideration.

Article III, Section 7 [["Fund's Acquisition of Gold"]], Alternative D [Greece]

Ambassador Varvaressos (Greece) called attention to III-7, [Alternative] D, and pointed out that this provision was intended to cover exceptional cases.

Article IV, Section 5 [["Uniform Changes in Par Values"]], Alternative A [U.S.]

The **Chairman** suggested that, since we have already discussed IV-1, [Alternative] A, "Initial Par Values of the Currencies of Member Countries," and that since some additional material is being prepared which relates to this provision and to provisions IV-2, IV-2 and IV-4 [on par values], we should proceed to a discussion of provision IV-5.

Article IV, Section 5, Alternatives A [U.S.] and B [Canada]

IV-5, [Alternative] A and IV-5, [Alternative] B constitute only changes in wording.

Article IV and additional section, "Protection of the Assets of the Fund," Alternative A [U.S.]

Mr. Luxford [U.S.] explained the purpose of this provision and called attention to the fact that the second paragraph of Alternative A should be deleted. Sir Wilfrid Eady inquired concerning the meaning of the term "has depreciated." The Chairman explained that there will be two types of changes in exchange rates: (a) changes undertaken under the provisions of the Fund and (b) de facto or market alterations, and that this provision is intended to cover both types of depreciation. Sir Wilfrid Eady (UK) felt that if a de facto depreciation occurred, other consequences would follow besides the necessity to compensate the Fund for the depreciation in the value of its assets. He felt that all provisions relating to de facto depreciation should be collected under an article on disciplinary measures. Since this question concerns the format of the draft, it was not discussed further.

Article IV, Additional Section, "Protection of the Assets of the Fund," Alternative B [Netherlands]

This provision was explained by Mr. de Iongh (Netherlands). Mr. [Dennis] Robertson (UK) remarked that he had thought that variations in colonial rates would be outside the jurisdiction of the Fund, and suggested that this provision should be considered more thoroughly. The Chairman agreed with Mr. de Iongh that colonial exchanges should be within the jurisdiction of the Fund.

Article V, Section 1 [["Use of Fund to Finance Capital Controls"]], Alternative B [Canada]

Mr. Rasminsky (Canada) pointed out that this provision is closely related to III-2 [["Limitations on Operations"], Alternative] B [Canada].

Article VI, Sections 1 and 2 [["Use of Fund to Finance Capital Controls" and "Capital and Current Controls"]], Alternative A [U.S.]

Mr. Bernstein (U.S.) pointed out that Section 1 of this provision introduces the concept of a general scarcity [of a currency]. The Chairman pointed out that this provision does not refer to the Fund's holdings of a currency but to general trends in international balances of payments. **Mr. Istel (France)** remarked that this question had been discussed at length in Committee 2 and that he felt that the present wording of the provision on scarce currencies constitutes an improvement over the provisions of the Joint Statement.

Mr. Bernstein (U.S.) pointed out the changes of substance and changes of emphasis in Section 2, "Scarcity of the Fund's Holdings." He called attention to the use of the phrase "seriously threatens." Thus the Fund can anticipate a scarcity of its holdings of any currency. He also called attention to the restriction introduced in the last line, "member countries shall have complete jurisdiction subject to the provisions of Article IX, Section 3."[266] Thus a country may not bring about a de facto depreciation of the exchange rate of another country by offering the country's currency at auction.

Sir Wilfrid Eady (UK) announced that the Management Committee met yesterday and would meet again today and that they expected to have a report ready for the consideration of the full group by tomorrow. Discussion of the provisions on management was deferred until that report has been submitted.

Article VII, Additional Section, "Depositories," Alternative A [U.S.]

Mr. Luxford (U.S.) explained this provision. **Mr. Rasminsky (Canada)** stated that the phrase in subsection (a) "in an amount not less than that deemed by the Fund to be necessary for its operation" was not necessary.

Dr. Beyen (Netherlands) felt that in subsection (b) of this provision it was not necessary to specify that one-half of the holdings of gold of the Fund should be deposited in that country in which the Fund has its principal office. **Prof. Smirnov (USSR)** read a provision on this point which the Russian delegation has just submitted to the Secretariat but which has not yet been distributed [Article VIII, additional Section, "Depositories," Alternative B?], and suggested that all further discussion of this point be reserved until the [Bretton Woods] Conference.

Dr. Beyen (Netherlands) inquired why the Fund's holdings of securities should be non-interest-bearing. He suggested that the Fund's holdings of securities should be interest-bearing and that the provisions

---

[266] Article IX, Section 3 [["Current Transactions"]] obligates members not to impose exchange controls on current transactions or engage in discriminatory currency practices.

on charges and commissions should be deleted. **Mr. Istel (France)** felt that, since it is desirable that there should be no inducement for the Fund to make a profit, the Fund's holdings of securities should be non-interest-bearing.

Mr. Rasminsky (Canada) felt that some distinction should be made between a country's initial currency subscription and subsequent currency contributions to the Fund as to whether these could be held in the form of securities, and called attention to the fact that there are different implications for country in contributing currency and in contributing securities. **Mr. Luxford (U.S.)** replied that the provisions on charges would prevent abuse of the provision that part of the Fund's holdings of member currency may be held in the form of securities.

*   *   *

The **Chairman** announced that we expect to complete the first discussion of Document F-1 [the IMF Articles of Agreement] tomorrow morning. We will then discuss the Bank proposal. A meeting of the Steering Committee was announced for 12:45 a.m., this morning [i.e., 12:45 p.m., this afternoon], in Mr. White's office.

The membership of the Subcommittee on the Obtaining of Information by the Fund was announced. This committee will be [chaired] by the USSR (Mr. [A.P.] Morozov) and will include representatives of India, the Netherlands, Brazil, Canada and United States ([August] Maffry).

The membership of the Subcommittee for Consideration of Certain Technical Problems was announced. This committee will be [chaired] by the United States ([Walter] Gardner) and will include representatives of the United Kingdom, Canada, the Netherlands, and Czechoslovakia.

A meeting of the Management Subcommittee was announced for 2:30 p.m. in room 206.

The **Secretary [Frank Coe, U.S.]** announced that documents relating to transportation [to Bretton Woods] are now available.

49

Formal Agenda Committee
Seventh meeting
Atlantic City
June 28, 1944 at 4:30 p.m.

Management of the Fund • Withdrawal from the Fund •
Obligations of member countries • Transitional arrangements •
Liquidation of the Fund

The committee concludes its discussion of Article VII of the draft IMF articles and moves through various provisions to Article X, which marks the end of the Joint Statement. The British delegation would strongly prefer that the IMF be located in London, or if not, in New York rather than in Washington, D.C., which they consider too close to the center of American political power. Lengthy consideration follows concerning the provisions that will apply to members that withdraw from the IMF and to the liquidation of the organization itself if necessary (which, 75 years later, still has not been). The committee then turns to the provisions concerning exchange controls on current payments and how long after the war members would be allowed to continue them. The British expected that they themselves would a transition period of five years rather than the three years that the Americans were pushing for, but John Maynard Keynes criticizes making the transitional period unlimited. In the IMF articles as the Bretton Woods conference approved them and as they exist today, though, the transitional period remains unlimited, and a few members still have exchange controls on current payments. After decades, the IMF agreement contains no requirement that members make their currencies free of controls for capital transactions, although many members, especially rich countries, have done so.

Two versions exist of the minutes of this meeting, both by the American delegation.

(Version by Henry J. Bittermann)

Sir Wilfrid Eady [UK] proposed Alternative B [UK] (page 23b) as an additional section to be included in Article VII ["Management of the Fund"]. This alternative provided that the Council [Board of Governors] should have power to make agreements with other international economic organizations and the world organization [the United Nations] to be constituted after the war, if its action is approved by three-fifths majority vote. **Mr. [Jan] Mládek (Czechoslovakia)** believed that a normal majority should be sufficient. **Sir Wilfrid Eady** agreed on behalf of the UK. **Mr. White** opposed this alternative on the grounds that the agreements and arrangements contemplated might limit the actions of the Fund and in consequence raise opposition to it. The U.S. would propose a new alternative at a later date and [he] suggested passing over this section.

The question of location of offices was raised and, at the suggestion of the **Chairman,** passed over. **Lord Keynes,** however, wished to make it clear that the UK did not accept the provisions of the draft. He believed that the location of the headquarters of the Fund would have to be considered in the light of the ultimate location of the Bank and other international institutions set up as the result of the war. For convenience in performing its work it might be necessary to have a Fund headquarters located outside of the U.S. He indicated that Great Britain might not be willing to discuss this question at the [Bretton Woods] conference and might reserve its position.

The next matter taken up was the distribution of net income as proposed in [VII, proposed additional section], Alternative A [U.S.] (page 23a). **Mr. Luxford [U.S.]** explained the proposal for using half of the net earnings for surplus and distributing the balance to the member countries with a 2 percent payment on the amount of currency used and with the balance in proportion according to quotas. **Lord Keynes** believed that the distribution of the net earnings should take place, but that the entire amount should be assigned to surplus. If, at some future time, the surplus became more than necessary or desirable, the distribution of earnings should be made at the discretion of the directors. **Mr. Beyen (Netherlands)** agreed with Lord Keynes's position. **Mr. Bernstein [U.S.]** argued that since half of the earnings were first assigned to surplus, the provisions for the security of the Fund would be entirely adequate. In the applying to an inquiry, it was suggested by the **Chairman** that the countries whose currencies were actively used by the Fund would incur a cost in providing their quotas, since the government would have to borrow on the open market. The elimination of the payments to the countries whose currencies were in use would be justifiable only if the quotas could be distributed without cost. **Lord Keynes** agreed that since all countries are burdened with a national debt, the provision of their currency would constitute a real burden.

At the **Chairman's** suggestion the miscellaneous powers provisions [VII, proposed additional section, Alternative A, U.S.] (page 23a), were passed over at the meeting and referred to a special committee.[267] **Mr. [Eric] Beckett (UK)** suggested that the same committee consider other questions of an essentially legal nature arising under the Fund, such as the immunities of the Fund, its legal power to begin suit, the question of extraterritoriality, etc.

The next question considered was the right of a member country to withdraw under [Australia's] Alternative B, Article VIII, Section 1 [["Procedure for Withdrawal"]], providing that the right of withdrawal from the Fund shall not be prejudiced by membership in the Fund being made a condition of membership of any other international body. **Mr. Melville [Australia]** favored this alternative on the grounds of the Fund should be completely independent of other institutions. **Mr. Luxford [U.S.]** suggested that it was important first to see what other institutions might be involved. **Sir Wilfrid Eady** and **Mr. Basch [Czechoslovakia]** joined in the opinion that the Fund agreement should not attempt to deal with membership in other international organizations. **Mr. Melville** agreed that the present provisions could not bind other organizations. **Mr. White** noted that in the Bank proposal, membership in the Fund was a prerequisite for membership in the Bank. This, he said, was appropriate to the Bank, but inherently there was no reason why membership in the Fund should be conditional upon membership in the Bank.

Mr. Luxford explained Alternative A [U.S.] (page 25), an additional section to Article VIII providing for the suspension of members failing to meet their obligations under the agreement. The proposal stipulated that a country would, during a period of suspension, be denied all the privileges of membership except that of withdrawal, while remaining subject to all the obligations. **Mr. Smirnov (USSR)** intimated the only privilege a country had under the agreement was that of withdrawal. **Mr. Mládek [Czechoslovakia]** inquired whether a country would be failing to meet its obligations if it were unable to provide transactions beyond the margins specified by IX-2 [["Foreign Exchange Dealings"]]. **Mr. Luxford** said that this would be one of the conditions, and if a country finds its obligations under IX-2 too onerous, it has the privilege of withdrawal. **Lord Keynes** favored Alternative B [UK], which provides for suspension of the use of the Fund's resources or compulsory withdrawal by simple majority of the votes. **Dr. Keilhau [Norway]** opposed this alternative on

---

[267] The Subcommittee for Consideration of Certain Technical Matters?

the grounds that suspension from membership is a matter affecting the national honor of the member. Therefore, suspension should not follow the analogy of a business organization and be determined by quotas, but should be determined by a vote [in] which each country has an equal voice, following the rules of international conferences. **Mr. Monteros [Mexico]** announced that Mexico supported the Norwegian position. **Mr. Luxford** pointed out that Alternative A is more inclusive than B since it applies to other matters than the use of the Fund's resources.

Mr. Monteros believed that the use of the Fund's resources, as an economic matter, might properly be determined by a vote according to quotas, but that suspension or compulsory withdrawal of a member, as a matter of national honor, must be voted by the entire Directorate [Board of Governors] representing the nations. **Lord Keynes,** on the other hand, believe that where its honor is involved, a country should voluntarily withdraw. The Fund, as a business organization, is not concerned with questions of national honor. **Mr. Varvaressos [Greece]** was of the opinion that a penalty of suspension of the use of the Fund's resources or compulsory withdrawal might be too severe and that, therefore, the Fund should be given authority to use lesser sanctions. **Mr. Rasminsky [Canada]** suggested that compulsory withdrawal might be conditional upon a vote of a majority of the members, including a majority of the quota votes. **Lord Keynes** accepted this provision on behalf of the UK. **Mr. Hexner [Czechoslovakia]** believed that the language of the alternative was too broad in that it permitted suspension for action contrary to the "purposes and policies of the Fund." He believed suspension should follow only on violation of the "provisions" of the agreement. **Lord Keynes** accepted the suggestion, along with Mr. Rasminsky's proposal, on behalf of the UK.

The Committee then discussed the settlement of accounts with countries ceasing to be members, Article VIII, Sections 2 and 3, Alternative A [U.S.]. **Sir Wilfrid Eady [UK]** stated that in his opinion, the requirement of settlement of accounts within three years of withdrawal is not adequate. **Mr. Hexner** objected to the clause requiring member countries desiring to obtain the currency of a former member country to purchase this currency from the Fund, on the grounds that this would limit the market for this currency and so accentuate depreciation which, in all probability, would be the principal occasion for suspension. After further discussion by **Mr. Varvaressos** and **Mr. Bernstein U.S.],** the **Chairman** suggested referring the whole matter of the Committee in charge of Article VIII [Subcommittee 3].

In discussing the liquidation of the Fund, [Article VIII, additional section], Alternative A [U.S.] (page 27), **Lord Keynes** held that the proposed plan was unworkable since it required gold payments by countries in debt to the Fund and these countries would not be likely to have gold available. **Mr. Keilhau [Norway]** opposed the provisions which would give the Executive Committee power to suspend the operation of the Fund. **Mr. Monteros,** agreeing, held that this should be a matter to be voted by all the countries on the Board of Directors [Governors], since only the countries which created the Fund by international action should have authority to suspend its operations by the same procedure. **Mr. Luxford,** however, pointed out that if, say, two big members withdrew from the Fund,[268] the whole scheme would in practice become unworkable. The Fund would not then be able to service functions and so all members would try to withdraw. Therefore, it was essential that the Executive Committee be empowered to suspend operations. **Baron Boël (Belgium)** announced that he was submitting an alternative to the proposed draft and suggested that the matter be deferred for later consideration.

Article IX, relating to the obligations of members, Section 2, Alternative A [U.S.], relating to prior values, and Section 3 (page 31), Alternative A [U.S.], were referred to the Technical Committee for consideration. **Lord Keynes** expressed his approval of Alternative A (page 31), providing for the repatriation of the proceeds of current international transactions. Article IX, [proposed additional section, Alternative A, U.S.], "Immunities of the Fund," was passed over for reference to a committee to be constituted at the [Bretton Woods] Conference.

Mr. Bernstein explained that Alternative A [U.S.] (page 33) combined the substance of the Joint Statement, Article X, Sections 1 and 2 [["Entry into Force" and "Transition Period"]]. **Lord Keynes** said that the UK could not accept the provisions for multilateral convertibility until the basic issues of the reconstruction period, particularly the matter of international debts, would be settled. He believed that the section should be redrafted. **Messrs. Istel [France]** and **White** suggested postponement of discussion. **Mr. Keilhau** inquired whether, under the terms of the agreement, a country would be required to secure the Fund's approval of exchange restrictions in the event of a new war. **Sir Theodore Gregory [India]** said that in case of war the Fund should be required to suspend its operations. **Mr. Keilhau** agreed that the Fund

---

[268] He has mind the United States and United Kingdom.

must have some emergency powers and on the **Chairman's** suggestion agreed to submit a draft covering his point.

The Committee passed to a discussion of Article X, Section 3 [Alternative B, UK] (page 34), relating to withdrawal of exchange restrictions and the transitional period. **Lord Keynes** emphasized that the UK would have to take advantage of these transitional period provisions. He believed that the five-year period would not necessarily be satisfactory, since under the draft the Fund might invoke penalties against a member which retained exchange controls contrary to the Fund's opinion. He agreed to consultation but opposed any mandatory action on the part of the Fund. **Messrs. Mládek** and **Keilhau** concurred. At the **Chairman's** suggestion, the matter was postponed until a new draft was submitted to the Committee.

(Version by Dorothy F. Richardson)

Article VII ["Management of the Fund"], Additional Sections, Alternative B [UK]

Sir Wilfrid Eady (UK) explained that the word "Council"[269] as used in this provision is not an acknowledged word. Responding to the question by **Mr. Mládek (Czechoslovakia)** concerning the requirement of a three-fifths majority vote, **Sir Wilfrid** explained that this was precautionary. **Mr. Mládek** felt that a simple majority vote was sufficient.

Article VII, Additional Sections, Alternative A, "Location of Offices" [U.S.]

Lord [John Maynard] Keynes (UK) stated that the UK delegation had no instructions on this provision and therefore reserved judgment. The **Chairman** requested that the UK delegation consult their Foreign Office on this matter.

---

[269] The British call the Council what became the Board of Governors, and they call the Board what became the Executive Directors.

Article VII, Additional Sections; Article VII, "Distribution of Net Income of the Fund" [Amendment A, United States]

Lord Keynes (UK) suggested that it would be preferable not to distribute any part of the net income of the Fund at the outset. He suggested that the phrase "at the discretion of the Board subject to overruling by the Council" should be added to the opening sentence of this provision. **Dr. Beyen (Netherlands)** supported this point. **Mr. Bernstein (U.S.)** pointed out that under this provision, 50 percent of the profits of the Fund would be assigned to surplus until the surpluses equal to 10 percent of the aggregate quotas, and that member countries' right to income was not cumulative.

Article VII, Additional Sections, Alternative A [U.S.], "Miscellaneous Powers"

Mr. [Eric] Beckett (UK) suggested that this section be referred to the Subcommittee on Questions of Immunities.[270]

Article VIII, Section 1 [["Procedure for Withdrawal"]], Alternative B [Australia]

Mr. Luxford (U.S.) suggested that this provision should be discussed in connection with the Bank proposal. **Mr. Basch (Czechoslovakia)** felt that this provision would interfere with the rights of countries which become members of the proposed Bank. **Sir Wilfrid Eady (UK)** expressed agreement with Mr. Luxford and with Mr. Basch. **Mr. Melville (Australia)** agreed that this clause could have no legal force.[271]

Article VIII, additional section, Alternative A [U.S.], "Suspension of Membership"

---

[270] We are unsure whether the conference had a separate subcommittee on this subject, which left no records, or whether Beckett is referring to Subcommittee 4, which among other topics dealt with immunities.

[271] Australia's proposal involved the stipulation *"the right of withdrawal shall not be prejudiced by membership of the Fund being made a condition of membership of any other international body."* Apparently this clause would have no legal force because it other international bodies would decide on their own rules, if any, with regard to members' participation in the IMF.

Mr. Luxford (U.S.) explained this provision. **Prof. Smirnov (USSR)** asked for an interpretation of the phrase "all the privileges of membership except that of withdrawal." **Lord Keynes (UK)** replied that this included the right of a member country to convert its holdings of the currencies of other member countries. **Mr. Mládek (Czechoslovakia)** inquired whether the obligations of provision IX-2 of the Joint Statement, "not to allow exchange transactions in its market in currencies of other members at rates outside a prescribed range based on the agreed parities," would continue in force.

Mr. Luxford (U.S.) replied that this obligation would continue in force until a country withdrew. The **Chairman** suggested that further discussion as to whether or not the privileges of multilateral convertibility should cease to operate in regards to a country which has been suspended from the Fund should be deferred.

Lord Keynes (UK) stated that the UK delegation agreed with the principle embodied in this provision but that they preferred the formulation set forth in [the UK's] Alternative B.

Article VIII, Additional Section, Alternative B [UK], "Suspension of Membership"

Prof. [Wilhelm] Keilhau (Norway) expressed the opinion that uniform voting was necessary in this connection since suspension from the Fund involves the honor of a member country. **Mr. Monteros (Mexico)** and **Mr. Melville (Australia)** supported Keilhau's suggestion.

Mr. Luxford (U.S.) stated that [a] certain confusion arises from the formulation set forth in Alternative B since it combines the declaration of a country [being] ineligible to use the resources of the Fund (provision [Article] III-2(d) of the Joint Statement), which is an operational matter, and suspension, which is in many aspects a political matter. Mr. Luxford also pointed out that the suspension provided for in Alternative A is in addition to suspension from for the use of the Fund's resources, and therefore provides a Fund with an additional form of penalty not provided for in Alternative B, while keeping a member under obligation to maintain its exchange rate.

Lord Keynes stated that he would not object to Alternative A if it were in addition to Alternative B, but that he felt that declaring a country ineligible to use the resources of the Fund was a penalty appropriate to other actions of a member country besides use the Fund's resources which are inconsistent with the purposes and policies of the Fund.

Ambassador Varvaressos (Greece) supported Alternative B. **Mr. Rasminsky (Canada)** also supported Alternative B but suggested that the decision on this matter should be by a majority both of the basic votes and of the member countries. **Lord Keynes (UK)** accepted this amendment.

Mr. Hexner (Czechoslovakia) inquired whether "purposes and policies" of the Fund would include general policies, such as trade policies. **Lord Keynes (UK)** replied that this phrase meant the provisions of the Fund. **Mr. Hexner (Czechoslovakia)** remarked that he felt that subsection 2 of Alternative B, under which the Fund may require a member country to withdraw, provided too strong a penalty.

Mr. Monteros (Mexico) stated that the Mexican delegation felt that questions of suspension should not be delegated to the Executive Committee.

Article VIII, Sections 2-3 [["Liquidation of Obligations" and "Deposal of Withdrawing Member's Currency"]], Alternative A [U.S.]

Sir Wilfrid Eady (UK) stated, in connection with the subsection of Alternative A, "Settlement of Accounts of Countries Ceasing to Be Members," that the length of the time period for settlement should be discretionary and should be left to the management of the Fund.

Mr. Hexner felt that the fourth paragraph of Alternative A, which provides that "Any member country desiring to obtain the currency of a former member country shall acquire the currency, if available, by purchase from the Fund," constituted a burden upon member countries.

Ambassador Varvaressos (Greece) felt that the third paragraph of this provision means in effect that if the Fund and a withdrawing country cannot reach an agreement upon a settlement of their accounts, that country will be deprived of all foreign exchange resources until the Fund has liquidated this claim against that country. He proposed that in case the Fund and a member country do not reach agreement upon settlement of their accounts, the country shall be obliged to liquidate any of the Fund's holding of its local currency in excess of the Fund's obligations to the country within a period of not less than three years to be determined by the Fund. That is to say, he proposed dropping all of Alternative A, after the first sentence of paragraph 3. **Mr. Melville (Australia)** also felt that Alternative A was too drastic.

Mr. Bernstein (U.S.) pointed out that paragraph 1 and the first sentence of paragraph 3 of Alternative A are inconsistent and stated that

287

the time period set forth in the first sentence of paragraph 3, "[within a period of note less than] three years to be determined by the Fund," was the period intended. He also stated that when no agreement is reached between the Fund and a member country, some method of orderly liquidation must be provided for.

Article VIII, Sections 2-3, Alternative B [UK]

Lord Keynes (UK) pointed out that Alternative B left decision of these questions of the future.

Mr. Luxford (U.S.) suggested that in view of the inadequacies of Alternative A and the brevity of Alternative B, this question should be referred to a committee for further discussion.

Article VIII, Additional Section, "Liquidation of the Fund" [U.S.]

Mr. Luxford (U.S.) suggested that this provision be referred to a committee. Lord Keynes (UK) opposed this suggestion.

Prof. Keilhau (Norway) felt that the suspension of the operations of the Fund should in no circumstances be delegated to the Executive Committee. Mr. Luxford (U.S.) pointed out the consequences of not giving the Executive Committee the power to suspend the operations of the Fund. If one of the major countries withdraws from the Fund at a time when the Board of Directors is not in session, there will result a race among the remaining members to withdraw. Therefore, in order to protect the assets of the countries remaining in the Fund, it is necessary to give the Executive Committee the power to suspend the operations of the Fund.

Mr. Monteros (Mexico) reported that the discussion of this matter and Subcommittee 3 had brought forth the impression that this matter was one in which voting should be uniform.

Article VIII, "Liquidation of the Fund," Alternative B [Belgium]

Baron [René] Boël (Belgium) expressed willingness to have Alternative B discussed in subcommittee.[272]

---

[272] We have not found the text of this alternative, which Belgium may have let die in the subcommittee.

Article IX, Sections 1-2 [["Gold Price" and "Foreign Exchange Dealings"]], Alternative A [U.S.]

Sir Wilfrid Eady (UK) pointed out that these provisions could not be adequately discussed until the report of the Subcommittee on Certain Technical Matters was heard. Discussion of these provisions was therefore postponed.

Article IX, Additional Section [4, "Exchange Controls on Current Payments"], Alternative A [U.S.]

This provision has already been discussed.

Lord Keynes (UK) expressed approval of this provision. **Mr. White (U.S.)** felt that the word "repatriation" should be replaced by some other word. **Mr. Rasminsky (Canada)** suggested that the substitution of the phrase "not to impose restrictions upon another members repatriation of the proceeds of current international transactions" would clarify the meaning of this provision.

Article IX, Additional Sections

It was decided to refer the additional provisions to Article IX which are set forth on page 32 of Document F-1 [IX, additional sections on legal immunities and exemption from taxation] to a committee of the formal [Bretton Woods] Conference.

Article X, Sections 1-2 [["Entry into Force" and "Transition Period"]], Alternative A [U.S.]

Mr. Bernstein (U.S.) explained that this alternative combined provisions X-1 and X-2 of the Joint Statement. **Lord Keynes (UK)** remarked that this alternative omits important parts of Article X-1 of the Joint Statement. This alternative is also open to criticism in that it seems to make the transitional period of unlimited duration. Lord Keynes stated that the UK delegation would attempt to redraft these provisions making clear that the transitional period should be a short as possible. **Mr. Istel (France)** and **Ambassador Varvaressos (Greece)** supported Lord Keynes's statement.

The **Chairman** agreed that since phraseology is so important in connection of these provisions, further discussion should be postponed until another draft was prepared.

Prof. Keilhau (Norway) inquired whether provision would be made through the member countries of the responsibilities which they undertake in connection with the Fund in case of the imminence of the outbreak of fresh hostilities. **Sir Theodore Gregory (India)** suggested that in such a case it would be the responsibility of the Executive Committee to meet and suspend the Fund. **Prof. Keilhau** felt it would be desirable for the Fund to continue operations even at the outbreak of a new war. The **Chairman** stated that the conference would be glad to consider a draft of such provisions.

Article X, Section 3 [["Restrictions on Exchange"]], Alternative A [U.S.]

Mr. Bernstein (U.S.) explained the changes involved in this alternative. The restrictions dealt with include several types of restrictions, whereas provision X-3 of the Joint Statement dealt only with restrictions on exchange rates. After three years, retention of restrictions is conditional upon approval of the Fund rather than [merely upon] consultation with the Fund.

Article X, Section 3, Alternative B [UK]

Lord Keynes (UK) pointed out that there should be a period after the phrase "still in force under (2) above." Lord Keynes explained that Alternative B makes the transitional period of uncertain duration to avoid [the] appearance of lack of good faith if a country is unable to accomplish the necessary adjustments within three years. The **Chairman** inquired whether Lord Keynes would be willing to provide the Fund with any authority to compel member countries to give up the retention of restrictions granted under Article X after a longer period, say ten years. **Lord Keynes** felt that such authority is given to the Fund under Article VIII, additional section [2], "Suspension of Membership," Alternative B [UK].

Mr. Mládek (Czechoslovakia) felt that a five-year period was realistic and that with the substitution of a five-year period for the three-year period he would prefer the drafting of this provision set forth in

290

Alternative A. **Lord Keynes (UK)** objected that a five-year period would not be reasonable for a country such as Argentina.[273]

The **Chairman** suggested that discussion of this provision indicated a tendency to forget that the Board of Directors of the Fund will represent the members and we should expect its judgment on these matters to be reasonable.

---

[273] The Allies did not invite Argentina to the Bretton Woods conference because they considered it too friendly to the Axis powers, but they expected it to become a member of the IMF eventually.

50

Formal Agenda Committee
Eighth meeting
Atlantic City
June 29, 1944 at 10:30 a.m.

Bretton Woods commissions • Subcommittee on Supplying Information • Subcommittee on Management • Subcommittee on Certain Technical Matters • Depreciation • Amendments • Interpretation • Par values • Purposes and policies of the Fund • Changes in par values

The last session at Atlantic City on the IMF opens with reports from several subcommittees. The Agenda Subcommittee recommends that the Bretton Woods conference should be organized into three "commissions," dealing with the Fund, the Bank, and other methods of international monetary cooperation. The commissions would have formal committees and could also appoint ad hoc subcommittees. These recommendations are like the plans the United States formulated for Bretton Woods some time before the Atlantic City conference.

Subcommittees on the information members will supply to the IMF, on management, and on certain technical matters then offer their reports to the Formal Agenda Committee. Discussion ensues about whether a matter referred to the Subcommittee for Consideration of Certain Technical Matters requires policing currency black markets.

The Formal Agenda Committee then proceeds to consider additional articles for the IMF agreement that are not in the Joint Statement. The articles concern amending the agreement, interpreting it, and bringing it into force. After that, committee chairman Harry Dexter White suggests that the committee discuss some provisions passed over at previous meetings. Several delegations bring up alternatives they have proposed. The purpose of the discussion is not so much to settle the matters they raise as to set them up for consideration at Bretton Woods.

Two versions exist of the minutes of this meeting, both by the American delegation.

(Version by Dorothy F. Richardson)

The **Chairman of the Agenda Subcommittee [Harry Dexter White, U.S.?]** reported that it was suggested that there should be three commissions [at Bretton Woods]. Commission I would deal with the Fund and would have four committees, each of would consider one aspect of the Fund. Commission II would deal with the Bank and would also have four committees. Commission III would deal with other methods of international monetary cooperation. All committees would be empowered to appoint ad hoc subcommittees. It is important that all resolutions to be discussed in the Third Commission be submitted to the Secretariat before noon. The Chairman stated that he expected the report of the subcommittee to be completed either this morning or this afternoon.

Mr. [A.P.] Morozov (USSR), chairman of the subcommittee for consideration of the provision empowering the Fund to obtain information from member countries, reported that the committee had completed its work and submitted the report of the committee to the Formal Agenda Conference. The **Chairman** accepted this report.[274]

Sir Wilfrid Eady (UK), chairman of the Subcommittee on Management, in submitting the report of this committee,[275] stated that while there had been little difficulty in reaching agreement over a large part of the field, there was some part of the field upon which no agreement had been reached. The **Chairman** proposed that the Agenda Committee accept this report and refer the matter to the formal conference [at Bretton Woods] for further consideration.

Mr. [Walter] Gardner (U.S.), chairman of the Subcommittee for Consideration of Certain Technical Matters, reported that the committee felt that it was not the proper one for consideration of IX-2(a) [["Foreign Exchange Dealings"]]. Although this provision involves technical matters, it also involves broader issues. **Mr. [Lionel] Robbins (UK)** suggested that the conference could discuss this provision most intelligently if the technical questions were previously dealt with. He asked Mr. Gardner what point of principle he had in mind. **Mr. Gardner** replied that he was thinking of the phrase "through appropriate measures authorized under this Agreement."

The **Chairman** felt that the obligation of member countries is to

---

[274] See chapter 81.
[275] Document F-6; see chapter 79.

purchase or sell gold. **Ambassador Varvaressos (Greece)** felt that member countries are not required to use their resources to prevent their exchange rates from depreciating if the transfers leading to depreciation are transfers of capital. He also pointed out that in some cases, use of the country's gold resources will not be enough to prevent depreciation, and the country will be obliged to take other legal measures to assure this. **Prof. Keilhau (Norway)** felt that the appropriateness of such measures would depend upon the relationship between the Fund and the monetary laws of each member country. He suggested that the discussion of the applications of this phrase be deferred until the formal conference.

Mr. E. E. Brown (U.S.) inquired whether a member country would be obligated to undertake policing measures to maintain the rates of exchange of other members' currencies, that is, to prevent within its borders black-market operations in other members' currencies. **Lord Keynes (UK)** suggested that member countries might be required to make such black-market operations illegal. Making such operations illegal would exclude currency acquired on the black market from the advantages of the convertibility provision.

Mr. E. E. Brown (U.S.) suggested that depreciation might be caused by the device of quoting different prices for commodities to different countries. The question of where the responsibility for the depreciation would rest in such a case was discussed. **Mr. Istel (France)** felt that the responsibility would be on the country which had introduced restrictions upon exchange transactions. **Mr. Monteros (Mexico)** felt that such cases as that envisaged by Mr. Brown (U.S.) would be rare.

The **Chairman** suggested that this question should be included in the agenda for the [Bretton Woods] conference.

XI ["Amendments"], Alternatives A [U.S.] and B [UK]

Sir Wilfrid Eady (UK) felt that Alternative A was too detailed and Alternative B was not sufficiently detailed. He suggested that both versions be remitted to their sponsors for redrafting. This suggestion was accepted.

XII ["Interpretation of the Agreement"], Alternative A [U.S.]

The section "Effect on Other International Commitments" was passed.

XIII ["Putting the Fund into Operation"], Alternative A [U.S.], All Sections thorough "Agenda of the Initial Meeting"

Mr. Bernstein (U.S.) explained this provision **Mr. Beckett (UK)** stated that the UK delegation had drafted an alternative for the first paragraph of this provision, that they had circulated this alternative, but that this alternative was not included here. Mr. Beckett explained that the UK delegation felt that the proposals should consist of two parts: a formal document which would concern only the member governments, and a set of statutes which would contain all the material which the directors or management would need to deal with. The **Chairman** inquired whether in such an arrangement both the formal document and the statutes would be integral parts of the same document. **Mr. Beckett (UK)** replied that they would.

Prof. Keilhau stated that if the initial meeting of the Board of Directors took place before the parliaments of countries now occupied by the enemy had a chance to meet, special arrangements for such countries should be made in this provision. The **Chairman** asked Prof. Keilhau to redraft this provision taking this into account.

[Proposed new] XIII, Alternative A [U.S.], "Fixing Initial Par Values"

Lord Keynes (UK) pointed out that there is no official value of the pound sterling in terms of gold. There is an official buying price for gold in terms of pounds and there is also an official pound-U.S. dollar rate. He felt that for the UK and for many other countries, the official rate on July 1, 1944 in terms of gold or a gold convertible currency would have no meaning.

The **Chairman** felt there were two problems involved. There exists an actual pattern of exchange rate for such transactions as are permitted. There is also a problem in how to describe a pattern of rates. There is also a problem in deciding whether or not we should accept this existing rate schedule.

Prof. Keilhau called attention to IV-1 [["Establishing Par Values,"] Alternative] B [UK] (page 13a). At the moment there are not real exchange rates for the currencies of many countries. It will be necessary for such countries to know what the dollar-sterling sterling rate will be before they can determine an appropriate rate for their currencies. Lord Keynes (UK) stated that it would not be possible to set the dollar-sterling rate for some time. He therefore proposed that countries which have been occupied shall be required to set a provisional rate for their currency within one month after their liberation but that this rate not be considered definite until the period of reconstruction is completed.

Lord Keynes (UK) stated that he supported provision IV-1, [Alternative] B.

Mr. Bernstein (U.S.) pointed out that we must not ignore the fact that many United and Associated Nations do not have exchange rates which have been in use for some time and which are fairly realistic. It is not necessary to refuse to use such partial solutions as a starting point merely because of difficulties of definition. If we assume the U.S. dollar is a gold convertible currency, it will be possible to determine a par value for any country which has a fairly meaningful dollar exchange rate. Furthermore, in order to avoid members acting unilaterally in regard to their exchange rates, the date chosen for determination of the de facto rate should be one before the Fund became imminent.

Mr. Luxford (U.S.) felt that the Fund, as well as member countries, should be empowered to question the suitability of an exchange rate. **Mr. Bernstein (U.S.)** suggested that in view of the provisions on alteration of exchange rates, there might also be some provision which would relieve the Fund from the responsibility of providing resources to support a rate which it feels is unsatisfactory.

Mr. [Louis] Rasminsky (Canada) felt that allowance should be made for changes in the rate of exchange of other countries' currencies if there should be changes in the dollar-sterling rate. The **Chairman** felt that this might be possible. **Lord Keynes (UK)** suggested that IV-1 [Alternative] B could be amended to make this point.

XIII [["Putting the Fund into Operation"]], Alternative B [UK]

The second paragraph of Article XIII, [Alternative] A, "Fixing Initial Par Values" [U.S.] and Article XIII, [Alternative] B [on the inauguration of the Fund], were passed.

[Provisions passed over]

The **Chairman** suggested that the remainder of the meeting be devoted to discussion of some of the provisions passed over. **Mr. Istel (France)** requested the discussion of III-2 [["Purchases of Another Member's

Currency"]], Alternative E [France]; **Mr. [Chintaman] Deshmukh (India)**[276] requested the discussion of I ["Purposes and Policies of the Fund"], Alternative D [India]; **Prof. Keilhau (Norway)**, I, Alternative G [Norway]; and **Mr. Melville (Australia)**, IV-2 [["Changes in Par Value"]], Alternative C [Australia].

I-4 [["Promote Exchange Stability"]], Alternative D [India]

Mr. [Chintaman] Deshmukh (India) explained that the addition of the phrase "to assist in the full utilization of the resources of economically underdeveloped countries" was needed to sharpen the meaning of the phrase "high level of employment and real income." **Mr. Monteros (Mexico)** supported this provision. **Mr. Melville (Australia)** suggested that this phrase be made a separate paragraph.

The **Chairman** suggested that the phrase "real income" adequately covered the case.[277] **Sir Jeremy Raisman (India)** disagreed. The **Chairman** replied that it was necessary to avoid criticism that the Fund was being used for purposes of reconstruction. **Lord Keynes (UK)** also felt that it was necessary to consider that this phrase did not overlap with the purposes of the Bank. **Mr. Mládek (Czechoslovakia)** suggested that a rephrasing of this provision could be accomplished which would accomplish Mr. Deshmukh's purpose without incurring the criticism that the Fund was being used for purposes of reconstruction.

I-4, Alternative G [Norway]

The purpose of dividing I-4 of the Joint Statement as is done here is to emphasize the fact that the purpose of the Fund is to promote exchange stability.

III-2 [["Purchases of Another Member's Currency"]], Alternative E [France]

This is an alternative to provision III-2(c) of the Joint Statement, and involves a substantial change in that provision. **Prof. Smirnov (USSR)**

---

[276] Deshmukh was not on board the *Queen Mary;* he joined the Indian delegation at Atlantic City.

[277] This phrase was already in the Joint Statement.

297

supported this provision since it affords more flexibility of resources to member countries.

IV-2-4 [["Changes in Par Value," etc.]], Alternative C [Australia]

Mr. Melville (Australia) explained that this Alternative assures security to raw material producing countries. It assures such countries that a fall in the prices of such raw materials will be considered a "fundamental [dis]equilibrium." The delegation from **India** strongly supported this alternative.

IV-2-4, Alternative D [USSR]

Prof. Smirnov (USSR) explained that in some cases, changes of a member's exchange rate will not affect the international transactions of other member countries.

IV-2-4, Alternative E [Greece]

Ambassador Varvaressos (Greece) stated that he would like to submit an amendment to this alternative.

[Meeting schedule]

There will be a meeting to discuss the Bank proposal this afternoon at 3:30 p.m. Lord Keynes (UK) will act as chairman of this meeting. The material for this meeting will be available at 2:30 p.m.. A second meeting on the Bank proposal will be held tomorrow morning at 10:30 a.m.

(Version by Henry J. Bittermann)

The Agenda Subcommittee reported that the [Bretton Woods] Conference should be divided into three Commissions: I. The International Monetary Fund; II. The Bank for Reconstruction and Development; III. Other Monetary and Financial Problems. The Commissions on the Fund and the Bank were to be subdivided into four Committees each, dealing respectively with: 1. Purposes, Policies and Quotas (Capital); 2. Operations; 3. Organization and Management; 4. Form and Status.

A committee on supplying information under the Fund agreement was appointed by the **Chairman** with **Mr. Morozov (USSR)** as chairman. The Committee on Management, with **Sir Wilfrid Eady [UK]** as chairman, submitted its report, Document F-6.[278] This report covered the points of agreement and the points of disagreement discussed by the Committee. By unanimous consent the report was laid on the table.

The Technical Committee, **Mr. Gardner [U.S.],** chairman, requested instructions from the General Committee regarding Article IX, Section 2 [["Foreign Exchange Dealings"]] (Document F-1, page 29), relating to the prohibition of exchange transactions outside the prescribed range from parity. **Mr. Keilhau (Norway)** believed that the [Bretton Woods] Conference and the Articles of Agreement should recommend appropriate measures for controlling this variation rather than prescribing regulations, which should be a matter of national legislation. **Mr. White** pointed out that a country could prevent appreciation of its currency by accepting gold, and [prevent] depreciation by selling gold. **Mr. Basch (Czechoslovakia)** raised questions about the rates of commission paid for the purchase and sale of currency. **Mr. [Edward] Brown (USA)** suggested that buying and selling gold is one [and the same] problem, that a country might be willing to permit gold transactions as a means of maintaining parity of its own currency, but he wished to know whether the wording of IX-2 required a country to take police measures to enforce the range provisions with respect to foreign currencies. **Lord Keynes** agreed with Mr. Brown that gold transactions would be sufficient to maintain the parity of a country's own currency, but he doubted that this would be adequate to control black market transactions in foreign currencies. If the U.S. were not to enforce the provisions against transactions beyond the prescribed range, the U.S. would become the principal black market. He suggested the substitution of the following words for the original provision: "A member country undertakes to render illegal currency transactions beyond the prescribed range within its own jurisdiction." He believed this would be adequate. It would make black market contracts unenforceable but would eliminate the necessity for police measures.

Mr. White reiterated Mr. Brown's position that the U.S. obligations would be discharged by accepting gold. **Mr. Brown** pointed out in answer to Lord Keynes that the problem is not merely the problem of the black market. American companies, he said, could make contracts in

---

[278] See chapter 79.

various currencies and violate the range provisions by quoting differential prices to buyers in different countries. **Mr. White** suggested that this problem was to be viewed from the standpoint of two countries. If both countries accept the convertibility principle there is no problem at issue. **Lord Keynes** returned to the question of illegal transactions. He pointed out that sterling was blocked for capital transactions, but that sterling exchange could be sold in the U.S. by a French national at a discount, and, unless the transactions were illegal under American law, this would make possible transactions beyond the prescribed range and would also constitute effective violation of British exchange control.

Mr. Espinosa de los Monteros (Mexico) agreed fully with Mr. Brown's main position but contended that further study should be made of the borderline cases of potential violation arising out of triangular transactions. **Mr. Istel (France)** said that cooperative agreements among the countries for mutual enforcement would be the only way in which this problem could be handled. **Mr. Luxford [U.S.]** asked Lord Keynes to explain whether his wording merely meant that illicit contracts would be unenforceable or whether it would require other implementation. **Lord Keynes** replied that the UK would be satisfied if the transactions were declared illegal. **Mr. Crena de Iongh (Netherlands)** pointed out that the black market problem would be particularly serious in view of the fact that not all countries would be members of the Fund and, therefore, many countries would not be obligated to protect the parities of currencies. **Mr. Luxford** indicated that there was no particular problem in connection with the depreciation of currency since this was covered by other provisions of the Fund agreement. **Mr. Varvaressos (Greece)** believed that the Fund's use of gold would not be adequate and that the member countries must adopt supplementary legal measures to protect the parities.

The Committee then considered Article IX [XI] (Document F-1, page 36) relating to the amendment of the Articles of Agreement. **Mr. Luxford** explained Alternative A (the U.S. proposal). **Sir Wilfrid Eady** argued that Alternative A was too cumbersome, whereas Alternative B (the British proposal) probably provided for too simple a procedure. He suggested that minor changes might be made in accordance with the terms of Alternative B while the procedure of Alternative A should be reserved for more important changes. The Committee referred the entire question back to the Subcommittee on Management for redraft. The **Chairman** suggested, and it was agreed, that Article XII ["Interpretation"] (page 37a) be passed over [at Atlantic City] for discussion at the [Bretton Woods] Conference. This article referred to the definitions and to the power of the Fund to give advice to the member countries.

The Committee then passed to Article XIII [["Putting the Fund into Operation"]], Alternative A [U.S.] (page 38a). **Mr. Bernstein [U.S.]** explained the provisions of the Alternative A. **Mr. Beckett (UK)** suggested that the convention adopted by the Conference should contain only the formal provisions directly concerning governments. The statutes of the Fund determining the operations and powers of the Fund should be, in his opinion, placed in an annex to the convention [the Articles of Agreement]. **Mr. Hexner (Czechoslovakia)** believed that the convention adopted should contain those portions of the plan which were to be non-amendable as part of an international obligation comparable to a treaty. The statutes of the Fund would contain the amendable portions, while the method of amendment would be covered by the terms of the convention. **Mr. Keilhau** pointed out that countries which were now occupied by the enemy might not be in a position to give parliamentary approval to the Fund agreement in time to participate in the initial meeting. The **Chairman** suggested that the Norwegian delegation submit a draft covering this point.

The Committee then took up the question of the initial par values [proposed new Article XIII, Section 5, "Fixing Initial Par Values," Alternative A, U.S.] (page 38a). **Mr. Bernstein** said that the parities existing on July 1, 1944 are to be regarded as the initial parities for the purposes of the Fund unless this rate were regarded as unsatisfactory either by the Fund or the countries concerned. Alternative A allowed a period of 90 days during which an agreement might be reached by the member and the Fund. If no agreement could be reached at that time, a member would be regarded as having withdrawn from the Fund. **Lord Keynes** objected to the wording of the alternative, since sterling had no official value in gold. British law merely provided a buying price of gold in pounds sterling. Alternative A, he said, made no provision for such a legal situation. In answer to a question, he said that the pound had no selling price in terms of gold. **Mr. Keilhau** called attention to [the UK's] Alternative B, Article IV, Section 1 [["Establishing Par Value"]] (Document F-1, page 13a), which provided that the U.S. and the UK would communicate the initial par values of their currencies expressed in gold. After the adoption of this rate, other member countries would take similar action before the Fund would begin operations. The occupied countries would be given a reasonable time to communicate their initial parities after the reconstruction of their monetary systems. **Lord Keynes** said that the UK preferred this arrangement to the provisions of

Alternative A. **Mr. Bernstein** argued that it would be undesirable to permit thirty countries to make changes in their rates in the early period since there were already in existence working parity rates among all the United Nations. **Mr. White** said that the U.S. would regard it as bad policy to open the matter of these rates for discussion. The consequences would be disastrous depreciation of many of the currencies.

Lord Keynes announced after considerable discussion that the UK agreed to the acceptance of the de facto rate as it existed on July 1, 1944. He believed that the Fund should not question the existing de facto rates as a matter of policy, but that a member country should be free to do so if it regarded it as essential to its interests. Whereupon **Mr. White** concluded that the only question remaining was to determine the date of the de facto rates. He pointed out that it was essential that the date be some past date so as to prevent unilateral action tending toward depreciation. **Mr. [Hendrik] Riemans (Netherlands)** asked whether the invaded countries and the non-invaded countries should be separated for this purpose, and Mr. White replied that this was understood. **Mr. Rasminsky (Canada)** said that countries must be free to change the rates if there is a change in the ratio between the pound and the dollar. Consequently, a provision must be made for changes of rates whenever the two most important currencies change their respective ratios. **Lord Keynes** suggested the following language as a substitute for the proposed alternatives: "An official rate expressed in terms of gold based on the de facto rates existing at the inauguration of the Fund shall be communicated by each member country to the Fund and shall be the par value of that currency for the purposes of the Fund." **Mr. Bernstein** suggested that the Fund should not be compelled to supply exchange to support a rate regarded as unsatisfactory by it. The **Chairman** directed that the question be referred to the [Bretton Woods] Drafting Committee for action.

The Committee then considered other alternative sections which had been passed over by common consent at previous meetings. **Mr. Istel** raised [France's] Alternative E, Article III, Section 2 [["Purchases of Another Member's Currency"]] (page 6b), relating to the purchase of currency from the Fund for capital transfer. **Sir Chintaman Deshmukh (India)** wished to have the committee consider [India's] Alternative D, Article I, Section 2 (page 1b), which provided for "The fuller utilization of the resources of economically underdeveloped countries" as one of the purposes of the Fund. **Mr. Keilhau** asked for consideration of

Alternative C [to Article I] (page 1c);[279] **Mr. Melville (Australia),** [Australia's] Alternative B, Article IV-2-4 [["Changes in Par Value," etc.]] (page 14b); **Mr. [Bulhões (Brazil)** wished to consider [Brazil's] Alternative C, [paragraph] (b), Article IV-2-4 (page 14c).

The Committee proceeded to the consideration of [Article I], Alternative D [India] (page 1b). **Sir Chintaman Deshmukh** spoke in favor of this alternative, which would have included among the purposes of the Fund "To assist the fuller utilization of the resources of underdeveloped countries." **Mr. Melville** suggested that this provision should be incorporated in an appropriate paragraph, while **Lord Keynes** contended that it was a function appropriate to the Bank rather than to the Fund. **Sir Jeremy Raisman (India)** inquired why India should be expected to undertake the obligation of the Fund unless the Fund was directed toward policies which would be beneficial to the Indian economy. **Mr. Monteros** expressed his full sympathy with the Indian proposition and favored consideration of this alternative. The **Chairman** suggested that the objective of the Indian proposition was fully covered in the original phraseology relating to a "high level of employment and real income." **Sir Jeremy Raisman** said that the term "full employment" would have significance only in an advanced country, but would be irrelevant to a backward country. The **Chairman** concluded the discussion by saying that the U.S. did not regard the use of the Fund for purposes of reconstruction and development as proper. These are matters for which the Bank was the proper agency.

Mr. Istel raised **[France's]** Alternative E, III-2 [["Purchases of Another Member's Currency"]] (page 6c). He argued that the Fund should not permit a member country to exceed 125 percent of its quota during the first, and 25 percent additional in each subsequent, year with a maximum of 200 percent. This device, he believed, would prevent a country from making sudden demands upon the Fund so as to use up its allowable share of the quota, and would require time to ration the purchases over an appropriate period. The **USSR** supported this position. The delegates of **Australia** and **India** supported the [UK's] Alternative B, Article IX, Section 3 [["Current Transactions"]] (page 14b), which provided *inter alia* that the Fund would not reject a requested change in par value necessary to meet "a serious and persistent deficit in the balance of payments on current account accompanied by a substantial adverse

---

[279] Possibly a mistake based on a mishearing. Alternative C was Brazil's; Alternative G was Norway's.

change in the terms of trade." The Committee then adjourned the discussion of the International Monetary Fund, with the Bank made the subject for the afternoon meeting.

51

Formal Agenda Committee
Ninth meeting
Atlantic City
June 29, 1944 at 3:30? p.m.

British redraft of Bank proposal • Guarantees versus direct loans • Level of risk • Membership in the Fund and the Bank • Unpaid subscriptions • Loan policy • Differences with American draft • Restrictions on capital movements • Organization and management

Harry Dexter White yields the chairmanship to John Maynard Keynes for the Formal Agenda Committee's sessions on the Bank for Reconstruction and Development. It is an action that acknowledges Keynes's great intellectual influence and emphasizes that the conference is not purely American-led.

The British introduce conference Document B-1, their proposed modifications to the American draft on the Bank. The British desire in particular that the Bank be able to borrow and re-lend funds additional to those that members provide; that it make more risky low-interest loans than the Americans might like; and that in the immediate postwar period it be allowed to make loans for general economic stabilization rather than only loans for specific projects. The committee then discusses various provisions of the British proposal that particularly interest the delegates.

The **Chairman [John Maynard Keynes],** in introducing the UK redraft of the Bank proposal,[280] stated that it was not intended to conflict in any important respect with the U.S. Treasury proposal. It differed in some details, and in a few matters of policy there were differences which could be reconciled by mutual agreement after discussion. He indicated the guarantee function would be the most important part of the Bank's activities, rather than direct loans. The resources of the Bank must be provided by the creditor countries. He debtors cannot provide funds, but

---

[280] Document B-1; see chapter 80.

in an international adventure should properly bear part of the risk. Consequently, the direct loans under the Bank's capital would be limited. The Bank, however, could borrow additional funds on the open market which could, in turn, be re-lent to the members. The debtor countries, as stockholders of the Bank, would be liable for their share of the debt so incurred. The loans which the Bank was to sponsor, whether by guarantee or direct loan, should be in large part those which could not be secured on a commercial basis.

Secondly, the Chairman continued, the Bank would be conducted with prudence, but it should not avoid taking risks. Under the proposed scheme the risk is pooled. Each loan, he said, should not be judged on a commercial basis, though the loans as a whole should be prudently made, so that there would be no impairment of the Bank's capital and no necessity to call upon the members to implement their guarantees. He believed that the loans made by the Bank should be made on substantially the same terms to all borrowers. To do otherwise would require the Bank to assess the credit of its members. This, he believed, would be impossible and impolitic for an international organization. Moreover, the Bank should not be conducted for profit. It is not to be a usurer trying to get as much as possible. If a country gets into difficulties, the Bank should come to its aid. It should aim at restoration rather than to enforce penalties on defaulting debtors. Finally, he suggested that the Bank should make loans to aid in the stabilization of currencies in the immediate postwar period. All other loans should follow the general outlines of the U.S. proposal contemplating the use of the Bank's resources only for specific projects of reconstruction and development.

The **Committee** generally agreed that in view of the short time at its disposal, it would be inadvisable to suggest amendments or modifications of the drafts submitted. Discussion on each point would necessarily be brief, and all disputed points would be deferred to the [Bretton Woods] conference for later discussion.

The first question raised was about the formula for subscription of stock to the Bank. On **Mr. White's** suggestion, this was deferred [to Bretton Woods].

Mr. Melville [Australia], referring to Article II, Section 3 [["Distribution of Shares"]],[281] inquired why membership in the Fund

---

[281] Note that although the discussion centers on the British Document B-1, references to articles and section are to the American draft of November 24, 1943 on the Bank, which is in chapter 3.

should be prerequisite to membership in the Bank. **Mr. White** replied that membership in the Fund was an assurance of the stability of a country's currency, and provide a greater prospect of the country's being able to meet its liabilities to the Bank. **Mr. Melville** objected, however, that this requirement of membership in the Fund practically made nugatory the right of a country to withdraw from the Fund. **Mr. White** made it clear that the U.S. failure to reply to this particular argument did not imply agreement with it. **Prof. Robbins (UK)** pointed out that in the Fund proposal, a member would be dropped only with a four-fifths vote. **Mr. Bernstein [U.S.]** inquired whether the Fund's resources could be used to implement guarantees under the terms of the UK draft. **Lord Keynes** replied that there was no obligation on the part of the Fund to permit this use of its resources.

The committee then considered Article II, Section 5 [["Unpaid Subscriptions"]], providing for the reservation of the unpaid subscriptions as a surety fund. **Mr. Louchheim [U.S.]** inquired whether any special restrictions were to be applied to currency provided to implement guarantees. Mr. Bernstein explained that no additional restrictions would apply to this other than those which applied to local currencies subscribed and paid in. In reply to **Mr. Gardner's [U.S.]** inquiry as to whether currency repaid to the Bank would be free exchange, **Lord Keynes** replied that the restrictions on currency applied only to the original payments on capital.

Questions of loan policy were raised by various members. **Mr. Beyen [Netherlands]** wished to know whether short-term loans were contemplated. The **Chairman** stated that in his opinion a reconstruction loan for a five-year period would not be precluded under the British draft. **Mr. White** replied that the U.S. draft had not contemplated making shorter or intermediate loans, but that it was the expectation of the American group that the Bank would concentrate on loans for a 20- or 30- year period. Long-term loans would require smaller amortization payments, and consequently could be adjusted more readily to the debtor country's ability to pay.

The **Chairman** stated that in the UK draft the American provisions of II-6 [["Excess Subscriptions"]] had been omitted as being needlessly detailed and probably unnecessary, considering the circumstances under which future calls for capital might be made. The provisions of II-7 [["Repurchase of Local Currency"]] were also omitted, since he expected that these provisions would be covered by other clauses requiring payment to be made in gold and convertible currency. With respect to Article III, Section 2 [["Guarantee against Depreciation"]], "The local currency assets of the Bank are to be guaranteed against any depreciation in the value in terms of gold," the Chairman stated that this had been omitted from the British draft through an oversight. The UK was in complete agreement with the U.S. on the necessity for this clause.

Lord Keynes explained III-6 of the UK draft, providing for stabilization loans. **Mr. Basch [Czechoslovakia]** inquired whether stabilization loans included not merely the provision of gold for currency purposes, but also the provision of stocks of raw materials and inventories. **Lord Keynes** agreed that provision should be made for such loans.

Passing to Article IV ["Powers and Operations"] of the UK version, the **Chairman,** in reply to a question raised by **Mr. Luxford [U.S.],** stated that the guarantees could not be paid from the originally subscribed capital, since the currency for the original subscription was subject to control by the member country providing it, while the guarantees must be paid in completely liquid funds. He further explained that the provisions of IV-4 of the UK draft [["Currency of Loans"]] were intended solely to provide additional necessary detail for the American draft. **Mr. White** further explained that in the International Monetary Fund, currency supplied by the members had to be free of restrictions upon their use. In the Bank, which did not face the same conditions, there was no necessity of exempting this currency from any restrictions placed upon capital movements by member countries.

The question of Bank organization and management was raised, but in view of the incompleteness of the draft was not given extended discussion.

52

Formal Agenda Committee
Tenth meeting
Atlantic City
June 30, 10:30 a.m.

Commissions at Bretton Woods • Continuation of discussion of British redraft of Bank proposal • Payment provisions • Guarantees • Withdrawal or suspension of membership • Distribution of net profits • Other powers

Keynes again chairs the committee, meeting for the last time before the conference closes and the delegates leave later in the day for Bretton Woods. After hearing the report of the Agenda Subcommittee, the committee considers the remainder of the agreement on the Bank for Reconstruction and Development, melding provisions from the American and British drafts into new whole. In particular, the committee considers provisions on payment, guarantees, suspension of membership, and distribution of net profits.

The report of the Agenda Subcommittee was submitted.[282] There will be three Commissions at the [Bretton Woods] conference. Commission I will deal with the Fund, Commission II will deal with the Bank, and Commission III will deal with other means of international financial cooperation. The Secretariat of the conference will be from the United States.

It was suggested that resolutions for discussion at the Third Commission be submitted to the Secretariat. **Mr. de Iongh (Netherlands)** suggested that the freezing controls[283] might be discussed in the Third Commission.

Lord Keynes, acting Chairman, accepted the report of the Agenda Subcommittee.

---

[282] We have not found the report.

[283] Possibly this phrase means blocked balances, such as the sterling balances.

The discussion of the UK draft of the Bank proposal which was begun at yesterday's meeting was continued.

IV-6(b) [["Payment Provisions"]] [284]

The first part of Section 6(b) is necessary because use of the international monetary unit has been dropped. The second part of this section replaces IV-10(c) [of the U.S. draft].

Mr. Bernstein (U.S.) remarked that if member countries are allowed to repay in any "convertible" currency rather than in the currency borrowed that the Bank will be burdened with conversion operations. Furthermore, there will be a serious problem if the currency in which the loan was made is a scarce currency in the Fund and the Bank wishes to convert the "convertible" currency which it receives in repayment. **Lord Keynes** thought that this provision would work out in about the same manner as the corresponding provisions in the U.S. draft. **Mr. Bernstein (U.S.)** requested a further discussion of this provision, of the corresponding provisions of the U.S. draft of November 1943, and of the gold repurchase provisions of the U.S. draft of November 1943 (II-7) [["Repurchase of Local Currency"]]. **Lord Keynes** deferred this discussion until we have completed the explanation of this draft.

Mr. Rasminsky (Canada) pointed out that in order for the Bank to convert currency required a repayment of loans to the Fund, it will be necessary to set up a special definition of "current transaction." **Lord Keynes** agreed.

IV-6(c) [[Payment Provisions]]

Section 6(c) replaces IV-10(d) of the U.S. draft. **Mr. Bernstein (U.S.)** remarked that provision 6(c)(1), which provides that if the service of a loan is paid in local currency, the Bank may require part of such currency to be transferred to another member country, in whose hands it shall be freely available to make payments or to purchase exports in the borrowing country, could operate as a mild sanction against the borrowing country, forcing it to cut down imports and increase exports. Therefore, great discretion would have to be exercised by the Bank in

---

[284] In this chapter, the British version of the Bank agreement is the baseline, so section headings are to it unless otherwise indicated, whereas in the previous chapter, the American version was the baseline.

connection with this provision.

Mr. Bernstein also suggested that the Bank might require member countries to take portions of this local currency instead of calling up guarantees. In reply to a question by **Mr. Basch (Czechoslovakia)**, **Lord Keynes** stated that the rate of exchange used in such cases would be the normal rate of exchange.

Ambassador Varvaressos (Greece) suggested that this provision might be mitigated by specifying time limits for the period during which a borrowing country which pays service and loans in local currency shall repurchase this local currency from the Bank.. He suggested that this period might be longer than three years. **Lord Keynes (UK)** stated that the three-year period referred to was not the period of repurchase, but the period during which the Bank may accept local currency in respect of payments for service on a loan.

Mr. Bernstein (U.S.) suggested that some definite rate of repurchase, such as is provided for under the provision on liquidation of the Fund, might be provided for. **Lord Keynes** agreed that this was a possibility. **Ambassador Varvaressos (Greece)** also felt that this was a possibility. **Mr. Mládek (Czechoslovakia)** remarked that this could lead to temporary forced investment in a country with an adverse balance of payments, but he felt that, on the whole, the paragraph had a great deal of merit.

IV-7 [["Guarantees"]]

In regard to Section 7, **Mr. [Louchheim (U.S.)** remarked that the wording seems to limit the loans which the Bank may guarantee to national governments.

Lord Keynes then called attention to the fact that the proceeds of loans made through the usual investment channels and guaranteed by the Bank must be fully transferable for purchases in any member country. **Mr. Bernstein (U.S.)** stated that he agreed that there was a difference between direct loans and guaranteed loans in this respect, but that there are political implications to be considered, and that he was not qualified to comment on this point.

Mr. Gardner (U.S.) commented upon the flat-rate commission provided for in this section. **Lord Keynes (UK)** pointed out that there will be a wide range of risks in connection with which the market will have little to base its judgment upon. Therefore, the pattern of the insurance factor in the rate of interest will be very erratic. The Bank will be asked to guarantee the unpopular loans, but that will not mean that the risk of default on these loans is greater than on other loans. **Mr. Bernstein (U.S.)** pointed out that the fact that the Bank charges a flat rate commission does not mean that the rate of interest on the loans will be the same.

Sir Theodore Gregory (India) asked whether the amount of the commission would continue the same during the life of a loan in spite of amortization. **Lord Keynes** replied that this had been intended. If the commission represented an actual rather than an average rate, the charge would be heaviest at the outset. This would be undesirable. **Mr. Bernstein (U.S.)** remarked that a flat rate commission could prove very burdensome, and that this burden would be different depending upon the length of the loan. **Lord Keynes** replied that this would depend partly upon whether the rate of interest was the same for all types of loans, and that he was more afraid of a country's being forced into a shorter-term loan than would otherwise be desirable than of their defaulting because of over-burdensome charges.

Mr. Bernstein stated that the U.S. delegation would present a statistical tabulation dealing with this matter. **Mr. de Iongh (Netherlands)** pointed out that the formation of price for loans in the market will be very much complicated by the establishment of this Bank. Firstly, the credit of this Bank must be correctly rated or else its operations will be hampered. Secondly, the relation of the loans guaranteed by the Bank to other loans which are not guaranteed must be considered. He suggested, therefore, that extensive studies of such technical matters should be undertaken.

IV-8 [["Limit on Guarantees"]]

Lord Keynes pointed out that although the meaning of this section, that lenders shall have no right to call upon the Bank to sell its nonliquid assets, is clear, the drafting is imperfect. **Mr. Bernstein (U.S.)** questioned the inclusion of profits derived from operations under 1(a) as part of the security against guarantees given under 1(b) and 1(c). **Mr. Luxford (U.S.)** suggested that it might be simpler to say that all defaults should first be met out of surplus and the Guarantee Fund.

IV-9 [["Covering Deficiencies"]]

Section 9 explains how guarantees are to be implemented.

IV-10 [["Suspension of Membership"]]

Section 10 replaces the first two paragraphs of provision V-8 of the U.S. draft.

IV-11 [["Withdrawal or Suspension from Bank"]

Section 11 replaces the third paragraph of provision V-8 of the U.S. draft. **Mr. Bernstein (U.S.)** remarked that the U.S. delegation had been working on this problem and would submit a redraft of this provision later today.

IV-12 [["Distribution of Net Profits"]]

Section 12 replaces provision V-9 of the U.S. draft. **Mr. Luxford (U.S.)** remarked that the U.S. delegation that also been considering a more conservative provision on this point. The problem of distribution of profit will not arise in connection with loans under IV-1(b) or IV-1(c). However, it will not be desirable to pile up profits resulting from loans under IV-1(a). **Mr. Bernstein (U.S.)** felt that a reserve limit should be set, but agreed that if the income from such loans should be reserved, they should be reserved as is provided for here.

V-1 to V-4 [["Other Powers"; "Agency Powers"; "Agencies Dealing with Bank"; "No Assistance to Suspended Members"]]

Article V, Section 1 replaces provision IV-15 of the U.S. draft [["Other Powers"]]; Section 2 replaces provision IV-16 of the U.S. draft [["Agency Powers"]]; Section 3 replaces IV-17 of the U.S. draft [["Agencies Dealing with Bank"]]; and Section 4 replaces IV-18 of the U.S. draft [["No Assistance to Suspended Members"]]. It was pointed out that Section 4 makes any country defaulting on one of the Bank's loans a financial outlaw. **Mr. Bernstein (U.S.)** replied that in the case of United States, a defaulting country would be prevented from use of the facilities of the Exchange Stabilization Fund, the Export-Import Bank,[285] and other

---

[285] The United States established the Exchange Stabilization Fund in 1934, patterning it after Britain's Exchange Equalisation Account. The Department of the Treasury administered the Exchange Stabilization Fund, thereby giving the president of the United States as an instrument of monetary policy independent

313

governmental institutions, but would not be prohibited from raising funds in the market.

V-8 and V-9 [of U.S. draft, ["Suspension of Membership"; Distribution of Net Profits"]]

Lord Keynes remarked that aside from provision V-8 and V-9 of the U.S. draft, which have been included under the article "Powers and Operations" in the UK draft [Article IV], the UK delegation have not yet considered questions of management.

Mr. Bernstein (U.S.) remarked that one of the essential differences in the UK and the U.S. draft[s] is the division of the Bank's capital into two distinct parts. He felt that this might involve legal difficulties. The U.S. delegation had intended to insert a clause limiting the amount of the Bank's capital which could be used for direct loans, and also intended providing that this part of the bank's capital should eventually consist only of gold and gold convertible currencies, so that there would be no necessity for tying loans. **Lord Keynes** remarked that Mr. Luxford (U.S.) had suggested that a provision might be worked out providing that such part of the bank's capital as is set apart for direct loans and is not so used could be gradually made available for guaranteeing. He felt that the suggestion would be more acceptable to the UK delegation. **Mr. Robbins (UK)** requested a draft provision embodying Mr. Bernstein's suggestion.

---

of the Federal Reserve System. On occasion, the fund made loans or extended lines of credit to foreign governments. The Export-Import Bank, also established in 1934, offered financing for trade deals that commercial lenders considered too risky to make on standard terms.

PART V

CONFERENCE MEETINGS: SUBCOMMITTEES

53

Subcommittee 1
IMF Purposes, Policies and Subscriptions
First meeting
Atlantic City
June 20, 1944, [morning] [286]

Chairman's welcome • Depositories and form of currency holdings

Subcommittee 1 covered IMF purposes, policies, and subscriptions (that is, capital contributions, or in IMF terminology, quotas). The subcommittee chairman, Tingfu Tsiang, was an experienced Chinese diplomat and bureaucrat who had obtained his good knowledge of English when he earned a Ph.D. in history at Columbia University two decades earlier. He would also be the chairman of the similar committee at Bretton Woods.

At its first meeting, the subcommittee considers questions concerning depositories, that is, the organizations or places in which the IMF will hold its assets. The debate is now mainly of interest as a historical reflection of power relations among prospective members of the IMF. The location of assets has little or no importance for trading today given the much reduced role of gold as a reserve asset; the freedom of capital movements that most major economies allow; inexpensive global communications; and computerized financial markets. Traders today can easily hold assets across the globe and trade them at the push of a button.

Except as noted, minutes of the meetings of all subcommittees are by American secretaries, stenographers, and typists.

The meeting opened with **Mr. [Tingfu] Tsiang [China, Chairman]**

---

[286] Present: Mr. [Tingfu] Tsiang of China, Chairman; Mr. [Octavio de] Bulhões of Brazil, Reporter; Mr. [Fyodor] Bystrov of Russia; Mr. [Robert] Mossé of France; Mr. [Wynne] Plumptre of Canada; Mr. [Antonín] Basch of Czechoslovakia; Mr. [James] Brigden of Australia; Messrs. [Frederick] Livesey, [Emanuel] Goldenweiser and [Emanuel "Duke"] Minskoff of the United States.

explaining that the purpose of the committee was to discuss and consider the problems raised in the flimsies and that there is no compulsion that any agreement be reached on the points involved, but that on the other hand, it was not necessary to disagree. He pointed out that any questions on which agreement was not reached will be referred to the meeting of the whole [the Agenda Committee].

Out of the three topics assigned, the committee considered only the flimsy dealing with "Depositories and Form of Currency Holdings."[287]

The following questions were discussed:

1. Was it intended that the Fund "designate" the depositary in each member country for local currency? It was agreed that:

(a) The language should be redrafted to make it clear that the central bank should be used whenever one was available, and

(b) That in the absence of a central bank, the country recommend the depository.

There was a minority view which preferred to remove the flexibility of the word "recommended" and substitute for the word "designate."

2. The question was raised in connection with the provision that a member country could use bills, notes, etc. in lieu of that part of its currency which was not needed by the Fund for its operations. The point was made that in view of the possibility that only a small percentage of a country's contribution might be held in currency, and a very large percentage in demand securities, that such country might be caught off balance by a sudden demand by the Fund for its currency, in lieu of the securities deposited.

The further point was made that such a provision makes it easier for countries to come in, but may make it difficult for them to meet their commitments. However, the general feeling was that the language which permitted substitution of nonnegotiable and noninterest-bearing demand securities was a little improvement.

3. The question was asked what the phrase "other assets," including gold, meant. The thought was expressed that other assets would be limited to collateral put up by the Fund, since any foreign exchange would really be local currency of some member country.

4. The question was raised with reference to the fact that the "four" countries having the largest quotas were particularly mentioned as

---

[287] See also proposed additional Section VII-6, Alternative A, U.S., in chapter 74. The other two topics that the Agenda Committee assigned to Subcommittee 1 were "form of subscription" and "statement of policies"; see chapter 38.

depositories for the Fund's gold holdings. Among other things, it was stated that:

(a) The number might be five, in accordance with the approach of Article VII [VII-1, ["Board and Executive Committee"]], or

(b) It might refer to countries having [at least] 10 percent of the aggregate quota [apiece], or

(c) It might refer merely to the largest countries.

After some discussion, the feeling was rather general that in view of the fact that the Fund would only be required to hold one piece of gold in three or four countries to meet this provision, that the designation is not particularly important.

5. A question was raised with respect to the provision that at least half of the Fund's holdings of gold were to be in the country having the largest quota.[288] After rather extended discussion of the various considerations, it was suggested that some language might be adapted to the fact that the Fund will distribute its holdings in accordance with such criteria as shipments, necessities of the Fund, and subscriptions, provided that at least 50 percent be held in the country with the largest quota. The general view, however, was to avoid reference to quotas or subscriptions.

---

[288] The United States.

54

Subcommittee 1
IMF Purposes, Policies and Subscriptions
Second meeting
Atlantic City
June 21, 1944, [morning] [289]

Depositories and form of currency holdings • Payment of subscriptions

The subcommittee concludes its work on depositories, then turns to payment of subscriptions. A Soviet delegate suggests a reduction in the first installment of subscriptions for countries that have been heavily damaged by the war — which, of course, is true of the Soviet Union. The subcommittee does not resolve the issue.

[Flimsy on] Depositories and Form of Currency Holdings

Having reported on Section 1 [of the flimsy] yesterday, the committee considered Section 2.

1. **[Robert] Mossé [France]** suggested new language for the first sentence for Section 2 to read as follows: "The Fund may hold other assets including gold in designated depositories in such member countries as the Fund may select having due regard to the probable needs of the Fund, size of the gold subscription of the member country and the shipment facilities." **Mr. [Emanuel] Goldenweiser [U.S.]** agreed with the suggestion. **Mr. [Fyodor] Bystrov, USSR,** insisted that the

---

[289] Present: Mr. Tsiang of China, Chairman; Mr. Bulhões of Brazil, Reporter; Mr. Bystrov of Russia; Mr. Mossé of France; Mr. Plumptre of Canada; Mr. Basch of Czechoslovakia; Mr. Brigden of Australia; Messrs. Livesey, Goldenweiser and Minskoff of the United States. [Also, not mentioned in this list but present in the minutes, Alice Bourneuf of the United States.]

paragraph remain intact. **Mr. [Wynne] Plumptre, Canada,** was willing to go along with Mossé's suggestion provided that they [i.e., the delegates favoring the suggestion] omitted the reference to quotas, otherwise he too would prefer the original language. **Mr. [Tingfu] Tsiang, China [Chairman]** also agreed to keep the paragraph intact. **Mr. [Octavio de] Bulhões [Brazil, Reporter]** and **Miss [Alice] Bourneuf [U.S.]** also opposed tying amounts of gold deposited in the various depositories to quotas or subscriptions of gold. The alternatives will be presented to the meeting as a whole.

The quotas being basic to Mossé's whole idea, obviously the suggestion was not acceptable. (At one time, gold subscriptions were included. This was changed to quotas.)

2. With respect to the second sentence of Section 2, Mr. Bystrov suggested that the words "at least one-half" be changed to read "about one-half." He wasn't concerned with the form; it was a change in substance. He felt that approximately one-half should be the outside United States. **Mr. Plumptre** objected to the word "about" as being stupid. After some discussion, it was decided this question should be presented to the meeting as a whole.

[Flimsy on] Payment of Subscriptions

3. Section 1 [of the flimsy] was approved.

4. **Mr. Bystrov** suggested that where a country has been damaged by enemy occupation and / or hostilities, that the 75 percent mentioned in the second paragraph of Section 2 be amended to read "between 75 percent and 50 percent," depending on the extent of damage caused by such hostilities and / or occupation. **Plumptre** pointed out that it would be extremely difficult to get 65 percent, 75 percent, etc., and argued that a fixed figure has much to commend it. **Goldenweiser** pointed out that the total gold subscription was only 10 percent of the country's holdings, and under the present provision [is] reduced to 7½ percent, and that the total holdings of the Fund in gold outside of United States contribution would be less than $1 billion. His argument was that this was a very small amount relatively. **Dr. Tsiang** of **China** agreed that the difference of China would be very small, but that the difference of the Fund [as a whole] might be important. This will also be presented to the committee as a whole [the Agenda Committee].

5. Section 3 was approved.

The committee has completed two of its three assignments and will begin its third assignment, "Purposes and Policies," at the next meeting.

55

Subcommittee 1
IMF Purposes, Policies and Subscriptions
Third meeting
Atlantic City
June 22, 1944, [morning] [290]

Purposes and policies

The subcommittee considers a flimsy related to the first article of the IMF Articles of Agreement, which enumerates the purposes and policies of the organization. The changes are not controversial at this stage.

Purposes and Policies [Article I]

1. The committee felt that Section 1 of Article I [["Promote International Monetary Cooperation"]] should be modified by omitting the subordinate clause reading "which provides for the machinery for consultation on international monetary problems." It was thought that the shortened sentence was broader and more meaningful.

2. Section 2 [["Balanced Trade, High Employment and Real Income"]] was approved as written.

3. Section 3 [["Lend to Members"]] was approved as written.

4. Section 4 [["Promote Exchange Stability"]] was approved as written.

5. Section 5 [["Assist with Multilateral Payments Facilities"]] was approved as written.

6. Section 6 [["Shorten Balance of Payments Disequilibrium"]] was approved as written. However, Section 6 was renumbered 4, and Section

---

[290] Present: Mr. Tsiang of China, Chairman; Mr. Bulhões of Brazil, Reporter; Mr. Bystrov of Russia; Mr. Mossé of France; Mr. Plumptre of Canada; Mr. Basch of Czechoslovakia; Mr. Brigden of Australia; Messrs. Livesey, Goldenweiser and Minskoff of the United States.

4 was renumbered 6.

7. It was suggested that an additional item be added to indicate that the Fund was not intended to be the cure-all for the world's economic needs, but rather to form a part of the pattern of organizations such as [the] Reconstruction Bank, etc. This would be suggested at the meeting of the whole [Agenda Committee]. It will probably take the form of a suggestion that a portion of the Foreword contained in paragraph 3 of the Foreword be utilized.

8. It will also be suggested, probably privately rather than at the general meeting, that there be, when the formal meetings start and the British have arrived, a statement or preferably a series of statements by **White** and **Keynes** and other members the senior delegations, concerning the "Fund at work" for the information and enlightenment of the delegates and technicians. The suggestion was made by **Mossé [France]** and **Plumptre [Canada]**.

The committee completed the assignment and will take up at the following meeting two new assignments.

56

Subcommittee 1
IMF Purposes, Policies and Subscriptions
Fourth meeting
Atlantic City
June 23, 1944, [morning] [291]

Statement of IMF policies • Obtaining information from members • Publication of reports • IMF recommendations to members

Subcommittee chairman Tingfu Tsiang proposes an artful phrase on the purposes and policies of the IMF that avoids committing member countries to those policies. The subcommittee then discusses the kinds of information that the IMF may require from its members. A delegate from the Soviet Union, which treats information about its economy as state secrets, wishes to minimize the information required. The Soviet delegate is also eager to prevent the IMF from making recommendations that would require a country to make fundamental changes to its economic system. Ultimately, because of concerns such as the Soviet delegate voices here, the Soviet Union would not join the IMF and World Bank. After the Soviet Union dissolved in 1991, its successor states all eventually joined, and all made fundamental changes leaving behind comprehensive centralized economic planning.

1. *Statement of policies.* The committee reverted to the question of the purposes and policies which had been previously considered [Article I] and, at the suggestion of the **Chairman,** agreed to amend the section on purposes and policies to begin as follows: "The purposes and policies of the member countries in establishing the Fund are as follows:"

This was rather an ingenious suggestion, intended to include both the

---

[291] Present: Mr. Tsiang of China, Chairman; Mr. Bulhões of Brazil, Reporter; Mr. Bystrov of Russia; Mr. Mossé of France; Mr. Plumptre of Canada; Mr. Basch of Czechoslovakia; Mr. Brigden of Australia; Messrs. Livesey, Goldenweiser and Minskoff of the United States.

obligation of the Fund that of the member countries, without making it too clear or too obvious that the member countries were undertaking any obligation. It was felt that this was preferable to any bald statement that the purposes and policies of the Fund shall be the purposes and policies of member countries.

2. *Obtaining information.*[292] **Mr. Plumptre [Canada]** objected to the tone of the language which demanded information, spoke of uniform information, required information, etc. Being an opportunist, the **Secretary [Emanuel "Duke" Minskoff, U.S.]** suggested that elimination of the second sentence (which we had previously already agreed-upon) might meet the point made by Mr. Plumptre. Upon further modification, the sense of the meaning was to adopt language along the following lines: "Member countries undertake to oblige the Fund with such information as is necessary for its operations. Information other than required information shall be furnished to the Fund by agreement with member countries."

Mr. [Fyodor] Bystrov [USSR], as may be expected, felt very strongly on the question of information, and suggested that the Secretariat indicate and itemize the types of information desired. It was thought that if the enumeration was satisfactory, the first sentence could include information and the second sentence would merely mention that information other than that enumerated might be required by agreement with member countries.

3. *Publication of reports* passed through unscathed.[293]

4. *Consideration of recommendations of the Fund.*[294] **Mr. Bystrov** wanted to know why we deviated from the language contained in the July [1943] draft.[295] The **Secretary** pointed out that the change is not substantive and

---

[292] There was a flimsy by this name, which includes as sections points 2-4 on this page. See also proposed new Section III-11, "Furnishing Information," Alternative A, U.S.

[293] See also VII-4 [["Publication of Financial Position"]], Alternative A, U.S..

[294] See also III, additional section following proposed Section 12, Alternative A, U.S.

[295] Bystrov is referring to the U.S. "Preliminary Draft Outline of a Proposal for an International Stabilization Fund of the United and Associated Nations," also known as the White plan after its chief drafter, Harry Dexter White. Article VII, section 6 of the White plan states that members undertake "To give consideration to the views of the Fund on any existing or proposed monetary or economic policy, the effect of which would be to bring about sooner or later a serious disequilibrium in the balance of payments of other countries."

really a matter of language and that the Secretary would have no objection to reverting to the original language used. It became clear that the question was merely an opening wedge; his objection was more fundamental. He desired to have a proviso that the Fund would not make representations which required a fundamental change in the economic stricture of a member country.

The sense of the meeting was that the following language would be presented to the committee of the whole [the full Preliminary Agenda Committee]: "The Fund shall have the right to make representations to any member country at any time on any existing or proposed economic policy of such member country which tends or may tend to produce a serious disequilibrium in the international balance of payments of member countries."

In addition, it will be noted that **Mr. Bystrov** suggests the proviso to the effect that the Fund shall not recommend a change in the fundamental economic structure of a country.

Mr. Mossé's [France] suggestion, the attention of the meeting will be called to the possibility of referring back to the language contained in the Joint Statement with reference to "domestic, social or political policies."

Mr. Mossé suggested that the committee should not consider the matters before it as not being germane to its assignment, but should enter into a consideration of the problem of quotas. The **Secretary,** supported by the **Chairman,** gently but firmly reminded Mr. Mossé that some of the flimsies were not ready, including that on quotas, and that it would not be really helpful to attempt unilaterally to change the orderly handling of assignments made to the various committees.

57

Subcommittee 2
Operations of the Fund
First meeting
Atlantic City
June 20, 1944 at 9:30 a.m.[296]

IMF purchases of a member's currency with gold • Member's purchase of IMF holdings of its currency with gold • Minimum proportion of gold in purchases of foreign currency from IMF

Subcommittee 2 covered the operations of the IMF, such as its purchases and sales of members' currencies and the related topic of exchange controls. The subcommittee chairman, André Istel of France, had been a prominent banker before World War II and was the author of a 1943 Free French plan for international monetary cooperation.

At its first meeting, the subcommittee considers questions concerning the relationship between member currencies and gold. Despite the intent, expressed elsewhere at the conference, to avoid a return to "the old gold standard," gold remained in the picture because it was internationally accepted and because it was large share of some countries' international reserve assets. For example, more than half of the Federal Reserve System's assets consisted of gold.

1. [The] meeting began over discussion of whether or not a member country is required to accept gold from the Fund in exchange for its own

---

[296] Present: Mr. [André] Istel of France, Chairman; Mr. [Louis] Rasminsky of Canada, Reporter; Mr. [Jacques] Polak of the Netherlands; Messrs. [A.P.] Morozov and [N.I.] Kuznetzov of the USSR; Mr. [Felipe] Pazos of Cuba; Mr. [Ts-Liang] Soong of China; Messrs. [Edward?] Brown, [Emilio] Collado, [August] Maffry, [Raymond] Mikesell and [Elting] Arnold of United States.

currency.[297] **Mr. [Louis] Rasminsky [Canada]** stated that although there is no explicit provision for acceptance of gold by a member country from the Fund, a country was actually obligated to accept gold in order to meet its obligation to the Fund to maintain its exchange rate. The acceptance of gold by the member countries from the Fund is also implicit in the provisions of the Fund [agreement] requiring the payment of gold to the Fund by the member country.

2. **Mr. [Jacques] Polak [Netherlands]** raised the question as to whether or not III-7(a) [["Fund's Acquisition of Gold"]] should be modified by a clause which stated that a member country would not have the right to repurchase its own currency with gold from the Fund if the Fund's supply of such currency were very low. It was the consensus of the meeting that such a provision was not necessary.

3. With respect to this III-7(b), **Mr. Rasminsky** raised the issue as to whether countries with gold and gold convertible foreign exchange in excess of their quotas should not be required to use all of such excess for the purchase of needed foreign exchange before buying foreign exchange from the Fund with its own currency, instead of only half as is provided under Section III-7(b). There was not full discussion on this point.

4. Certain ambiguities in the language of Section III-7(b) were discussed, and the **Chairman [André Istel, France]** appointed **Mr. [Elting] Arnold [U.S.]** to draft new language which would maintain the subsidy [substance] of meaning but would reflect the views of the committee with regard to the elimination of these ambiguities.

---

[297] From the flimsy "Acquisitions of Gold by the Fund." See also III-7, [["Fund's Acquisition of Gold"]].

58

Subcommittee 2
Operations of the Fund
Second meeting
Atlantic City
June 21, 1944 at 10 a.m.[298]

Scarce currencies • IMF acquisition of currencies from third parties • IMF acquisition of gold from war-damaged countries

The subcommittee addresses scarce currencies, a potential problem that took up much thought and time but turned out not to be important in the actual operations of the IMF. To repeat what we have said elsewhere, it was expected that for at least a few years after World War II, many IMF members would have inconvertible currencies, as they continued with exchange controls to avoid devaluing to market-clearing levels and incurring the inflation that would result. The IMF's effectively usable resources would be limited to its holdings of gold and fully convertible currencies — in practice, overwhelmingly U.S. dollars. If each member drew (borrowed) convertible currency up to the amount of its quota (contribution), there would not be enough for all.

The subcommittee also considers whether the IMF must buy a currency only from the issuing country, and whether members may sell the currencies of other countries to the IMF. Latin American delegates favor more latitude than delegates of other countries. Also, a Soviet delegate presses for delaying the requirement for countries heavily damaged by the war that when their external reserves increase, they must exchange some of the additional reserves for the IOUs they have given the IMF. For countries whose currencies are inconvertible, such as the Soviet Union, the IOUs are in practice nearly worthless.

---

[298] Present: Mr. Istel of France, Chairman; Mr. Rasminsky of Canada, Reporter; Mr. Polak of the Netherlands; Messrs. Morozov and Kuznetzov of the USSR; Mr. Pazos of Cuba; Mr. Soong of China; Messrs. Brown, Collado, Maffry, Mikesell and Arnold of United States.

1. Committee 2 has covered the entire section on scarce currencies, the Fund's power to acquire needed foreign exchange, and has completed the discussion of acquisitions of gold by the Fund and began the discussion of III-5 [["Obligations of a Purchasing Country"]] under the topic "Provisions Concerning Multilateral Clearing."[299]

Two points [were] raised:

(a) In regard to scarce currency, **Mr. [August] Maffry [U.S.]** stated that he was of the opinion that Article VI-2 [["Rationing of Scarce Currency"]] should be subject to the provisions of Article IX-3 [["Current Transactions"]] as well as IX-2 [["Foreign Exchange Dealings"]]. It was pointed out that this would be inconsistent with the purposes of article VI-2.

(b) **[Ts-Liang] Soong [China], [André] Istel [France]** and **[Antonio Espinosa de los] Monteros [Mexico]** believed that the issue of a report with regard to scarce currency might cause a run on the currency which was scarce. It was decided to include a provision to the effect that the timing of the report would be at the discretion of the Fund. It was also decided that the report mentioned in VI-1 [["Fund Warning of Scarcity"]] should be permissive on the part of the Fund, whereas a report and recommendations must be made at the time a currency is declared scarce.

(c) The question was raised as to whether the Fund should have the right to buy from a member country the currency of a third member country. **Mr. Rasminsky [Canada]** supported the view of the Joint Statement with regard to the passivity of the Fund. **Monteros** and **[Felipe] Pazos [Cuba]** thought that the Fund should be allowed to buy or borrow dollars from Cuba and Mexico with the permission of the lending country.

(d) An important question was raised as to whether the authorization to restrict transactions and scarce currency should apply to the member country whose currency was scarce. **Mr. [Edward?] Brown [U.S.]** took the view that a country whose currency was declared scarce should be permitted to restrict operations in its own currency.

(e) **Mr. [A.P.] Morozov of the USSR** stated that III-7(b) [["Fund's Acquisition of Gold"]] [should] be amended so as not to apply during the

---

[299] The flimsies and the parts of the IMF draft agreement related to them are "Scarce Currencies" (Article VI), "Acquisitions of Gold by the Fund" (III-7, [["Fund's Acquisition of Gold"]]), and "Provisions Concerning Multilateral Clearing" (III-5, [["Obligations of a Purchasing Country"]]).

first five years of the Fund's operations to countries which were occupied or devastated, and also that III-7(c) should not be applied during the period of restoration [reconstruction] in the case of occupied or devastated countries in the case of acquisitions of newly mined gold. There was little discussion on this point, except to point out that section 7(c) would not apply to a country unless it had a net accumulation of gold and gold convertible exchange, which would not be likely to occur in the case of devastated countries.

(f) **Mr. Rasminsky** suggested that we should stick to the substance of the topics rather than to the language, and that we should avoid any attempt to redraft provisions in exact language.

(g) **Dr. Pazos** raised the question as to why Cuba should not sell Brazilian currency directly to the Fund rather than having to require Brazil to buy back its own currency. The answer given emphasized the passivity of the Fund, and the responsibility of each member country for the Fund's holdings of its currency and the handling of its balance of payments position.

59

Subcommittee 2
Operations of the Fund
Third meeting
Atlantic City
June 22, 1944 at 9:30 a.m.[300]

Reciprocal obligations of members to purchase one another's currencies • Multiple exchange rates • Distinguishing current account from capital account transfers • IMF approval of discriminatory currency practices

The subcommittee considers various provisions related to exchange controls.

The three provisions set forth in the attached memorandum [the flimsy "Provision Concerning Multilateral Clearing"] were discussed:

1. Points raised concerning provision III-5 [["Obligations of a Purchasing Country"]]:

a. The phrase "of a current account nature" should be deleted and the word "any" inserted before the word "transactions" in order to clarify that holdings accumulated as a result of capital transactions effected before the removal of restrictions of the early postwar period should not become subject to the operations of this provision.

b. There was considerable discussion as to whether the phrase "payments and transfers" covered adequately all transfers which were intended to be covered. The consensus of the group seemed to be that this phrase is satisfactory.

2. Points raised concerning provision IX-3 [["Current Transactions"]]:

---

[300] Present: Mr. Istel of France, Chairman; Mr. Rasminsky of Canada, Reporter; Mr. Polak of the Netherlands; Messrs. Morozov and Kuznetzov of the USSR; Mr. Pazos of Cuba; Mr. Soong of China; Messrs. Brown, Collado, Maffry, Mikesell and Arnold of United States.

a. **Mr. [Antonín] Basch [Czechoslovakia]** inquired whether it was intended that any multiple currency practices were to be permitted under the Fund, and pointed out that this phrase is worded would allow this. It was suggested that multiple currency practices might be allowed for such purposes as encouraging student travel. Mr. Basch another stated firmly that they believed such things should be encouraged by other means and that the door should not be open to such practices.

b. There is also considerable discussion of the problem of distinguishing between transfers of a current account nature and transfers of a capital account nature. The **Secretary [Raymond Mikesell, U.S.]** explained that we consider that there is a difference between exchange control and exchange restriction. The **Chairman [André Istel, France]** suggested that in order to control capital transactions, something further than overall scrutiny would be necessary, and that restrictions would be involved.

Rasminsky [Canada] stated that he preferred the language of the original draft, which includes the cause "other than those involving capital transactions or in accordance with VI, above," because of such things as contractual amortization.

It was agreed that the language of the draft needed clarification and that Mr. Rasminsky should report on this point.

3. Points raised concerning [proposed new] provision IX-4 [["Relation to Other Commitments"]].

a. **Mr. Rasminsky** stated that if this provision means that countries are given complete jurisdiction in regard to imposing restrictions on currencies declared scarce, etc., only within the limits of all existing treaties, that he felt we should consider the whole matter of provision VI-2 [["Rationing of Scarce Currencies"]] before discussing this point. He felt in particular that this provision is couched in much too general terms. It was agreed that Mr. Rasminsky should report on this point.

60

Subcommittee 2
Operations of the Fund
Fourth meeting
Atlantic City
June 23, 1944 at 9:30 a.m.[301]

Role of silver • Current account and capital account movements •
Unofficial markets in foreign currencies

At its fourth and final meeting, the subcommittee completes its discussion of capital movements. A Mexican delegate asks that the Bretton Woods conference consider the monetary role of silver, of which Mexico is a leading producer. The committee concludes with a discussion of exchange controls, which most of the countries present had at the time of the Atlantic City conference and which they expected to continue for some time after the war.

1. Committee No. 2 completed the discussion of the flimsy on capital movements [titled "Capital Movements"].

2. At the beginning of the meeting, **Mr. Monteros [Mexico]** stated that he would like to have silver included on the agenda of the international monetary conference and proposed that there be included under "transactions of the Fund" the following points:

   a. The Fund shall determine the proper role of silver in the operations of the Fund.

   b. The Fund is authorized to follow whatever policy it deems appropriate for silver.

   c. Member countries agree to act in accordance with the principles

---

[301] Present: Mr. Istel of France, Chairman; Mr. Rasminsky of Canada, Reporter; Mr. Polak of the Netherlands; Messrs. Morozov and Kuznetzov of the USSR; Mr. Pazos of Cuba; Mr. Soong of China; Messrs. Brown, Collado, Maffry, Mikesell and Arnold of United States.

with respect to silver which the Fund adopts.

3. There was considerable discussion as to how capital movements might be controlled without imposing overall controls with respect to all exchange transactions. It was pointed out that the requirement not to impose restrictions on payments arising out of current international transactions did not prevent a country from adopting exchange controls, and in fact in some instances overall exchange controls might be necessary.

4. It was the view of **Rasminsky [Canada], Istel [France]** and other members of the committee that Article X-2 [["Transition Period"]] was somewhat ambiguous with respect to the obligation of a member country. The principles involved in X-2 were explained by the **Secretary [Raymond Mikesell, U.S.]**, and there was no disagreement here, but the language was not thought to clearly indicate this principle.

5. **Rasminsky** asked whether or not a country would be meeting its obligation of the Fund if it required its exporters to receive payment in dollars, thereby making it impossible for nonresidents to use previously accumulated balances for payment of imports from that country. Mr. Rasminsky inquired further as to whether or not the Fund would permit an unofficial market in such blocked balances in another country and inquired as to whose responsibility, if any, it would be to maintain a rate of exchange respect to such balances. This point was discussed at some length and will be referred to in the larger [Agenda] Committee.

61

Subcommittee 3
Organization and Management of the Fund
First meeting
Atlantic City
June 20, 1944 at 10 a.m.[302]

Executive Directors • Voting

Subcommittee 3 covered the internal organization of the IMF, including the sensitive matter of how Executive Directors would be chosen. The subcommittee chairman, Alexei Smirnov, was a professor at the Institute of Foreign Trade in Moscow.

At its first meeting, the subcommittee recommends that alternate Executive Directors only be allowed to vote when their Executive Directors are absent. It then considers which powers the Board of Governors should not be allowed to delegate to the Executive Directors. The Board of Governors will consist of representatives of all IMF members, whereas the Executive Directors will be a limited body in which most small members will lack direct representation. Finally, the subcommittee considers part of the formula for votes, which will consist of a uniform number of basic votes plus a variable number of votes determined largely by economic size. The higher the number of basic votes, the greater the relative influence of small countries. The variable number of votes would be a matter of extensive debate and haggling at the Bretton Woods conference.

1. Board of Directors[303]

(a) **Mr. [Aleksei] Smirnov [USSR]** opened the meeting with a

---

[302] Present: Mr. [Aleksei] Smirnov of the USSR, Chairman; Mr. [Antonio Espinosa de los] Monteros of Mexico, Reporter; Mr. [Rodrigo] Gómez of Mexico; Mr. [Kuo-Ching] Li of China; Mr. [Raoul] Aglion of France; Mr. [James] Brigden of Australia; Messrs. [Walter] Gardner, Brown, [Karl] Bopp and [Elting] Arnold of the United States.

[303] The flimsy the subcommittee discussed in this session was "Governing Board and Executive Committee." Numbers refer to sections of the flimsy.

discussion on the Governing Board and Executive Committee. Committee recommends the insertion of the words "except that they may vote only in the absence of their respective directors" at the close of sentence 3.

(b) Delete the word "annual" from line 2.

Question was raised as to limitations on the power of the Board of Governors to "delegate" its powers with respect to certain fundamental questions. The questions that were mentioned specifically were:

(1) General change in the price of gold.

(2) Suspension of a member.

(3) To liquidate the Fund.

The following wording was suggested. Insert at the end of the first sentence the words "except powers to change the price of gold, to suspend a member country, or to liquidate the Fund."

(c) Question was raised as to whether to include a provision similar to Section VI-10 of the [U.S. "White plan"] July 10, 1943 draft requiring the chairman to call a meeting if requested to do so by members casting one-fourth of the votes.

It was suggested that the provision of Section VI-10 of the July 10, 1943 draft requiring that "not more than one annual meeting in any five-year period shall be held within the same member country" should be reinstated.[304]

(d) No change.

(e) No change.

2. Voting

Paragraph 1. Question was raised as to why the number 25 [votes] has been substituted for 100, as stated in the draft of July 10, 1943 and whether 100 should be restored.

It was agreed that if a new monetary unit is adopted by the Fund, the

---

[304] Section VI-10 of the White plan read as follows:

"The Board of Directors shall hold an annual meeting and such other meetings as it may be desirable to convene. The annual meeting shall be held in places designated by the Executive Committee, but not more than one annual meeting in any 5-year period shall be held within the same member country.

"On request of member countries casting one-fourth of the votes, the Chairman shall call a meeting of the Board for the purpose of considering any matters placed before it."

words "1 million U.S. dollars of the weight and fineness in effect on July 1, 1944" should be replaced with the appropriate number of the new monetary units. This change should be made wherever applicable.

Paragraph 2. The language of this paragraph should be clarified to indicate clearly circumstances under which a vote is required, either by listing occasions or by indicating the operations which do not require a vote.

Question was raised as to whether the limitation of one-fifth of the aggregate votes cast should be applicable also to voting under this paragraph.

62

Subcommittee 3
Organization and Management of the Fund
Second meeting
Atlantic City
June 21, 1944 at 12 p.m.[305]

Executive Directors

The subcommittee considers the procedure for electing Executive Directors. The countries with the largest quotas at the IMF will get to appoint their own directors. These countries are expected to be the five major Allied powers — the United States, United Kingdom, Soviet Union, China, and France – and possibly India. The remaining countries will need to form coalitions to elect Executive Directors to represent multiple countries, and the details of calculating which coalitions are sufficient to get a directorship are complex.

The entire session was devoted to a discussion of the Executive Committee of the Fund.[306]

Mr. [Antonio Espinosa de los] Monteros [Mexico] said the provision for proportional representation achieved by the election procedure meets the needs of small countries so far as method of voting is concerned, but he feels the number of votes distributed outside the quota should be increased.

Mr. Smirnov [USSR] said the procedure was very complicated and he would work on a simpler method.

It was agreed that a proposal to provide for rotation among elected directors should be presented for discussion. There was general

---

[305] Present: Mr. Smirnov of the USSR, Chairman; Mr. Monteros of Mexico, Reporter; Mr. Gómez of Mexico; Mr. Li of China; Mr. Aglion of France; Messrs. Gardner, Brown, Bopp and Arnold of the United States.

[306] Section 3 of the flimsy "Governing Board and Executive Committee."

agreement upon or indifference to such a provision.

It is agreed upon the suggestion of **Mr. [Raoul] Aglion [France]** on that the words "in which the person receiving the lowest number of votes shall be ineligible for election and" should be deleted from page 3, section [paragraph] (b), lines 8-9 of the flimsy.

The committee agreed to return to a discussion of the topic at 12 noon on June 22.

63

Subcommittee 3
Organization and Management of the Fund
Third meeting
Atlantic City
June 22, 1944 at 9:30 a.m.[307]

Executive Directors • Managing Director • Monetary unit

The subcommittee continues its discussion about the method of calculating which coalitions of countries have sufficient votes to elect Executive Directors to represent them. A question arises whether Executive Directors represent the general interest of the IMF as an institution or the particular interest of their members. The matter is not resolved at this meeting. A provision concerning the Managing Director, the top manager of the IMF, passes, apparently with little discussion. Finally, the subcommittee discusses what unit of account the IMF shall use. As a practical matter, the choice is between gold and the U.S. dollar, the only fully convertible major currency. In 1969 the IMF would create its own unit of account, the Special Drawing Right (SDR), which was initially equal to the U.S. dollar but later diverged in value as the dollar depreciated. The IMF continues to use the SDR as its unit of account today; for example, loans to members are denominated in SDRs.

Points discussed:

(1) Executive Committee[308]

(2) Managing Director – O.K. [VII-2, 3 Alternative A., U.S., and B., UK]

(3) Monetary unit [IV-1, ["Establishing Par Value"], Alternative A. U.S.]

---

[307] Present: Mr. Smirnov of the USSR, Chairman; Mr. Monteros of Mexico, Reporter; Mr. Gomez of Mexico; Mr. Li of China; Mr. Aglion of France; Messrs. Gardner, Brown, Bopp and Arnold of the United States.

[308] Section 3 of the flimsy "Governing Board and Executive Committee."

(1) **Mr. [Jacques] Polak [Netherlands]** said the device of the five permanent directors discriminated in favor of large countries, and that the method of determining "excess votes" discriminated in favor of the smallest countries, and that together they discriminated against the middle-sized countries.

Methods of avoiding a possible deadlock on the selection of the sixth elected director without embarrassment to any candidate were discussed. Use of a plurality vote either by statement in the Agreement or by authorization granted to the Board of Directors were mentioned as possibilities.

The advantages and disadvantages of rotation were discussed but no firm convictions were expressed.

Important. The fundamental question was raised as to whether a director represented each of his constituents or whether he should vote in the general interest as he saw it. **Mr. Aglion [France]** felt the director should vote in the general interest. **Mr. Smirnov [USSR]** said that a member should have the right to be represented at any meeting at which a matter of vital or direct importance was to be considered and that its director should have the right to cast that country's vote on the question.

(2) Managing Director – O.K.

(3) Unit of account

Mr. Smirnov raised these questions:

(a) Should there be a unit of account?

(b) If so, should it be expressed in terms of gold, per se? The advantage of this method is primarily political. **Mr. Monteros** said **Mexico** would never adopt a definition of the peso in terms of gold.

(c) If there is to be a unit of account, should it be expressed in terms of a single currency – practically the U.S. dollar. The advantage of this method would be in simplicity of accounts and unyielding great quotations similar to existing quotations.

(d) How should par values be expressed – directly in terms of gold, or in a unit of account which is expressed in gold[?]

Will consider tomorrow: withdrawal, suspension, liquidation.

64

Subcommittee 3
Organization and Management of the Fund
Fourth meeting
Atlantic City
June 23, 1944 at 9:30 a.m.[309]

Withdrawal by a member • Suspension of a member • Settlement of a member's accounts with the IMF • Liquidation of the IMF

The subcommittee addresses questions regarding the withdrawal or suspension of members from the IMF and of the liquidation of the IMF itself. This is the last meeting for which we have found minutes, but there is a reference to a future meeting.

Topics considered: [310]
1. Withdrawal
2. Suspension
3. Settlement of accounts
4. Liquidation

1. Withdrawal – O.K.

2. Suspension of membership.
Suggest deletion of word "any" in line 1.
A question was raised as to the definition of the words "privileges" and "obligations." **Mr. Monteros [Mexico]** felt that obligations should be restricted to financial obligations.

---

[309] Present: Mr. Smirnov of the USSR, Chairman; Mr. Monteros of Mexico, Reporter; Mr. Gómez of Mexico; Mr. Li of China; Mr. Aglion of France; Messrs. Gardner, Brown, Bopp and Arnold of the United States.
[310] From the flimsy "Withdrawal and Suspension of Member Countries; Liquidation of the Fund."

3. Settlement of accounts.

Paragraphs 1 and 2 are O.K.

In paragraph 3 the sentence "The country further guarantees such currency against exchange appreciation until it has been used or redeemed as aforesaid" should be reworded to indicate that the Fund should be protected against loss resulting from the depreciation of a member's currency and that it should repay any profits resulting from the appreciation of the member's currency. It should be made clear that the member country should be permitted to reimburse the Fund for any loss resulting from depreciation by payment of additional amounts of the country's currency.

4. Liquidation of the Fund.

The addition of the words "any majority of the member countries, each of which for this purpose shall have one vote."

Recommend the deletion of the word "all" in line 3 of paragraph 1.

The process of liquidation was discussed in a preliminary way and will be resumed at the next meeting.[311]

---

[311] We have found no minutes of the meeting and suspect that no meeting took place.

65

Subcommittee 4
Establishment of the Fund
First meeting
Atlantic City
June 20, 1944 at 10 a.m.[312]

*Setting up the Fund • Beginning operations • Agreeing on
exchange rates • Beginning exchange transactions*

*Subcommittee 4 covered matters related to setting up the IMF and beginning its
operations. The subcommittee chairman, John Deutsch, was a former official of the
Bank of Canada who had moved into an important position in the Canadian foreign
ministry.*

*At its first meeting, the subcommittee considers various questions about acceptance
of membership in the IMF, the IMF's initial meeting, and the beginning of exchange
transactions under the terms of the IMF's Articles of Agreement.*

**[Flimsy] "Setting up the Fund, Beginning Operations, Agreeing on
Exchange Rates and Beginning Exchange Transactions"**

The following points were made in connection with the section on
acceptance of membership in the Fund:

1. Does acceptance of membership clearly mean that the agreement is
binding upon the accepting country? **([Ervin] Hexner,
[Czechoslovakia, Reporter])**

2. Since no commitments will be made by governments at the

---

[312] Present: Mr. [John] Deutsch of Canada, Chairman; Mr. [Ervin] Hexner of
Czechoslovakia, Reporter; Mr. [Daniël Crena] de Iongh of the Netherlands; Mr.
[Jean] de Largentaye of France; Mr. [Redvers] Opie of United Kingdom; Messrs.
[Hawthorne] Arey, [Walter] Louchheim, [Joseph] Dreibelbis, [John Parke] Young
and [Richard] Brenner of United States.

conference, when will commitments be made? **([John] Deutsch, [Canada, Chairman])**

(a) What obligations will be incurred on the date of acceptance of membership?

(b) What is the order in which the obligations attach after acceptance of membership?

3. The provisions considered presuppose that quotas will be determined at the conference and will be set forth in other provisions of the agreement.

4. The suggestion is to be made to the general meeting [Agenda Committee] that a committee be formed to consider the relations of the Fund with nonmember countries and the countries represented at the conference accepting membership after operations have begun. **([Daniël Crena] de Iongh, [Netherlands])**

The section providing for calling the initial meeting of the Fund states that countries will be represented by the directors *and* alternates. The question was raised whether alternates as well as director should attend in order to keep themselves informed or whether they should attend only in the absence of the directors. **([Redvers] Opie, [UK])**

The following points relate to be provisions for the agenda of the initial meeting and the beginning of exchange transactions:

1. Article IV, Section 1 [["Establishing Par Values"]] of the Joint Statement of Principles provides that the prior value of a member's currency shall be agreed with the Fund when it is admitted to membership. In the draft under consideration, the countries are first admitted to membership and subsequently agree with the Fund upon the par values of the currencies. **(Hexner)**

2. Since countries do not agree on a par values until after they have accepted membership, it will be necessary to limit the time within which par values may be agreed upon. **(Hexner)**

3. The draft under consideration requires the Board at the initial meeting to "make provision for agreeing with the member countries upon the par values of their currencies expressed in terms of gold." The suggestion was made that this language might be clarified to indicate clearly that it refers to the setting up of machinery with the purpose of reaching agreement on par values. Verification might include a provision that a special committee be selected for this purpose, or the matter might be left to the Board of Directors. **(Opie)**

4. In what form will the payment of 1/20 of 1 percent of the quota be payable? And what form will the balance of subscriptions be payable? **(Deutsch)**

5. The draft under consideration postpones exchange transactions until at least three months after the Fund shall have determined that hostilities in the present conflict have ceased. **(Hexner)** It was suggested that either of the following might be more appropriate tests:

(a) When the Fund determines that world conditions are suitable for the commencement of exchange transactions. **(Opie)**

(d) When a fixed extraordinary majority of the votes agrees to begin transactions. **(Deutsch)**

It was suggested that more importance attaches to the subsequent provision that exchange transactions shall not begin until par values have been agreed upon for currencies of members having 60 percent of the aggregate quotas then attaches to the cessation of hostilities. **(Opie)**

66

Subcommittee 4
Establishment of the Fund
Second meeting
Atlantic City
June 21, 1944 at 10:30 a.m.[313]

Transitional arrangements

This meeting is entirely devoted to the transition period during which members who do not wish to make their currencies convertible will not be required to do so. For the founders of the IMF, convertibility meant the absence of exchange controls on current account transactions such as international trade in goods and services. The founders were comfortable with permanent exchange controls on capital account transactions such as cross-border purchases and sales of bonds. As matters stand 75 years later, the IMF allows members who have not made their currencies convertible for current account transactions to delay convertibility indefinitely, but once a country declares current account convertibility, it is not supposed to reimpose exchange controls, and the unofficial norm for all high-income countries and many others is full convertibility, including for capital account transactions.

Committee 4 discussed transitional arrangements and began by pointing out that the flimsy ["Transitional Arrangements"] had a number of changes in it from the Joint Statement. **Mr. Opie [UK]** suggested that the changes be pointed out and then ignored.

Mr. de Iongh [Netherlands] suggested that in removing exchange controls, consideration be given to the establishment of priorities in favor of nonresidents over residents.

---

[313] Present: Mr. Deutsch of Canada, Chairman; Mr. Hexner of Czechoslovakia, Reporter; Mr. de Iongh of the Netherlands; Mr. de Largentaye of France; Mr. Opie of United Kingdom; Messrs. Arey, Louchheim, Dreibelbis, Young and Brenner of the United States.

Dr. [Antonín] Basch [Czechoslovakia] questioned the relationship between the prohibition against exchange controls and the fact that the imposition of import controls would be permitted. **Mr. Opie** answered this by pointing out that the conference was the second to be held pursuant to Article VII of the Mutual Aid Agreements, which is a starting point for all economics discussions among the United Nations. He said that he would like to see a strong reference to Article VII in the opening address at the conference, since he felt that it had been unfortunate that this relationship was not clear at Hot Springs.[314]

Mr. [John] Deutsch [Canada] noted that the phrase "restrictions on multilateral clearing" had been left out and other language substituted for it. This led to an hour's discussion of the meaning of multilateral clearing as expressed in III-5 [["Obligations of a Purchasing Country"]]. There was considerable confusion as to what was intended, and even more confusion as to what the language of III-5 meant. At the conclusion of the meeting it was decided that the reporter should state that multilateral clearing was discussed but should not present any details at the meeting.

The last clause of Section 2 of the flimsy states that member countries taking advantage of the transitional arrangement shall, after three years, "retain exchange controls only with the approval of the Fund." This was not in the Joint Statement, and it was agreed that the new clause would give a definite limit to the transitional period. It was the understanding of the foreign [i.e., non-American] members of the committee that the length of the transition period with respect to each country was to be determined by it, and that its acceptance of III-5 and its lifting of exchange controls were to be postponed throughout the period. The general policy question was raised as to whether a country should be permitted to use the Fund's resources if it took advantage of the transitional arrangements. It was decided that this was a general policy question which should not be decided or discussed by the committee.

Mr. [Ervin] Hexner [Czechoslovakia, Reporter] pointed out that in both the Joint Statement and the flimsy, countries are permitted during the transitional period to "maintain and adapt" controls. He felt that this

---

[314] On Article VII of the Mutual Aid Agreements, see the footnote in chapter 41. "Hot Springs" refers to the United Nations Conference on Food and Agriculture, at Hot Springs, Virginia, May-June 1943. It was the first step in the founding of the Food and Agricultural Organization of the United Nations and the first conference with the participation of dozens of countries that aimed at establishing organizations to promote international cooperation after World War II.

language is unsatisfactory for countries now occupied, since they have to introduce new controls.

Mr. Opie pointed out that the last paragraph of the flimsy used the words "making decisions on requests," instead of "deciding on its attitude." It was agreed that this change conformed to the last clause of the preceding paragraph, which gave a definite limit on the transitional period. It was also pointed out that this paragraph affected the entire Joint Statement and not merely the transitional arrangements. Mr. Opie suggested that the problem was really whether the consultative provisions were to be depended upon generally, or whether the Fund was to have power to impose sanctions. He felt that this was a question of faith, and that if member countries had faith that in the Fund, the mere fact that the Fund disagreed with a particular country would have considerable persuasive power.

The entire flimsy on transitional arrangements was covered, but no effort was made to discuss any major policy problems.

67

Subcommittee 4
Establishment of the Fund
Third meeting
Atlantic City
June 22, 1944 at 9:30 a.m.[315]

Taxation and immunities

The subcommittee discusses the extent to which the IMF and its staff should be exempt from national taxes and enjoy certain legal immunities characteristic of embassies and foreign diplomats.

[Flimsy "]Taxation and Immunities [Provisions"]

1. The provisions should be preceded by a general statement that the Fund has extraterritorial rights and immunities such as those accorded to foreign governments. Particular immunities should then be listed, with immunity of assets being first. (Suggested by **Mr. Hexner [Czechoslovakia, Reporter]** and agreed to by the committee.)

It was suggested that reference be made to the ILO Document No. 1 issued at its recent meeting,[316] which deals with this problem generally.

2. Salaries and remuneration paid by the Fund be exempt from taxation of all countries rather than subject to taxation by the country of citizenship.

3. Sentence proposing discriminatory taxation on salaries and remunerations should be omitted.

---

[315] Present: Mr. Deutsch of Canada, Chairman; Mr. Hexner of Czechoslovakia, Reporter; Mr. de Iongh of the Netherlands; Mr. de Largentaye of France; Mr. Opie of United Kingdom; Messrs. Arey, Louchheim, Dreibelbis, Young and Brenner of United States.

[316] The International Labor Organization's May 1944 conference in Philadelphia.

4. Wording that securities should be free from taxation because of origin should be clarified to indicate origin in the Fund.

5. **Mr. Hexner** suggested that assets be given complete immunity and that the Fund waive such immunity whenever it felt such waiver to be proper. **Mr. de Iongh [Netherlands]** suggested that this was too broad an immunity and **Mr. [Jean] de Largentaye [France]** took the same position. **Mr. Deutsch [Canada, Chairman]** appeared to agree with Mr. Hexner.

6. The question was raised whether free use of the Fund's holdings of gold and currency for the purpose[s] of the Fund would be covered elsewhere. It was the consensus of the committee that provision for this should be made in the immunity section.

7. The committee agreed that immunity from suit should apply only to national courts, not to international courts.

8. It should be made clear that official acts of employees, directors, etc. would be immune from suit.

9. The status of the staff, the directors, and the Executive Committee should be specified. Are they to have diplomatic status and, if so, how far down the line will such status apply?

The entire flimsy was covered and the committee has no further assignments to take up.

68

Subcommittee 4
Establishment of the Fund
Fourth meeting
Atlantic City
June 23, 1944, [morning] [317]

Protection of the Fund's assets • Transferability and guarantees of the Fund's assets • Distribution of the Fund's income

At its final meeting, the subcommittee discusses how to protect the IMF's assets and distribute surplus income.

The committee considered protection of the assets of the Fund, transferability and guarantees of the assets of the Fund, and distribution of income of the Fund. [318]

1. Protection of the assets covers changes made as authorized by the Fund and also de facto changes.

2. Transferability of assets involves interpretation of X-2 [["Transition Period"]]. There is some question as to the transferability of a currency of a country imposed X-2 during the transition period. If each country is permitted to purchase exchange from the Fund, will its currency be sold by the Fund without being subject to restrictions? There was also a question concerning gold held in such a country. Should it be freely transferable regardless of whether it is contributed by the country or some other country?

---

[317] Present: Mr. Deutsch of Canada, Chairman; Mr. Hexner of Czechoslovakia, reporter; Mr. de Iongh of the Netherlands; Mr. de Largentaye of France; Mr. Opie of the United Kingdom; Messrs. Arey, Louchheim, Dreibelbis, Young and Brenner of the United States.

[318] The flimsies the subcommittee discussed were "Protection of the Assets of the Fund," "Taxation and Immunities Provisions," and "Distribution of Profits of the Fund."

3. The point is to be raised at the meeting [of the whole Agenda Committee] whether income should be distributed according to quotas or according to use of assets.

4. It was pointed out that in (d) under "distribution of income," a portion should be determined in accordance with the average amount of currency held during the year.

The committee completed discussion of these three items and has no assignments remaining unfinished.

69

Steering Committee
Second? meeting
Atlantic City
June 26, 1944 at 10:30 a.m.[319]

*Schedule of meetings on the IMF • Flimsies • Membership of
Steering Committee • Committee on Management of the Fund •
Commission III at Bretton Woods*

*The Steering Committee consisted of delegates from the United States, United
Kingdom, Soviet Union, China, Mexico, and later France. Harry Dexter White was
the chairman. The purpose of the committee was to help the Atlantic City conference
work smoothly by overseeing the schedule of meetings and other organizational matters.*

*These minutes are from British files. We found no other minutes for the committee,
although minutes from the American Technical Group's meeting of June 22 (chapter
13) imply that it may have met before this, and these minutes imply that it had one
later meeting.*

1. It was agreed that to push on rapidly with consideration of the Fund
proposals and for that purpose to hold two meetings [of the Formal
Agenda Committee] daily, at 10:30 and 4:30.

2. The system of compiling a loose-leaf folder containing alternative
versions of all the changes with any new clauses was approved.

3. It was decided that the Chairman should co-opt two further
members to the Steering Committee, of whom one would probably
represent France.

4. It was decided to appoint a small committee on Management of the
Fund: chairman Sir Wilfrid Eady [UK] (with Mr. [Eric] Beckett [UK] and

---

[319] Present: Dr. [Harry Dexter] White [U.S., Chairman]; Lord [John Maynard]
Keynes [UK]; Dr. [Aleksei] Smirnov (Russia); Dr. [Tingfu] Tsiang (China); Mr.
[Antonio Espinosa de los] Monteros (Mexico); Mr. [Frank] Coe [U.S.] (Secretary);
Mr. [H.E.] Brooks [UK] (Deputy Secretary).

Mr. [George] Bolton [UK] as advisers), Mr. [Ansel] Luxford [U.S.] (with advisers) and, say, four other countries to be chosen. **Dr. Monteros [Mexico]** said he would be interested; China and Russia reserve their position. **Lord Keynes** proposed that Dr. Beyen [Netherlands] should also be invited to serve.

5. It was confirmed that Commission III at Bretton Woods would deal with "other forms of international monetary cooperation," i.e., it would be the clearing place for every other proposal outside [the] Fund and Bank.

6. **Mr. Smirnov [USSR]** asked whether it was intended to discuss quotas.

70

Subcommittee on Management
Atlantic City
Fourth meeting
June 27, 1944 at 2:30 p.m. [320]

Levels of management at the IMF • Choosing governors and alternates • Choosing Executive Directors • Meetings of Executive Directors

The Steering Committee created a Subcommittee on Management to clarify the relationship and workings of the IMF management structure outlined in Article VIII of the Joint Statement. The subcommittee chairman was Sir Wilfrid Eady, the second-highest career official in the British Treasury. The IMF's management was to have three layers. The Board of Governors would include all countries and would meet annually to make high-level decisions. The Executive Directors would have representatives from a small group of countries to approve or disapprove loans and supervise staff. The General Manager, or as he was ultimately called, the Managing Director, would be the top official in charge of day-to-day operations.

Minutes for this meeting exist in both American and British versions. The British version states that this is the fourth meeting of the committee. We have no records of the first three meetings.

(American version by Richard H. Brenner)

A number of management provisions [Article VII, "Management of the Fund"] were discussed and the **Chairman [Sir Wilfrid Eady, UK]** asked

---

[320] Present: The American version lists Sir Wilfrid Eady (Chairman) [UK]; Messrs. [Eric] Beckett, [A.W. "Peter"] Snelling and [George] Bolton of the United Kingdom; Dr. [Te-Mou] Hsi of China; Mr. [Jan Willem "Wim"] Beyen of the Netherlands; Mr. [Antonio Espinosa de los] Monteros of Mexico; Messrs. [Ansel] Luxford and [Richard] Brenner of the United States. The British version lists additionally Rodrigo Gómez of Mexico and Fyodor Bystrov of the USSR.

357

each country represented for its view on each problem. It was made clear that the assent of the United States to provisions was only for the purpose of having the matters presented to the general meeting [the Formal Agenda Committee].

1. There are to be three tiers of management — a board having representatives of each member country, a committee selected from the board and possibly from outside, and a staff to be employed by the Fund.

2. The names are to be:

(a) Board of Governors.

(b) Executive Directors (or Governors if selection is limited to the Board).

(c) General Manager and inferior employees.

3. Choosing governors and alternates — accepted U.S. draft [VII-1, ["Board and Executive Committee"] Alternative A, U.S., Section 1(a)].

4. Activities of alternates — two points of view:

(a) Can participate but only vote when governor is absent.

(b) Can participate only in absence of governor. Presence at the meeting to be a matter for Board to decide.

5. Choosing Executive Directors. Consensus favored choosing from the Board but the possibility of choosing outsiders was not completely rejected.

6. Tenure of office of governors. U.S. draft accepted [VII-1, ["Board and Executive Committee"] Alternative A, U.S., Section 1(a)].

7. Chairman of Board of Governors. Consensus favored not spelling out that Board should select a chairman. Prefer leaving matter to the Board.

8. Meetings. Accept the U.S. draft [VII-1, ["Board and Executive Committee"] Alternative A, U.S., Section 1(c)] but wish to change provision that no country should be meeting place for more than once in five years, to wording that would leave Board free to choose meeting place.

9. Polling Board. Accepted U.S. draft [VII-1, ["Board and Executive Committee"] Alternative A, U.S., Section 1(d)] but preferred wording making it applicable only for extraordinary problems.

10. Pay of governors and alternates. Accepted U.S. draft [VII-1, ["Board and Executive Committee"] Alternative A, U.S., Section 1(e)].

11. **UK** and **Dutch** opposed provision that Executive Directors be in continuous session [as in VII-1, ["Board and Executive Committee"] Alternative A, U.S., Section 2(a)]]. Question reserved.

12. Election of Executive Directors. Reserved method of election but

agreed to short tenure such as three years [as] in U.S. draft [VII-1, ["Board and Executive Committee"] Alternative A, U.S., Section 2(a)]. Third proposal (Belgium) to be presented in subcommittee and possibly to the general meeting.

13. Inconclusive discussion as to whether General Manager should be chairman of Executive Directors. Problem rests upon decision as to whether Executive Directors are to be in continuous session and this, in turn, depends on allocation of powers among board, Executive Directors and General Manager. Allocation of powers to be taken up first at next meeting.

(British version, no attribution)

1. The meeting had before it the proposals for the Management of the Fund set out on pages 20 to 23b of Document F-1 [VII, "Management of the Fund" in the draft IMF articles].

General Organization of the Management

2. It was generally agreed that the Management of the Fund should consist of three tiers: first, the body on which every member country would be represented; second, a smaller body consisting of representatives of about 11 or 12 Governments; third, a General Manager or Managing Director.

3. **Mr. Monteros [Mexico]** raised the question whether there should be a fourth body which would give birth to the Fund and have power to change its constitution later on. His own view was that there should not be such a body, and that it should be possible for the first body to reach decisions upon amendments of the constitution ad referendum to Governments. This view also met with general approval.

Nomenclature

4. **Mr. Luxford [U.S.]** explained that, for political reasons in the United States, it was highly desirable to give the Fund the appearance of a business organization rather than an intergovernmental political institution on, say, the League of Nations model. This lay behind the nomenclature suggested by the United States, which was designed to use terms that would be familiar to business men in the United States. **Mr.**

Beyen [Netherlands] pointed out, however, that there was a great difference in business nomenclature between different countries and that terms familiar in one country would be liable to be misleading in another. After some discussion, it was agreed that for the time being the first body should be referred to as "the Board of Governors"; the second body as the "Executive Directors," or, if it should be decided that only Governors should be eligible to be Directors, the "Executive Governors"; and the third as "the General Manager."

Appointment of the Board of Governors

5. There was general agreement that the Government of each member country should appoint one Governor and that the Government should be free to choose whom they would appoint.

6. Some discussion took place on the proposals regarding alternates in page 20 of Doc. F-1. There was a considerable measure of support for the view that it would be useful to have alternates for educational purposes, but **Mr. Beyen** pointed out that the American suggestion that the alternates should "participate in all activities of the Board" was a novel one; he and **Sir Wilfrid Eady** were inclined to doubt the wisdom of it. It was agreed —

(a) that alternates should not vote, except in the absence of their Governments, and

(b) that the question whether or not alternates should participate in the work of the Board should be referred to the main Conference.

Selection of Executive Directors

7. **Sir Wilfrid Eady** pointed out that the United States proposals laid down, in the new terminology, that the Executive Directors would be Governors ((a) on page 20a [VII-1, ["Board and Executive Committee"], Alternative A, U.S.], whereas the UK proposals left Governments with freedom to appoint as Executive Directors persons who were not Governors ((b) on page 20d [VII-1, Alternative B, UK]). **Mr. [Richard] Brenner [U.S.]** explained that the American conception was that the Executive Directors would be a selection of Governors; no effort was being made to bring in new blood at the Director level. **Mr. [George] Bolton [UK]** saw disadvantages in such an arrangement: he thought, for instance, that, as Executive Directors might have to be ready to devote a good deal of time to the Fund, countries represented on the Executive would, under the U.S. proposal, be unable to appoint such persons as

Ministers of Finance to be Governors. **Sir Wilfrid Eady** mentioned that there was a possibility of appeals to the Board of Governors from decisions by the Executive Directors and he thought that, if the same people served on both bodies, this appellate function of the Board of Governors could not be properly exercised.

8. It was agreed to state to the main Conference the two alternatives: (i) that only Governors shall be eligible for appointment as Executive Directors or (ii) that the persons chosen as Executive Directors need not be Governors.

Duration of Appointment of Governors

9. It was agreed that the best course would probably be that suggested by the United States, i.e. that Governors should serve for five years subject to the pleasure of their respective Governments and that they should be eligible for reappointment.

Chairman of the Board of Governors

10. It was agreed to leave for the time being, as a matter to be settled by the Board of Governors itself, the proposal in the United States draft that "the Board shall select from its members a Chairman who shall serve for a period of two years."

Meetings of the Board of Governors

11. It was agreed that paragraph (c) on page 20 [on annual meetings of the Board of Governors] was acceptable, subject to the deletion of the last sentence and of the substitution of "It shall not be necessary for annual meetings always to be held in the same place."

Provision for Polling Governors

12. Some discussion took place as to the wisdom of the provision at (d) on page 20 that Governors could be polled by the Executive Directors in the absence of the former. **Sir Wilfrid Eady** thought that such a provision might be dangerous, not only because Governors ought only to vote after hearing debate on the pros and cons of propositions, but also because it might prove more difficult than imagined to get quick decisions by this means. **Mr. [George] Bolton [UK]** thought that it would be

impossible to conduct a poll by cable on questions like the withdrawal of facilities from, or the expulsion of, a member. **Mr. Beyen** agreed that these difficulties existed, but pointed out how awkward it would be if a situation arose such as had occurred in the Bank for International Settlements in 1939 because of absence of provisions for a poll.[321] It was generally agreed that the principle in (d) on page 20 should be accepted, but that the paragraph should be drafted more tightly.

Executive Directors

13. Some discussion took place on the questions whether Directors should devote their whole time to the work of the Fund and should reside at its headquarters. Mr. Beyen thought that such an arrangement would have very undesirable consequences. It would be impossible to find proper full-time work for 11 or 12 Directors; if they had to be brought into the machine, the business of management would become very cumbersome. There was also the danger that they would get out of touch with their own countries. He thought an arrangement on the lines of the BIS [Bank for International Settlements] might work very well where under Directors met in Basle for three day each month. Questions requiring quick decisions rarely arose out of the blue, and emergency meetings could, of course, be called as necessary.

Constitution of the Executive

14. It was agreed that two years was probably about the right period for which elected Directors should serve.

Some discussion took place about the chairmanship of the Executive. The United Kingdom proposals placed greater emphasis on this post than did the United States proposals. The UK view was that Governments might be willing to give to a single General Manager the enormous powers which it would be necessary for him to possess in order to deal with emergencies, but that they might be more willing to see those powers split between the General Manager and the Chairman of the Executive. **Mr. Beyen** and **Mr. Hsi Te-Mou [China]** supported this view, but **Mr. Monteros** suggested that, before it could be considered

---

[321] Beyen had been the president of the bank from 1937 to 1939. After World War II began in September 1939, representatives from countries that had entered the war ceased attending the bank's meetings.

fully, it would be necessary to examine more closely the question of the functions of the Executive. It was therefore agreed to resume at this point on the following day.

71

Subcommittee on Management
Atlantic City
Fifth meeting
June 28, 1944 at 2:30 p.m.[322]

Allocation of powers • Delegation of authority by Executive Directors • Election of Executive Directors • Managing Director

At its second meeting, the subcommittee agrees that the Board of Governors should retain certain important powers and not delegate them to the Executive Directors. British and Dutch delegates oppose the Executive Directors meeting continuously rather than only, say, quarterly like a typical corporate board. The British and Dutch would lose that battle. The subcommittee also discusses whether Executive Directors should be responsible to particular governments. In practice, they have been.

The subcommittee's report (chapter 79) mentions that it met three times, but we have found no minutes of the third meeting.

1. Allocation of Powers to the Several Administrative Bodies [VII-1, ["Board and Executive Directors,"] and alternatives]

It was agreed that all powers would be in the larger body (the Board of Governors) and that all but a limited power could be delegated to the smaller body (the Executive Directors). The powers which may not be delegated are:

(a) Uniform changes in par values;

(b) Suspension of membership;

(c) Decision to liquidate the Fund;

---

[322] Present: Chairman: Sir Wilfrid Eady; Messrs. Bolton, Beckett, Snelling of the United Kingdom; Mr. Hsi Te-Mou of China; Messrs. [Rodrigo] Gómez and Monteros of Mexico; Mr. Beyen of the Netherlands; Messrs. Luxford and Brenner of the United States.

(d) Admission of new members;

(e) Revision of quotas;

(f) Suspension and expulsion the members;

(g) Decisions on appeals from interpretations made by the Executive Directors on appeal from member countries;

(h) Agreements to cooperate with other international agencies.

No agreement was reached as to whether the power to suspend the use of the Fund's resources should be delegated. The thought that **British** this should not be delegated, but the **Dutch** and the **U.S.** thought it should be. In the event that provision is made for amendments of the agreement or for the extension of the transition period, these matters are to be nondelegable.

2. Delegation of Authority by the Executive Directors

The decision as to whether this small body should delegate its powers rests on the question of whether it is to be in continuous session. There was a fundamental disagreement on this issue, with the **UK** and the **Dutch** opposing continuous session. It was suggested that compromise might be made on the basis of continuous sessions for the first five years, and the decision of whether future administration should be the same might be left to the Executive Directors.

3. Election of Executive Directors

There was fundamental disagreement on the schemes for electing directors. The **British** felt that the director should not be responsible to particular governments and the view of the **United States** was that there should be proportional representation. The **Dutch** do not like the idea of directors being responsible to governments, but they are not willing to accept the possibility of the entire elected directorate being chosen by the same majority of votes. The **Mexicans** indicated that this procedure, which is the British proposal, would not be acceptable to small countries.

4. Managing Director

It was agreed that the Managing Director should not be responsible to any one country. The question of whether or not he should be chairman of the Executive Directors was thought to be unimportant if the representation and continuous session principles are adopted.

72

Special Committee on Furnishing Information
Atlantic City
Only meeting
June 28, 1944, [morning?] [323]

Types of information members will furnish to IMF

The Steering Committee appointed the Special Committee on Information to develop a list of the kinds of economic data that members would submit to the IMF. John Maynard Keynes was among those who thought that the IMF could greatly deepen understanding of the world economy by gathering and publishing comprehensive statistics. The Soviet Union, however, treated many kinds of data on its centrally planned economy as state secrets. To placate the Soviet Union, one of its delegates, A.P. Morozov, chief of the Monetary Division of the People's Commissariat for Foreign Trade, was appointed the chairman of the subcommittee. The Soviet Union later signed the IMF Articles of Agreement at Bretton Woods but did not ratify them and did not join the IMF because of concerns about disclosure of information, among other issues. This meeting seems to have been the only one the subcommittee held. It produced a report, found in chapter 81.

Section, "Furnishing Information" [proposed new Section III-11, Alternative A, U.S.]

The Fund may require member countries to furnish it with such information as it deems necessary for its operations. In requesting information the Fund shall, however, take into consideration the ability of individual countries to furnish the data asked for. The minimum amount of information necessary for the due carrying out of the Fund's duties include the following:

---

[323] Membership: Mr. [A.P.] Morozov of the USSR, Chairman; Mr. [August] Maffry of the U.S., Reporter; Mr. [John] Deutsch of Canada; Mr. [Jacques] Polak of the Netherlands; Sir Theodore Gregory of India.

(list 1)

1. Official holdings of (a) gold at home and abroad, (b) gold convertible currencies, distributed by currencies, and (c) other currencies distributed by currencies, as defined for purposes of the Fund.

2. Holdings by banking and financial agencies other than official agencies of (a) gold at home and abroad, (b) gold convertible currencies distributed by currencies, and (c) other currencies, distributed by currencies, as defined for purposes of the Fund.

3. Production of gold.

4. Gold exports and imports, distributed by countries of destination and origin.

5. Total exports and imports of merchandise, in terms of local currency values, distributed by countries of destination and origin.

6. International balance of payments, including (a) trade in goods and services, (b) gold movements, and (c) capital transactions.

7. International investment position, i.e., investments within the country owned abroad and investments abroad owned by residents of the country.

8. National income.

9. Price indexes. (Indexes of commodity prices in wholesale and retail markets and of export and import prices as available from official sources.)

10. Buying and selling rates for foreign currencies.

11. Exchange controls. (Comprehensive statement of exchange controls in effect at the time of assuming membership in the Fund and changes thereafter as they occur.)

12. Where official exchange controls exist, arrearages for commercial or financial remittances in terms both of the time lag in remittances and total amounts in arrears by types of arrearage.

(list 2)

1. Gold holdings of the central bank and the treasury and their changes.

2. Gold convertible exchange holdings of the central bank and the treasury.

3. Movement of capital.

4. Foreign trade data.

5. Other items of the balance of payments.

6. Rates of exchange and their changes.

73

Editors' note on other subcommittee meetings

The minutes of the Atlantic City conference indicate the existence of these other subcommittees, for which we have found no records:

- The Subcommittee for Consideration of Certain Technical Matters (mentioned in chapters 48, 49, and 50).

- The Subcommittee on Questions of Immunities (mentioned in chapter 48); rather than a separate subcommittee, this may simply have been a reference to Subcommittee 4, which among other things dealt with immunities.

- The Agenda Subcommittee (mentioned in chapters 44, 50, and 52).

Where indications of their meetings exist, we have listed them in Appendix B.

PART VI

CONFERENCE DOCUMENTS

74

Document F-1
(Bretton Woods Document 32, with additions)
Preliminary Draft of Suggested
Articles of Agreement for the Establishment of an
International Monetary Fund

*I. Purpose and Policies of the Fund • II. Subscription to the Fund •
III. Transactions with the Fund • IV. Par Values of Member
Currencies • V. Capital Transactions • VI. Apportionment of Scarce
Currencies • VII. Management of the Fund • VIII. Withdrawal from
the Fund • IX. Obligations of Member Countries • X. Transitional
Arrangements • XI. Amendments • XII. Interpretation of the
Agreement*

*The draft IMF Articles of Agreement, Document F-1 (F standing for "Fund") was
the document on which the Atlantic City conference spent most of its time. The initial
Atlantic City version was distributed on June 26.[324] The Atlantic City conference did
not print a final version of the document, but the initial version at Bretton Woods was
approximately the final version at Atlantic City.*

*Here, we reprint the initial Bretton Woods version of the document with some
additions. The document consists of these parts:*

*(a) The "Joint Statement by Experts on the Establishment of an International
Monetary Fund," the document from which the Atlantic City conference started.*

*(b) Alternatives proposed at Atlantic City and incorporated into the initial Bretton
Woods draft. The Bretton Woods draft does not identify the proposing countries, but
we were usually able to do so from a master list from the U.S. National Archives[325]
and from committee minutes at Atlantic City. Appendix D summarizes the
alternatives.*

---

[324] Dates of distribution for this and the other conference documents in this
section are from U.S. National Archives, RG 56, Box 1, Folder A-3, "Assignment
of Document Numbers."
[325] RG 56, Box 20, Folder A-11, "Check List of Pages in Doc. F-1."

(c) Some material proposed at Atlantic City but modified or omitted by the time of the initial draft at Bretton Woods.

(d) A bit of material in the initial draft at Bretton Woods but apparently not proposed at Atlantic City.

Page numbers in brackets refer to the Atlantic City version of Document F-1 in the U.S. National Archives, RG 56, Box 1, Folder A-3; page numbers in parentheses are numbers in a loose-leaf version supplied to the delegates at Bretton Woods in 1944 to enable them to analyze, debate, and amend the document more easily. Text in brackets listed from Atlantic City is material from the June 27, 1944 draft that differs from the text of Bretton Woods Document 32.

There is attached a preliminary draft of provisions which have been submitted to the Secretariat.

At the top of each page there is set forth the pertinent provision of the Joint Statement of Principles. Immediately below appear alternative and supplementary texts submitted to the Secretariat. It is expected that further suggestions will be made and as they are presented to the Secretariat, they will be distributed for inclusion in the attached draft.

The Secretariat has attempted to put the various proposals together in a manner which would be helpful in the consideration of the alternative provisions suggested. The order adopted conforms in general to the Joint Statement but is in no way indicative of where the provisions might appropriately appear in a final document.

The Secretariat is aware of the possibility that errors and omissions have been made in the attached draft, despite the care employed in its preparation. Accordingly, the Secretariat requests the indulgence of any delegation whose proposals may have been partially or wholly omitted or improperly presented. If the attention of the Secretariat is called to any error or omission, such error or omission will be corrected promptly.

Three types of alternatives have been submitted: (1) Suggestions that do not appear to make substantial changes in the Joint Statement provisions but merely modify the language for purposes of clarity, (2) suggestions that substantially modify the Joint Statement provisions, and (3) suggestions that supplement the provisions of the Joint Statement. For the convenience of the reader, the Secretariat has used symbols to indicate the character of the alternative provisions submitted. In each case the characterization is that of the Secretariat and, if errors have been made, the proper characterization (p. ii) should be communicated to the Secretariat by the delegation proposing the alternative provision so that corrections can be made. The symbols employed are:

* = No substantial change
& = Substantial change
# = Supplementary material

[p. 1] (p. 1)

JOINT STATEMENT I
I. Purpose and Policies of the Fund

The Fund will be guided in all its decisions by the purposes and policies set forth below:

1. To promote international monetary cooperation through a permanent institution which provides the machinery for consultation on international monetary problems.

2. To facilitate the expansion and balanced growth of international trade and to contribute in this way to the maintenance of a high level of employment and real income, which must be a primary objective of economic policy.

3. To give confidence to member countries by making the Fund's resources available to them under adequate safeguards, thus giving members time to correct maladjustments in their balance of payments without resorting to measures destructive of national or international prosperity.

4. To promote exchange stability, to maintain orderly exchange arrangements among member countries, and to avoid competitive exchange depreciation.

5. To assist in the establishment of multilateral payments facilities on current transactions among member countries and in the elimination of foreign exchange restrictions which hamper the growth of world trade.

6. To shorten the periods and lessen the degree of disequilibrium in the international balance of payments of member countries.

7/1/44 J.S. Art. I

(p. 1a)

Alternative A [United States]

[Atlantic City: There is hereby established the International Monetary Fund, hereinafter referred to as the "Fund." It shall be guided in all its decisions by the following purposes and policies:]

The purposes of the International Monetary Fund are:

* 1. To promote international monetary co-operation by providing permanent machinery for consultation on international monetary

problems.

* 2. To facilitate the expansion and balanced growth of international trade and to contribute thereby to the maintenance of high levels of employment and real income, as a primary objective of economic policy.

* 3. To give confidence to member countries by making the Fund's resources available to them under adequate safeguards, thus giving them time to correct maladjustments in their balance of payments without resort to measures destructive of national or international prosperity.

* 4. To promote exchange stability, to maintain orderly exchange arrangements among member countries, and to avoid competitive exchange depreciation.

* 5. To assist in the establishment of a multilateral system of payments in respect of current transactions between members and in the elimination of foreign exchange restrictions which hamper the growth of world trade.

* 6. To shorten the periods and lessen the degree of disequilibrium in the international balance of payments of members.

\# The Fund shall be guided in all its decisions by the purposes set forth above.

7/1/44 J.S. Art. I

[p. 1a] (p. 1b)

Alternative B [Australia]

(Substitute for Joint Statement I, subdivisions 2, 3, 4 and 6)

* 2. To facilitate the expansion and balanced growth of international trade and to contribute to a high level of employment and real income which must be a primary objective of economic policy.

& 3. To make the Fund's resources available to members under adequate safeguards and to assist them to correct maladjustments in their balance of payments without resort to measures destructive of national or international prosperity.

& 4. To secure orderly changes in exchange rates among member countries where necessary to correct exchange disequilibrium, thus promoting exchange stability and avoiding competitive exchange depreciation.

* 6. *In accordance with the above principles*, to shorten the periods and lessen the degree of disequilibrium in the international balance of payments of member countries.

[p. 1b]

Alternative C [India; Atlantic City Alternative D]
(Substitute for Joint Statement I, subdivision 2)

& 2. To facilitate the expansion and balanced growth of international trade, *to assist in the fuller utilization of the resources of economically underdeveloped countries* and to contribute thereby to the maintenance in the world as a whole of a high level of employment and real income, which must be a primary objective of economic policy;

Alternative D [Norway; Atlantic City Alternative F]
(Substitute for Joint Statement I, subdivision)

& 4. To promote exchange stability and avoid competitive exchange depreciation by securing, where necessary to correct exchange disequilibrium, orderly changes in exchange rates among member countries.

7/1/44 J.S. Art. I

(p. 1c)

Alternative E [Norway; Atlantic City Alternative G]
(Substitute the following for Joint Statement I, subdivision 4)

& 4. To promote exchange stability.

& 5. To avoid competitive exchange depreciation by securing, where necessary to correct fundamental disequilibria, orderly changes in par values of member currencies.

Alternative F [Brazil; Atlantic City Alternative C]
(Add as a new subdivision)

To correlate procedures for exchange stability with a policy for the promotion of international investment by other international financial agencies and to evolve a working relationship with such agencies.

[p. 1c]

Alternative G [India; Atlantic City Alternative E]
(Add as a new subdivision)

To promote and facilitate the settlement of abnormal indebtedness arising out of the war.

7/1/44 J.S. Art. I

[p. 2] (p. 2)

JOINT STATEMENT II, 1
II. *Subscription to the Fund*

1. Member countries shall subscribe in gold and in their local funds amounts (quotas) to be agreed, which will amount altogether to about $8 billion if all the United and Associated Nations subscribe to the Fund (corresponding to about $10 billion for the world as a whole).

Alternative A [United States]

Section 1. *Countries Eligible for Membership.*

The members of the Fund shall be those of the countries represented at the United Nations Monetary and Financial Conference whose governments accept membership in the Fund [Atlantic City: as provided in Article XIII].

Membership in the Fund shall be open to other countries at such times and in accordance with such terms as may be prescribed by the Fund.

Section 2. *Quotas.*

Each member shall be assigned a quota. The quotas of the countries represented at the United Nations Monetary and Financial Conference shall be those set forth in Schedule A. [Atlantic City second sentence: The quotas of the countries represented at the United Nations Monetary and Financial Conference shall be as follows, in terms of the United States dollar of the weight and fineness In effect on July 1, 1944.]

(Schedule A to be added later)

Quotas of other countries which become members of the Fund shall be determined by the Fund.

Section 3. *Time and Place of Payment.*

Each member shall provide the Fund at the appropriate depository with the full amount of its quota on or before the date fixed for exchange transactions in its currency to begin. [Atlantic City: Each country which becomes a member before the date fixed for the operations of the Fund to begin shall pay to the Fund a the appropriate depository with the full amount of its quota on or before such date fixed by the Fund for such payment to be made.] Any member whose quota is increased shall provide the full amount of the increase within thirty days of the date on which the member approves the increase in its quota.

7/1/44 J.S. Art. II, Sec. 1

[p. 2a] (p. 2a)

Alternative B [Czechoslovakia]

(It is suggested to add to the text of Alternative A:)

\# Notwithstanding the fundamental principles on payment of quotas particular arrangements may be made with countries whose currency system has been disrupted as a result of enemy occupation. Such arrangements may not extend over more than nine months i.e., after nine months, at the latest, the obligations of the country will be the same as they would have been if such an exception had not been granted. The government of the respective country has to guarantee by a specific act that the fund will not suffer any loss because of that particular arrangement.

7/1/44 J.S. Art. II, Sec. 1

[p. 3] (p. 3)

JOINT STATEMENT II, 2

2. The quotas may be revised from time to time but changes shall require a four-fifths vote and no member's quota may be changed without its assent.

Alternative A [United States]

* Section 4. *Adjustment of Quotas.*

The Fund may, at intervals of five years, adjust the quotas of the members. It may also, if it thinks fit, consider at any other time the adjustment of any particular quota at the request of the member concerned. A four-fifths majority vote shall be required for any change in quotas and no quota shall be changed without the consent of the member concerned. [Atlantic City: The Fund shall examine, at intervals of five years, the need for adjustment of quotas. Changes in quotas shall require a four-fifths vote and the quota of a member country may not be changed without its consent.]

7/1/44 J.S. Art. II, Sec. 2

[p. 4] (p. 4)

JOINT STATEMENT II, 3

3. The obligatory gold subscription of a member country shall be fixed at 25 percent of its subscription (quota) or 10 percent of its holdings of

gold and gold convertible exchange, whichever is the smaller.

Alternative A [United States]

* Section 5. *Initial Payments.*

Each member shall pay in gold the smaller of (a) twenty-five percent of its quota or (b) ten percent of its official holdings of gold and gold convertible exchange[326] on ---------- [Atlantic City: January 1, 1944]. [Following sentence not in Atlantic City version:] In the case of any member occupied by the enemy whose holdings are not ascertainable as of ----------, the Fund shall fix an appropriate alternative date. The data necessary to determine official holdings of gold and gold convertible exchange shall be furnished by the members as provided in this Agreement [Atlantic City: as provided in Article III, Section 11].

Each member shall pay the balance of its quota in its own currency.

\# Section 6. *Payments When Quotas are Changed.*

(a) Each member whose quota is increased shall pay twenty-five percent of the increase in gold. Each member shall pay the balance of any increase in its own currency. [Following sentence not in Atlantic City version:] If, however, on the date the member approves an increase, its holdings of gold and gold convertible exchange are less than its new quota, the Fund may reduce the portion of the increase to be paid in gold.

(b) Each member whose quota is reduced shall receive from the Fund within thirty days of the reduction [Atlantic City: omits "within thirty days of the reduction"] an amount in its own currency or gold equal to the reduction. In making this payment, [Atlantic City: omits "In making this payment,"] the Fund shall pay to such member only the amount of gold necessary to prevent reducing the holdings of the Fund of that currency below seventy-five percent of such new quota of the member.

7/1/44 J.S. Art. II, Sec. 3

(p. 4a)

Alternative B [Union of Soviet Socialist Republics]

(Add at the end of Joint Statement II, 3)

& Any country represented at the United Nations Monetary and

---

[326] The phrase "gold and gold convertible exchange" is subject to definition and to such change in terminology as may be agreed. [Note in Bretton Woods conference proceedings; not in Atlantic City document.]

Financial Conference whose home areas have suffered from enemy occupation and hostilities during the present war, may reduce its gold payment to between seventy-five and fifty percent of the amount it would otherwise have to pay, dependent on the extent of the damage caused to it by the enemy occupation and hostilities.

[p. 4a]
Alternative C [United States; Atlantic City Alternative D]
(Add to Joint Statement II, 3)

& Any country represented at the United Nations Monetary and Financial Conference whose home areas have suffered substantial damage from enemy action or occupation during the present war, may reduce its initial gold payment to ---------- percent of the amount it would otherwise have to pay.
7/1/44 J.S. Art. II, Sec. 3

[Atlantic City Alternative C, United Kingdom; not in Bretton Woods document]
(Substitute for Joint Statement II, 3)

3. The obligatory gold subscription of a member country shall be fixed at 25 percent of its subscription (quota) or 10 percent of its monetary reserves, whichever is the smaller.[327]

[p. 5] (p. 5)
JOINT STATEMENT III, 1
III. *Transactions with the Fund*

1. Member countries shall deal with the Fund only through their Treasury, Central Bank, Stabilization Fund, or other fiscal agencies. The Fund's account in a member's currency shall be kept at the Central Bank of the member country.

Alternative A [United States]
* Section 1. *Agencies Dealing with the Fund.*

Each member country shall deal with the Fund only through its Treasury, Central Bank, Stabilization Fund or other similar fiscal agency

---

[327] *Editors' note:* "Monetary reserves" are defined as net official holdings of gold and convertible exchange in the Atlantic City section on definitions.

and the Fund shall deal only through the same agencies.
(Second sentence of J.S. dealt with elsewhere)
7/1/44 J.S. Art. III, Sec. 1

[p. 6] (p. 6)

JOINT STATEMENT III, 2

2. A member shall be entitled to buy another member's currency from the Fund in exchange for its own currency on the following conditions:

(a) The member represents that the currency demanded is presently needed for making payments in that currency which are consistent with the purposes of the Fund.

(b) The Fund has not given notice that its holdings of the currency demanded have become scarce in which case the provisions of VI, below, come into force.

(c) The Fund's total holdings of the currency offered (after having been restored, if below that figure, to 75 percent of the member's quota) have not been increased by more than 25 percent of the member's quota during the previous 12 months and do not exceed 200 percent of the quota.

(d) The Fund has not previously given appropriate notice that the member is suspended from making further use of the Fund's resources on the ground that it is using them in a manner contrary to the purposes and policies of the Fund; but the Fund shall not give such notice until it has presented to the member concerned a report setting forth its views and has allowed a suitable time for reply.

The Fund in its discretion and on terms which safeguard its interests waive any of the conditions above.
7/1/44 J.S. Art. III, Sec. 2

[p. 6a] (p. 6a)

Alternative A [United States]

Section 2. *Conditions upon which any Member may Purchase Currencies of other Members.*

A member shall be entitled to buy the currency of another member from the Fund in exchange for its own currency subject to the following conditions:

* (1) The member *initiating the purchase* represents that the currency *requested* is presently needed for making payments in that currency which are consistent with the *provisions of this Agreement;* [Atlantic City: consistent

with the purposes and policies of the Fund]

* (2) The Fund has not given notice under Article VI that its holdings of the currency *requested* have become scarce;

* (3) The total holdings of the Fund in the currency of the member *initiating the purchase* (after having been restored, if below that figure, to seventy-five percent of the quota of such member) have not increased during the previous twelve months by more than twenty-five percent of the quota of such member and do not exceed two hundred percent of the quota; and

& (4) The Fund has not previously declared under Section 3 of this Article that the member initiating the purchase is ineligible to use the resources of the Fund [Atlantic City: omits "Section 3 of"]. The Fund may, in its discretion, and on terms which safeguard its interests, waive any of these conditions. In special circumstances, where the Fund considers it necessary, it may require collateral security as a condition of such waiver.

& Section 2a. *Conditions Governing Purchases for Capital Transfers.* [Atlantic City: alternative does not include this section.]

If the Fund's holdings of the currency of a member have remained below 75 percent of its quota for a period not less than six months such member shall be entitled, notwithstanding the provisions of Article V, Section 1, to buy the currency of another member from the Fund for its own currency for any purpose, including capital transfers, provided, however, that (p. 6b) purchases for capital transfers may not have the effect of raising the Fund's holdings of the currency of such member above 75 percent of its quota, or reducing the Fund's holdings of the currency purchased below 75[328] percent of the quota of the member whose currency is purchased.

& Section 3. *Declaring Members Ineligible to Use the Resources of the Fund.*

Whenever the Fund is of the opinion that [Atlantic City: determines that] any member is using the resources of the Fund in a manner contrary to the purposes and policies of the Fund, it shall present to the member a report setting forth the views of the Fund and stating a suitable time for reply. After presenting such a report to a member the Fund may limit the use of its resources by the member. If no reply to the report is received

---

[328] Should this figure be 60, 75 or 100 percent? [Footnote in Bretton Woods conference proceedings.]

from the member within the stated time, or the reply received is unsatisfactory, the Fund may continue to limit the member's use of the Fund's resources or, after giving reasonable notice to the member, declare it ineligible to use the resources of the Fund [Atlantic City: the Fund may limit the use of its resources by the country]. [Atlantic City: order of second and third sentences is reversed.]

[p. 6b] (p. 6b)
[Atlantic City Alternative B; Canada; not in Bretton Woods draft]
(Add at end of Joint Statement III, 2(a).)

If the Fund's holdings of a member country have remained below 75 percent of its quota for a period not less than six months such member country shall be entitled, notwithstanding the provisions of V, 1, to buy another member's currency from the Fund for its own currency for any purpose, including capital transfers, provided, however, that purchase for capital transfers may not have the effect of raising the Fund's holdings of the currency of such member above 75 percent of its quota.

Alternative B [Australia; Atlantic City Alternative C]
(Substitute for Joint Statement III, 2(c).)

& (c) The Fund's total holdings of the currency offered (after having been restored, if below that figure, to 75 percent of the member's quota) have not been increased by more than *33-1/3* percent of the member's quota during the previous 12 months and do not exceed 200 percent of the quota.
7/1/44 J.S. Art. III, Sec. 2

(p. 6c)
Alternative C [Czechoslovakia; Atlantic City Alternative D]
(Amend Joint Statement III, 2 as follows(c)

* It is suggested to change the term "consistent with the purposes of the Fund" to "consistent with the purposes and provisions of the Fund."

[p. 6c]
Alternative D [France; Atlantic City Alternative E]
(Substitute for Joint Statement III, 2(c).)

& The total holdings of the Fund in the currency of the member country initiating the purchase shall not exceed 125 percent of the quota during the first, 150% of the quota during the second, 175% of the quota during the third year of the operations of the Fund in that particular

currency and 200% thereafter.
7/1/44 J.S. Art. III, Sec. 2

[p. 7] (p. 7)
JOINT STATEMENT III, 3

3. The operations on the Fund's account will be limited to transactions for the purpose of supplying a member country on the member's initiative with another member's currency in exchange for its own currency or for gold. Transactions provided for under 4 and 7, below, are not subject to this limitation.

Alternative A [United States]

* Section 4. *Limitation on the Operations of the Fund.*
Except as otherwise provided in this Agreement, operations for the account of the Fund shall be limited to transactions for the purpose of supplying a member, on the initiative of such member, with the currency of another member in exchange for the currency of the member initiating the transactions or for gold.
7/1/44 J.S. Art. III, Sec. 3

[p. 8] (p. 8)
JOINT STATEMENT III, 4

4. The Fund will be entitled at its option, with a view to preventing a particular member's currency from becoming scarce:
(a) To borrow its currency from a member country;
(b) To offer gold to a member country in exchange for its currency.

Alternative A [United States]
Section 5. *Operations for the Purpose of Preventing Currencies from becoming Scarce.*
* The Fund may, if it deems such action appropriate to prevent the currency of any member from becoming scarce, take either or both of the following steps:
& (1) Propose to the member that it lend such currency to the Fund or, with the approval of the member, borrow such currency within that country from some other source, but no member shall be under any obligation to lend its currency to the Fund or to approve the Fund's borrowing its currency from any other source.

* (2) Offer to buy the currency of that member with gold.

Alternative B [Netherlands]
(Substitute for Joint Statement III, 4(b))
& To *sell* gold to a member country in exchange for its currency.
7/1/44 J.S. Art. III, Sec. 4

[p. 9] (p. 9)

JOINT STATEMENT III, 5

5. So long as a member country is entitled to buy another member's currency from the Fund in exchange for its own currency, it shall be prepared to buy its own currency from that member with that member's currency or with gold. This shall not apply to currency subject to restrictions in conformity with IX, 3 below, or to holdings of currency which have accumulated as a result of transactions of a current account nature effected before the removal by the member country of restrictions on multilateral clearing maintained or imposed under X, 2 below.

Alternative A [United States]
& Section 6. *Multilateral International Clearing.*
Each member shall buy balances of its currency held by another member with currency of that member or, at the option of the member buying, with gold, if the member selling represents either that the balances in question have been currently acquired or that their conversion is needed for making currency payments which are consistent with the provisions of the Fund. This obligation shall not relate to transactions involving:

(a) capital transfers, except those transactions referred to in the second and third sentences of V, 1, below; or

(b) holdings of currency which have accumulated as a result of transactions effected before the removal by a member of restrictions on multilateral clearing maintained or imposed under X, 2, below; or

(c) the provision of a currency which has been declared scarce under VI, above; or

(d) holdings of currency acquired as a result of dealings illegal under the exchange regulations of the member which is asked to buy such currency;

nor shall it apply to a member which has ceased to be entitled to buy currencies of other members from the Fund in exchange for its own currency.

Nothing in this section shall be deemed to modify or affect the obligation of a member under IX, 2 and 3, below.

(Proposed to be transferred in final draft to Article IX as Section 3)

[Atlantic City alternative reads as follows: A member country shall be entitled to sell the currency of a second member country to such member and obtain payment in its own currency or gold so long as the second member country can buy the currency of the first from the Fund with its own currency.

This requirement shall be without prejudice to exchange restrictions with are authorized under this Agreement or requested by the Fund, and shall not apply to holdings of currencies of member countries which have accumulated as a result of transactions of a current account nature effected before the removal by the member country of restrictions on payments or transfers maintained or imposed during the early post-war transition period.]

[p. 9a]

[Atlantic City Alternative B; United Kingdom; transferred to IX-3 in Bretton Woods draft]

3. To buy balances held with it by another member with that member's currency or, at the option of the member buying, with gold, if that member represents either that the balances in question have been currently acquired or that their conversion is needed for making current payments which are consistent with the provisions of the Fund. This obligation shall not relate to transactions involving:

(a) capital transfers, except those transactions referred to in the second and third sentences of V(1):

or (b) holdings of currency which have been accumulated as a result of transactions effected before the removal of the member country of restrictions on multilateral clearing maintained or imposed under X (2) below:

or (c) the provision of a currency which has been declared scarce under VI above:

or (d) holdings of a currency which has been illicitly obtained:

nor shall it apply to a member who has ceased to be entitled under III(2) or VIII above to buy other members' currencies from the Fund in exchange for its own currency.

(To be transferred to Article IX as Section 3.)

[p. 9b]

[Atlantic City Alternative C; Czechoslovakia; not in Bretton Woods draft]

(Substitute the following for (c) in Alternative B.)

(c) Holdings of currency acquired as a result of dealings which by the country's exchange regulations are considered illicit.

(Provision (c) which appears in Alternative B should follow as (d).)

[p. 9c]

(With respect to Alternative B:)

It is suggested to add to Alternative B instead of (c): "Holdings of currency acquired as a result of dealings, which by the country's exchange regulations are considered illicit," and change the old (c) into (d), etc.

7/1/44 J.S. Art. III, Sec. 5

[p. 10] (p. 10)

JOINT STATEMENT III, 6

6. A member country desiring to obtain, directly or indirectly, the currency of another member country for gold is expected, provided that it can do so with equal advantage, to acquire the currency by the sale of gold to the Fund. This shall not preclude the sale of newly-mined gold by a gold-producing country on any market.

Alternative A [United States]

* Section 7. *Acquisition by Members of the Currencies of Other Members for Gold.*

Any member [Atlantic City: Any member country] desiring to obtain, directly or indirectly, the currency of another member [Atlantic City: another member country] for gold *shall,* provided that it can do so with equal advantage, acquire the currency by the sale of gold to the Fund. *Nothing in this Section shall be deemed* to preclude any member from selling in any market the new production of gold from mines located within territory subject to its jurisdiction.

7/1/44 J.S. Art. III, Sec. 6

[p. 11] (p. 11)

JOINT STATEMENT III, 7

7. The Fund may also acquire gold from member countries in accordance with the following provisions:

(a) A member country may repurchase from the Fund for gold any part of the latter's holdings of its currency.

(b) So long as a member's holdings of gold and gold convertible exchange exceed its quota, the Fund in selling foreign exchange to that country shall require that one-half of the net sales of such exchange during the Fund's financial year be paid for with gold.

(c) If at the end of the Fund's financial year a member's holdings of gold and gold convertible exchange have increased, the Fund may require up to one-half of the increase to be used to repurchase part of the Fund's holdings of its currency so long as this does not reduce the Fund's holdings of a country's currency below 75 percent of its quota or the member's holdings of gold and gold convertible exchange below its quota.

Alternative A [United States]

Section 8. *Other Acquisitions of Gold by the Fund.*

(To be submitted later.)

[Atlantic City: (a) Any member country may at any time repurchase with gold any part of its currency held by the Fund.

(b) So long as a member country's official holdings of gold and gold convertible exchange exceed its quota, the Fund in selling to that country the currencies of other member countries shall require that one-half of such sales be currently paid for in gold.

If during any financial year of the Fund, the payments in gold under this provision exceed one-half of the net increase in the Fund's holdings of such currency, the Fund shall arrange to repurchase the currency of that country with gold to the extent of the excess.

(c) If at the end of any financial year of the Fund the official holdings of gold and gold convertible exchange of any member country have increased, the fund may require up to one-half of the increase during the year to be used to repurchase with gold part of the holdings of the fund of the currency of such country provided that the repurchase will not reduce the holdings of the fund of the currency of such country below seventy-five percent of its quota, or the official holdings of gold and gold convertible exchange of such country below its quota.]

[p. 11a]
Alternative B [Union of Soviet Socialist Republics]
(Add to Joint Statement III, 7(b))

\# This provision shall not be applied during [the] five-year period from the beginning of the operations of the Fund to member countries who suffered particularly great damage from enemy occupation and hostilities.

(Add to Joint Statement III, 7(c))

\# This provision shall not be applied during the period of restoration of economy to the newly-mined gold of member countries, whose home areas particularly suffered from enemy occupation and hostilities.
7/1/44 J.S. Art. III, Sec. 7

[p. 11c] (p. 11a)
Alternative C [Belgium; Atlantic City Alternative D]
Substitute for Joint Statement III, 7(c))

& (c) If at the end of any financial year of the Fund, the official holdings of gold and gold convertible exchange of any member country have increased as compared to that member's official holdings of gold and gold convertible exchange at the moment of joining the Fund, the Fund may require...etc....

[p. 11d]
Alternative D [Greece; Atlantic City Alternative E]
(Substitute for Joint Statement III, 7(b))

& So long as a member's holdings of gold and gold convertible exchange exceed its quota, the Fund in selling foreign exchange to that country shall require that one-half of the net sales of such exchange during the Fund's financial year be paid for with gold or gold convertible exchange. *The Fund, however, may in its discretion waive this condition with respect to any particular country if its application would reduce the facilities accorded by the Fund to that Country in a way contrary to the purposes and policies of the Fund and in particular to the purpose stated in I(3).*
7/1/44 J.S. Art. III, Sec. 7

[p. 11b]

[Atlantic City Alternative C, part 1; United Kingdom; not in Bretton Woods draft]

(b) If, at the end of the Fund's financial year, a member's monetary reserves exceed its quota, and the Fund's holdings of its currency of increased, the Fund may require that it shall use a part of these reserves to repurchase currency up to the point when its reserves have fallen by an amount not less than the amount by which, under this adjustment, the Fund's holdings of its currency have increased. Furthermore, if, after this adjustment (if called for) has been made a member's monetary reserves have increased during the year, the Fund may require it, whether or not the Fund's holdings of the currency have increased during the year, to use half of this increase for a further repurchase of its currency from the Fund; provided, always, that these adjustments do not bring its reserves below its quota and the second adjustment does not bring the Fund's holdings of its currency below 75 percent of its quota.

(Or alternatively, substitute for both subdivisions)

(1) If, at the end of any year, a member's monetary reserves after deducting its holdings of convertible exchange exceed its quota, and if the Fund's holdings of its currency exceed 75 percent of its quota, the Fund may require it to use its holdings of gold to reduce the Fund's holdings of its currency by half of the excess of such holdings over 75 percent of its quota.

[Atlantic City Alternative C, part 2; United Kingdom; not in Bretton Woods draft]

(Add at end of section.)

In estimating the amount of a member's monetary reserves for the purpose of the preceding paragraph, its holdings of a foreign currency, which has become convertible for the first time during the year in question, shall not be counted, provided that and insofar as the member possessed these holdings at the beginning of that year.

[p. 12] (p. 12)

JOINT STATEMENT — No Provisions

The following material has been suggested as an addition to Article III.

Alternative A [United States]

Section 9. *Transferability and Guarantee of the Assets of the Fund.*

(a) All assets of the Fund shall, to the extent necessary to carry out the operations prescribed by this Agreement, be free from restrictions, regulations and controls of any nature imposed by members [Atlantic City: by member countries].

(b) The currency of a member purchased from the Fund shall always be accepted by that member in payment of current account obligations due to that member.

(c) All assets of the Fund shall be guaranteed by each member against loss resulting from failure or default on the part of the depository designated by such member. [Atlantic City: Paragraphs (b) and (c) are part of paragraph (a).]

7/1/44 J.S. Art. III, Additional Section (9)

(p. 13)

JOINT STATEMENT — No Provisions

The following material has been suggested as an addition to Article III.

Alternative A [United States]

Section 10. *Charges and Commissions.*

(a) Any member buying the currency of any other member from the Fund in exchange for its own currency shall pay a service charge in addition to the parity price.

(b) The Fund may levy a reasonable handling charge on any member buying gold from the Fund or selling gold to the Fund.

(c) The Fund shall prescribe charges uniform among members which shall be payable by any member on the amount of its currency in excess of its quota held by the Fund, as follows: (to be inserted later) [Atlantic City has the following: not less than one per cent per annum on amounts up to twenty-five percent; not less than one and one-half per cent per annum on amounts between twenty-five and fifty per cent; and charges similarly increased by not less than one-half per cent per annum for every additional bracket of twenty-five percent of the quota, except that on amounts held by the Fund in excess of two hundred percent of the quota of a country charges need not be uniform among all member countries. A further uniform charge on amounts in excess of the quota held by the Fund shall be levied as follows: a charge of not less than one-half of one per cent per annum on amounts held between one and two years; not less

390

than one per cent per annum on amounts held between two and three years; and charges similarly increased by one-half of one percent per annum for each additional annual period. Amounts held and periods which they [p. 12a] have been held shall be determined by averaging the holdings of the Fund according to rules to be established by the Fund.]

(d) All charges and commissions shall be paid in gold. [Atlantic City omits the following sentence:] If, however, the member's holdings of gold and gold convertible exchange are less than one-half of its quota, it shall pay in gold that proportion which such holdings bear to one-half of its quota, and shall pay the balance in its own currency.

[p. 12b]

Alternative B [Union of Soviet Socialist Republics]
(Substitute for Section 10(c) of Alternative A)

The Fund shall levy a charge uniform to all countries, at a rate not more than 1 percent per annum, payable in gold, against any country on the amount of its currency held by the Fund in excess of the quota of that country. An additional charge, payable in gold, shall be levied by the Fund against any member country on the Fund's holdings of its currency in excess of 200 percent of the quota of that country.

7/1/44 J.S. Art. III, Additional Section (10)

[p. 12a] (p. 14)

JOINT STATEMENT — No Provisions

The following material has been suggested as an addition to Article III.

Alternative A [United States]

Section 11. *Furnishing Information.*

The Fund may require members to furnish it with such information as it deems necessary for its operations. In requesting information the Fund shall, however, take into consideration the ability of individual members to furnish the data asked for. The minimum amount of information necessary for the due carrying out of the Fund's operations includes the following: (List of required information to be inserted)

The Fund may arrange to obtain further information by agreement with the members.

[Atlantic City: The Fund may require members to furnish it with such information as follows:

1. Official holdings of (a) gold at home and abroad, (b) gold convertible currencies distributed by currencies, and (c) other currencies distributed by currencies as defined for purposes of the Fund. (To be reported monthly)

2. Holdings, other than official, of (a) gold at home and abroad, (b) gold convertible currencies distributed by currencies, and (c) other current is distributed by currencies is defined for purposes of the Fund. (To be reported monthly)

3. Foreign-owned balances and short-term funds distributed by countries. (To be reported monthly)

4. Production of gold. (To be reported monthly)

5. Gold exports and imports distributed by countries of destination and origin. (To be reported monthly)

6. Foreign trade in terms of local currency values as follows:

a. Total exports and imports distributed by countries of destination and origin. (To be reported monthly and annually)

b. Total exports and imports distributed by commodities. (To be reported monthly and annually)

c. Exports and imports of all classified commodities distributed by countries of destination and origin. (To be reported at least annually)

d. Exports and imports and trade with individual countries distributed by all classified countries. (To be reported at least annually)

7. International balance of payments, including (a) trade in goods and services, (b) gold movements, and (c) capital transactions. (To be reported at least annually)

8. International investment position, i.e., investments within the country owned abroad and investments abroad owned by residents of the country. (To be reported at least annually)

9. National income. (To be reported at least annually)

10 industrial production. (To be reported at least quarterly)

11. Price levels. (Indexes of commodity prices in the wholesale and retail markets and of export and import prices to be reported as available from official sources)

12. Buying and selling rates for foreign currencies. (Daily quotations to be reported weekly)

13. Exchange controls. (Comprehensive statement of exchange controls in effect at the time of assuming membership in the Fund and changes thereafter as they occur)

14. Arrearages for commercial or financial remittances in terms both of the lagging remittances and total amounts in arrears by types of

arrearage. (To be reported monthly)

The Fund may arrange to obtain further information by agreement with member countries.]

Alternative B [not in Atlantic City draft]
(Substitute for list to be inserted in Alternative A)

1. Gold holdings of the Central Bank and the Treasury and their changes.

2. Gold convertible exchange holdings of the Central Bank and the Treasury.

3. Movement of capital.

4. Foreign Trade data.

5. Other items of the balance of payments.

6. Rates of exchange and their changes.

7/1/44 J.S. Art. III, Additional Section (11)

(p. 15)

JOINT STATEMENT — No Provisions

The following material has been suggested as an addition to Article III.

Alternative A [United States?; not in Atlantic City draft]
Section 12. *Consideration of Representations of the Fund.*

The Fund may make representations to a member on monetary or economic conditions and developments in such member which tend, or may tend, to produce a serious disequilibrium in the international balance of payments of members. A representative of the member country involved shall participate in the preparation of the Fund's representations. The Fund shall not make representations which would involve changes in the fundamental structure of the economic organization of members.

Alternative B [United Kingdom; in Atlantic City draft as part of Article XII, Alternative B]
The Fund shall have at all times the right to communicate its views informally to any member on any matter arising under this Agreement.

7/1/44 J.S. Art. III, Additional Section (12)

[Atlantic City Alternative A; United States; not in Bretton Woods draft]

#Section. *Consideration of Recommendations of the Fund.*

Each member country shall give consideration to the views and recommendations of the Fund on any existing or proposed monetary or economic policy of such member country which tends, or may tend, to produce a serious disequilibrium in the international balance of member countries.

[p. 12b]

[Atlantic City Alternative C; Union of Soviet Socialist Republics; not in Bretton Woods draft]

(Insert the following in place of the fourth "section" [sentence] of Alternative A.)

The Fund may make presentation to a member country on any existing or proposed monetary or economic policy of such member country which tends, or may tend to produce a serious disequilibrium in the international balance of payments of member countries.

The Fund shall not make such presentations which would require changes in the fundamental structure of the economic organization of a member country.

[p. 13] (p. 16)

JOINT STATEMENT IV, 1

IV. *Par Values of Member Currencies*

1. The par value of a member's currency shall be agreed with the Fund when it is admitted to membership, and shall be expressed in terms of gold. All transactions between the Fund and members shall be at par, subject to a fixed charge payable by the member making application to the Fund, and all transactions in member currencies shall be at rates within an agreed percentage of parity.

Alternative A [United States]

& Section 1. *Par Values of the Currencies of Members.* [Atlantic City: *Initial Par Values of the Currencies of Member Countries.*]

The par value of the currency of each member shall be expressed in terms of gold, *as a common denominator, or in terms of a gold convertible currency unit of the weight and fineness in effect on July 1, 1944. All computations relating to currencies of members for the purpose of applying the provisions of this Agreement shall*

394

be on the basis of their par values. [Atlantic City: The par value of the currency of each member country shall be expressed in terms of gold or a gold convertible currency unit of the weight and fineness in effect on July 1, 1944.]

[Additional Atlantic City section not in Bretton Woods draft: *Transactions Governed by Par Values.*

All transaction in the currencies of member countries shall be at rates of exchange within a stated percentage of parity fixed by the Fund.

All computations relating to currencies of member countries for the purpose of applying the provisions of this Agreement shall be on the basis of their par value.]

7/1/44 J.S. Art. IV, Sec. 1

[p. 13a]
[Atlantic City Alternative B; United Kingdom; not in Bretton Woods draft]

& Section 1. The government of the UK and the Government of the United States will communicate to the Monetary Fund at its inauguration, the initial par value of their respective currencies, expressed in terms of gold. Within one month (or in the case of occupied countries, within one month of liberation) the other member countries wishing to adhere to the Convention will make corresponding communications. Notwithstanding this rule, member countries that have been occupied by the enemy need not make a definitive communication of the initial par value in the above sense until the reconstruction of their monetary system has been completed and the initial communication may be limited to giving a provisional par value. If the Directorate of the Fund finds a communicated initial or par value reasonable, such par value shall come into force immediately for the purpose of the Fund. If, however, the Directorate should deem the communicated par value to be open to criticism, the question shall be the subject of further consideration with the member country in question, and the facilities of the Fund shall not be available to the member until agreement has been reached. All transactions between the Fund and members shall be at par subject to a fixed charge payable by the member making application to the Fund; and all transactions in member currencies shall be at rates within an agreed percentage of parity.

[p. 14] (p. 17)

JOINT STATEMENT IV, 2, 3, 4

2. Subject to 5, below, no change in the par value of a member's currency shall be made by the Fund without the country's approval. Member countries agree not to propose a change in the parity of their currency unless they consider it appropriate to the correction of a fundamental disequilibrium. Changes shall be made only with the approval of the Fund, subject to the provisions below.

3. The Fund shall approve a requested change in the par value of a member's currency, if it is essential to the correction of a fundamental disequilibrium. In particular, the Fund shall not reject a requested change, necessary to restore equilibrium, because of the domestic social or political policies of the country applying for a change. In considering a requested change, the Fund shall take into consideration the extreme uncertainties prevailing at the time the parities of the currencies of the member countries were initially agreed upon.

4. After consulting the Fund, a member country may change the established parity of its currency, provided the proposed change, inclusive of any previous change since the establishment of the Fund, does not exceed 10 percent. In the case of application for a further change, not covered by the above and not exceeding 10 percent, the Fund shall give its decision within 2 days of receiving the application, if the applicant so requests.

7/1/44 J.S. Art. IV, Secs. 2-4

[p. 14a] (p. 17a)

JOINT STATEMENT IV, 2-4
(All alternatives to be supplied later)

[Atlantic City Alternative A; United States; not in Bretton Woods draft]

Section. Restrictions against Changes in Par Values.

No change in the par value of the currency of any member country shall be made by the Fund without the approval of the country.

Each member country agrees not to propose a change in the par value of its currency which affects its international transactions unless it considers such action appropriate to the correction of a fundamental disequilibrium.

Section. *Conditions on Which Changes in Par Values May be Made.*

Changes in the par values of the currencies of member countries shall be made only with the approval of the Fund, subject to the provisions below:

(1) The Fund shall approve a proposed change in the par value of the currency of a member country if in the judgment of the Fund that change is essential to the correction of a fundamental disequilibrium. In particular, the Fund shall not reject a proposed change, necessary to restore equilibrium, because of the domestic social or political policies of the member country or because its economic policies insofar as these contribute to the maintenance of a high level of employment and real income;

(2) In considering proposed changes in the par value of the currencies of member countries, the Fund shall take into consideration extreme uncertainties prevailing at the time the par values of the currencies of the member countries were initially agreed upon;

(3) After consultation with the Fund, any member country may change the par value of its currency, provided the proposed change, plus all previous changes, whether increases or decreases, since the par value of such currency was initially agreed with the Fund, do not exceed 10 percent of the initial par value of such currency; and

(4) Upon the request of a member country proposing a change in the par value of its currency, the Fund shall approve or reject the proposed change within two business days of receiving a request; provided that the proposed change, plus all previous changes, whether increases or decreases, made under this paragraph, not exceed 10 percent of the initial par value of that currency, or in the case of a country which changed the par value of its currency under (3) above, 10 percent of the initial par value of that currency plus percentage of change made under (3) above.

[p. 14b]

[Atlantic City Alternative B; Australia; not in Bretton Woods draft]

3. The Fund shall approve a request the change in the par value of a member's currency, if it is essential to the correction of a fundamental disequilibrium. In particular, the Fund shall not reject a requested change, necessary to restore equilibrium, because of the domestic social or political policies of the country applying for the change *nor one designed to meet a serious and persistent deficit in the balance of payments on current account accompanied by a substantially adverse change in the terms of trade.* In considering a requested change, the Fund shall take into consideration the extreme uncertainties prevailing at the time the parities of the currencies of the

member countries were initially agreed upon.

[p. 14c]
[Atlantic City Alternative C; Brazil; not in Bretton Woods draft]
(Replace the last sentence of section 3 with the following.)

In considering the requested change, the Fund shall take into consideration,

(a) The extreme uncertainties prevailing at the time the parities of the currencies of the member countries were initially agreed upon, and

(b) that the applicant country is been unable to obtain adequate resources to restore the equilibrium of its balance of payments from an international investment agency with which the Fund is in working relationship.

[Atlantic City Alternative D; Union of Soviet Socialist Republics; not in Bretton Woods draft]
(Substituted in place of section 2.)

Subject to 5, below, no change in the par value of a member's currency shall be made by the Fund without the country's approval. Member countries agreed not to propose a change in the parity of their currency unless they consider it appropriate to the correction of a fundamental disequilibrium.

Changes in the par value shall be made only with the approval of the Fund, subject to the provisions below if such changes would affect international transactions of member countries.

[p. 14d]
[Atlantic City Alternative E; Greece; not in Bretton Woods draft]
(It is suggested to add at the end of section 2 the following.)

In particular, the Fund shall take into full account that in a country where large-scale monetary disintegration will prevail at the end of the war, the fixing of exchange rates during the period of transition will be of a tentative nature.

7/3/44 J.S. Art. IV, Secs. 2-4

[p. 15] (p. 18)
JOINT STATEMENT IV, 5

5. An agreed uniform change may be made in the gold value of member currencies, provided every member country having 10 percent or

more of the aggregate quotas approves.

Alternative A [United States]

* Section 5. *Uniform Changes in Par Values.*

Notwithstanding the provisions of Section 3 of this Article, the Fund *by majority vote* may make uniform proportionate changes in the par values of the currencies of all the members, provided each such change is approved by every country which has ten percent or more of the aggregate quotas. *Such uniform changes shall be excluded from consideration in applying the provisions of Sections 4(3) and (4) of this Article.* (J.S. IV, 4).

[Atlantic City Alternative B; Canada; not in Bretton Woods draft]

A uniform change may, by majority vote, be made in the gold value of member currencies, provided every member country having 10 percent or more of the aggregate quotas approves.

7/1/44 J.S. Art. IV, Sec. 5

[p. 16] (p. 19)

JOINT STATEMENT — No Provisions

The following material has been suggested as an addition to Article IV.

Alternative A [United States]

Section 6. *Protection of the Assets of the Fund.*

No change in the foreign exchange value of the currency of any member shall alter the gold value of the assets of the Fund. Whenever [Atlantic City: omits clause (i)] (i) the par value of a currency of a member is reduced, or (ii) the foreign exchange value of the currency of any member has depreciated within its jurisdiction to a significant extent in the opinion of the Fund, the member shall compensate the Fund by paying to the Fund within a reasonable time an amount of its own currency equal to the reduction in the gold value of the currency of such member held by the Fund. Whenever the par value of the currency of any member has been increased the Fund shall compensate such member by returning, within a reasonable time, an amount in the currency of such member equal to the increase in the gold value of the currency of such member held by the Fund.

7/1/44 J.S. Art. IV, Additional Section

(p. 20)

JOINT STATEMENT — No Provisions

The following material has been suggested as an addition to Article IV.

Alternative A [United States]

Section 7. *Separate Currencies within a Member's Jurisdiction.*

\# A member proposing a change in the par value of its currency shall be deemed, unless it declares otherwise, to be proposing a corresponding change in the par value of the currencies of all territories under its jurisdiction. It shall however be open to a member to declare that its proposal relates either to the metropolitan currency alone, or to one or more specified subordinate currencies alone, or to the metropolitan currency and one or more specified subordinate currencies.

Alternative B [Netherlands]

(Add to Joint Statement IV)

\# If separate currencies are used in different parts of the territory of a member country, the provisions of this article shall apply to each of these currencies.

7/1/44 J.S. Art. IV, Additional Section

[p. 17] (p. 21)

JOINT STATEMENT V, 1
V. *Capital Transactions*

1. A member country may not use the Fund's resources to meet a large or sustained outflow of capital, and the Fund may require a member country to exercise controls to prevent such use of the resources of the Fund. This provision is not intended to prevent the use of the Fund's resources for capital transactions of reasonable amount required for the expansion of exports or in the ordinary course of trade, banking, or other business. Nor is it intended to prevent capital movements which are met out of a member country's own resources of gold and foreign exchange, provided such capital movements are in accordance with the purposes of the Fund.

Alternative A [United States]

& Section 1. *Use of the Resources of the Fund for Transfers of Capital.*

A member may not use the resources of the Fund to meet a large or sustained outflow of capital, and the Fund may request a member to exercise controls to prevent such use of the resources of the Fund. If after receiving such request, a member fails to exercise appropriate controls the Fund may declare such member ineligible to use the resources of the Fund.

This Section is not intended to prevent the use of the resources of the Fund for capital transactions of reasonable amount required for the expansion of exports or in the ordinary course of trade, banking or other business. [Atlantic City: Nor is it intended to prevent] Capital movements which are met out of a member's own resources of gold and foreign exchange, are not affected by this section, but members undertake that such capital movements will be in accord with the purposes of the Fund.
7/1/44 J.S. Art. V, Sec. 1

[Atlantic City Alternative B; Canada; not in Bretton Woods draft]

A member country may not *make use of* the Fund's resources to meet a large or sustained outflow of capital, and the Fund may require a member to exercise controls to prevent such use of the resources of the Fund. This provision is not intended to prevent the use of the Fund's resources for capital transactions of reasonable amount required for the expansion of exports or in the ordinary course of trade, banking or other business, or in accordance with the provisions of the second sentence of III, 2(a).

[p. 18] (p. 22)

JOINT STATEMENT V, 2

2. Subject to VI below, a member country may not use its control of capital movements to restrict payments for current transactions or to delay unduly the transfer of funds in settlement of commitments.

Alternative A [United States]

* Section 2. *Limitation on Controls of Capital Movements.*

Members [Atlantic City: Member countries] *may control international capital movements* but no member [Atlantic City: member country] may exercise such controls in a manner which will restrict payments for current transactions or which will unduly delay the transfer of funds in settlement of commitments, except as provided in [Atlantic City: Article] VI, 2 and in [Atlantic City: Article] X.
7/1/44 J.S. Art. V, Sec. 2

[p. 19] (p. 23)

JOINT STATEMENT VI, 1, 2
VI. *Apportionment of Scarce Currencies*

1. When it becomes evident to the Fund that the demand for a member country's currency may soon exhaust the Fund's holdings of that currency, the Fund shall so inform member countries and propose an equitable method of apportioning the scarce currency. When a currency is thus declared scarce, the Fund shall issue a report embodying the causes of the scarcity and containing recommendations designed to bring it to an end.

2. A decision by the Fund to apportion a scarce currency shall operate as an authorization to a member country, after consultation with the Fund, temporarily to restrict the freedom of exchange operations in the affected currency, and in determining the manner of restricting the demand and rationing the limited supply among its nationals, the member country shall have complete jurisdiction.

7/1/44 J.S. Art. VI, Sec. 1 & 2

[p. 19a] (p. 23a)
JOINT STATEMENT VI, 1 and 2
Alternative A [United States]
Section 1. *General Scarcity.*

If the Fund finds that a general scarcity of a particular currency is developing, the Fund may so inform members [Atlantic City: member countries] and may issue a report setting forth the causes of the scarcity and containing recommendations designed to bring it to an end. *In the preparation of such report there shall participate a representative of the member the currency of which is involved.*

& Section 2. *Scarcity of the Fund's Holdings.*

If it becomes evident to the Fund that the demand for a member's [Atlantic City: member country's] currency seriously threatens the Fund's ability to supply that currency, the Fund, whether or not it has acted under Section 1 above, shall formally declare such currency scarce and shall thenceforth apportion the existing and accruing supply of the scarce currency *with due regard to the relative needs of members* [Atlantic City: member countries] *and the general international economic situation and any other pertinent considerations.* The Fund shall also issue a report concerning its action. [Atlantic City: The Fund shall issue a report either before or after declaring such a currency scarce.] The formal declaration shall operate as an authorization to each member [Atlantic City: member country], after consultation with the Fund, temporarily to restrict the freedom of exchange operations in the affected currency; and, in determining the manner of restricting the demand and rationing the limited supply among its nationals, the members [Atlantic City: member country] shall have complete jurisdiction *subject to the provisions of Article IX, Section 2.* (J.S.). 7/1/44 J.S. Art. VI, Secs. 1 & 2

[p. 20] (p. 24)

JOINT STATEMENT VII, 1
VII. *Management of the Fund*

1. The Fund shall be governed by a board on which each member will be represented and by an executive committee. The executive committee shall consist of at least nine members including the representatives of the five countries with the largest quotas. (As to Executive Committee see p. 25)

Alternative A [United States]

Section 1. *Board of Governors* [Atlantic City: Board of Directors].

(a) The administration of the Fund shall be vested in a Board of Governors consisting of one governor [Atlantic City: director] and one alternate appointed by each member [Atlantic City: member country] in such manner as it may determine. Governors [Atlantic City: Directors] and alternates shall serve for five years, subject to the pleasure of their respective governments, and may be reappointed. No alternate may vote except in the absence of his governor. The Board shall select a chairman from its members. [Atlantic City: Any alternate may participate in all activities of the Board but he shall not vote except in the absence of his director. The Board shall select from its members a chairman who shall serve for a period of two years.]

(b) The Board of Governors may delegate to the Executive Directors authority to exercise any powers of the Board, except:

(1) Determining what new members may be admitted and the conditions of their admission;

(2) Approving a revision of quotas;

(3) Approving an agreed uniform change in the par value of the currencies of all member countries;

(4) Requiring a member to withdraw;

(5) Deciding appeals against interpretations of the Agreement by the

Executive Directors given on application by a member country;

(6) Making agreements to cooperate with other international organizations;

(7) Deciding to liquidate the Fund.

[Atlantic City: The Board of Directors may delegate to the Executive Committee authority to exercise any powers of the Board, except, except the power to make uniform change in the par values of the currencies of all member countries, the power to suspend countries from membership, and the power to liquidate the Fund. Delegated powers shall be exercised in a manner consistent with the purposes and policies of the Fund and the general practices of the Fund.]

7/1/44 J.S. Art. VII, Sec. 1 (Board of Directors)

(p. 24a)

(c) The Board of Governors [Atlantic City: Board of Directors] shall hold an annual meeting and such other meetings as may be provided for by the Board or convened by the Executive Directors [Atlantic City: Executive Committee]. Meetings of the Board shall be convened by the Executive Directors [Atlantic City: Executive Committee] whenever requested by one quarter of the members or by members having one quarter of the aggregate votes. [Atlantic City: by member countries having twenty-five percent of the aggregate vote. Annual meetings shall not be held in the same country more than once in five years.]

(d) The Board may by regulation establish a procedure whereby the Executive Directors [Atlantic City: Executive Committee], when they deem such action to be in the best interests of the Fund, may obtain a vote of the governors on a specific question in lieu of calling a meeting of the Board. [p. 20a]

(e) Governors [Atlantic City: Directors] and alternates shall serve as such without compensation from the Fund, but the Fund shall pay such reasonable expenses as are incurred by the governors and alternates in attending any meetings [Atlantic City: any meetings of the Fund or any committee of the Fund.]

[p. 20c]

Alternative B [United Kingdom]

(Substitute the following for section 1(c) of Alternative A:)

(a) The Board of Governors [Atlantic City: Board of Directors] shall hold an annual meeting and such other meetings as may be provided for by the Board or convened by the Executive Directors. Meetings of the Board shall be convened by the Executive Directors whenever requested *by five member countries.* Annual meetings shall not be held in the same country more than once in five years.

7/1/44 J.S. Art. VII, Sec. 1 (Board of Directors)

[p. 20a] (p. 25)

JOINT STATEMENT VII, 1[329]

1. The Fund shall be governed by a board on which each member will be represented and by an executive committee. The executive committee shall consist of at least nine members including the representatives of the five countries with the largest quotas. (As to Board of Directors see p. 25)

Alternative A [United States]

\# Section 2. *The Executive Directors.* [Atlantic City: *The Executive Committee.*]

\# (a) There shall be twelve Executive Directors, namely, the General Manager, the governors representing the five member countries having the largest quotas, and six other governors elected biennially by the governors who are not automatically Executive Directors. The General Manager shall be chairman of the Executive Directors. The Executive Directors shall exercise all authority delegated to them by the Board of Governors and shall be in continuous session at the principal office of the Fund for at least the first three years of operations. In the absence of any Executive Director, his alternate on the Board of Governors may serve in his place. Executive Directors shall be compensated by the Fund in an amount fixed by the Board of Governors.

Whenever a member country not having a governor among the Executive Directors has requested action or will be directly affected by a decision of the Executive Directors, the governor representing such country shall be entitled to be present at the meeting of the Executive Directors considering such request or decision, but he shall not be entitled to vote.

\# (b) In balloting for the elective Executive Directors, each governor eligible to vote shall cast for one governor all of the votes to which he is entitled under the first paragraph of Section 3 of this article. (J.S. VII, 2)

---

[329] *Editor's note:* In the text as printed at Bretton Woods, this section appears twice. We have left it as is.

405

The six persons receiving the greatest number of votes shall be Executive Directors, except that no person who receives less than sixteen percent of the aggregate eligible votes shall be considered elected. When six persons are not elected on the initial balloting, a (p. 25a) second balloting shall be held in which the person receiving the lowest number of votes shall be ineligible for election and in which there shall vote only those governors who vote for a person not elected and these governors all or part of whose votes for a person elected are deemed to have raised the votes cast for such person above [p. 20b] seventeen per cent of the aggregate eligible votes. In determining whether any part of the votes cast by a governor raised the total of any person above seventeen per cent, there shall be considered as not forming part of the excess the votes of the governor casting the largest number of votes for such person, then the votes of the governor casting the next largest number, and so on until the total reaches seventeen per cent. Any governor whose votes are partly not in excess and partly in excess shall be eligible to vote in the second balloting only to the extent of the votes in excess. If enough additional persons are not elected on the second balloting to bring to six the total number each of whom has received at least sixteen per cent of the aggregate eligible votes, further ballots shall be taken on the same principles until six such persons have been elected, provided that after five persons are elected the sixth may be elected by a simple majority of the remaining votes and shall be deemed to have been elected by all such votes.

(c) Each governor who is automatically an Executive Director shall be entitled to cast the number of votes allotted under Section 3 of this Article (J.S. VII, 2) to the country which he represents. Each elected Executive Director shall be entitled to cast the number of votes to which the governors who elected him would be entitled. A member whose election is due in part to his having received a portion of the votes of a particular governor shall be entitled to vote only those votes of such governor which contributed to his election. When the provisions of the second paragraph of Section 2 of this Article are applicable to a vote (p. 25b) on any question the votes to which an Executive Director would otherwise be entitled shall be increased or decreased proportionately. The General Manager shall have no vote.

(d) The Executive Directors may appoint such committees as they deem advisable. Membership of such committees need not be limited to governors and alternates.

[Atlantic City version:

The Executive Committee.

(a) There shall be an [E]xecutive Committee consisting of the Managing Director, the directors representing the five member countries having the largest quotas and six other directors elected biennially by the directors who are not automatically members of the Committee. The Managing Director shall be chairman of the Committee. The Committee shall exercise all authority delegated to it by the Board of Directors, and shall be in continuous session at the principal office of the Fund. In the absence of any member of the Committee, his alternate on the Board may serve in his place. Members of the Committee shall be compensated by the Fund in an amount fixed by the Board.

Whenever a member country not having a director on the Executive Committee, has requested action or will be directly affected by a decision of the Executive Committee, the director representing such country shall be entitled to be present at the meeting of the Committee considering such request or decision, but he shall not be entitled to vote.

(b) Balloting for the elected members of the Committee, each director eligible to vote shall cast for one director all of the votes to achieve is entitled under the first paragraph of Section 2 of this Article. The six persons receiving the greatest number of votes shall be members of the Committee, except that no person who receives less than sixteen per cent of the aggregate eligible votes shall be considered elected. When six persons are not elected on the initial balloting, a second balloting shall be held in which the person receiving the lowest number of votes shall be ineligible for election and in which there shall vote only those directors whose vote for a person not elected and those directors all are part of whose vote for person elected are deemed to have raised the votes cast for such person above [p. 20b] seventeen per cent of the aggregate eligible vote. In determining whether any part of a director's votes raised a total of any person above seventeen per cent, there shall be considered as not forming part of the excess the votes of the director casting the largest number of votes for such person, then the votes of the director casting the next largest number, and so on until the total reaches seventeen per cent. Any director whose votes are partly not in excess and partly in excess shall be eligible to vote in the second balloting only to the extent of the votes in excess. If enough additional persons are not elected on the second balloting to bring to six the total number each of whom has received at least sixteen per cent of the aggregate eligible votes, further ballots shall be taken on the same principles until six such persons have been elected, provided that after five persons are elected the sixth may be elected by a symbol majority of the remaining votes and shall be deemed to have been elected by all such votes.

(c) Each director who is automatically a member of the Committee shall be entitled to cast the number of votes allotted under Section 2 of this Article to the country which he represents. Each elected member shall be entitled to cast the number of votes to which the directors who elected him would be entitled. A member whose election is due in part to his having received a portion of the votes of a particular director shall be entitled to vote only those votes of such director which contributed to his election. When the provisions of the second paragraph of Section 2 of this Article are applicable to a vote on any question, the votes to which a member of the Executive Committee would otherwise be entitled shall be increased or decreased proportionately. The Managing Director shall have no vote.

(d) The Executive Committee may appoint such committees as it deems advisable. Membership of such committees need not be limited to directors and alternates.]

7/1/44 J.S. Art. VII, Sec. 1 (Executive Committee)

(p. 25b)

Alternative B [United Kingdom]

(b) There shall be twelve Executive Directors, of whom x shall be appointed by the members having the x largest quotas, (the remaining y seats being filled by Executive Directors appointed by members chosen for this purpose by all the Governors excluding those representing the members with the x largest quotas). The members so chosen shall have the power of appointment of directors for two years; at the end of this period any of the members may be chosen again or other members may be chosen. The persons chosen as Executive Directors need not be Governors. The Executive Directors shall meet not less than once every three months.

(c) The Executive Directors shall appoint as *Chairman* a suitable person who is not a Director. The Chairman may appoint a Director to act for him as Deputy Chairman. The Chairman of the Executive Directors, if he is not a Governor, may attend and speak at meetings of the Board. He shall be eligible to be elected as Chairman of the Board of Governors.

(b)[330] *Executive Directors.*

The Executive Directors shall conduct all of the business of the Fund delegated to them by the Board of Governors.

(c) *The Chairman.*

(i) the Chairman shall reside at the Headquarters of the Fund and the Deputy Chairman must reside there at those times when he is acting for the Chairman;

(ii) the Executive Directors may delegate to the Chairman or Deputy Chairman the power of performing on their behalf any of the functions delegated to them except the following, supposing they have been so delegated:

(p. 25c)

(1) waiver of any of the conditions in III(2);

(2) the exercise of the options of the Fund in III(4);

(3) all decisions on the par value of member currencies in IV(1-4);

(4) all action relating to the apportionment of scarce currencies (VI);

(5) decision on the use of the resources of the Fund by a member who has withdrawn (VIII (4) as revised);

(6) decision on X(3) as revised and X(4) as revised;

(7) a formal interpretation of the Statute.

(d) *Voting.*

On questions before the Executive Directors, the Director appointed by the United States shall cast 6 votes, the Director appointed by the United Kingdom shall cast 3 votes, the Director appointed by the USSR shall cast 2 votes, and all the other Directors shall cast 1 vote each. The appointed Chairman shall only have a casting vote in case of an equal division in the voting.

In order to constitute a quorum for the Executive Directors there must be present Directors representing not less than one-half of the total voting power of the Executive Directors and not less than six in number.

[p. 20d] [Atlantic City version:

Amend the wording to provide for the following:

VII (a) A *Governing Council*, consisting of Councilors appointed by all the Member Countries, each Member appointing one Councilor. Each Councilor may appoint a substitute if he is unable to be present. The

---

[330] Editors' note: Because of a printer's error, this and the subsequent sections of the alternative are mislabeled in the original. We have left them as they are.

Council shall meet at least once a year.

(b) A *Directorate*, consisting of 12 Directors, of whom, say 6 shall be appointed by the Members having the 6 largest quotas, (the remaining 6 Seats being filled by Directors appointed by Members chosen for this purpose by all the Councilors excluding those representing the members with the six largest quotas[)]. The right of appointment by the members chosen for the purpose shall be for two years; at the end of this period any of the members may be chosen again or other members may be chosen. The persons chosen as Directors need not be Councilors. The Directorate shall meet not less than once every three months.

(c) The Directorate shall co-opt as *Chairman* a suitable person who is not a Director. The Chairman may appoint a director to act for him as Deputy Chairman. The Chairman of the Directorate, if he is not a Councilor, may attend and speak in meetings of the Council. He shall be eligible to be elected as chairman of the Council.

(d) The *Directorate* shall appoint a *General Manager*, being a person of knowledge and experience of the business.

(e) The Chief Assistants of the General Manager shall be appointed by the Directorate, on the proposal of the General Manager. The General Manager and Chief Assistants shall be appointed under contract determinable by six months' notice on either side. The continuance of the service of each of these are officials shall be considered by the Directorate after every period of five years. [p. 20e]

(f) The Chairman, the General Manager and all the members of the staff shall be paid such salaries and expenses and serve under such conditions as the Directorate may determine.

Voting.

(b) On the Directorate, the Director appointed by the United States shall cast three votes, the Director appointed by the United Kingdom shall cast two votes, and all other Directors shall cast 1 vote each. The co-opted Chairman should only have a casting vote.

In order to constitute a quorum for the Directorate there must be present Directors representing not less than one-half of the total voting power of the Directorate and not less than six and number.

Rules of Procedure.

The Council and the Directorate shall draw up such Rules of Procedure as are necessary for the conduct of their business, in conformity with the provisions of the Statutes. The Council's Rules of

Procedure shall, inter alia, determine the manner in which annual and other meetings of the Council shall be summoned, and the method of voting for the election of Directors.

Functions.

(a) *Council.* In addition to the appointment of the Directorate, the Council shall have the following functions:

(i) Power to invite non-signatory countries to become members;

(ii) the approval of original quotas (II(2));

(iii) the approval of an agreed uniform change in the gold value of the currencies of members (IV(5));

(iv) the suspension of a member from the facilities of the Fund (III(2)(d);

(v) the requirement to a member to withdraw from the Fund (VII(1) as revised);

(vi) decisions on the interpretation of the Statute given on application by a member; [p. 20f]

(vii) receiving the Statement of Accounts and the Report of the Directorate at the Annual Meeting;

(viii) to review the working of the Fund in the light of its Purposes and Policies (I);

(ix) agreements for co-operation with other international organizations.

(b) *Directorate.*

The conduct of all the business of the Fund, other than that belonging, as above, to the Council, and other than that delegated by the Director to the chairman, as provided below.

(c) The *Chairman.*

(i) the chairman shall reside at the Headquarters of the Fund;

(ii) the Directorate may delegate to the Chairman or Deputy Chairman the power of performing on their behalf all their functions except

(1) waiver of any of the conditions in III(2);

(2) the exercise of the options of the Fund in III(4);

(3) all decisions on the par value of member currencies in IV (1-4);

(4) all action related to the appointment of scarce currencies (VI)[;]

(5) decision on the use of the resources of the Fund by a member who has withdrawn (VIII(4) as revised);

(6) decision on X(3) as revised and X(4) as revised;

(7) a formal interpretation of the Statute.

(d) The *General Manager* shall conduct, under the general direction of the Chairman, the ordinary business of the Fund's work. Subject to the general control of the Directorate, he shall be responsible for internal organization and the appointment and dismissal of subordinate staff. The General Manager shall be responsible to the Directorate for the accounts.

[p. 20g]

[Atlantic City Alternative C; Australia, Canada, or Netherlands?; not in Bretton Woods draft and perhaps not distributed at Atlantic City]

The Executive Committee is going to be the most important body of the Fund. Various proposals have been put forth as to its composition. These proposals were based on the principle that members representing the biggest quotas had a definite title to membership on this Executive Committee, whereas other member should one way or another share there are many available seats among themselves. I should like to submit the following suggestions:

While being in complete agreement of the most important quota holders, notwithstanding the geographic location of their countries, should be entitled to a permanent seat, the importance of the quotas in the geographic distribution of the other member country should, I believe, be taken into consideration also for the disposal of the other seats.

The suggestions referred to above have considered wise to limit the number of members to from 9 to 12. I should like to retain the latter figure, to be allotted as suggested below.

The five largest quota holders would be entitled to a permanent seat each, and taking as a basis the British suggestion regarding quotas, they would represent a quota holding of 6,100 million dollars.

Of the seven remaining seats, I would give three to be shared among the countries having each a quota of 300 million dollars or more, and four to the other countries. This would mean that 3 seats should be allotted the following members: Australia, Canada, South Africa, India, Belgium, and the Netherlands, it being understood that the three British Dominions and the Government of India would share two of the seats and Belgium and Holland the third. These six countries together represent a quota holding of 1,900 million dollars. The 4 remaining seats of the allotted to the remaining [version of document in U.S. National Archives file is cut off here; we assume that at least one of the missing words is "countries"].

7/1/44 J.S. Art. VII, See. 1 (Executive Committee)

[p. 21] (p. 26)

JOINT STATEMENT VII, 2, 3[331]

2. The distribution of voting power on the board and the executive committee shall be closely related to the quotas.

3. Subject to II, 2 and IV, 5, all matters shall be settled by a majority of the votes.

Alternative A [United States]

& Section 3. *Voting*

Each member shall have two hundred fifty votes plus one additional vote for each part of its quota equivalent to one hundred thousand United States dollars of the weight and fineness in effect on July 1, 1944.

Whenever a vote is required under Article III, each member shall be entitled to a number of votes modified from its normal number:

(a) By the addition of one vote for the equivalent of each two hundred thousand United States dollars of the weight and fineness in effect on July 1, 1944 of net sales of its currency by the Fund (adjusted for its net transactions in gold), and

(b) By the subtraction of one vote for the equivalent of each two hundred thousand such United States dollars of its net purchases of the currencies of other member countries from the Fund (adjusted for its net transactions in gold).

Except as otherwise specifically provided all matters before the Fund shall be decided by a majority of the aggregate votes cast.

7/1/44 J.S Art. VII Sec. 2 & 3

[p. 21a] (p. 26a)

Alternative B [United Kingdom]

(Substitute for Joint Statement VII, 2 and 3.)

& (a) On the Board of Governors [Atlantic City: General Council] the number of votes which each governor [Atlantic City: Councillor] can cast shall be related to the quota of the member appointing the governors [Atlantic City: the Councilor];

[Additional clause in Atlantic City version: Where under the Statutes a

---

[331] Editors' note: Because of a printer's error, mistakenly labeled "III 2, 3" in the original.

special majority (e.g. four-fifths, etc.) of votes is required for a decision taken by the Council, this means four-fifths of the total voting power.]

A quorum for the Board shall consist of not less than two-thirds of the total voting power of the governors [Atlantic City: the Councilors]. 7/1/44 J.S. Art. VII, Sec. 2 and 3

(p. 27)

JOINT STATEMENT — No Provisions

The following material has been suggested as an addition to Article VII.

[p. 20c]

Alternative A [United States?]

Section 4. *The General Manager.*

The Board of Governors shall appoint and fix the compensation of a General Manager of the Fund and one or more Assistant General Managers. The General Manager shall be chief of the operating staff of the Fund and shall be a member *ex officio* of the Board of Governors.

Alternative B [United Kingdom?; not in Atlantic City draft]

(d) The Executive Directors shall appoint a *General Manager*, being a person of knowledge and experience of the business.

(e) The Chief Assistants of the General Manager shall be appointed by the Executive Directors, on the proposal of the General Manager. The General Manager and his Chief Assistants shall be appointed under contract determinable by six months' notice on either side. The continuance of the service of each of these officials shall be considered by the Executive Directors after every period of 5 years.

(f) The *General Manager* shall conduct, under the general direction of the Chairman, the ordinary business of the Fund's work. Subject to the (p. 27a) general control of the Executive Directors, he shall be responsible for internal organization and the appointment and dismissal of subordinate staff. The General Manager shall be responsible to the Executive Directors for the accounts.

The Chairman, the Deputy-Chairman, the General Manager and all the members of the staff shall be paid such salaries and expenses and serve under such conditions as the Fund may determine. 7/1/44 Article VII, Additional Section (4)

[p. 22] (p. 28)

JOINT STATEMENT VII, 4

4. The Fund shall publish at short intervals a statement of its position showing the extent of its holdings of member currencies and of gold and its transactions in gold.

Alternative A [United States]

Section 5. *Publication of Reports.*

The Fund shall publish an annual report containing an audited statement of its accounts and shall issue at intervals of three months or less, a summary statement of its transactions and its holdings of gold and currencies of members.

The Fund may publish such other reports as it deems desirable for carrying out its purposes and policies.

7/1/44 J.S. Art. VII, Sec. 4

[p. 23] (p. 29)

JOINT STATEMENT — No Provisions

The following material has been suggested as an addition to Article VII.

Alternative A [United States]

Section 6. *Depositories.*

(a) Each member country shall designate its central bank as a depository for all the Fund's holdings of its currency or, if it has no central bank, it shall designate such other institution as may be acceptable to the Fund.

[Atlantic City: (a) Each member country shall designate as a depository for the Fund its central bank or, if it has no central bank, such other institution as may be acceptable to the Fund. The holdings of the Fund of the currency of each member country in an amount not less than that deemed by the Fund to be necessary for its operations, shall be deposited in an account in the name of the Fund in the depository in that country.

The Fund shall accept from any member country in lieu of any part of the currency of that country not needed by the Fund in its operations, notes or other form of indebtedness, issued by the Government of the country, which shall be non-negotiable, non-interest bearing and payable at their par value on-demand by a

415

credit to the currency account of the Fund in that country.]

(b) The Fund may hold other assets, including gold, in designated depositories in the four members having the largest quotas and in such other depositories as the Fund may select. At least one-half of the holdings of gold of the Fund shall be held in the designated depository in the member in which the Fund has its principal office. [Next sentence not in Atlantic City draft:] In an emergency, the Executive Directors may transfer all or any part of the Fund's holdings of gold to any place where it can be adequately protected.

Section 7. *Form of Holdings of Currency.*

The Fund shall accept from any member in lieu of any part of the currency of that country not needed by the Fund in its operations, notes or similar obligations issued by the Government of the country or the depository designated by such member, which shall be non-negotiable, non-interest bearing and payable at their par value on demand by a credit to the currency account of the Fund in that country.

7/1/44 J.S Art. VII, Additional Sections (6 & 7)

(p. 29a)
Alternative B [Union of Soviet Socialist Republics?]
(Substitute for (b) under Section 6 of Alternative A)

(b) Sums payable to the Fund in gold shall be placed at the disposal of the Fund at a depository indicated by the Fund. In indicating a depository the Fund shall pay regard to the convenience of the member, the costs of transport, and the expected requirements of the Fund. Gold and assets other than holdings of currency belonging to the Fund may be held in or moved to any depository as the Fund may determine.

[p. 23b]
Alternative C [Netherlands]
(Substitute the following for subdivision (b) of Alternative A)

(b) Other assets of the Fund, including gold, shall be held in designated depositories, as a general rule, in the four member countries having the largest quotas.

About one-half of the holding of gold of the Fund shall be deposited in the designated depository in the country in which the Fund has its principal office.

7/1/44 J.S. Art. VII, Additional Section (6)

(p. 30)

JOINT STATEMENT — No Provisions

The following material has been suggested as an addition to Article VII.

Alternative A [United States?; not in Atlantic City draft]

Section 8. *Relationship to Other International Organizations.*

The Fund, within the terms of this Agreement, shall cooperate with any general international organization and with public international organizations having specialized responsibilities in related fields. Any arrangements for such cooperation which would involve a modification of any of the provisions of this Agreement may be effected only after amendment to this Agreement in conformity with the procedure set forth in Article ----------.

[p. 23b]

[Atlantic City Alternative B; United Kingdom; not in Bretton Woods draft]

The Council shall have power to make such arrangements or agreements as may be necessary or desirable for cooperation between the Fund on the one hand and other International Economic Organizations and the World Organization on the other hand.

These arrangements or agreements must be approved by a 3/5 majority vote.

7/1/44 J.S. Art. VII, Additional Section (7)

(p. 31)

JOINT STATEMENT — No Provisions

The following material has been suggested as an addition to Article VII:

[p. 23]

Alternative A [United States]

Section 9. *Location of Offices.*

The principal office of the Fund shall be located in the member having the largest quota, and agencies or branch offices may be established in any member or members [Atlantic City: member country or member countries].

417

Alternative B [United Kingdom?; not in Atlantic City draft]

The location of the principal office of the Fund shall be decided by the Fund at the first meeting of the Board of Governors, which shall take place in the territory of the member having the largest quota.

7/1/44 J.S. Art. VII, Additional Section (9)

(p. 32)

JOINT STATEMENT — No Provisions

The following material has been suggested as an addition to Article VII.

Alternative A [United States]

The Fund shall determine annually what part of its net income shall be placed to reserve and what part, if any, shall be distributed.

7/1/44 J.S. Art. VII, Additional Section (10)

(p. 32a)

(Alternative B [A] continued)

If any part is distributed, two per cent noncumulative shall be paid, as a first charge against the distribution of any year, to each member on the average amount during the year by which 75 percent of its quota exceeds the holdings by the Fund of its currency; and the balance to the members in proportion to their quotas. Payments to each member shall be made in its own currency.

[p. 23a]

[Atlantic City: #*Distribution of Net Income of the Fund.*

Net income of the Fund shall be distributed annually in the following manner:

(1) Fifty per cent to surplus until the surplus is equal to ten per cent of the aggregate quotas;

(2) Such amount to each member country it will give it a return of two percent on the average annual amount during the year by which seventy-five per cent of its quota exceeds the holdings of the Fund of its currency; and

(3) The balance to the member countries in proportion to their quotas.

When the surplus has reached ten per cent of the aggregate quotas, all of the net income shall be distributed to the member countries as provided in (2) and (3)

above. Payments to each member country shall be made in its own currency.]
7/1/44 J.S. Art. VII, Additional Section (10)

(p. 33)

JOINT STATEMENT — No Provisions

The following material has been suggested as an addition to Article VII.
Section 11. *Miscellaneous Powers.*

In order to carry out its purposes, the Fund may:

(1) Make contracts;

(2) Acquire and dispose of real and personal property;

(3) Institute legal proceedings in any court of competent jurisdiction;

(4) Employ such staff as shall be necessary to conduct the business of the Fund; and

(5) Adopt such rules or regulations as may be necessary or appropriate to conduct the business of the Fund.

[Atlantic City: Alternative A; United States]

[In order to carry out its purposes and policies, the Fund shall have the following powers in addition to those specified elsewhere in this Agreement:

(1) To adopt, alter and use an official seal;

(2) To make contracts;

(3) to acquire, own, lease or dispose of such real and personal property as may be necessary to conduct the business of the Fund;

(4) To sue and complain in any court of competent jurisdiction;

(5) To select, employ and fix the compensation of such officers, employees, attorneys, and agents as shall be necessary to conduct the business of the Fund; to define their authority and duties, require bonds of them and fix the penalties thereof, and to dismiss at pleasure such officers, employees, attorneys, and agents; and

(6) To promulgate, amend, and repeal bylaws, rules and regulations necessary or appropriate to further the purposes and policies of the Fund.]
7/1/44 J.S. Art. VII, Additional Section (10)

[p. 24] (p. 34)

419

JOINT STATEMENT VIII, 1
VIII. *Withdrawal from the Fund*

1. A member country may withdraw from the Fund by giving notice in writing.

Alternative A [United States]

* Section 1. *Right of Members to Withdraw.*

Any member may withdraw from the Fund at any time by serving written notice on the Fund at its principal office. *Withdrawal shall become effective on the date such notice is received.*

[Atlantic City: Any member country may withdraw from membership in the Fund at any time by serving written notice on the Fund at its principal office. Withdrawal shall become effective on the date such notice is received.]

Alternative B [Australia]

& A member country may withdraw from the Fund by giving notice in writing *and the right of withdrawal shall not be prejudiced by membership of the Fund being made a condition of membership of any other international body.*

7/1/44 J.S. Art. VIII, Sec. 1

[p. 25] (p. 35)

JOINT STATEMENT — No Provisions

The following material has been suggested as an addition to Article VIII.

Alternative A [United States]

Section 2. *Suspension of Membership or Compulsory Withdrawal.*

(To be inserted later.)

[Atlantic City: *Suspension of membership.*

A member country failing to meet any of its obligations under this Agreement may be suspended from membership by decision of the majority of the member countries, each of which for this purpose shall have one vote, to be cast by its director or alternate. At the end of one year from the date of suspension, the country shall automatically cease to be a member of the Fund unless a majority of the member countries, voting in the same manner as for suspension, as previously restored the country to good standing.

While under suspension, a country shall be denied all the privileges of membership except that a withdrawal, but shall be subject to all of its obligations.]

[Atlantic City Alternative B; United Kingdom; not in Bretton Woods draft]

If the Fund finds that a member persists, after having received a special notice from the Fund, and acting in a manner inconsistent with the purposes and policies of the Fund, the Fund may, at its option, either:

(a) give notice that the member is suspended from making further use of the Fund's resources without the approval the Fund, or

(b) require that member to withdraw from the Fund.

7/1/44 J.S. Art. VIII, Additional Sec. (2)

[p. 26] (p. 36)

JOINT STATEMENT VIII, 2 & 3

2. The reciprocal obligations of the Fund and the country are to be liquidated within a reasonable time.

3. After a member country has given notice in writing of its withdrawal from the Fund, the Fund may not dispose of its holdings of the country's currency except in accordance with the arrangements made under 2, above. After a country has given notice of withdrawal, its use of the resources of the Fund is subject to the approval of the Fund.

Alternative A [United States]

Section 3. *Settlement of Accounts with Countries Ceasing to be Members.*

(To be inserted later)

[Atlantic City: When a country ceases to be a member, settlement of reciprocal accounts between the Fund and such country shall be made with reasonable dispatch, not to exceed three years from the date the country ceases to be a member.

The Fund shall be obligated to pay to such country the amount of its quota plus any other amounts due to it from the Fund, less any amounts due to the Fund from such country – including charges accruing after the country ceases to be a member – but no payment shall be made before six months from the date it ceased to be a member. Such payments shall be made in the currency of the country held by the Fund and, in the event the holdings of such currents are insufficient, the remainder shall be paid in gold or in such other manner as may be agreed. Currency of the country to be used to meet the Fund's obligation to it shall be set aside for that purpose; but no payment shall be made to the country until the Fund's holdings of its currency in excess of the Fund's obligations the currency are redeemed.

If the Fund and the country do not reach agreement promptly on a method of settling their account, the country shall be obligated to redeem such excess currency and gold or gold convertible exchange within a period of not less than three years to be determined by the Fund. Pending redemption by the country of its excess currency, but not before six months from the date the country ceases to be a member, the Fund may liquidate such currency in an orderly manner in any market; and the country unconditionally guarantees the unrestricted use of such currency in the purchase of goods or in the [p. 26a] payment of other obligations to it or to its nationals. The country further guarantees such currency against exchange depreciation until it has been used or redeemed.

Any member desiring to obtain the currency of a former member country shall acquire the currency, if available, by purchase from the Fund.

In the event the fund goes into liquidation within six months of the date upon which any country ceases to be a member, all rights of such member shall be determined by the provisions governing liquidations that of the provisions governing settlement of accounts with countries ceasing to be members of the Fund.]

Alternative B [United Kingdom]
(To be inserted later)

[Atlantic City: 3. On the withdrawal of a member under (1) or (2) above, the reciprocal obligations of the Fund and the member are to be liquidated within a reasonable time.

4. On the withdrawal of a member under (1) or (2) above, the Fund may not dispose of the member's currency except in accordance with arrangements under (3) above. After the withdrawal of a member under (1) or (2) above, its use of the resources of the Fund is subject to the approval of the Fund.]

7/1/44 J.S. Art. VIII, Secs. 2 & 3

[p. 27] (p. 37)

JOINT STATEMENT — No Provisions

The following material has been suggested as an addition to Article VIII.

Alternative A [United States]

Section 4. *Liquidation of the Fund.*

(To be inserted later)

[Atlantic City: The Fund may be voted into liquidation only by a majority of the aggregate votes. In an emergency, the Executive Committee may by a majority vote temporarily suspend all transactions of the Fund pending an opportunity for further consideration and action by the Board.

Upon being voted into liquidation, the Fund shall forthwith cease engaging in activities except those incident to an orderly liquidation of its assets in the settlement of its obligations.

The obligations of the Fund, other than the repayment of quotas, shall be a prior claim on all the assets of the Fund. In meeting each such obligation the Fund shall use its holdings of the currency in which the obligation is due. If these holdings are insufficient, it shall use its gold. This is insufficient to complete the payment, the remainder shall be covered by drawing on the currencies held by the Fund as far as possible in proportion to the quotas of those countries.

The net assets of the Fund remaining to be distributed as follows:

(a) The fund shall determine a percentage for each country by dividing its holdings of the currency of such country by the quota of such country.

(b) All countries shall have returned to them in their own currencies a proportion of their quotas equal to the smallest percentage determined in (a).

(c) The country having the next lowest percentage under (a) above shall then have returned to it the remainder of its currency held by the Fund and the country whose currency holdings have been exhausted shall have returned to it an [p. 27a] equivalent proportion of its quota in gold. If there is not sufficient gold, then the currency of the country having the second lowest percentage of the divided between the two countries in such manner that each will have been repaid the same proportion of its quota. All other countries shall have paid to them amounts in their respective currencies which represent the same proportion of their quotas.

(d) Further distributions shall be made in the manner provided in (c) above until the currencies of all countries have been exhausted.

Each member country shall redeem in gold or gold convertible exchange its currency held by another member country as a result of liquidation. Such redemptive shall be made with reasonable dispatch and, in any event, within three years unless the member country receiving such currency shall extend the period. Pending redemption of such currency in the aforesaid manner, a member country receiving it may liquidate it in any market at a rate not exceeding in any quarterly period one-twelfth of the amount held, and the member company obligated to redeem such currency unconditionally guarantees its unrestricted use in the purchase of goods or in the payment of other obligations to such country or to its nationals. Such country further guarantees such currency against exchange rate depreciation until it is been used or redeemed as aforesaid.]

[p. 27b]
Alternative B [Belgium?]
(To be inserted later)
7/1/44 J.S. Art. VIII, Additional Section (4)

[p. 28] (p. 38)
JOINT STATEMENT IX, 1
IX. *Obligations of Member Countries*

1. Not to buy gold at a price which exceed the agreed parity of its currency by more than a prescribed margin and not to sell gold at a price which falls below the agreed parity by more than a prescribed margin.

Alternative A [United States]
\# Section 1. *Purpose and Scope of Additional Undertakings*
(To be inserted later)
[Atlantic City: In order to support the activities of the Fund and to foster the accomplishment of its purposes and policies, each member country, in addition to commitments appearing elsewhere in this Agreement, undertakes the performance of and agrees to the stipulations set forth below. This undertaking agreement shall continue to be binding upon each member country during any periods of ineligibility to use the resources of the Fund and during suspension of membership, but it shall not be binding on any country after the termination of membership.]

* Section 2. *Gold Purchases Based on Parity Prices*

No member country shall buy or sell gold from or to the monetary authorities of another member at prices which vary from the agreed parity of its currency by more than a prescribed margin. [Atlantic City: No member country shall buy or sell gold at prices which vary from the agreed parity of its currency by more than a prescribed margin.]

7/1/44 J.S. Art. IX, Sec. 1

[p. 29] (p. 39)

JOINT STATEMENT IX, 2

2. Not to allow exchange transactions in its market in currencies of other members at rates outside a prescribed range based on the agreed parities.

Alternative A [United States]

& Section 3. *Foreign Exchange Dealings Based on Par Values.*

(a) The Fund shall prescribe maximum and minimum rates for exchange transactions in the currencies of members, which shall not differ by more than _____ percent from parity.

(b) Each member undertakes, through appropriate measures authorized under this Agreement, not to permit within its jurisdiction an appreciation or depreciation of the exchange value of its own currency in terms of gold beyond the range prescribed under (a) above. A member whose monetary authorities in fact freely buy and sell gold within the prescribed range, to settle international transactions, shall be deemed to be fulfilling this undertaking.

(c) Exchange transactions in the territory of one member involving the currency of any other member, which evade or avoid the exchange regulations prescribed by that other member and authorized by this Agreement, shall not be enforceable in the territory of any member.

[Atlantic City entire section: Every country undertakes, through appropriate measures authorized under this Agreement, not to permit within its jurisdiction an appreciation or depreciation of the exchange rate of its own currency in terms of gold beyond the prescribed range of parity.]

[Atlantic City Alternative A; United Kingdom; not in Bretton Woods draft]

3. To buy balances held with it by another member with that member's currency or with gold, if the member represents either that the balances in question have been currently acquired or that their conversion is needed for making current payments which are consistent with the provisions of the Fund. This obligation shall not relate to transactions involving:

(a) capital transfers.

(b) holdings of currency which have accumulated as result of transactions of a current account nature effected before the removal of the member country of restrictions on multilateral clearing maintained or imposed under X(2) below;

(c) the provision of a currency which has been declared scarce under VI above;

nor shall it apply to remember was seized to be entitled under III(2) or VIII above to by other members' currencies from the Fund in exchange for its own currency.

7/1/44 J.S. Art. IX, Sec. 2

[p. 30]

[Atlantic City:] (Transfer Article III, Section 5, rephrased as follows, to Article IX, as section 3)

Alternative A [United States]

3. To buy balances held with it by another member with that member's currency or with gold, if that member represents either that the balances in question have been currently acquired or that their conversion is needed for making current payments which are consistent with the provisions of the Fund. This obligation shall not relate to transactions involving:

(a) capital transfers.

(b) holdings of currency which have been accumulated as a result of transactions effected before the removal of the member country of restrictions on multilateral clearing maintained or imposed under X(2) below:

(c) the provision of a currency which has been declared scarce under VI above:

or (d) holdings of a currency which has been illicitly obtained:

nor shall it apply to a member who has ceased to be entitled under III(2) or VIII above to buy other members' currencies from the Fund in

426

exchange for its own currency.

[p. 31] (p. 40)

JOINT STATEMENT IX, 3

3. Not to impose restrictions on payments for current international transactions with other member countries (other than those involving capital transfers or in accordance with VI, above) or to engage in any discriminatory currency arrangements or multiple currency practices without the approval of the Fund.

Alternative A [United States]

* Section 4. *Exchange Controls on Current Payments.*

No member shall impose restrictions on the transfer into the currency of another member of the proceeds of current transactions with that member, or engage in any discriminatory currency arrangements or multiple currency practices unless authorized under this Agreement, or approved by the Fund. [Atlantic City: No member country shall impose restrictions on another member's repatriation of the proceeds of current international transactions with other member countries, or to [sic] engage in any discriminatory currency arrangements or multiple currency practices unless authorized under this Agreement, or approved by the Fund.]

Alternative B [United Kingdom]

* 4. Not to impose restrictions save as otherwise provided on payments for current international transactions with other member countries, or to engage in any discriminatory currency arrangements or multiple currency practices without the approval of the Fund.

7/1/44 J.S. Art. IX, Sec. 3

[p. 32] (p. 41)

JOINT STATEMENT — No Provisions

The following material has been suggested as an addition to Article IX:

Alternative A [United States]

* Section 5. *Immunity of Assets of the Fund.*

The Fund and its assets of whatsoever nature shall, wheresoever located and by whomsoever held, be exempt and immune from search, seizure, attachment, execution, requisition, confiscation, moratorium and

427

expropriation in the territory of any member [Atlantic City: expropriation by any member country or any political subdivision thereof].
7/1/44 J.S. Art. IX, Additional Sec. (5)

(p. 42)

JOINT STATEMENT — No Provisions

The following material has been suggested as an addition to Article IX:

\# Section 6. *Immunity from Suit.*
The Fund shall be immune from suit except when it consents to be sued.
7/1/44 J.S. Art. IX, Additional Sec. (6)

(p. 43)

JOINT STATEMENT — No Provisions

The following material has been suggested as an addition to Article IX:

\# Section 7. *Restrictions on Taxation of Fund, its Employees and Obligations.*
(a) The Fund, its assets, property, income, activities, operations and transactions of whatsoever nature shall be exempt and immune from all taxation or liability for the collection or payment of any tax, including without limitation by reason of this enumeration, excises, duties, and imposts, imposed by any member or any political subdivision or taxing authority thereof.

(b) No member [Atlantic City: member country], or any political subdivision or taxing authority thereof shall impose or collect any tax on or measured by salaries or remunerations for personal services paid by the Fund to persons who are not citizens of such country.

(c) (Provision concerning taxation of securities issued by the Fund to be inserted later.)

[Atlantic City: (c) No member country, or any political subdivision or taxing authority thereof, shall impose or collect taxation on any obligation or security issued by the Fund or any dividend or interest thereon, by whomsoever held or received, which discriminates against such obligation, dividend, or interest, because of its origin, or which is applicable with respect such obligation, security, dividend, or interest because of the place or currency in which it is issued, made payable or paid, or because of the location of any office or place of business maintained by the

Fund.]
7/1/44 J.S. Art. IX, Additional Sec. (7)

[p. 33] (p. 44)

JOINT STATEMENT X, 1-4
X. *Transitional Arrangements*

1. Since the Fund is not intended to provide facilities for relief or reconstruction or to deal with international indebtedness arising out of the war, the agreement of a member country to provisions III, 5 and IX, 3 above, shall not become operative until it is satisfied as to the arrangements at its disposal to facilitate the settlement of the balance of payments differences during the early post-war transition period by means which will not unduly encumber its facilities with the Fund.

2. During this transition period member countries may maintain and adapt to changing circumstances exchange regulations of the character which have been in operation during the war, but they shall undertake to withdraw as soon as possible by progressive stages any restrictions which impede multilateral clearing on current account. In their exchange policy they shall pay continuous regard to the principles and objectives of the Fund; and they shall take all possible measures to develop commercial and financial relations with other member countries which will facilitate international payments and the maintenance of exchange stability.

3. The Fund may make representations to any member that conditions are favorable to withdrawal of particular restrictions or for the general abandonment of the restrictions inconsistent with IX, 3 above. Not later than 3 years after coming into force of the Fund any member still retaining any restrictions inconsistent with IX, 3 shall consult with the Fund as to their further retention.

4. In its relations with member countries, the Fund shall recognize that the transition period is one of change and adjustment, and in deciding on its attitude to any proposals presented by members it shall give the member country the benefit of any reasonable doubt.

Alternative A [United States]
(To be inserted later)

[Atlantic City: [1.] Since the Fund is not intended to provide facilities for relief or reconstruction of the deal international indebtedness arising out of the war, member countries, during the early postwar transition period may, notwithstanding the provisions of III, 5 and IX, 3, maintain and adapt to changing circumstances and introduced, where necessary, in the case of countries which have occupied by the enemy, exchange regulations and currency arrangements and practices which impede payments and transfers for international transactions and current account. They undertake to withdraw as soon as possible by progressive stages all such restrictions, arrangements and practices. In their exchange policies member country shall pay continuous regard to the purposes and policies of the Fund and shall take all possible measures to develop commercial and financial relations with other member countries which will facilitate international payments and the maintenance of exchange stability.

[No alternative provision to Section 2.] [p. 34]

3. [Atlantic City: *Withdrawal of Exchange Restrictions.*] The Fund may at any time make representations to any member country that conditions are favorable for the withdrawal of particular restrictions on exchange transactions or particular ringtones and practices, or for the general abandonment of such restrictions, arrangements and practices which are inconsistent with III, 5 or IX, 3. Not later than three years after the date on which the operations of the Fund commence any member country still retaining restrictions, arrangements or practices inconsistent with III, 5 or IX, 3 shall consult with the Fund as to their further retention and shall retain them only with the approval of the Fund. [p. 35]

4. *Policy of the Fund During the Transition Period.* In its relations with member countries, the Fund shall recognize that the early postwar transition period will be one of change and adjustment, and in making decisions in requests presented by any member country it shall give the benefit of any reasonable doubt to such country.]

Alternative B [United Kingdom]

(To be inserted later)

[Atlantic City: 3. After the establishment of the Fund, but before it commences operations, members shall notify the Fund whether or not they intend to avail themselves of the optional transitional arrangements under (1) or (2) above; and whether they are prepared to accept the obligations of IX (3) and (4). At any subsequent date a member may notify its acceptance of these obligations. Not later than three years from the coming into force of the Fund, and each year thereafter, the Fund shall report on the restrictions still enforced under (3) above, five years after the coming into force of the Fund, and each year thereafter, each member still retaining any restrictions and consistent IX(3) and (4) shall consult the Fund as to their further retention. [p. 35]

4. *Policy of the Fund During the Transition Period.* In its relations with

member countries, the Fund shall recognize that the early postwar transition period will be one of change and adjustment over a term of uncertain duration, and in making decisions or requests presented by any member country it shall give the benefit of any reasonable doubt to such country.]

7/1/44 J.S. Art. X, Secs. 1-4

[p. 36] (p. 45)

JOINT STATEMENT — No Provisions

The following material has been suggested as part of an additional Article (XI).

[Alternative A [United States]]
Article XI — *Amendments*

Any governor or executive director desiring to introduce modifications in this Agreement shall communicate his proposal to the Chairman of the Board of Governors who shall bring the proposal before the Board of Governors. If the proposed amendment is approved by the Board of Governors by a majority of the aggregate votes, the Fund shall prepare a protocol, by dated circular letter, to the governments of all the members asking whether they accept the proposed modifications. When the governments of members having four-fifths of the aggregate votes, have accepted the proposed amendment, or, in the case of modifications of the right to withdraw from the Fund, when the governments of all of the members have accepted, the Fund shall certify the fact by means of a *procès verbal,* which it shall communicate to the governments of all members. The protocol will enter into force between all members three months from the date of the *procès verbal* unless a shorter period is specified in the protocol.

[Atlantic City: Any member country which desires to introduce modifications in this agreement shall communicate its proposals to the Fund. The Fund, if four-fifths of the aggregate votes deem it advisable, shall prepare a protocol, by dated circular letter, to the governments of all the member countries, asking whether they accept the proposed modifications. When the governments of member countries having four-fifths of the aggregate votes, have acceded, the Fund shall certify the fact by means of a *procès verbal,* which it shall communicate to the governments of all the member countries. The protocol will enter into force between all the member countries three months from the date of the *procès verbal*, unless a shorter period is specified in the protocol.

Alternative B [United Kingdom]
(Add the following to Alternative A)

Notwithstanding the foregoing provisions (of Alternative A) amendments may be made to the following provisions of this Agreement, namely (unimportant provisions will be inserted later) by a four-fifths majority vote of the Board of Governors.

[Atlantic City: The Council shall have power to repeal, amend or add to the provisions of the statutes by decisions taken by a 3/5 majority except that

(a) a decision concurred in by all countries shall be required for

_____

(b) the Council shall have no power by any repeal, amendment or addition to _____

7/1/44 J.S. Art. XI (Additional Article)

[p. 37] (p. 46)

JOINT STATEMENT — No Provisions

The following material has been suggested as part of an additional Article (XII) on interpretation of the Agreement.

Alternative A [United States]
Article XII — *Interpretation of the Agreement*
Section 1. *Interpretation.*

All questions of interpretation of the provisions of this Agreement between two or more member countries shall be resolved by the Fund. Whenever a disagreement arises between the Fund and a country which has ceased to be a member, or between the Fund and any member country after liquidation of the Fund, such disagreement shall be submitted to arbitration.

[Atlantic City: All disagreements between two or more member countries concerning the interpretation of any of the provisions of this Agreement or of any amendments thereto, or of any rules, regulations or by-laws promulgated by the Fund, shall be settled by the Fund. Whenever a disagreement arises between the Fund and a country which has ceased to be a member, or between the Fund and any member country after liquidation of the Fund, such disagreement shall be submitted to arbitration.]

Alternative B [United Kingdom]

(1) All questions which arise involving doubts or differences relating to the interpretation of the provisions of this Agreement shall be submitted to the Executive Directors of the Fund for their opinion. If the question is one which involves a dispute affecting particularly one (or more) member (s) and that (or those) member (s) are not represented among the Executive Directors by a Director appointed by it (or them) then that (or those) member(s) may appoint a representative to take part in the discussions of this question of the Executive Directors on the same footing as the Directors.

(2) In any case where the Executive Directors have given an opinion under paragraph (1) above, a member may require that the question be submitted to the Board and the opinion of the Board is final. Pending the result of the reference to the Board of Governors, the Fund may (so as is necessary) act on the basis of the opinion of the Executive Directors.

[Atlantic City: (1) The Fund shall have at all times a right to tender informal advice to any member in any matter arising under these statutes.

(2) All questions which arise involving doubts or differences relating to the interpretation of the provisions of these Statutes shall be submitted to the Directorate of the Fund for their opinion. If the question is one which involves a dispute affecting particularly one (or more) member(s) and where that (or those) member(s) are not represented on the Directorate by a Director appointed by it (or them) then that (or those) member(s) may appoint a representative to take part in the discussions of this question in the Directorate on the same footing as the Directors.

(3) In any case where the Directorate has given an opinion under para. (2) above, a member may require that the question be submitted to the Council and the opinion of the Council is final. Pending the result of the reference to the Council, the Fund may (so as is necessary) act on the basis of the opinion of the Directorate.
7/1/44 Art. XII, Sec. 1 (Additional Article)

[p. 37 lower] (p. 47)

JOINT STATEMENT — No Provisions

The following material has been suggested as part of an additional Article (XII) on interpretation of the Agreement.

Alternative A [United States]

Section 2. *Definitions.*

(To be inserted later)

[Atlantic City: (a) The term "currency" means every form of medium of exchange used within a member country which is defined in terms of the monetary unit of such country, including without limitation:

(1) All paper money and coin issued or coined in accordance with the laws of such country;

(2) All demand deposits in banks within such country; and

(3) All bills, notes or other forms of indebtedness substituted by member countries for part of the Fund's holdings of their currencies.

(b) The term "gold convertible exchange" means any foreign currency, as defined above, or any evidences of indebtedness expressed in such currency having maturities of less than one year, available for use by the monetary authorities of a country, directly or indirectly, for the purchase of gold.

(c) The term "official holdings" means the holdings of a member country's government and central bank and of any governmental department, agency, establishment or corporation; without reduction for any liabilities, whether such liabilities are actual or potential, general or specific, internal or external.

All non-official holdings of gold and all non-official holdings of gold convertible exchange in excess of one-fourth of the quota of the [p. 37a] member country shall be deemed to be official holdings for the purposes of III, 7(a) and (b).

(Further definitions to be added)]

[p. 37c]

Alternative B [United Kingdom; Atlantic City Alternative D]

(To be inserted later)

[Atlantic City: (The following has been suggested as an alternative to (b) and (c) of the new Section on definitions in Alternative A.)

(b) The term "monetary reserves" means the sum of a country's net official holdings of gold and gold convertible exchange. "Official holdings" include the holdings of a Central Bank, Treasury, or other

434

Government Institution, and also the holdings of any other banks, which in the particular circumstances of the case it is agreed between the Fund and the member country should properly come within the "official" category. This interpretation shall not, however, include, for example, holdings of authorized dealers in exchange not in excess of normal working balances; but they include holdings of banks other than Central Banks when in practice some part of the members' reserves in foreign currency in excess of working balances is normally held in the name of such banks.

"Convertible exchange" means the currencies of members who have accepted the obligation of convertibility under IX(3). Where a member declares that this obligation is accepted from the outset, that member's currency shall be reckoned as convertible for the purpose of the official subscription.

"Net" official holdings shall be calculated by deducting the liabilities of other official holders in gold or convertible currencies from the gross official holdings of gold and convertible currency, so as to provide that gold and convertible currencies do not count twice, first in respect of a country holding convertible currency and second in respect of gold held against that by the country having this liability. Accordingly, convertible exchange reckoned as part of the official holdings of one country shall be deductible in reckoning the net official holdings of the country whose exchange is involved.

(*NOTE.* These provisions are in substitution for the "Note on Certain Definitions" circulated as Doc. F-5.)]

[p. 37b]
Alternative C [Union of Soviet Socialist Republics]
(To be inserted later)
[Atlantic City: (Insert the following in place of subdivision (c) in the second section of Alternative A.)

As holdings of gold and gold convertible exchange shall be considered the holdings of a member country's Central Bank and Treasury.]
7/1/44 Art. XII, Sec. 2 (Additional Article)

[p. 37 lower] (p. 48)
JOINT STATEMENT — No Provisions

The following material has been suggested as part of an additional Article (XII) on interpretation of the Agreement.

Alternative A [United States]

Section 3. *Effect on Other International Commitments.*

(To be inserted later)

[Atlantic City: Nothing in this Agreement shall be deemed to affect in any way any existing or future international commitments regarding the non-discriminatory application of exchange restrictions or international undertakings for the progressive relaxation of barriers to trade.]

7/1/44 Art. XII, Sec. 3 (Additional Article)

p. 38] (p. 49)

JOINT STATEMENT — No Provisions

The following material has been suggested as an additional Article (XIII) on putting the Fund into operation:

Alternative A [United States]

Section 1. *Entry into Effect.*

(To be inserted later)

[Atlantic City: Section [1]. *Acceptance of Membership in the Fund.*

This agreement shall be presented by the delegates to their respective governments for acceptance of membership. Each government that accepts membership shall sign this agreement and, as soon as possible, deposit evidence of its acceptance with the Government of the United States of America, which shall transmit certified copies of all evidences of acceptance to the governments of all the countries represented at the United Nations Monetary and Financial Conference.

The Government of the United States of America shall also notify by telegram, cablegram or radiogram the governments of all such countries immediately upon the deposit with that of such evidence of acceptance.

At the time it accepts membership, each government shall transmit to the Government of the United States of America one-twentieth of one percent of its quota in gold or gold convertible exchange for the purpose of meeting administrative expenses. The Government of the United States of America shall hold such funds in a special deposit account and shall transmit them to the Board of Governors of the Fund when the initial meeting has been called. If the initial meeting has not been called by January 1, 19 , the Government of United States of America shall return such funds to the government that transmitted them.

Section 2. *Effective Date of the Agreement.*
(To be inserted later)

[Atlantic City: As soon as the evidences of the acceptance of membership by countries having sixty-five percent of the aggregate quotas established in II, I, have been deposited, this Agreement shall come into force in respect of such countries.

Thereafter this agreement shall come into force between the countries which shall have accepted membership and each country which subsequently deposits its evidence of acceptance on the date of such deposit. [p. 38a]

Section 3. *Calling the Initial Meeting of the Fund.*
(To be inserted later)

[Atlantic City: Immediately after receipt of the evidences of acceptance of countries having sixty-five percent of the aggregate quotas established in II. 1, the government of the country accepting membership which has the largest quota shall invite to the initial meeting of the Fund, to be held in that country sixty days after the date of such invitation, all of the countries which shall have accepted membership in the Fund. Such countries shall be represented at the meeting by the directors or alternates they appoint to the Board of Directors of the Fund.]

Section 4. *Agenda of the Initial Meeting.*
(To be inserted later)

[Atlantic City: At the initial meeting of the Board of Directors, the Board shall make provision for the organization of the Fund. In addition to such other action as it may deem appropriate, it shall elect a chairman, elect an Executive Committee, and set a date for the operations of the Fund to begin, subject to Section 5 of this article.]

Section 5. *Fixing Initial Par Values.*
(To be inserted later)

[Atlantic City: The official value on July 1, 1944, of the currency of each member country in terms of gold or gold convertible currency shall be the par value of that currency for purposes of the Fund, unless either the Fund or the member country concerned signifies within a period of ninety days from the effective date of this Agreement that such par value for a given currency is unsatisfactory. If either so signifies, the Fund and the member country shall, during this period or during an extended period to be determined by the Fund in the light of all relevant circumstances of the member country, agree upon a suitable rate. If agreement between the member country and the Fund is not reached during such period, as extended, a member country shall be deemed to have withdrawn from the Fund as of the date of the termination of such period.

The Fund shall begin exchange transactions at such date as it may determine after par values have been established for the currencies of members having sixty percent of the aggregate quotas fixed in II, 1, but in no event until one-hundred twenty days after the effective date of this [p. 38b] Agreement, or until the Fund shall have determined that major hostilities in the present conflict have ceased, whichever is the later. Exchange transactions in a currency, the par value of which is not become established when exchange transactions begin, shall begin when agreement has been reached with the Fund on a par value.]

Alternative B [United Kingdom]

I A. *Entry into Effect.*

(To be inserted later)

[Atlantic City: *Inauguration of the Fund.*

1. When the Convention comes into force, the first meeting of the Council shall be held as soon as possible. The Councilor appointed by the Government in whose country the first meeting takes place shall take the Chair until the Council have appointed a Chairman.

2. The Council shall then proceed to the election of the Directors and shall arrange for the first meeting of the Directorate to take place as soon as possible.

3, The Directorate at their first meeting shall appoint the Chairman and General Manager, shall request the payment by each member of such proportion of its subscription as is required, in the opinion of the Directorate, for the preliminary expenses of the Fund, and shall instruct the General Manager to make the necessary arrangements with regard to the taking of offices and the engaging of staff.

4. The Directorate shall then, as soon as may be, take steps to determine the par value of members' currencies in accordance with IV and the provisions of IV shall come into operation.

5. Thereafter the Directorate shall, as soon as seems to them expedient, call up such further proportion of the subscription of each member as in their judgment is immediately required to provide facilities currently required by members, and as from the date of this call the whole of the provision of this Statute shall come into operation.

6. For the purposes of taking action under 4 and 5 above, the assent of Directors representing four-fifths of the total voting power of the Directorate shall be required. [p. 38c]

7. Thereafter the Directorate may, from time to time, call up such further instalments of the subscriptions due by members as may be required for the operation of the Fund.]

7/1/44 J.S. Art. XIII, Sec. 1 (Additional Article)

[p. 39]
JOINT STATEMENT — No Provisions [United States; Atlantic City article not in Bretton Woods draft]

The following material has been suggested as part of an additional Article concerning execution of the Agreement:

\# [Article XIV.] *Execution of the Agreement*

IN FAITH WHEREOF the undersigned have executed this Agreement.

Done at Washington in a single copy which will remain deposited in the archives of the United States of America, and of which certified copies will be transmitted through the diplomatic channel to the other countries represented at the United Nations Monetary and Financial Conference.

75

Document F-2

International Monetary Fund
Mexico's Memorandum on Silver
[June 24, 1944]

1. In order to attain a large measure of international cooperation in the monetary field, it seems obvious that the Fund must take into account the monetary habits, needs and practices of all the member countries.

2. Among the United and Associated Nations, there are some countries which, besides keeping a gold reserve sufficiently ample to maintain their exchange rates, traditionally have had and must continue to have, large silver stocks hoarded by their nationals.

3. It is a fact that these silver stocks constitute for these countries a monetary reserve as real as are the foreign exchange and gold holdings of any country, which stocks, moreover, operate much in the same manner as these holdings, in the settlement of international balances.

4. The very existence of large silver recordings in some countries has definite international monetary effects which must not be disregarded by the Monetary Conference of the United and Associated Nations which avowedly must face, and offer adequate solutions for, problems of this very same nature.

5. Consequently, Mexico respectfully requests that the following provisions be included in the Agenda section relative to "Transactions of the Fund" and that they be given due consideration:

A. That the Fund shall determine the proper role and function of silver within the international monetary structure.

B. That the Fund is authorized to carry out whatever policy it deems appropriate for silver.

C. That member countries agree to act in accordance with the Fund's policy on silver.

Document F-3

International Monetary Fund
Amendment [on Investment] to Joint Statement of
Principles Proposed by the Representative of Brazil
[June 26, 1944]

Correlation of Exchange Stability and Investment

It is suggested that a general provision for the correlation of exchange stability and investment be included in the Purposes and Policies of the Fund, Article I, by adding a paragraph 7 as follows:

"To correlate procedures for exchange stability with a policy for the promotion of international investment by other international financial agencies and to evolve a working relationship with such agencies."

It is further suggested that this statement of policy be implemented by amending the last sentence of paragraph 3, Article IV, Par Values of Member Currencies, to read as follows:

"In considering a requested change, the Fund shall take into consideration,

(a) the extreme uncertainties prevailing at the time the parities of the currencies of the member countries were initially agreed upon, and

(b) that the applicant country has been unable to obtain adequate resources to restore the equilibrium of its balance of payments from an international investment agency with which the Fund is in working relationship."

Document F-4

Minimum Percentage Charges Payable by a Country on Fund's Holdings of Its Currency in Excess of Its Quota
[June 27, 1944]

Marginal Charges

Amount of country's currency held by Fund as percentages of country's quota	Percent per annum payable on excess currency during					
	First year Fund holds it	Second year	Third year	Fourth year	Fifth year	Additional years
100-125	1	1½	2	2½	3	Corresponding increases
125-150	1½	2	2½	3	3½	
150-175	2	2½	3	3½	4	
175-200*	2½	3	3½	4	4½	
200-225	3	3½	4	4½	5	
Additional amounts	Corresponding increases					

*Full use of quota.

78

Document F-5

[British] Note on Certain Definitions
[June 27, 1944]

1. Whenever in the Joint Statement of Principles the words "gold and gold convertible exchange" appear, this should be replaced by the words "monetary reserves."

2. In an interpretation clause, monetary reserves should be defined as the sum of a country's net official holdings of gold and convertible exchange.

3. Official holdings should be further defined as including the holdings of a Central Bank, Treasury, or other Government institution, and also the holdings of any other banks, which in the particular circumstances of the case it is agreed between the Fund and the member country should properly come within the "official" category. This interpretation should not be operated so as to include, for example, the holdings of authorized dealers in exchange which do not exceed normal working balances; but should include the holdings of banks other than Central Banks when in practice some part of the country's reserves of foreign currency in excess of working balances is normally held in the name of such banks.

4. Convertible exchange should be interpreted to mean the currencies of members which have accepted the obligation of convertibility under IX-3 [["Current Transactions"]]. Where a member declares that he accepts this obligation from the outset, his currency would be reckoned as "convertible" for the purpose of the initial subscription.

5. "Net" official holdings should be tabulated by deducting liabilities to other official holders in gold or convertible currencies from the gross official holdings of gold and convertible currency. That is to say, gold and convertible currencies should not count twice, first of all in respect of the country holding the convertible currency, and secondly, in respect of the gold held against it by the country having this liability. Accordingly, convertible exchange reckoned as part of the official holdings of one country shall be deductible in reckoning the net official holdings of the country whose exchange is involved.

Document F-6

Report of the Committee on
the Management of the Fund

The Board of Governors • Executive Directors

1. The Committee appointed to consider questions relating to the management of the Fund has held three meetings which have been attended by members of the delegations of China, Mexico, the Netherlands, the UK, the U.S., and the USSR. The Committee has, in particular, considered the alternatives on pages 20-20(f) of Doc. F-1 [Article VII of the draft IMF agreement, "Management of the Fund"], and has agreed to the following report upon its deliberations.

2. The Committee is in general in agreement that the management of the Fund should consists of — (i) a Governing Body, which in this report is provisionally called the "Board of Governors," on which every member country would be represented; (ii) an executive body provisionally called "Executive Directors," of about 11 or 12 Directors. There would also be a Managing Director (or General Manager), responsible, among other things, for the internal organization and its staff, and the routine business of the Fund.

The Board of Governors

3. The Committee is in agreement that each member country should appoint one Governor. It is also agreed that it would be useful for alternates to be appointed by the member countries and that alternates should not vote accept the absence of the respective Governors. There is a division of opinion whether or not this implies that alternates should be present with their Governors and participate in all activities of the Board.

4. The Committee agrees that Governors and alternates should serve for five years, subject the pleasure of the members appointing them, and

that they should [be] eligible for reappointment. It is also agreed that the Board of Governors shall hold an annual meeting and such other meetings as may be provided for by the Board or convened by the Executive Directors; that meetings of the Board shall be convened by the Executive Committee whenever requested either by member countries having 25 percent of the aggregate votes or by a specified number of member countries; and that it shall not be necessary for annual meetings of the Board always to be held in the same place.

5. The Committee considers that all the powers of the Fund are vested in the Board of Governors, and that the Board should not be permitted to delegate any of the following functions; –

(i) power to invite non-signatory countries to become members;

(ii) approval of a revision of quotas (II-2);

(iii) approval of an agreed uniform change in the gold value of the currencies of members (IV-5);

(iv) expulsion of a member from the Fund;

(v) decisions on appeals from the Executive Directors about the interpretation of a Statute given an application by member;

(vi) agreements for co-operation with other international organizations;

(vii) a decision to liquidate the Fund.

There is a difference of opinion whether the power to suspend a member from the facilities of the Fund under III-2(d) [["Purchases of Another Member's Currency"]] could be delegated to the Executive Directors, and also whether an appeal by a member against the decision of the Executive Directors on a requested change of par values should lie to the Board of Governors. It is agreed that the conduct of all business of the Fund, other than that belonging, as above, to the Board of Governors, may be delegated by that Board.

Executive Directors

6. There is a difference of opinion in the Committee on the question of whether or not Governors alone should be eligible for appointment as Executive Directors. On view is that the Executive Directors should be regarded as forming part of the Board of Governors, and that only Governors should therefore be eligible for appointment as Executive Directors. The other view is that member countries should be able to appoint as Executive Directors persons who are not Governors.

7. The Committee agrees that, say, five Executive Directors should be

appointed by the five member countries having the largest quotas and that, say, six other Directors should be elected biennially.

8. There is a difference of opinion in the Committee on a number of questions relating to the Executive Directors and to the need or desirability of requiring them to reside at the Headquarters of the Fund during the period of their appointment.

9. There is general agreement that the work of the Fund has important consequences for all member countries and that many of the decisions require great judgment and experience. It is therefore essential that men appointed to the Directorate shall be men of high standing and knowledge. There is also agreement that some of the important decisions to be taken by the Executive Directors will be urgent, and that countries may be damaged by delay.

10. From this general agreement two differing lines of thought have shown themselves. The first is that the decisions requiring the collective judgment of the Executive Directors will be so numerous and continuous that the conception of a full Directorate regularly and in residence must be envisaged as a necessity of the Fund. Moreover, urgency requires a regular presence of a sufficient Directorate.

11. The alternative line of thought is that, after the initial period when admittedly there will be a heavy volume of work upon the Executive Directors, the work of the Fund will consist of regular matters which, though they are technically important, do not raise questions of general policy on which the collective view of the Executive Directors is required, together with important issues which cannot be decided except on the considered judgment of the Directors as a whole, but will only arise intermittently.

12. If this second view is an accurate forecast of the development of the Fund, two consequences, it is suggested, would follow from a decision that the Directors should be whole-time persons resident at the Headquarters. Men of standing and experience would not be content to remain if they had not regular work of importance to perform, and the withdrawal of any Director on such grounds would obviously prejudice the standing of the Fund. Moreover, there is a risk that Executive Directors, however much knowledge they may have from their past conduct with financial affairs, may lose touch with the current of the actual business and trends proceeding in the international markets, which must form the background of exchange dealings. As regards the difficulty of urgency, it is suggested that this can be met under modern conditions of transportation by a system of a quorum.

13. The Committee have to record a divergence of opinion on another

matter affecting the provision of the Executive Directors. This concerns the relationship of the Directors, respectively to the Fund and to the country which appointed them.

14. There is general agreement that the aim is that Executive Directors should exercise a corporate responsibility to all the member countries. One view assumes that this can more certainly be achieved if the Directors, whether representing the countries with the largest quotas or elected by the other members, regard themselves, when elected, much as the directors of a commercial organization, i.e. representing the shareholders as a body, not the sectional interest of any one country which they are expected to safeguard at the deliberations of their corporate body. The other view is that in practice it is assumed that each of the Executive Directors will be looking after the interests of his own country, or group of countries. This view requires that the method of election of those Directors who are elected shall be such as to make them truly representative of the quota strength and interests of those member countries who do not possess the right to nominate Directors. Furthermore, it is felt that the only way to secure this is by proportionate voting on the lines proposed in (b) on pages 20(a) and 20(b) of Doc. F-1.[332]

15. The Committee feel that they have no competence to make a recommendation on these questions of principle, which are more appropriate for consideration by a wider Conference.

16. The Committee agrees that Governors, Directors and alternates should receive expenses and that Directors should receive salaries from the Fund.

(Signed) W. Eady [UK, Chairman]
28th June, 1944

---

[332] VII-1 ["Board and Executive Committee"], Alternative A, U.S., giving seats to the five member countries with the largest quotas and to six directors elected by coalitions of other countries.

Document B-1

The Reconstruction Bank [British proposal] June 29, 1944

Preamble • I. The Purposes of the Bank • II. Capital Structure of the Bank • III. General Provisions for Loans to Member Countries • IV. Powers and Operations • V. Miscellaneous Provisions • VI. Management

On the trip aboard the Queen Mary, *the British delegation devised its own draft proposal for the Bank for Reconstruction and Development. Upon reaching Atlantic City and talking to the American delegation, the delegations found that they were close enough to produce a compromise draft to be the basis for discussion of the Bank at Bretton Woods. The Full Agenda Committee devoted its ninth and tenth meetings to considering the British proposal and melding it with the American proposal.*

The British proposal has names for articles, but not for sections. We have inserted our own section names in double brackets, [[ ]]. We use the section names in other chapters to help readers understand more easily what topics the delegates to the Atlantic City conference are discussing.

DRAFT OUTLINE OF A PROPOSAL FOR
A BANK FOR RECONSTRUCTION AND DEVELOPMENT
U.S. draft of November 1943 incorporating
suggestions made by UK Delegation

Preamble

1. As in U.S. draft.
2. " " " ".
3. " " " ".
4. " " " ".

I. The Purposes of the Bank

1. *[[Cooperate with Private Agencies in Reconstruction and Development.]]* As in U.S. draft.
2. *[[Provide Capital when Private Agencies Do Not.]]* " " " ".
3. *[[Assist in Transition to Peacetime.]]* " " " ".
4. *[[Raise Productivity.]]* " " " ".
5. *[[Promote Trade.]]* " " " ".

II. Capital Structure of the Bank

1. *[[Capital.]]* As in U.S. draft.
2. *[[Shares.]]* " " " ".
3. *[[Distribution of Shares.]]* " " " ".
4. *[[Payments on Subscriptions.]]* The subscribed capital of the Bank shall be divided into two parts as follows:-

(a) 20 per cent of the subscription of each member country shall be callable by the Bank as and when required, some portion of which (not to exceed 20 per cent) shall be paid in gold and the remainder in local currency. The proportions to be paid in gold and local currency shall be graduated according to an agreed upon schedule which shall take into account the adequacy of the gold and free foreign exchange holdings of each member country. These subscriptions shall be available for direct loans made by the Bank out of its own funds under IV-1(a) below.

(b) The remaining 80 per cent shall be callable by the Bank, as and when required to implement, where necessary, guarantees given by the Bank under IV-1(b) and (c) below and shall not be callable for any other purpose. Amounts callable under this clause shall be paid either in the currency required to implement the guarantee or in gold or in currency which is convertible under the terms of the IMF.

5. *[[Expenditure of Local Currency Subscribed.]]* The local currency subscribed under II-4(a) above shall not be expended except with the permission of the member country under IV-4 below. Member countries agree that all other local currency holdings and other assets of the Bank located in their country, provided that they have been acquired or borrowed with their permission, shall be free from any special restrictions as to their use.

6. *[[Use of Resources.]]* (II-9 of U.S. draft.) The resources and the facilities of the Bank shall be used exclusively for the benefit of member countries.

449

III. General Provisions for Loans to Member Countries

1. *[[Loans.]]* (IV-1 in U.S. draft.) To achieve the purposes stated in Section I, the Bank may guarantee, participate in, or make loans to any member country and through the government of such country to any of its political subdivisions or to business or industrial enterprises therein under conditions provided below:

(a) (IV-1(a) in U.S. draft.) The payment of interest and principal is fully guaranteed by the national government.

(b) (IV-1(b) in U.S. draft.) The borrower is otherwise unable to secure the funds from other sources, even with the national government's guarantee of repayment, under conditions which in the opinion of the Bank are reasonable.

(c) A competent committee has made a careful study of the merits of the project or the program and, in a written report, concludes that the loan would serve directly or indirectly to raise the productivity of the borrowing country.

(d) The bank shall make arrangements to assure the use of the proceeds of any loan which it guarantees, participates in, or makes, for the purposes for which the loan was approved, with due attention to considerations of cheapness and efficiency regardless of political or other noneconomic influences or considerations.

(e) The Bank shall guarantee, participate in, or make loans at reasonable rates of interest and commission with a schedule of repayment appropriate to the character of the project and the balance of payments prospects of the country of the borrower.

2. *[[Noncompetition with Private Investment.]]* (IV-6 in U.S. draft.) The Bank shall make no loans or investments that can be placed through the usual private investment channels on reasonable terms. The Bank shall by regulation prescribe procedure for its operations that will assure the application of this principle.

3. *[[Spending of Proceeds of Loans.]]* (IV-7 in U.S. draft.) The Bank shall impose no condition upon a loan as to the particular member country in which the proceeds of the loan must be spent; provided, however, that the proceeds of a loan may not be spent in any country which is not a member country without the approval of the Bank.

4. *[[Currency of Loans.]]* (IV-8 in U.S. draft.) The Bank in making loans shall provide that:

(a) The foreign exchange in connection with the project or program shall be provided by the Bank in the currencies of the countries in which the proceeds of the loan will be spent, and only with the approval of such countries.

(b) The local currency needs in connection with the project shall be largely financed locally without the assistance of the Bank.

(c) In special circumstances, where the Bank considerers that the local part of any project cannot be financed at home except on very unreasonable terms, it can lend that portion to the borrower in local currency.

(d) Where the developmental program will give rise to an increased need for foreign exchange for purposes not directly needed for that program, yet resulting from the program, the Bank will provide an appropriate part of the loan in gold or desired foreign exchange.

5. *[[Accounting.]]* (IV-9 in U.S. draft.) When a loan is made by the Bank, it shall credit the account of the borrower with the amount of the loan. Payment shall be made from this account to meet drafts covering audited expenses.

6. *[[Stabilization Loans.]]* In general, loans made or guaranteed by the Bank, shall be for the purpose of specific projects of reconstruction and development, and except as otherwise provided in this plan, the proceeds of loans shall only be made available to meet specific purposes. In exceptional circumstances, however, the Bank, acting in agreement with the International Monetary Fund, may make or guarantee a loan which provides the borrowing country with gold or foreign exchange for the purpose of establishing its exchanges and allowing a breathing space for the recovery of its economy and the balancing of its international payments.

7. *[[Lending Policy.]]* In making or guaranteeing a loan the Bank shall pay due regard to the prospects of the borrowing country being in a position to service the loan; and in determining the destination, the character and the volume of its loans it shall act prudently in the interests both of the borrowing member country and also of the guaranteeing members. At the same time, it shall not seek to avoid the incurring of some measure of reasonable risk (taking account of the commission chargeable — see below) where the loan is in the general interests of reconstructing or developing the world's resources or expanding international trade along mutually advantageous lines; and shall seek to conduct its operations taken as a whole in such manner as to avoid, so far as possible, the calling up of the capital reserved for guarantees, rather than seek full security from risk in each transaction taken separately. These considerations shall govern the lending policy of the Bank

especially in approving reconstruction loans to countries which have suffered from the war.

8. *[[Role in International Finance.]]* It shall be a primary duty of the Bank to secure that loans are not made haphazard[ly] but that the more useful and urgent schemes are dealt with first; also to coordinate international lending, in the case of loans made or guaranteed by the Bank, with loans through other channels; and in short to see that international lending is on a more wisely conceived plan that it was after the last war.

IV. Powers and Operations

1. *[[Loans.]]* The Bank may facilitate the provision of loans to any member country, which satisfy the general conditions of III, in any of the following ways:

(a) By direct loans out of the Bank's own capital subscribed under II-4 (a).

(b) By direct loans out of funds raised by the Bank as a charge of a member country; against its reserves and uncalled capital (see 8 below) in the market.

(c) By guaranteeing in whole or in part loans made by private investors through the usual investment channels.

2. *[[Loan Participations.]]* The old IV-3.

3. *[[Equity Investment.]]* The old IV-4.

4. *[[Currency of Loans.]]* In the case of loans under 1(a) above, the borrowing country shall notify the Bank in which member countries it desires to incur expenditure to be met out of the loan, and the Bank shall make the required currencies available out of its subscribed capital, provided that the country whose local currency is to be supplied has agreed in each case. If local currency subscribed under II-4(a) is not available in whole or in part, the Bank shall make it available out of its holding of gold or other free resources, if it possesses an adequate amount of such resources and is satisfied that, without this position, the country in which the borrowing country desires to place the order, would have difficulty in maintaining the equilibrium of its international balance of payments. Otherwise it shall request the borrowing country to transfer its proposed expenditure to another member country. Furthermore, at the request of the countries in which portions of the loan are spent, the Bank will repurchase for gold or needed foreign exchange a part of the sum expended in the currencies of those countries made by the borrower from the proceeds of the loan.

5. *[[Exchange Restrictions.]]* The Bank shall not borrow funds under 1(b) above or guarantee loans under 1(c) above raised in the market of a member country, except with that member's approval and only if that member agrees that the proceeds of the loan may be expended in any member country without restriction. It follows that, in the case of loans to member countries out of such funds or under such guarantees, there will be no exchange obstacle to the expenditure of the proceeds in the market of any member country in accordance with the preference of the borrowing country.

6. *[[Payment Provisions.]]* Loans made directly by the Bank to the borrowing country under 1(a) or (b) above shall contain the following payment provisions:-

(a) The annual service of the loan shall be made up of three parts, namely:

(i) A standard rate of interest fixed by the Bank and the same to all borrowers but modifiable from time to time for new loans;

(ii) An annual commission at a flat rate fixed at 1 per cent in the first instance but alterable by the Bank from time to time at its discretion for new loans in the light of experience, the same to all borrowers, to cover the general expenses of the Bank, and as a provision against risk (but the particular expenses of investigation, etc., attaching to the individual loan, may be charged separately against the borrowing country and may be paid out of the proceeds of the loan).

(iii) An annual contribution to amortization either at a flat, or a progressive, rate sufficient to repay the capital within a determined number of years, the length of which shall be fixed with regard not only to the character and purpose of the loan, but also (especially in the case of reconstruction loans) to the conditions in the borrowing country which may delay the time within which the country can repay the loan — not normally exceeding 30 years but extensible to 50 years in particular cases.

(b) The loan and its annual service shall be fixed in whatever currency may be stipulated by the Bank when making the loan, and shall be paid, at the option of the borrowing country, in a convertible IMF currency or in gold, or at the discretion of the Bank, in any other currency acceptable to it at the prevailing rate of exchange of the currency in which the service has been fixed.

(c) In the event of the borrowing country suffering from an acute exchange stringency, so that it is unable to provide the service of the loan in the stipulated manner, it may appeal to the Bank for a relaxation of the conditions of payment. If the Bank is satisfied that some relaxation is in the interests of the borrowing country and of the operations of the Bank

453

and the other member countries as a whole it may take action under all, or any, of the following headings in respect of the whole, or part, of the annual service:-

(i) The Bank may in its judgment accept payments in respect of the service of the loan for periods not exceeding three years at a time in local currency. The Bank shall arrange with the borrowing country for the repurchase of such local currency over a period of years on appropriate terms that safeguard the Bank's holdings of such currency. The Bank may also require that the whole, or part of such currency, may be transferred to another member country in whose hands it shall be freely available to make payments or to purchase exports in the borrowing country (see (9) below).

(ii) The Bank may rearrange the installments of amortization so as to increase the amount due in later years or to prolong the life-time of the loan.

7. *[[Guarantees.]]* The Bank may guarantee loans to member countries through the usual investment channels, charging a flat rate commission of 1 per cent per annum (or other flat rate fixed by the Bank from time to time) payable to it direct by the borrowing country, provided that the Bank is satisfied as to the terms and conditions and purposes of the loan and that its proceeds will be freely transferable for purchases in any member country.

8. *[[Limit on Guarantees.]]* All guarantees given by the Bank under 1(b) or (c) above shall be secured only by its receipts from commissions and other profits and by the whole of its uncalled capital.

9. *[[Covering Deficiencies.]]* If there is any interruption in the service of a loan provided out of the proceeds of a loan guaranteed by the Bank under 1(b) above, or guaranteed by it under 1(c) above, the Bank shall first meet its obligations out of its net current or accumulated receipts from commissions or other profits. If this source is insufficient, it shall then call up from each member *pro rata* an appropriate amount of its uncalled capital, which shall be returned to the members meeting the guarantee if the arrears of the loan service are subsequently recovered. Subject to the approval of the Bank, a member part of whose subscription is being called up, to implement a guarantee given by the Bank, may purchase from the bank the local currency of the country in arrears in lieu of paying up a part of its uncalled subscription.

10. *[[Suspension of Membership.]]* A member country failing to meet its financial obligations to the Bank may be declared in default and it may be suspended from membership during the period of its default provided a majority of the member countries so decide. While under suspension, the

country shall be denied the privileges of membership, but shall be subject to the obligations of membership. At the end of one year the country shall be automatically dropped from membership in the Bank unless it has been restored to good standing by a majority of the member countries. Any member country that withdraws or is dropped from the International Stabilization Fund [IMF], shall relinquish its membership in the Bank unless three-fourths of the member votes favor its remaining as a member.

11. *[[Withdrawal or Expulsion from Bank.]]* If a member country elects to withdraw or is dropped from the Bank, it shall be repaid any part of its local currency subscribed under II-4 (a) above which remains in the hands of the Bank, and it shall not be liable to pay up any part of tis uncalled subscription except such amount as may be required to implement guarantees given during the period of its membership (after allowing for commissions received in respect of guarantees given during the same period). Any further divided, in respect of its interest arising from the part of its local currency originally subscribed and not returned to it as above, shall be paid in such amounts and at such times as the Bank, in its free discretion, may judge to be fair.

12. *[[Distribution of Net Profits.]]* The yearly net profits shall be carried to a reserve to meet subsequent losses under guarantees or otherwise, and shall not be distributed except under the authority of a 75 per cent vote of the Governing Body or on liquidation.

V. Miscellaneous Provisions

1. *[[Other Powers.]]* (IV-15 in U.S. draft.) With the approval of the representatives of the governments of the member countries involved, the Bank may engage in the following operations:

(a) It may issue, buy or sell, pledge, or discount any of its own securities and obligations, or securities and obligations taken from its portfolio, or securities which it has guaranteed.

(b) It may borrow from member governments, fiscal agencies, central banks, stabilization funds, private financial institutions in member countries, or from international financial agencies.

(c) It may buy or sell foreign exchange, after consultation with the International Stabilization Fund [IMF], where such transactions are necessary in connection with its operations.

2. *[[Agency Powers.]]* (IV-16 in U.S. draft.) The Bank may act as agent or correspondent for the governments of member countries, their central banks, stabilization funds and fiscal agencies, and for international

financial institutions.

The Bank may act as trustee, registrar, or agent in connection with loans guaranteed, participated in, made, or placed through the Bank.

3. *[[Agencies Dealing with Bank.]]* (IV-17 in U.S. draft.) Except as otherwise indicated, the Bank shall deal only with or through:

(a) The governments of member countries, their central banks, stabilization funds, and fiscal agencies.

(b) The International Stabilization Fund and any other international financial agencies owned predominantly by member governments.

The Bank may, nevertheless, with the approval of the member of the Board representing the government of the country concerned, deal with the public or institutions of member countries in the bank's own securities or securities which it has guaranteed.

4. *[[No Assistance to Suspended Members.]]* (IV-18 in U.S. draft.) If the Bank shall declare any country as suspended from membership, the member governments and their agencies agree not to extend financial assistance to that country without approval of the Bank until the country has been restored to membership.

5. *[[Political Neutrality.]]* The Bank and its officers shall scrupulously avoid interference in the political affairs of any member country. This provision shall not limit the right of an officer of the Bank to participate in the political life of his own country.

The Bank shall not be influenced in its decisions with the respect to applications for loans by the political character of the government of the country requesting a loan. Only economic considerations shall be relevant to the Bank's decisions.

The Bank, acting with the strictest imparity, shall pay particular regard, both in selecting the places of its borrowing and of its lending and when facilitating the choice of the place of expenditure under IV-4, to maintaining the equilibrium of the international balances of payments of member countries.

VI. Management

The UK Delegation have not yet considered these provisions in detail.

81

Report of the Special Committee on Furnishing Information of the Pre-Conference Agenda Committee, June 28, 1944

Page numbers in brackets are from the original document; page numbers in parentheses are from the Bretton Woods conference proceedings published in 1948, where this report was Document 129.

The Special Committee on Furnishing Information met on June 28 under the Chairmanship of Mr. [A.P.] Morozov of the USSR The other members of the Committee were Sir Theodore Gregory of India, Mr. [John] Deutsch of Canada, Mr. [Jacques] Polak of the Netherlands, and Mr. [August] Maffry of the United States as Reporter.

The Committee considered the advisability of a general provision which would require member countries to furnish information needed for the operations of the Fund as against a listing of required information. Several members of the Committee (p. 142) would have been willing to accept a general provision on the assumptions that the Fund would be reasonable in its demands for information and that it would make allowances for the position of countries the statistical services of which are less well developed than those of others.

It was decided to attempt a listing of information essential for the operations of the Fund with an escape clause which would permit a country to plead inability to supply certain information but not unavailability of information in its possession. Such a clause was considered necessary because some countries cannot now furnish some of the information which would be considered essential to the operations of the Fund.

It was recognized that a listing of required information would have the positive advantage of putting member countries on notice as to what was required and in this way of promoting the development of new statistical and other information.

The Committee did not reach full agreement on required items of information and has therefore submitted two lists as given below. It should be noted that items 3, 6(b), (c), and (d), and 10, which appeared in Alternative A submitted to the Committee for consideration were deleted and that the exact phrasing of items 1 and 2 on List I will depend upon the final definition of terms.

The Committee discussed at some length the question of requiring information on gold production. It was pointed out that gold production may be inferred, although with some margin of error, from data on gold holdings and gold movements, and could not be shown to be required under any specific provision of the draft agreement. The opposing view was that it would be very useful and indeed essential for the Fund to know current additions to gold supply as a result of new production independently of factors such as movements into and out of private hoards. The longer list given below includes gold production as an item of required information.

Section —. *Furnishing Information*

The Fund may require member countries to furnish it with such information as it deems necessary for its operations. In requesting information the Fund shall, however, take into consideration the ability of individual countries to furnish the data asked for. The minimum amount of information necessary for the due carrying out of the Fund's duties includes the following: [p. 2]

1. Official holdings of (a) gold at home and abroad, (b) gold convertible currencies distributed by currencies, and (c) (p. 143) other currencies distributed by currencies, as defined for purposes of the Fund.

2. Holdings by banking and financial agencies other than official agencies of (a) gold at home and abroad, (b) gold convertible currencies distributed by currencies, and (c) other currencies distributed by currencies, as defined for purposes of the Fund.

3. Production of gold.

4. Gold exports and imports distributed by countries of destination and origin.

5. Total exports and imports of merchandise, in terms of local currency values, distributed by countries of destination and origin.

6. International balance of payments, including (a) trade in goods and services, (b) gold movements, and (c) capital transactions.

7. International investment position, i.e., investments within the country owned abroad and investments abroad owned by residents of the country.

8. National income.

9. Price indexes. (Indexes of commodity prices in wholesale and retail markets and of export and import prices as available from official sources).

10. Buying and selling rates for foreign currencies.

11. Exchange controls. (Comprehensive statement of exchange controls in effect at the time of assuming membership in the Fund and changes thereafter as they occur.) [p. 3]

12. Where official exchange controls exist, arrearages for commercial or financial remittances in terms both of the time lag in remittances and total amounts in arrears by types of arrearage.

(List 2)

1. Gold holdings of the Central Bank and the Treasury and their changes.

2. Gold convertible exchange holdings of the Central Bank and the Treasury.

3. Movement of capital.

4. Foreign trade data.

5. Other items of the balance of payments.

6. Rates of exchange and their changes.

82

British Report on the International Monetary Fund

I. Par values • II. Definition of "gold convertible" • III. Obligations of a purchasing country • IV. Article VIII, Withdrawal • V. From Joint Statement to IMF statutes • Annex A: List of delegates etc. participating in discussions during the voyage (omitted) • Annex B: Amended version of Clause [Article] IV • Annex C: Amendments to Clause [Article] X-3 • Annex D: Instruments to be produced at Bretton Woods • Annex E: Suggestions regarding management

Aboard the Queen Mary *the British delegation discussed in detail the Joint Statement (reproduced in chapter 3). Because the United States would be providing the bulk of the funds that Britain and most other prospective members were hoping to borrow if the need arose, the Joint Statement was much closer to Harry Dexter White's plan for an International Stabilization Fund than to John Maynard Keynes's more expansive plan for an International Clearing Union. The Atlantic City and Bretton Woods conferences offered a final opportunity for the British to bend the design of the IMF a little more in their desired direction within the confines the Americans would allow. The introduction (chapter 1) discusses the degree to which they succeeded.*

21st June 1944

INTERNATIONAL MONETARY FUND
Report by the United Kingdom Delegation on the preliminary conversations with other delegates, and suggestions for the amendment of the agreed Statement of Principles.

I. [[Par values]]

1. During the voyage to America four meetings were held of the delegates on board at which the IMF was discussed. A full list of those

participating in these meetings is attached as Annex A,[333] and the UK Delegation desire to set on record their appreciation of the contributions made to the discussions by the other Delegations, which have greatly assisted the clarification of their own proposals. The suggested amendments to the Statement of Principles which are set out below are however made on the sole responsibility of the UK Delegation, though the great majority of them have been well received by the other participating delegations. The latter retain complete freedom to express their own views and to suggest other amendments if they desire, while for its part the UK delegation does not regard its suggestions as necessarily final or in any sense comprehensive.

2. Clause[334] IV of the Joint Statement ["Par Values of Member Currencies"], taken in conjunction with VIII-1 [["Procedure for Withdrawal"]], was intended to safeguard the ultimate authority of member countries over their own exchanges. The particular arrangements proposed is, however, open to two objections. The first is that the effect of the Statement taken as a whole is not easily made sufficiently clear to the general public and to members of Parliament who are not familiar with the proposals in all their details. Particular anxiety is felt in the United Kingdom, and probably also in other countries, as to whether the ultimate independence of the domestic policy of a country from outside dictation is fully safeguarded. A more forthright clause to this effect will, therefore, be extremely helpful, even if the substantial difference is not very great.

3. The second criticism is on the ground that the sanction provided when there is a difference of opinion between the Fund and the member, is not necessarily the most appropriate one. At present, if the Fund and the member ultimately disagree on exchange policy, the member can leave the Fund without notice, and, in effect, without penalty. Both from the point of view of the Fund and of the member, this may prove in practice not to be the most convenient course. For one thing, it releases the member from a number of other engagements. It is neither desirable nor necessary that the relationship between the member and the Fund should be severed so completely. In the second place, the dispute might prove to be of a temporary character; and it might be very much easier to find a subsequent compromise and an accommodation between the opposing

---

[333] Omitted; see page before first page of chapter 20 for a list of these and other persons who traveled on the *Queen Mary*.

[334] The British often call the articles of the Joint Statement "clauses."

views if the member had not actually left the Fund, but had remained in contact with it. For these reasons, it is suggested that the appropriate sanction in the case of a country taking its own course in the matter of its exchanges, is that it should be suspended from the facilities of the Fund. This might prove a particularly appropriate remedy in the case of just those countries where a dispute between the member and the Fund is perhaps the most likely. The right retort of the Fund, if the member decides to resume freedom of action in the matter of its exchanges, is that it should be suspended from the benefits of the Fund, whilst still remaining subject to other obligations, as, for example, the obligation of convertibility, and in general the obligations under IX ["Obligations of Member Countries"].

4. A revised version of IV ["Par Values of Member Currencies"] is annexed (Annex B) as a means of carrying out the above purposes. It will be seen that IV-1 [["Establishing Par Values"]] and 3 [["Fund's Approval of Changes in Par Values"]] are substantially unchanged; IV-2 [["Changes in Par Values"]] has lost its first and last sentences and its second sentence has been added to IV-3. [IV-]3 and 4 have been reworded here and there so that "concurrence" is substituted for "approval" etc. Also an additional Clause has been introduced. In the new [IV-]3 the opportunity has been taken to clear up the ambiguity (as it has appeared to some) whether changes [of exchange rates] in excess of 20 per cent will ever be permissible.

II. [[Definition of "gold convertible"]]

5. The phrase "gold convertible" occurs in three sections, namely, II-3 [["Gold Subscriptions"]], III-7(b) and III-7(c) [["Fund's Acquisition of Gold"]], but all our researches into the technical legal position and the opinions of the experts we have consulted support the view that no such currency at present exists. If this is correct, clearly changes in the wording of these sections are necessary, and in fact the consequences seen likely to reach further than a simple verbal substitution. It is proposed that the concept of currencies convertible into gold should be replaced by the concept of currencies which are convertible in terms of IX-3 [["Current Transactions"]]. Textually this involves the substitution of "convertible" for "gold convertible," and adding an interpretation clause explaining that "convertible exchange" means the currency of any country which has accepted the convertibility obligation under IX-3. When the Fund is established, members will be asked to declare whether or not they desire to avail themselves of the transitional arrangement for postponing the

obligation of convertibility. The currencies of those which accept it from the outset, will constitute "convertible exchange." For the purpose of the initial obligatory gold subscription and under Clause III-7 [["Fund's Acquisition of Gold"]], holdings of foreign currency would gradually become "convertible exchange" *pari passu* with members ceasing to take advantage of the transitional arrangements.

6. The concept of "holdings of convertible exchange" also raises certain questions of definition, which are indicated in the following proposals:-

a. "Holdings" should mean "official holdings," i.e. it should include the holdings of a Central Bank, a Treasury, or other Government institution, and also the holdings of such other Banks, which, in the particular circumstances of the case, it is agreed between the Fund and the member should properly come within the "official" category. It is suggested that this interpretation should not be operated so as to include, for example, the holdings of authorized dealers in exchanges when the latter do not exceed normal working balances; but should include the holdings of Banks other than Central Banks, when in practice some part of a country's reserves of foreign currency in excess of working balances are normally held in the name of such Banks.

b. The official holdings thus defined should presumably relate to "net official holdings," i.e. convertible currency and gold held against it should not both count, first of all, in respect of the country owning the convertible currency, and secondly in respect of the gold held against it by the country having this convertible liability. Accordingly, a convertible exchange, reckoned as part of the official holdings of one country, shall be deductible in reckoning the net official holdings of the country whose exchange is involved.

7. Textually these involve references in the proposed interpretation clause defining "net," "official" and "convertible." It is suggested, further, that the term "net official holdings of gold and convertible exchange," having been thus defined, should be for convenience, expressed in the text as "monetary reserves."

8. The existing draft of III-7(b) and (c) [["Fund's Acquisition of Gold"]] is unsatisfactory for the following reason. If a member is due to pay gold to the Fund under 7(b) (and the same applies to payments under 7(c) if the member has used the Fund during the year), it can in fact evade any such obligation merely by increasing its turnover with the Fund, as is shown in the following example:

A member has reserves x, x being in excess of its quota. In the year it has an adverse balance y, and draws on the Fund to that extent. The result is that at the end of the year it has to release $y/2$ of its reserves to the Fund, so that its reserves fall to $x - y/2$. This is the intention of the draft. But in order to defeat this intention all the member has to do is draw $2y$ from the Fund in the course of the year, with the result that its reserves rise to $x + y$, of which it has to surrender y to the Fund, thus ending up just as if the clause had not existed.

9. The desired result could, however, be attained and the two clauses expressed more clearly in a single formula by the following redraft:-

"If, at the end of the Fund's financial year, a member's monetary reserves exceed its quota, and the Fund's holdings of its currency have increased, the Fund may require that it shall use a part of these reserves to repurchase its currency up to the point when its reserves have fallen by an amount not less than the amount by which, after this adjustment, the Fund's holdings of its currency have increased. Furthermore, if, after this adjustment (if called for) has been made, a member's monetary reserves have increased during the year, the Fund may require it, whether or not the Fund's holdings of its currency have increased during the year, to use half of this increase for a further repurchase of its currency from the Fund; provided, always, that these adjustments do not bring its reserves below its quota and the second adjustment does not bring the Fund's holdings of its currency below 75 percent of its quota."

10. Under the above, a member can pay either in gold or in convertible exchange at its option, and need not pay solely in gold. This might have the effect of choking the Fund with exchanges it did not require, but it seems inevitable if "convertible exchange" is brought into the picture. If, on the other hand, the substance of these sections is limited to gold holdings two anomalies would result:-

(i) There would be an inevitable swing into holding reserves in convertible currencies at the main international centers, instead of in gold.

(ii) A financial center would be precluded from accumulating adequate gold reserves against an increase in its convertible liabilities.

11. We believe, therefore, that the superposition of III-7(b) and (c) [["Fund's Acquisition of Gold"]] on III-6 [["Purchase of Another Member's Currency with Gold"]] and V-1 [["Use of Fund to Finance Capital Outflows"]]) is doubtfully advantageous, and that it might be better to depend on III-6 and V-1 alone for gradually increasing the Fund's holdings of gold and for protection from abuse in the use of the Fund's resources. If, however, anything further is required, something like the following would be unobjectionable:-

"If, at the end of any year, a member's monetary reserves after deducting its holdings of convertible exchange exceed its quota, and if the

464

Fund's holdings of its currency exceed 75 percent of its quota, the Fund may require it to use its holdings of gold to reduce the Fund's holdings of its currency by half of the excess of such holdings over 75 percent of its quota."

12. If [III-]7(b) is retained, a temporary provision is required to deal with the sudden discontinuity which will arise, for example, when existing balances of Sterling, which had not previously been reckoned as convertible exchange, suddenly become such, at the date when the UK accepts the obligation of convertibility. There should, therefore, be a temporary clause to the effect that when exchange becomes convertible for the first time, the amount of such exchange held at the beginning of the year does not reckon as an increase in a member's holdings of convertible exchange if, during the year, the exchange in question has become convertible for the first time. Otherwise, the Fund might become choked with sterling and the UK might find itself under the necessity to postpone action. On the other hand, it may help to advance the date at which the acceptance of the obligation of convertibility becomes possible, if the new liabilities thus arising are immediately taken into account in reckoning "monetary reserves"; so that no corresponding temporary provision is proposed to cover this.

III. [[Obligations of a purchasing country]]

13. A doubt has been raised whether the drafting of III-5 [["Obligations of a Purchasing Country"]] could not be read in a manner inconsistent with III-2(a) [["Purchase of Another Member's Currency"]] or, at any rate, more widely than the latter provision, since III-2(a) explicitly states that it relates to payments presently needed for purposes which are consistent with the purposes of the Fund. III-5 is not expressly so limited so far as the first sentence is concerned. It is believed that the second sentence of III-5 was intended to bring the ambit of the two provisions within the same field. But it does so by reference and not very clearly. It is thought that it will be better therefore to bring III-5 into more direct connection with IX-3 [["Current Transactions"]].

14. This can be effected by a change which will also bring about a more logical drafting. III-5 does not, like the rest of Clauses of III, relate to the title of III, namely "Transactions with the Fund." It is really a part of [Article] IX, namely "The Obligations of Member Countries." This opportunity might also be taken to make small change in III-2(a), by substituting "the provisions of the Fund" for "the purposes of the Fund." In this context, "purposes" is not intended to refer back to the

"Purposes" of [Article] I, but relates rather to the actual provisions of the Fund.

15. III-5 should be deleted, and its substance incorporated in IX as follows in place of the existing IX-3 [["Current Transactions"]]:-

"3. To buy balances held with it by another member with that member's currency or with gold, if that member represents either that the balances in question have been currently acquired or that their conversion is needed for making current payments which are consistent with the provisions of the Fund. This obligation shall not relate to transactions involving:

(a) Capital transfers.

(b) Holdings of currency which have accumulated as a result of transaction of a current account nature effected before the removal by the member country of restrictions on multilateral clearing maintained or imposed under X-2 [["Transition Period"]] below:

(c) The provision of a currency which has been declared scarce under VI ["Apportionment of Scarce Currencies"] above;
nor shall it apply to a member who has ceased to be entitled under III-2 [["Purchase of Another Member's Currency"]] or VIII ["Withdrawal from the Fund"] above to buy other members' currencies from the Fund in exchange for its own currency.

4. Not to impose restrictions save otherwise provided on payments for current international transactions with other member countries, or to engage in any discriminatory currency arrangements or multiple currency practices without the approval of the Fund."

IV. [[Article VIII, Withdrawal]]

16. It is felt that VIII ["Withdrawal from the Fund"] could be stiffened with advantage to provide sanctions against the member who persistently refuses to abandon restrictions inconsistent with IX-3 [["Current Transactions"]] though able in the Fund's opinion to do so. The following redraft is suggested for consideration:

VIII. Withdrawal

1. If the Fund finds that a member persists, after having received a special notice from the Fund, in acting in a manner inconsistent with the purposes and policies of the Fund, the Fund may, at its option, either:

(a) give notice that the member is suspended from making

466

further use of the Fund's resources without the approval of the Fund, or

(b) require that member to withdraw from the Fund.

2. A member country may withdraw from the Fund by giving notice in writing.

3. On the withdrawal of a member under (1) or (2) above, the reciprocal obligations of the Fund and the member are to be liquidated within a reasonable time.

4. On the withdrawal of a member under (1) or (2) above, the Fund may not dispose of the member's currency except in accordance with arrangements made under (3) above. After the withdrawal of a member under (1) or (2) above, its use of the resources of the Fund is subject to the approval of the Fund.

V. [[Length of transition period]]

17. Under Clause X ["Transitional Arrangements"] members do not undertake to accept the obligation of convertibility under X-3 [["Restrictions on Exchange"]] and 4 [["Adjustments during Transition Period"]] at any specified date. But it has seemed to some critics that the reference to "three years from the coming into force of the Fund" in X-3 implies an expectation that the transitional period may very well come to an end within three years. In the case of the UK, it is considered very unlikely that the full assumption of the obligation of convertibility can be assumed as soon as that. It is feared, therefore, that the present phrasing may, on the one hand, excite expectations which will be disappointed, and on the other hand, alarms which are unnecessary.

18. It is suggested therefore that X-3 might be redrafted as in Annex C. The opportunity of the redraft has been taken to use words which will be convenient in connection with the definition of "convertible currency" in the interpretation clause.

19. It is also suggested that the uncertainty of duration of the transitional period should be emphasized by the introduction of a few worlds.

VI. [[From Joint Statement to IMF statutes]]

20. The following additional paragraphs are self-explanatory but would make it possible to convert the Joint Statement in its ultimate form into "The Statutes of the IMF," constituting the Fund Annex to the

Convention which we contemplate in the paper attached as Annex D. Annex E contains our provisional views regarding Clause VII [["Management of the Fund"]], but we have not attempted to determine how much needs to go into the proposed "Statutes."

[New Article] XI. (1) The Fund shall have at all times the right to tender informal advice to any member on any matter arising under these Statutes.

(2) All questions which arise involving doubts or differences relating to the interpretation of the provisions of these Statutes shall be submitted to the Directorate of the Fund for their opinion. If the question is one which involves a dispute affecting particularly one (or more) member(s) and that (or those) member(s) are not represented on the Directorate by a Director appointed by it (or them) then that (or those) member(s) may appoint a representative to take part in the discussions of this question in the Directorate on the same footing as the Directors.

(3) In any case where the Directorate has given an opinion under paragraph (2) above, a member may require that the question be submitted to the Council and the opinion of the Council is final. Pending the result of the reference to the Council, the Fund may (so as is necessary) act on the basis of the opinion of the Directorate.

XII. The Council shall have power to make such arrangements or agreements as may be necessary or desirable for cooperation between the Fund on the one hand and other International Economic Organizations and World Organizations on the other hand. These arrangements or agreements must be approved by a 3/5 majority vote.

XIII. The Council shall have power to repeal, amend or add to the provisions of these Statutes by decision taken by a 3/5 majority except that

(a) a decision concurred in by all Councilors shall be required for _____

(b) the Council shall have now [no?] power by any repeal, amendment or addition to _____

These three clauses have not been discussed with the Allied delegations travelling with us.

List of Annexes to I.M.C. (44) F.11

ANNEX
A. List of Delegates, etc. Participating in Discussions during the Voyage.
B. Amended Version of Clause IV.
   Text as in Annex to I.M.C. (44) F.1.
C. Amendments to Clause X (3).
   Text as in Annex to I.M.C. (44) F.4.
D. Instruments to be Produced at Bretton Woods
   Text is Mr. Beckett's paper I.M.C. (44) F.7 as amended.
E. Suggestions Regarding Management.
   Text is I.M.C. (44) F.8 as amended in discussion.

Annex A: List of Delegates, etc. Participating in Discussions during the Voyage

[Omitted; see page before first page of chapter 20 for a list of these and other persons who traveled on the *Queen Mary*.]

Annex B

Revised Version of Clause [Article] IV (Statement of Principles, International Monetary Fund)

IV. Par Values of Member Currencies

1. The Government of the UK, and the Government of the United States will communicate to the Monetary Fund at its inauguration, the initial par value of their respective currencies, expressed in terms of Gold. Within one month (or in the case of occupied countries, within one month of liberation) the other member countries wishing to adhere to the Convention will make corresponding communications. Notwithstanding this rule, member countries that have been occupied by the enemy need not make a definitive communication of the initial par value in the above sense until the reconstruction of their monetary system has been completed and the initial communication may be limited to giving a provisional par value. If the Directorate of the Fund finds a communicated initial or provisional par value reasonable, such par value shall come into force immediately for the purpose of the Fund. If, however, the Directorate should deem the communicated par value to be open to criticism, the question shall be the subject of further consideration with the member country in question, and the facilities of the Fund shall not be available to the member until agreement has been reached. All transactions between the Fund and members shall be at par subject to a fixed charge payable by the member making application to the Fund; and all transactions in member currencies shall be at rates within an agreed percentage of parity.

2. Subsequent changes in the par value of a member's currency shall not be made except at its own proposal. Member countries agree not to propose such a change unless they consider it appropriate to correct a fundamental disequilibrium. The Fund shall concur in a proposed change in the par value of a member's currency if it is shown to be essential to correct a fundamental disequilibrium. In particular, the Fund shall not dissent from a proposed change necessary to restore equilibrium because of domestic social or political policies of the country proposing the change. In considering a proposed change the Fund shall take into consideration the extreme uncertainties prevailing at the time the parties of currencies of member countries were initially agreed upon.

3. The Fund shall concur in a change proposed by a member country provided it does not exceed 10 percent, inclusive of any previous change

since the establishment of the Fund. In the case of a proposal for a further change not covered by the above and not exceeding 10 percent, the Fund shall give or withhold its concurrence within two days of receiving the application, if the applicant so requests. For a change larger than 20 percent the Fund will expect reasonable notice.

4. Nothing in the above provisions shall affect the right of members to modify their exchange rates as they may consider necessary or advisable. But a modification of rates shall not be made except after consultation with the Fund, and in the event of action being taken by a member without the Fund having expressed concurrence under the terms of the preceding Clauses, the Fund may, if it considers the action unjustified having regard to the proper working of the Fund, suspend the facilities of the Fund under III-2 [["Purchases of Another Member's Currency"]]; whist keeping alive the obligation of the member so long as it remains a member of the Fund, under all Clauses except IV ["Par Value of Member Currencies"].

5. An agreed uniform change may be made in the gold value of member currencies, provided every member county having 10 percent or more of the aggregate quotas approves.

19th June, 1944

Annex C

Amendments to Clause [Article] X

X. Transitional Arrangements

1. Renumber 4 [["Adjustments during Transition Period"]] so that it becomes 3 [["Restrictions on Exchange"]] and after "change and adjustment," add the words, "over a term of uncertain duration."

2. For 3 substitute the following:-

"4. After the establishment of the Fund, but before it commences operations, members shall notify the Fund whether or not they intend to avail themselves of the optional transitional arrangements under (1) [["Entry into Force"]] or (2) [["Transition Periods"]] above; and whether they are prepared to accept the obligations of IX-3 and 4. At any subsequent date a member may notify its acceptance of these obligations. Not later than three years from the coming into force of the Fund, and in each year thereafter, the Fund shall report on the restrictions still in force under (2) above, five years after the coming into force of the Fund, and each year thereafter, any member still retaining any restrictions inconsistent with IX-3 and 4 shall consult the Fund as to their further retention."

Annex D

International Monetary Fund
The Instruments to be Produced by the Conference

I. These suggestions are made on the assumption

(1) that it is desired that the Bretton Woods Conference should produce definite proposals for submission to Governments;

(2) that, while it is desired that the proposals should be as definitive as possible, it is also necessary that they should leave the Conference in such a form that, if any Government has important amendments to make before it can accept them finally, it should be possible for these amendments to be discussed and, if approved, incorporated subsequently;

(3) that ultimately before the scheme for the Fund can come finally into force in the form of international obligations between the Governments it will have to be, at any rate so far as some countries are concerned, ratified in accordance with their constitutional procedures.

II. It is suggested that the results of the Bretton Woods Conference should be in the form of a "Final Act." A Final Act is technically a formal signed record of what took place at a Conference. A delegate in signing it only commits himself technically to approving it as a correct record. It is a most convenient form of instrument because all sorts of different things can be put into it under various Resolutions etc., which are recorded. The Final Act would in the ordinary way record that a Conference had been held between certain dates, the delegations who attended it and describe, so far as is desired, what happened including, as the most important part, a record of Resolutions adopted.

III. One, and the most important Resolution, might be a Resolution adopting and submitting to Governments a Draft Convention with an Annex thereto embodying all of the most important part of the work on the Fund.

IV. A second paragraph of this Resolution might charge (? the United States Government as a Headquarter Government) with the duty of collecting the replies of Governments on the Draft Convention and Annex and of deciding in the light of these replies and after any necessary consultation whether the Draft Convention can be opened for signature or whether a further Conference will be necessary in order to decide upon amendments to the drafts which have been proposed.

V. Another Resolution might submit in the form of an Annex attached to it such preparatory work as has been done on the Bank.

VI. It is suggested that the Draft Convention relating to the Fund should be extremely short, consisting of short Articles on the following points:-

(a) an Article setting out that the high contracting parties accept the Annex to the Convention and undertake to abide by its provisions;

(b) that the Convention shall be ratified, ratifications to be deposited at -----

(c) that as soon as X ratifications and accessions have been deposited (including those of the USA and UK) or on the 1st August, 1945, whichever is the latter, the Convention will come into force. The Fund will thereupon come into operation by stages in the manner provided in 1A of the Annex;*

(d) that the provisions of the Annex, or certain specified provisions thereof might be altered or added to subsequently with the consent of Y proportion of the votes which can be cast on the Council.

VII. The Annex to the Convention would be the joint statement about the Fund set out in a proper form suitable as a definition of the obligations of the Member Governments, etc.

VIII. If it were desired that the Bretton Woods Conference should set up some machinery, in the form of a provisional Secretariat or Bureau, which should consider all the replies of Governments on the Draft Convention and Annex and advise the United States Government as to future action *vide* paragraph IV above, this could be done by a short protocol or agreement which might be signed at the Bretton Woods Conference or even perhaps by a separate Resolution to this effect included in the Final Act.

*Note: A further paper will be submitted showing *inter alia* the relation of the date on which the Fund starts business to the date of the inauguration of the Fund, as provided above.[335]

22nd June, 1944

---

[335] We are aware of no relevant British paper other than Annex E, on the next page.

Annex E

International Monetary Fund
Management and Inauguration

I. Management[336]

1. On 12 April we made the following proposals to the United States:

(a) The Fund shall be governed by a Board of Directors, perhaps of 5 appointed by the countries with the 5 largest quotas, and 4 appointed from all other countries by the Governing Council of members. These directors should be men of standing and each should have power to appoint an alternate from his own country.

(b) The directorate should chose a General Manager — being a man of standing an experience in the business of the Fund. The General Manager should submit for the approval of the Directorate of his Chief Assistants or Heads of Departments, chosen for their technical knowledge.

We urged the importance of getting the general principles of this system of management settled before the general Conference met.

2. Dr. White thought it might be diplomatically wiser to leave details to the General Conference. But he agreed that there should be (i) a general body of all members. We call this the Governing Council but the United States call it a Board; (ii) a governing body which we call Board but United States Executive Committee; and (iii) a management. (ii) would be chosen by (i).

He agreed that (ii) should have at least 9 members, but in a later communication it has been suggested that 12 might be more acceptable.

3. It is still our view that the general principles of governing management should be settled at the Drafting Committee — otherwise there is risk of undue time at the [Bretton Woods] Conference being devoted to the question, which also includes the subject of voting rights.

4. The working of the Monetary Fund has been designed to be largely automatic, with defined obligations both on the Fund and the Members, thereby avoiding the need for the frequent exercise of discretion or discrimination by the governing body. (In this respect it differs essentially from the Reconstruction Bank, where a large element of discretion and

---

[336] The document has no part II. It is dated June 20, 1944 in some copies.

judgment must, from the nature of the work, rest with the governing body.)

But the Fund also has important questions of discretion for the governing body, some of which arise at the beginning, and others occasionally.

At the beginning arises the agreement on the par value of members' currencies (IV-1). The whole handling of adjustments in exchange rates is clearly a matter of high policy calling for real judgment on the part of the governing body, especially having regard to IV-3 [["Latitude for Change in Par Value"]].

At later stages as occasion arises the governing body has to exercise its discretion under III-2 [["Purchases of Another Member's Currency"]] to waive the conditions of [III-]2. Also it presumably has to exercise discretion on its option under III-4 [["Scarce Currencies"]] and on the purchase of gold under III-7 [["Fund's Acquisition of Gold"]]. It has to exercise judgment on V-1 [["Use of Fund to Finance Capital Outflows"]]to ensure that the resources of the Fund are not being used to meet an outflow of capital, and at the same time to permit capital transactions of a reasonable amount for trade etc.

It has a difficult responsibility on VI on the apportionment of scarce currencies and still more difficult responsibilities in its relationship with member countries under X, Transitional Arrangements.

In addition, it has the general responsibility for interpretation of the instrument governing the Fund.

5. But while these exercises of discretion involve large issues of judgment, it does not appear that the regular work of the Fund will call for frequent decisions on matters of policy, certainly not to the extent of requiring a very high-powered Directorate permanently in residence. Nor will it be necessary to contemplate a large and high-powered management. Experience in other international institutions, particularly the BIS [Bank for International Settlements], has shown that if there are too many high-powered people for the regular business of the institution intrigues and "national" questions tend to arise within the organization itself. Further, if the management is larger than the work calls for, then questions of the distribution of the appointments among the various Nations introduce political factors which we want to keep out of the working of the Fund. So far as is practicable, we want to aim at a governing structure doing a technical job and developing a sense of corporate responsibility to all members, and not the need to guard the interests of particular countries.

6. After reviewing a number of factors the following set-up is

suggested:

(a) A *Governing Council,* consisting of Councilors appointed by all the Member Countries, each Member appointing one Councilor.

(b) A *Directorate,* consisting say of 12 Directors, of whom, say, 6 shall be appointed by the Members having the 6 largest quotas, i.e. USA, UK, Russia, China, France, India (in accordance with USA proposals for Quotas).

The remaining 6 seats being filled by Directors appointed by Members chosen for this purpose by all the Councilors excluding those representing the members with the 6 largest quotas. This right of appointment by the members chosen for the purpose shall be for two years; at the end of this period any of the members may be chosen again or other members may be chosen.

(c) The *Directorate* shall appoint a *Chairman* from among the Directors (? or co-opt as Chairman a suitable person who is not a Director).

(d) The Directorate shall appoint a *General Manager,* being a person of knowledge and experience of the business.

(e) The *General Manager* shall appoint his Chief Assistants with the approval of the Directorate. The *General Manager* and his Chief Assistants shall be appointed for a period of 5 years and shall be eligible for reappointment. (To be clarified)

7. Voting.

(a) On the *General Council* the number of votes which each Councilor can cast shall be related to the quota of the member appointing the Councilor;

Where under the governing instrument a special majority (e.g. 4/5th etc.) of the total voting power.

A quorum for the *Council* shall consist of not less than 2/3rd of this total vital power of the Councilors.

(b) On the *Directorate,* the Director appointed by the United States shall cast 3 votes, the Director appointed by the United Kingdom shall cast 2 votes, and all other Directors shall cast 1 vote each. (A Chairman, if co-opted, shall only have a casting [tie-breaking] vote).

A quorum for the Directorate shall consist of not less than ½ of the total voting power and one-half of the number of Directors.

8. Functions.

(a) *Council.* In addition to the appointment of the Directorate, the Council shall have the following functions:-

(i) Power to invite non-signatory countries to become members;

(ii) the approval of a revision of quotas (II-2 [["Revisions to Quota"]]);

477

(iii) the approval of an agreed uniform change in the gold value of the currencies of members (IV-5 [["Uniform Changes in Par Values"]]);

(iv) all action relating to the apportionment of scarce currencies (VI);

(v) the suspension of a member from the facilities of the Fund (III-2(d) [["Purchases of Another Member's Currency"]]);

(vi) the requirement to a member to withdraw from the Fund (VII-1 [["Board and Executive Committee"]]) as revised);

(vii) ? certain decisions on the interpretation of the governing instrument;

(viii) receiving the Statement of Accounts and the Report of the Directorate at the Annual Meeting;

(ix) to review the working of the Fund in the light of its Purposes and Policies (I);

(x) alteration of Statutes;

(xi) cooperation with other bodies.

(b) *Directorate*

(i) The conduct of all the business of the Fund, other than that belonging, as above to the Council, and other than that delegated by the Directorate to the Chairman, Deputy Chairman, or the General Manager as provided below. (add reference to frequency of meetings)

(c) *the Chairman*

(i) the Chairman shall reside at the Headquarters of the Fund;

(ii) the Directorate may delegate to the Chairman or Deputy Chairman the power of performing on their behalf all their functions except

a. waiver of any of the conditions in III-2 [["Purchases of Another Member's Currency"]];

b. the exercise of the options of the Fund in III-4 [["Scarce Currency"]];

c. all decisions on the par value of member currencies in IV 1-4;

cc. an action relating to the appointment of scarce currencies;

d. decision on the use of the resources of the Fund by a member who has withdrawn (VIII-4 as revised);

e. decisions on X-3 as revised [old X-4, ["Adjustments during Transition Period"]] and X-4 as revised [old X-3, ["Restrictions on Exchange"]];

f. a formal interpretation of the governing instrument;

(iii) the Chairman shall have the right to attend Council meetings and participate therein, and may if be desired be its Chairman.

(d) General Manager

The General Manager shall be the Executive head of the organization and shall conduct the routine business of the Fund's work, and be responsible to the Directorate for internal organization and all questions of establishment, including the appointment and dismissal of subordinate staff. (To be clarified)

83

Proposal for a
Bank for Reconstruction and Development
(Bretton Woods Document 169)

*I. Purposes of the Bank • II. Membership in and Capital of the
Bank • III. General Provisions Relating to Loans • IV. Operations •
V. Management • VI. Withdrawal and Suspension of Membership
and Liquidation • VII. Additional Undertakings on the part of
Member Countries • [VIII. No Text] • IX. Amendments •
X. Miscellaneous Provisions • XI. Final Provisions*

*When the British delegation arrived at the Atlantic City conference with its draft of
proposals for the Bank for Reconstruction and Development, it found that it was not
far apart from the ideas of the U.S. delegation. The conference accordingly drafted a
proposal on the Bank for the Bretton Woods conference. Though less polished than the
draft Articles of Agreement of the IMF, the proposal was useful enough to be the basis
for Articles of Agreement of the International Bank for Reconstruction and
Development signed at Bretton Woods.*

*As with the IMF articles, the Atlantic City conference did not print a final version
of its proposal for the Bank, but the initial version at Bretton Woods was
approximately the final version at Atlantic City.*

*Page numbers in parentheses refer to the document as circulated at Bretton Woods
in 1944. In the Bretton Woods text, marginal notes indicate whether various
provisions are taken from the American proposal (reproduced in chapter 3), the British
proposal (reproduced in chapter 81), or are new. We have inserted the notes into the
text in parentheses at the end of the appropriate sections.*

The Agenda Committee of Commission II propose that the attached
draft should be taken as the initial basis for discussion and amendment. It
is not to be regarded as the proposal of any Delegation, nor is any
Delegation committed to it.

Delegations are invited to send to the Secretariat (Mr. Upgren, Room
147) by 7 o'clock on Saturday, 8th July, any amendments, suggestions or
proposals which they may have ready by that time for incorporation in

the first edition of a text incorporating alternatives to be circulated for discussion. This will not preclude any Delegation from submitting further proposals at a later time. Papers received by the time named above will be assembled by the Secretariat and considered by a meeting of the Agenda Committee at 5 p.m. on Sunday, 9th July.

It will be much appreciated if, where this can be done without inconvenience, Delegations will supply the Secretariat with 25 copies of any papers they send in.

The Agenda Committee suggests, having regard to the shortness of time available, that Delegations need not be at the trouble of attempting to draft their proposals in legal form. It will be sufficient if the substantial intention of any addition or amendment which they wish to have discussed is communicated to the Agenda Committee at this stage. There will be a later opportunity of casting them into proper form. (p. 1)

AGREEMENT TO ESTABLISH A BANK FOR RECONSTRUCTION AND DEVELOPMENT

Article I. *Purposes of the Bank*

The bank shall be guided in all its decisions by the following purposes: (IMF I)

1. *To* assist in the reconstruction and development of member countries by facilitating provision of long-term investment capital for productive purposes through private financial agencies, *by means* of guaranteeing and participating in the loans made by private investors; (US I slightly revised (UK I, 1-5))

2. *To* supplement private financial agencies by providing capital for productive purposes out of its own resources, on conditions that amply safeguard its fund, when private capital is not available on reasonable terms;

3. *To* promote the long-range balanced growth of international trade by encouraging international investment for the development of the productive resources of member countries;

4. *To* coordinate loans made or guaranteed by it with revised) international loans through other channels so that the more useful and urgent projects will be dealt with first; (UK III, 8 (moved and revised))

5. *To* conduct its operations with due regard to the effect of international investment on business conditions in member countries and, in the immediate post-war years, to assist in bringing about a smooth

transition from a wartime to a peacetime economy.

NOTE: Symbols used in marginal notes [here, inserted by the editors at the end of a section in parentheses].

U.S. — Printed plan of November 24, 1943.

UK — Mimeographed draft outline of June 25, 1944.

I.M.F. — Latest mimeographed version of Agreement for Fund using Alternative A in all cases. (p. 2)

Article II. *Membership in and Capital of the Bank*

Section 1. *Countries Eligible for Membership.*

The members of the Bank shall be those members of the International Monetary Fund which accept membership in the Bank. (IMF III, 1)

Section 2. *Authorized Capital.*

The authorized capital stock of the Bank shall be $10,000,000,000, in terms of United States dollars of the weight and fineness in effect on ----- -------------. The capital stock shall be divided into 100,000 shares having a par value of $100,000 each, which shall be available for subscription only by members. (US II, 1 slightly revised)

The capital stock may be increased when the Bank deems it advisable by four-fifths of the aggregate votes. (New)

Section 3. *Subscription for Stock.*

Each member shall subscribe for shares of stock. The minimum numbers of shares to be subscribed by countries represented at the United Nations Monetary and Financial Conference shall be those set forth in Schedule A. (Schedule A to be added later.) The minimum number of shares for other countries which become members of the Bank shall be determined by the Bank

Any member may subscribe for additional shares of stock in accordance with rules to be established by the Bank, except that a part of the authorized capital shall be reserved by the Bank for minimum subscriptions of countries not represented at the United Nations Monetary and Financial Conference. (U.S. III, 3 revised)

Section 4. *Availability of Subscribed Capital.*

The subscription of each member country shall be divided into two parts as follows:

(a) Twenty percent shall be callable by the Bank as needed for any of its operations.

(b) The remaining 80 percent shall be callable by the Bank only when required to implement obligations of the Bank created under IV (1) (b) and (c) below.

Calls on unpaid subscriptions shall be uniform on all shares. (Cf. UK II, 4) (p. 3)

Section 5. *Payment of Subscription.*

(a) Payments under Section 5 (a) shall be partly in gold and partly in local currency. The proportions to be paid in gold and local currency shall be graduated according to an agreed upon schedule which shall take into account the adequacy of the gold and free foreign exchange holdings of each member country. The portion to be paid in gold shall not in any event exceed 20 percent of the total payment. (UK II, 4)

(Schedule to be inserted)

(b) Payments under Section 5 (b) shall at the option of the member be made either in gold or in the currency required to implement the obligations with respect to which a call is made. (Omits payment in currency convertible under IMF)

(c) The initial payment on each share issued shall be such as to equal the total amount per share already called on outstanding shares adjusted for the amount by which the issue price of the share differs from par value. (New)

(NOTE: UK Section 5 eliminated on ground it is covered by IV, 4 and 5 and VII, 2, below).

Section 6. *Issue Price of Shares.*

Shares of stock included in the initial subscription of a member represented at the United Nations Monetary and Financial Conference shall be issued at par if the subscription is received not later than one year after the date set for operations of the Bank to begin. Other shares shall be issued at par or such other price as may be fixed by three-fourths vote of the Bank. (New)

Section 7. *Limitation on Liability.*

Liability on shares shall be limited to the unpaid portion of the issue price of the shares. (U.S. II, 2)

Section 8. *Disposal of Shares Limited.*

Shares shall not be pledged or encumbered in any manner whatever and they shall be transferable only to the Bank. (U.S. II, 2)

Section 9. *Return of Subscriptions.*

When the liquid resources of the Bank are substantially in excess of prospective needs, the Bank may return, subject to call, uniform amounts on all shares of stock outstanding. (U.S. II, 6) (p. 4)

Article III. *General Provisions Relating to Loans* (Title derived from UK)

Section 1. *Use of Resources Restricted.*

The resources and the facilities of the Bank shall be used exclusively for the benefit of members. (US II, 9)

Section 2. *Agencies Dealing with the Bank.*

Except as otherwise indicated in this Agreement, the Bank shall conduct its business only with or through the governments of the members, their central banks, stabilization funds and other similar fiscal agencies, the International Monetary Fund, and other international agencies participated in primarily by governments of members. (U.S. IV, 17)

Section 3. *Limitation on Loans and Guarantees.*

The total amount of guarantees, participations in loans, and loans and other investments made by the Bank shall not exceed at any one time ----- ------- percent of the subscribed capital and surplus of the Bank. (New)

Section 4. *Conditions on which Bank may Guarantee or Make Loans.*

The Bank may guarantee, participate in, or make loans to the government of any member, political subdivisions thereof, and business and industrial enterprises therein, subject to the following conditions: (U.S., cf. UK III, 1)

(1) The government of the member in which the project is located, the central bank of such member, or some comparable agency fully guarantees the payment of interest on the loan and repayment of the principal. (UK confines to national gov.)

(2) The borrower is unable to secure the funds from other sources under conditions which, in the opinion of the Bank, are reasonable.

(3) A competent committee, after a careful study of the merits of the project, has submitted a written report concluding that the project would serve to increase the productivity of the member country in which it is located. (Omits "directly or indirectly" from UK) (Omits "favorable prospects" from U.S.)

(4) In the opinion of the Bank, the rate of interest is reasonable and such rate and the schedule for repayment of the principal are appropriate to the project and to the balance of payments prospects of the member country in which the project is located.

(5) In guaranteeing a loan made by other investors, the Bank receives compensation for its risk. (p. 5)

ALTERNATIVE A
PART (1)

In general, loans made or guaranteed by the Bank, shall be for the purpose of specific projects of reconstruction and development, and except as otherwise provided in this plan, the proceeds of loans shall only be made available to meet specific purposes. In exceptional circumstances, however, the Bank, acting in agreement with the International Monetary Fund, may make or guarantee a loan which provides the borrowing country with gold or foreign exchange for the purpose of establishing its exchanges and allowing a breathing space for the recovery of its economy and the balancing of its international payments. (UK III, 6 (new matter))

PART (2)

In making or guaranteeing a loan the Bank shall pay due regard to the prospects of the borrowing country being in a position to service the loan; and in determining the destination, the character and the volume of its loans it shall act prudently in the interests both of the borrowing member country and also of the guaranteeing members. At the same time it shall not seek to avoid the incurring of some measure of reasonable risk (taking account of the commission chargeable — see below) where the loan is in the general interests of reconstructing or developing the world's resources or expanding international trade along mutually advantageous lines; and shall seek to conduct its operations taken as a whole in such manner as to avoid, so far as possible, the calling up of the capital reserved for guarantees, rather than seek full security from risk in each transaction taken separately. These considerations shall govern the lending policy of the Bank especially in approving reconstruction loans to countries which have suffered from the war. (UK III, 7 (new matter))

NOTE — UK III, 2, taken directly from P.P. IV, 6 has been omitted as essentially duplicative of Art. III, Sec. 4, subdiv. (2) above.

Section 5. *Provision of Currencies for Loans.*

When the Bank makes loans it shall:

(a) Furnish the borrower with the currencies of members other than that of the member in which the project is located which are needed by the borrower in connection with the loan;

(b) Finance the expenditures of the borrower in the member in which the project is located only as follows, (1) under exceptional circumstances when the local currency required cannot be raised on reasonable terms in the country where the project is located, the Bank may provide an appropriate part of the loan in that currency, or (2) if the development program or project gives rise to an increased need for foreign exchange, the Bank may make available to the borrower an appropriate amount of gold or foreign exchange not to exceed the borrower's expenditure in the member in which the project is located; (p. 6)

(c) Make available at the request of a member in which a portion of a loan is spent an amount of gold or foreign exchange not to exceed the amount by which the expenditure of the loan in that member gives rise to an increased need for foreign exchange. (U.S. IV, 8 revised (cf. UK II, 4))

Section 6. *Use of Loans Guaranteed, Participated in or Made by the Bank.*

(a) The Bank shall impose no conditions as to the particular member in which the proceeds of a loan shall be spent.

(b) The Bank shall make arrangements to assure that the proceeds of any loan are used only for the purposes for which the loan was granted, with due attention to considerations of economy and efficiency regardless of political or other non-economic influences or considerations

(c) In addition to any other action which the Bank may take to implement the provisions of subsection (b) above with respect to loans it makes, it shall credit the account of the borrower with the amount of the loan and shall make payment from the account only to meet expenses as they are actually incurred. (p. 7) (U.S. III, 5 revised (cf. UK III, 1(4)))

Article IV. *Operations*

Section 1. *Methods of Facilitating Provision of Loans.*

The Bank may facilitate the provision of loans which satisfy the general conditions of Article III in any of the following ways:

(a) By direct loans out of the Bank's own capital subscribed under

Article II, Section 4(a).

(b) By direct loans out of funds raised by the Bank in the market of a member.

(c) By guaranteeing in whole or in part loans made by private investors through the usual investment channels. (UK IV, 1)

Section 2. *Loans from Subscribed Capital.*

The Bank shall make loans from currency subscribed under Article II, Section 4(a), only with the approval in each case of the member whose currency is to be loaned. If the currency required by the borrowing country is not available in whole or in part out of capital so subscribed, the Bank may supply such currency from its holdings derived from other sources or may supply gold, subject to Article III, Section 5, and Section 8 of this Article. (New)

ALTERNATIVE A

In the case of loans under Section 1 (a) of this Article, the borrower shall notify the Bank in which members it desires to incur expenditure to be met out of the loan, and the Bank shall make the required currencies available out of its subscribed capital, provided that the country whose currency is to be supplied has agreed in each case. If local currency subscribed under II (4) (a) is not available in whole or in part, the Bank shall make it available out of its holdings of gold or other free resources, if it possesses an adequate amount of such resources and is satisfied that, without this provision, the country in which the borrowing country desires to place the order, would have difficulty in maintaining the equilibrium of its international balance of payments. Otherwise it shall request the borrowing country to transfer its proposed expenditure to another member country. Furthermore, at the request of the countries in which portions of the loan are spent, the Bank will repurchase for gold or needed foreign exchange a part of the sum expended in the currencies of those countries made by the borrower from the proceeds of the loan. (UK IV, 4) (p. 8)

Section 3. *Loans from Borrowed Funds and Guarantees.*

The Bank shall borrow funds under Section 1 (b) of this Article or guarantee loans under Section 1 (c) only with the approval of the member in the market of which the funds are raised and only if that member agrees that the proceeds may be expended in any member without restriction. (UK IV, 5)

Section 4. *Payment Provisions for Direct Loans.*

Loans made directly by the Bank under Section 1(a) or (b) of this Article shall contain the following payment provisions (UK IV, 6)

(a) The annual service of the loan shall be made up of three parts, namely:

(i) a standard rate of interest fixed by the Bank and the same to all borrowers but modifiable from time to time for new loans;

(ii) an annual commission at a flat rate fixed at one percent in the first instance but alterable by the Bank from time to time at its discretion for new loans in the light of experience, the same to all borrowers, to cover the general expenses of the Bank, and as a provision against risk, but the particular expenses of investigation, etc., attaching to the individual loan, may be charged separately against the borrowers. (Could items (i) and (ii) be combined?)

(iii) an annual contribution to amortization either at a flat, or at a progressive rate sufficient to repay the capital within a determined number of years, the length of which shall be fixed with regard not only to the character and purpose of the loan, but also, especially in the case of reconstruction loans, to the conditions in the country of the borrower which may delay the time within which the borrower can repay the loan. The time normally shall not exceed thirty years but may be extended to fifty years in particular cases.

(b) The loan and its annual service shall be fixed in whatever currency may be stipulated by the Bank when making the loan, and may be paid, at the option of the borrower, in gold, or at the discretion of the Bank, in any other currency of a member. (Omits convertible IMF currency)

(c) In the event of the country of the borrower suffering from an acute exchange stringency, so that the service of the loan cannot be provided in the stipulated manner, the country may appeal to the Bank for a relaxation of the conditions of payment. If the Bank is satisfied that some relaxation is in the interests of the country of the borrower and of the operations of the Bank and the other members as a whole it may take action under either, or both, of the following headings in respect of the whole, or part, of the annual service: -

(i) The Bank may in its judgment accept payments in respect of the service of the loan for periods not exceeding three years at a time in local currency. The Bank shall arrange with the borrowing country for the repurchase of such local currency over a period of years on appropriate terms that safeguard the Bank's holdings of such currency. The Bank may also require that the whole, or part of such currency, may be transferred to another member in whose hands it shall be freely available to make payments or to purchase exports in the borrowing country. (Should this sentence be included?)

(ii) The Bank may rearrange the installments of amortization so as to increase the amount due in later years or to prolong the life-time of the loan. (U.S. IV, 10(d))

(d) Payments of interest, commissions, and principal, whether made in currency or in gold, must be equivalent to the gold value of the loan and of the contractual interest and commissions thereon.

Section 5. *Participations.*

The Bank may participate in loans with any of its resources except those subscribed under Article II, Section 4(a). Loans participated in by the Bank shall be placed through the usual investment channels. (U.S. IV, 3 revised)

Section 6. *Guarantees.*

In guaranteeing a loan placed through the usual investment channels, the Bank shall charge a commission on the entire original amount of the loan at a flat rate fixed at one percent per annum in the first instance but alterable by the Bank from time to time at its discretion for new guarantees in the light of experience. Commissions shall be paid direct to the Bank by the borrower. (Rewritten from UK IV, 7) (p. 10)

Section 7. *Order of Meeting Obligations.*

The obligation of the Bank on borrowings or guarantees under Section 1 (b) and (c) of this Article shall be met first from its receipts from commissions and other profits, then from a call on unpaid subscriptions, and finally from paid-in capital. When there is any interruption in the service of a loan guaranteed by the Bank, it shall assume the service. If losses of the Bank are recovered the funds received shall be returned pro rata to members responding to any calls by which the obligations of the Bank were met. With the approval of the Bank, a member subjected to a call, may, in lieu of paying the call, purchase from the Bank currency of the country the default of which or of a borrower in which has necessitated the call but in such case the amount returnable to the member if the loss is recovered shall be appropriately reduced. (UK IV, 7 & 8 rewritten and combined)

Section 8. *Miscellaneous Operations.*

In addition to the operations specified elsewhere in this Agreement, the Bank shall have the power:

(1) To issue, buy and sell (i) its own securities including securities collateralized by loans or investments it has made, (ii) securities it has guaranteed and, (iii) securities in which it has invested, but the Bank shall obtain the approval of the member in which securities are to be issued, bought or sold, and when the Bank buys securities it has issued, it shall also obtain the approval of the member whose currency will be paid for such securities. (U.S. IV, 15(a) revised; UK V, 1)

(2) To guarantee securities in which it has invested for the purpose of facilitating the sale of such securities; (U.S. IV, 5)

(3) To borrow the currency of any member with the approval of such country; and (U.S. IV, 15(a) revised) (p. 11)

(4) After consultation with the International Monetary Fund, *to* buy *and* sell *gold and the currencies of members whenever* such transactions are necessary in connection with *the* operations *of the Bank but with respect to each transaction other than any undertaken to pay creditors, the Bank shall obtain the approval of the member in which the transaction takes place and the member currency of which is disposed of by the Bank.* (U.S. IV, 15(c) revised)

In exercising the powers conferred by this Section, the Bank may deal with any person, partnership, association, corporation or other legal entity in any member country.

(NOTE: UK V, 2, taken from U.S. IV, 18 has been omitted) [This would have been Section 9.)

Section 10. *Warning to be Placed on Securities.*

Every security guaranteed or issued by the Bank shall bear on its face a conspicuous statement that it is not an obligation of the government of any country other than any expressly stated to be obligated on the security. (New)

Section 11. *Political Activity Prohibited.*

The Bank and its officers shall scrupulously avoid interference in the political affairs of any member. This provision shall not limit the right of an officer of the Bank to participate in the political life of his own country. (U.S. IV, 19)

The Bank shall not be influenced in its decisions with respect to applications for loans by the political character of the government of the member concerned with the loan. Only economic considerations shall be relevant to the Bank's decisions.

The Bank, acting with the strictest impartiality, shall pay particular regard, both in selecting the place of its borrowing and of its lending to maintaining the equilibrium of the international balance of payments of members. (UK V, 5) (p. 12)

Article V. *Management*

Section 1. *Board of Governors.*

(a) The administration of the Bank shall be vested in a Board of Governors consisting of one governor and one alternate appointed by each member country in such manner as it may determine. Governors and alternates shall serve for five years, subject to the pleasure of their respective governments, and may be reappointed. No alternate may vote except in the absence of his governor. The Board shall select a chairman from its members.

(b) The Board of Governors may delegate to the Executive Directors authority to exercise any powers of the Board, except:

(1) Determining what new members may be admitted and the conditions of their admission;

(2) Increasing the capital stock;

(3) Requiring a member to withdraw;

(4) Deciding appeals against interpretations of the Agreement by the Executive Directors given on application by a member;

(5) Making agreements to cooperate with other international organizations;

(6) Deciding to liquidate the Bank.

(c) The Board of Governors shall hold an annual meeting and such other meetings as may be provided for by the Board or convened by the Executive Directors whenever requested by five members or by one quarter of the aggregate votes.

(d) The Board may by regulation establish a procedure whereby the Executive Director, when they deem such action to be in the best interest of the Bank may obtain votes of the governor on a specific question in lieu of calling a meeting of the Board.

(e) Governors and alternates shall serve as such without compensation from the Bank, but the Bank shall pay such reasonable expenses as are incurred by the Governors and alternates in attending any meetings.

Section 2. *Voting.*

Each member shall have ------------ votes plus one additional vote for each share of stock held.

Except as otherwise specifically provided, all matters before the Bank shall be decided by a majority of the aggregate votes. (p. 12a)

Section 3. *The Executive Directors.*

(a) The Executive Directors shall be responsible for the conduct of the general operations of the Bank, and for this purpose, shall exercise all the powers delegated to them by the board of governors.

(b) There shall be eleven Executive Directors, of whom five shall be appointed by the five members holding the largest number of shares and six shall be elected biennially, in accordance with the provisions of Schedule B, by all the Governors other than those appointed by the members having the five largest number of shares. Persons chosen as Executive Directors need not be Governors.

(c) Every Executive Director may appoint an alternate with full power to act for him when he is not present. When the Executive Directors appointing them are present, alternates may participate in meetings but shall not vote.

(d) The Executive Directors shall be in continuous session at the principal office of the Bank.

(e) In order to constitute a quorum for any meeting of the Executive Directors, there must be present a majority of the Directors representing not less than one-half of the voting power of all the Executive Directors.

(f) Each Executive Director appointed by one of the members with the five largest quotas shall be entitled to cast the number of votes allotted under Section 2 of this Article to the member appointing him. Each elected Executive Director shall be entitled to cast only the number of votes which actually count toward his election. Each Executive Director shall cast all of the votes to which he is entitled as a single unit.

(g) The Board of Governors shall make regulations containing provisions under which a member which is not entitled to appoint an Executive Director under (b) above shall be permitted to send a representative to attend any meeting of the Executive Directors when a request made by, or a matter particularly affecting, that member is under consideration.

(h) The Executive Directors shall appoint a President who shall not be a Governor or an (p. 12b) Executive Director. The President shall be

Chairman of the Executive Directors, but shall have no vote except a casting vote in case of an equal division. He may participate in meetings of the Board of Governors, but shall not vote at such meetings. He shall, however, be eligible for election as Chairman of the Board of Governors. The President shall hold office at the pleasure of the Executive Directors,

(i) The President shall be chief of the operating staff of the Bank and shall conduct under the direction of the Executive Directors, the ordinary business of the Bank's work. Subject to the general control of the Executive Directors, he shall be responsible for the internal organization of the Bank's staff and the appointment and dismissal of its staff. The Managing Director shall be responsible to the Executive Directors for the accounts.

(j) The Executive Directors may appoint such committees as they deem advisable. Members of such committees need not be limited to Governors or Executive Directors or their alternates.

(k) The Board of Governors shall determine the remuneration to be paid to the Executive Directors and the salary and terms of service of the President.

SCHEDULE B

(a) In balloting for the elective Executive Directors, each governor eligible to vote shall cast for one person all of the votes to which he is entitled under Section 2 of this article. The six persons receiving the greatest number of votes shall be Executive Directors, except that no person who receives less than sixteen percent of the aggregate eligible votes shall be considered elected.

(b) When six persons are not elected on the first ballot, a second ballot shall be held in which the person receiving the lowest number of votes shall be ineligible for election and in which there shall vote only those governors who voted on the first ballot for a person not elected and those governors all or part of whose votes for a person elected are deemed to have raised the votes cast for that person above seventeen percent of the aggregate eligible votes. (p. 12c)

(c) In determining whether any part of the votes cast by a governor are to be deemed to have raised the total of any person above seventeen percent, there shall be considered as not forming part of the excess over seventeen percent the votes of the governor casting the largest number of votes for such person, then the votes of the governor casting the next largest number, and so on until the total reaches seventeen percent.

(d) Any governor whose votes are partly not in excess and partly in excess shall be eligible to vote in the second balloting only to the extent of the votes in excess.

(e) If on the second ballot, six persons have not been elected, further ballots shall be taken on the same principles until six persons have been elected, provided that after five persons are elected, the sixth may be elected by a simple majority of the remaining votes and shall be deemed to have been elected by all such votes. (p. 13)

Section 3. *Advisory Council.*

There shall be an Advisory Council of seven persons, elected by the Fund from outstanding representatives of banking, business, labor and agricultural interests, who are citizens of members, but only one citizen of any member shall serve on the Council at any one time. The Council shall advise with the Bank on matters of general policy. The Council shall meet annually and on such other occasions as the Bank may request.

Councilors shall serve for two years, and may be reelected. They shall be paid their reasonable expenses incurred in behalf of the Bank.

Section 4. *Loan Committees.*

The committees required to report on loans under Article I, Section 5, shall be appointed by the Bank, except that such committee shall include an expert selected by the Governor representing the member in which the project is located, who may or may not be from the technical staff of the Bank. The majority of each committee shall be from the technical staff.

Section 5. *Relationship to Other International Organizations.*

The Bank, within the terms of this Agreement, shall cooperate with any general international organization and with public international organizations having specialized responsibilities in related fields. Any arrangements for such cooperation which would involve a modification of any of the provisions of this Agreement may be effected only after amendment to this Agreement in conformity with the procedure set forth in Article IX.

Section 6. *Location of Offices.*

The principal office of the Bank shall be located in the member holding the greatest number of shares and agencies or branch offices may be established in any member or members.

Section 7. *Depositories.*

(a) Each member shall designate its central bank as a depository for all the Bank's holdings of its currency or, if it has no central bank, it shall designate such other institution as may be acceptable to the Bank. (p. 14)

(b) The Bank may hold other assets, including gold, in designated depositories in the four members holding the greatest number of shares and in such other depositories as the Bank may select. At least one-half of the holdings of gold of the Bank shall be held in the designated depository in the member in which the Bank has its principal office. In an emergency, the Executive Directors may transfer all or any part of the Bank's holdings of gold to any place where it can be adequately protected.

Section 8. *Form of Holdings of Currency.*

The Bank shall accept from any member in lieu of any part of the currency of that member not needed by the Bank in its operations, notes or similar obligations issued by the Government of the member or the depository designated by such member, which shall be nonnegotiable, non-interest bearing and payable at their par value on demand by a credit to the currency account of the Fund in that member.

Section 9. *Protection of the Assets of the Bank.*

No change in the foreign exchange value of the currency of any member shall alter the gold value of the assets of the Bank. Whenever (i) the par value of a currency of a member is reduced, or (ii) the foreign exchange value of the currency of any member has depreciated within the jurisdiction to a significant extent in the opinion of the Bank, the member shall compensate the Bank by paying to the Bank within a reasonable time an amount of its own currency equal to the reduction the gold value of the currency of such member held by the Bank. Whenever the par value of the currency of any member has been increased the Bank shall compensate such member by returning, within a reasonable time, an amount in the currency of such member equal to the increase in gold value of the currency of such member held by the Bank.

Section 10. *Publication of Reports.*

The Bank shall publish an annual report containing an audited statement of its accounts and shall issue at intervals of three months or less a summary statement of its financial position and a profit and loss statement showing the results of its operations.

The Bank may publish such other reports as it deems desirable for carrying out its purposes and policies. (p. 15)

Section 11. *Allocation of Income.*

The Bank shall determine annually what part of its net income shall be placed to reserve and what part, if any, shall be distributed.

Section 12. *Distribution of Income.*

If any part is distributed, two per cent non-cumulative shall be paid, as a first charge against the distribution of any year, to each member on the average amount during the year by which 75 per cent of its quota exceeds the holdings by the Fund of its currency; and the balance to the members in proportion to their quotas. Payments to each member shall be made in its own currency.

Section 13. *Miscellaneous Powers.*

In order to carry out its purposes, the Bank may:

(1) Make contracts;

(2) Acquire and dispose of real and personal property;

(3) Institute legal proceedings in any court of competent jurisdiction;

(4) Enter into such compromises or settlements of obligations due to or by the Bank as in the judgment of the Board are to the best interests of the Bank;

(5) Employ such staff as shall be necessary to conduct the business of the Bank; and

(6) Adopt such rules or regulations as may be necessary or appropriate to conduct the business of the Bank. (p. 16)

Article VI. *Withdrawal and Suspension of Membership and Liquidation*

Section 1. *Right of Members to Withdraw.*

Any member may withdraw from the Bank at any time by serving written notice on the Bank at its principal office. Withdrawal shall become effective on the date such notice is received.

Section 2. *Suspension of Membership.*

A member country failing to meet any of its obligations to the Bank may be suspended from membership by decision of a majority of the member countries, each of which for this purpose shall have one vote, to be cast by its director or alternate. At the end of one year from the date of suspensions, the country shall automatically cease to be a member of the Bank unless a majority of the member countries, voting in the same manner as for suspension, restores the country to good standing.

While under suspension, a country shall be denied all of the privileges of membership except the right of withdrawal, but shall be subject to all of its obligations.

3. *Financial Assistance to be Withheld.*

If any country is suspended from membership, the members agree that they and their agencies will not extend financial assistance to that country during the period of suspension without approval of the Bank.

Section 4. *Cessation of Membership in International Monetary Fund.*

Any member which ceases to be a member of the International Monetary Fund shall immediately cease to be a member of the Bank.

ALTERNATIVE A

Any member country that withdraws or is dropped from the International Monetary Fund, shall relinquish its membership in the Bank unless three-fourths of the member votes favor its remaining as a member.

Section 5. *Settlement of Accounts with Countries Ceasing to be Members.*

(a) When a country ceases to be a member, the Bank shall arrange to repurchase its shares as a part of the settlement of accounts with such country. The repurchase price of the shares shall be the amount (p. 17) at which such shares are carried on the books of the Bank on the day the country ceases to be a member of the Bank plus a pro rata share of any surplus existing on that date.

(b) The payment for shares repurchased by the Bank under this section shall be governed by the following conditions:

(1) No amount shall be paid for shares prior to six months from the date upon which the country ceases to be a member nor thereafter so long as the country, its central bank or any of its agencies remain liable, directly, or contingently, to the Bank, except as to liability of the country resulting from its subscription for shares, and any amount so withheld may, at the option of the Bank, be applied on any matured obligation. Payments for shares shall be made from time to time to the extent by which the amount due as the repurchase price exceeds the aggregate of such liabilities until the former member has received the full repurchase

price.

(2) Payments shall be made in the currency of the country receiving payment and any deficiency shall be paid in gold or gold convertible exchange at the option of the Bank.

(c) In the event the Bank goes into liquidation within six months of the date upon which any country ceases to be a member of the Bank, all rights of such country shall be determined by the provisions governing liquidation.

Section 6. *Assessments to Meet Losses.*

(a) In the event any loss is sustained by the Bank on any guarantee, participation in a loan, or loan which was outstanding on the date the country ceased to be a member of the Bank, and the amount of such loss exceeds the amount of the reserve existing on the date the country ceased to be a member, such country shall be obligated to repay upon demand that amount by which the repurchase price of its shares would have been reduced if the loss had been taken into account when the repurchase price was determined. In addition, the (p. 18) former member country shall remain liable on any call for unpaid subscriptions to the extent that it would have been required to respond if the impairment of capital had occurred and the call had been made at the time the repurchase price of its shares was determined.

(b) Repayment to the Bank under this section shall be in currency and gold or gold convertible exchange in the same proportion as the payments by the Bank for the repurchase of the shares.

Section 7. *Liquidation.*

In an emergency, the Executive Committee by a majority vote, temporarily may suspend the operations of the Bank, pending an opportunity for further consideration and action by the Board.

The Bank may be voted into liquidation by a majority of the aggregate votes.

Upon being voted into liquidation, the Bank shall forthwith cease engaging in any activities except those incident to the orderly liquidation, conservation and preservation of its assets and the settlement of its obligations.

The liability of all member countries for uncalled subscriptions to the capital stock of the Bank and their guarantees with respect to the depreciations of their own currencies shall continue until all claims of creditors including all contingent claims shall have been discharged.

Upon liquidation of all creditors holding direct claims shall be paid immediately if the Bank has sufficient assets, and if the assets are not sufficient, the Executive Committee shall pay such creditors as soon as possible out of payments to the Bank or calls on subscriptions, but before making any payments to holders of direct claims, the Committee shall make such arrangements as are necessary, in its judgment, to insure a distribution to holders of contingent claims ratably with creditors holding direct claims.

No distribution shall be made to a member country on account of its capital subscription until all claims of creditors, including all contingent claims, have been discharged or have been provided for by the Executive Committee having made arrangements sufficient, in its judgment, to accomplish that purpose.

(Detailed provisions relating to method of distribution to shareholders will be supplied later on basis of principles provided for liquidating the International Monetary Fund.) (p. 19)

Article VII. *Additional Undertakings on the Part of Member Countries*

Section 1. *Purposes and Scope of Undertakings.*

In order to support the activities of the Bank and to foster the accomplishment of its purposes and policies, each member country, in addition to commitments appearing elsewhere in this Agreement, undertakes the performance of and agrees to the stipulations set forth herein, all of which shall remain binding during suspension or after termination of membership.

Section 2. *Immunities of the Bank.*

(a) The Bank and its assets of whatsoever nature shall, wheresoever located and by whomsoever held, be exempt and immune in the territory of any member from:

(i) search, seizure, attachment, execution, requisition, confiscation, moratorium and expropriation, except as provided in 3, below; and

(ii) any exchange, debt, or export controls, except such as are consented to by the Bank.

(b) All governors, executive directors, officers and employees of the Bank shall, with respect to their official acts, be exempt from suit except when the Bank consents.

(c) The archives of the Bank shall be inviolable.

NOTE. There are certain other minor privileges or immunities which will also be required such as courier facilities. Further material will be supplied completing this section in this respect.

Section 3. *Suits against the Bank.*

Suits may be brought against the Bank only in a court of competent jurisdiction in a member in which the Bank has an office, and only by litigants other than members and those acting for or deriving claims from members. The Bank and its assets of whatsoever nature shall, wheresoever located and by whomsoever held, be exempt and immune from seizure, attachment and execution in advance of final judgment.

Section 4. *Restrictions on Taxation of Bank, its Employees and Obligations.*

(a) The Bank, its assets, property, income, activities, operations and transactions of whatsoever nature shall be exempt and immune from all taxation or liability for the collection or payment of any tax, including without limitation by reason of this enumeration, excises, duties, and imposts, imposed by any member or any political subdivision or taxing authority thereof. (p. 20)

(b) No member, or any political subdivision or taxing authority thereof, shall impose or collect any tax on or measured by salaries or remunerations for personal services paid by the Bank to persons who are not citizens of such member.

(c) No member, or any political subdivision or taxing authority thereof, shall impose or collect any taxation on any obligation or security issued by the Bank or any dividend or interest thereon, by whomsoever held or received, which discriminates against such obligation, dividend, or interest, because of its origin, or which is applicable with respect to such obligation, security, dividend, or interest because of the place or currency in which it is issued, made payable or paid, or because of the location of any office or place of business maintained by the Bank. (p. 21)

[Article VIII. *No Text*] [337]

Article IX. *Amendments*

Any governor or executive director desiring to introduce

---

[337] *Editors' note:* Because of a misprint, the original document has no Article VIII.

modifications in this Agreement shall communicate his proposal to the Chairman of the Board of Governors who shall bring the proposal before the Board of Governors. If the proposed amendment is approved by the Board of Governors by a majority of the aggregate votes, the Fund shall prepare a protocol, by dated circular letters, to the governments of all the members asking whether they accept the proposed modifications. When the governments of members having four-fifths of the aggregate votes, have accepted the proposed amendment, or, in the case of modifications of the right to withdraw from the Fund when the governments of all of the members have accepted, the Fund shall certify the fact by means of a *procès verbal,* which it shall communicate to the governments of all members. The protocol will enter into force between all members three months from the date of the *procès verbal* unless a shorter period is specified in the protocol. (p. 22)

Article X. *[[Miscellaneous Provisions]]*

Section 1. *Interpretation.*

All questions of the interpretation of the provisions of this Agreement between two or more member countries shall be resolved by the Bank. Whenever a disagreement arises between the Bank and a country which has ceased to be a member, or between the Bank and any member after liquidation of the Bank, such disagreement shall be submitted to arbitration.

Section 2. *Definitions.*

(To be supplied later)

Section 3. *Approval Deemed Given.*

Whenever the approval of any member is required before any act may be done by the Bank approval shall be deemed to have been given unless the member presents an objection within such reasonable period as the Bank may fix in notifying the member of the proposed act. (p. 23)

Article XI. *(Final Provisions)*

(To be supplied later)

APPENDICES

Appendix A

Conference participants

Delegations • Officers of the conference • Subcommittees

The delegate list is mainly from room directories.[338] Biographical details are mainly from Kurt Schuler and Mark Bernkopf's paper "Who Was at Bretton Woods?" The attribution of delegation chairmen is in some cases our unofficial designation, which may be wrong. Usually the most prominent member of the delegation is listed first in the June 26 directory.

Latin American names sometimes include two family names, the father's and then the mother's. At the time of the conference, the standard way of writing Chinese names in English was to use the Wade-Giles system of romanization and often to write personal name, then family name. The current standard is to use the pinyin system of Romanization and to write family name, then personal name.

Delegations

AUSTRALIA
Chairman: Leslie Galfreid Melville (1902-2002), Economic Adviser to the Commonwealth Bank of Australia; later Executive Director, IMF (1950-1953); Executive Director, World Bank (1950-1953); Alternate Governor, IMF (1951-1952)

---

[338] U.S. National Archives RG 56, Box 1, Folder A-3, room directory of foreign delegates as of June 20, 2044; RG 82, Box 42, Folder "Atlantic City Drafting Committee," room directories of U.S. delegates as of June 24 and foreign delegates as of June 26; RG 82, Box 1, Folder A-9, "List of Those Present at the Meeting of the Pre-Conference Agenda Committee at Atlantic City, June 24-June 30, 1944." RG 56, Box, Folder A-5 contains a document called "Administrative and Secretarial Staff, U.S. Delegation," but we think it is for Bretton Woods rather than Atlantic City, because it contains several names not listed in the Atlantic City room directory.

James Bristock "Jim" Brigden (1887-1950), Financial Counselor, Australian Legation, Washington; economist noted for contributions to trade, national income, and statistics in Australia

Arthur Harold Tange (1914-2001), Commonwealth Department of External Affairs; later Secretary (top career official), Commonwealth Department of Defense (1970-1979); knighted

Frederick Henry Wheeler (1914-1994), Commonwealth Department of the Treasury; later Secretary (top career official), Commonwealth Department of the Treasury (1971-1979); knighted

BELGIUM

Baron René Boël (1899-1990), Counselor of the Belgium Government; prominent banker and industrialist; later delegate to first meeting of IMF and World Bank (1946); President, European League for Economic Cooperation

Secretary: Hélène Van Gelder[339]

BRAZIL

Octávio Gouvea de Bulhões (1906-1990), Chief, Division of Economic and Financial Studies, Ministry of Finance; later Alternate Executive Director, IMF (1946-1947); Minister of Finance (1964-1967)

CANADA

Chairman: William Archibald Mackintosh (1895-1970), Special Assistant to the Deputy Minister of Finance; later Director, Bank of Canada

John James Deutsch (1911-1976), Special Assistant to the Under Secretary of State of External Affairs; later Alternate Governor, World Bank (1952-1953); senior official in multiple positions, including Chairman, Economic Council of Canada (1963-1967)

(Arthur FitzWalter) Wynne Plumptre (1907-1977), Financial Attaché, Canadian Embassy, Washington; later Alternate Governor, World Bank (1953-1965); Assistant Deputy Minister, Department of Finance (1953-1965); Executive Director, IMF (1962-1965)

Louis Rasminsky (1908-1998), Chairman (alternate), Foreign Exchange Control Board; later Executive Director, IMF (1946-1962); Executive Director, World Bank (1946-1962); Alternate Governor, IMF (1950, 1955, 1958, 1960-1968); Deputy Governor, Bank of Canada (1955-1961); Governor, Bank of Canada (1961-1973)

---

[339] The Atlantic City directory says "Miss Van Gilden," but based on the Bretton Woods directory and other records we think our identification above is correct.

CHILE

Hermann Max Coers (1893-1974), Technical Adviser, Central Bank of Chile; Professor, University of Chile

(The June 20 directory says "and 3 others," who were later at Bretton Woods, but the June 26 directory lists only Coers)

CHINA[340]

Chairman: Tingfu Fuller Tsiang [Jiang Tingfu] (1895-1965), Chief Political Secretary of Executive Yuan (cabinet); previously Ambassador to the USSR (1936-1938); later Permanent Representative of China to the United Nations[341] and Ambassador to the United States

Tsu-Yee Bei (also spelled "Pei") [Bei Zuyi] (1893-?), Director, Bank of China

Te-Mou Hsi [Xi Demao], Representative of the Ministry of Finance in Washington; later Alternate Executive Director, World Bank (1951)

Yu-Chung Hsi, Secretary to the Representative of the Ministry of Finance in Washington

Yee-Chun Koo [Gu Yiqun] (1901-1992), Vice Minister of Finance; later Executive Director, IMF (1946-1950); Treasurer, IMF (1953-1966)

Mun-Ho Leung

Cho-Ming Li, Professor of Economics, Southwestern Associated Universities, Kunming

Kuo-Ching Li [Li Guoqin] (1892-?), Adviser to the Ministry of Finance; General Manager, Wah Chang Trading Corporation, New York

Wan-Sen Lo, Secretary to the Representative of the Ministry of Finance in Washington

Ts-Liang Soong [Song Ziliang], General Manager, Manufacturers Bank of China; later Alternate Governor, World Bank (1946-1950)

Kai-Kwan Tsien

Ting-Sen Wei [Wei Tingsheng], Member, Legislative Yuan

Secretaries

Louise McConnell

Pearl Dorain

---

[340] Brackets list pinyin romanization for some delegates given in Jin (2015). Ping-Wen Kuo [Guo Bingwen], China's vice minister of finance, was on the *Queen Mary* with his wife and at Bretton Woods but apparently not at Atlantic City.

[341] The Nationalist Chinese government, later based in Taiwan, filled China's seat at the United Nations until 1971.

CUBA

Felipe Pazos y Roque (1912-2001), Commercial Attaché, Cuban Embassy, Washington; later an IMF official; President, Banco Nacional de Cuba (1950-52, 1959); and an Alliance for Progress and Inter-American Development Bank official

CZECHOSLOVAKIA

Chairman: Ladislav Karel Feierabend (1891-1969), Minister of Finance (1941-1945); previously Minister of Justice (1938); Minister of Agriculture (1938-1939)

Antonín Basch (1896-1971), Department of Economics, Columbia University; previously an official of the Czechoslovak National Bank; later Chief Economist, World Bank (1947?-1957)

Ervin Paul Hexner (1893-1968), Professor of Economics and Political Science, University of North Carolina; later Senior Counselor and Assistant General Counsel, IMF (1946-1958)

Jan Viktor Mládek (1911-1989), Ministry of Finance; later Executive Director, IMF (1946-1948); Governor, IMF (1946-1947); senior IMF official (1953-1977), including head of Paris office (1953-1961) and Director, Central Banking Service (1964-1977)

FRANCE (FRENCH COMMITTEE OF NATIONAL LIBERATION)

Chairman: André Istel (1887-1966), Technical Counselor to the Department of Finance; prominent banker; previously coauthor of a Free French plan for international monetary cooperation (1943)

Raoul Aglion (1904-2004), Legal Counselor; previously Professor of Economic History, École des Hautes Études Sociales (1930); later French diplomat and author

Jean Rioust de Largentaye (1903-1970), Inspector of Finance; previously translator of John Maynard Keynes's *General Theory of Employment, Interest and Money* into French (1942); later Alternate Executive Director, IMF (1946); Executive Director, IMF (1946-1964)

Robert Mossé (1906-1973), Professor of Economics, New School for Social Research, New York; later Professor of Economics, School of Law, University of Grenoble, and author of books on international monetary issues

Secretaries

Gaston Mallet

Jacqueline Mailhot

Gertrude Picard

Marguerite Vincent

GREECE

Chairman: Kyriakos Varvaressos, Governor of the Bank of Greece (1939-1941, 1941-1944, 1945) and Ambassador Extraordinary for Economic and Financial Matters; previously Deputy Governor of the Bank of Greece (1933-1939); later Executive Director, World Bank (1946-1948)

Alexander Loverdos, Ministry of Finance; later Alternate Governor, IMF (1946-?); Alternate Governor, World Bank (1946-?); Head, Greek Office of Economic Research, New York (circa 1946)

Athanase (Athanasios) Ioannou "A.J." Sbarounis (1892-?), Director General, Ministry of Finance; later Governor, World Bank (1946-1947)

INDIA

Chairman: Sir (Abraham) Jeremy Raisman (1892-1978), Member (minister) of Finance, Government of India (1939-1945); British subject

Sir Chintaman Dwarakanath Deshmukh (1896-1982), Governor, Reserve Bank of India (1943-1949); later Governor, IMF (1946-1955); Governor, World Bank (1946-1947, 1950-1956); Minister of Finance (1950-1957)

Sir Theodore Emanuel Guggenheim Gregory (1890-1970), Economic Adviser to the Government of India; sometime Professor of Banking and Currency, London School of Economics and Political Science; British subject

MEXICO

Chairman: Rodrigo Gómez (1897-1970), Manager, Banco de México; later Director General, Banco de México (1952-1970); Executive Director, IMF (1946-1948, 1958-1960); Alternate Governor, IMF (1946-1947, 1953-1956, 1960-1968); Governor, IMF (1957-1959)

Antonio Espinosa de los Monteros (1903-1959), Executive President, Nacional Financiera, and Director, Banco de México; later Ambassador to the United States (1945-1948); Governor, IMF (1946-1947); Governor, World Bank (1946-1948)

NETHERLANDS

Chairman: Johan Willem "Wim" Beyen (also spelled "Beijen") (1897-1976), Financial Adviser to the Netherlands Government; Director, Unilever; previously Alternate to the President, Bank for International Settlements (1935-1937); President, Bank for International Settlements (1937-1939); later Executive Director, World Bank (1946-1952); Executive Director, IMF (1948-1952); Minister of Foreign Affairs (1952-1956)

Daniël Crena de Iongh (1888-1970), President, Board for the Netherlands Indies, Surinam, and Curaçao in the United States; previously President, Nederlandsche Handel-Maatschappij (Netherlands Trading Company)

(1934-1939); later Alternate Executive Director, IMF (1946); Alternate Executive Director, World Bank (1946-1947); Treasurer, IMF (1946); Treasurer, World Bank (1947-1953); Executive Director, IMF (1953-1955); Executive Director, World Bank (1953-1955)

Jacques Jacobus "Koos" Polak (1914-2010), Economist, Netherlands Economic, Financial, and Shipping Mission to the United States; previously a League of Nations official; later a senior IMF official (1947-1979); originator of the "Polak model" of the monetary approach to the balance of payments (1957); Executive Director, IMF (1981-1986)

Hendrik Riemens, Financial Attaché, Netherlands Embassy, Washington

Secretary

Miss B. Thielen

NORWAY

Wilhelm Christian Ottesen Keilhau (1888-1954), Director, Norges Bank (Bank of Norway), pro tempore, London; previously Professor of Economics, University of Oslo

UNION OF SOVIET SOCIALIST REPUBLICS (USSR, Soviet Union)

Chairman: A.P. Morozov, Chief, Monetary Division of the People's Commissariat for Foreign Trade (also transliterated as "Morosov")

Aleksei Mikhailovich Smirnov, Professor, Institute of Foreign Trade; later author, *Normalization of World Trade and the Monetary Problem* (1952)

Fedor (also transliterated "Fyodor") Petrovich Bystrov, Professor of Finance, Institute of Foreign Trade

N.I. Kuznetzov (also transliterated as "Kuznetsov")

Miss A.W. Pougacheva (listed as "A.K. Pugacheva" at Bretton Woods)

Mrs. L.J. Gouseva (also transliterated as "Guseva")

UNITED KINGDOM

Chairman: John Maynard Keynes (1883-1946), Lord Keynes, Economic Adviser to the Chancellor of the Exchequer; Director, Bank of England; most influential economist of the 20th century; created Baron Keynes of Tilton (1942); later Governor, IMF (1946); Governor, World Bank (1946); Vice President, World Bank (1946)

(William) Eric Beckett (1896-1966), chief Legal Adviser, Foreign Office; chief British legal expert at Bretton Woods; later knighted (1948)

George Lewis French Bolton (1900-1982), Adviser, Bank of England; later Executive Director, IMF (1946-1952); Alternate Governor, IMF (1952-1956); Executive Director, Bank of England (1948-1957); Director, Bank of England (1957-1968); knighted

H.E. Brooks, United Kingdom Treasury

Charles H. Campbell, First Secretary, British Embassy, Washington

Sir (Crawfurd) Wilfrid Griffin Eady (1890-1962), Joint Second Secretary (second-highest career position) and head of Overseas Finance, United Kingdom Treasury; highest-ranking British official at Atlantic City and Bretton Woods; previously Deputy Under Secretary of State, Home Office (1938-1940)

Arthur S. Gambling, Treasury

M. Harris

Redvers Opie (1900-1984), Counselor, British Embassy, Washington; economist

Lionel Charles Robbins (1898-1984), Head, Economic Section, War Cabinet Office; Professor, London School of Economics and a leader in its rise to international eminence; later created Baron Robbins of Clare Market (1958)

Dennis Holme Robertson (1890-1963), Economic Adviser, United Kingdom Treasury; previously and later Cambridge University monetary economist; later knighted; the best writer economics has ever produced

Arthur Wendell "Peter" Snelling (1914-1996), Dominions Office; later High Commissioner in Ghana (1959–1961); Deputy Under Secretary of State, Foreign and Commonwealth Office (1961–1969); Ambassador to South Africa (1970-1973); knighted

Secretaries

Florence Fadzzen

Miss M.F. Houlden

Jean C. Gregory

Miss F.N. Macey

Miss Peek

Miss Page

Miss L.D. Simpson

Miss I. Storey

Additional attendee: Lydia Lopokova (1892-1981), Baroness Keynes, wife of John Maynard Keynes

UNITED STATES OF AMERICA

Chairman: Harry Dexter White (1892-1948), Assistant to the Secretary of the Treasury; chief American negotiator on international monetary matters during World War II; main originator of the ideas in the IMF agreement; previously Professor of Economics, Lawrence College (1932-1934); Director, Division of Monetary Research, U.S. Department of the Treasury (1938-1945); Assistant Secretary of the Treasury (a Senate-confirmed position) (1945-1946); Executive Director, IMF (1946-1947); passed secrets to USSR

Hawthorne Arey (1905-1972), Vice President, Export-Import Bank of the United States; previously attorney, Reconstruction Finance Corporation; later Member of Board of Directors, Export-Import Bank of the United States (1949-1953, 1954-1961); Director, Operations Division, Inter-American Development Bank (?-1968)

(Harry) Elting Arnold (1912-1988), Legal Staff, Treasury Department; Assistant General Counsel, Treasury Department (1948-1960); Acting Director, Foreign Assets Control, Treasury Department (1950-1960); General Counsel, Inter-American Development Bank (1960-1971)

Edward Morris "Eddie" Bernstein (1904-1996), Assistant Director of Monetary Research, Treasury Department, Executive Secretary of the Delegation; later Director, Research Department, IMF (1946-1958)

Henry J. Bittermann, U.S. Treasury Department; previously Associate Professor of Economics, Ohio State University (1930s-1943); later Director, Office of International Financial Policy Coordination, U.S. Treasury Department

Karl Richard Bopp (1906-1979), Federal Reserve Board; later President, Federal Reserve Bank of Philadelphia (1958-1970)

Alice Bourneuf (1912-1980), Federal Reserve Board; later Professor of Economics, Boston College

Richard B. Brenner (1918-1955), U.S. Treasury Department; later Assistant General Counsel, IMF (1946-1955)

Edward Eagle "Ned" Brown (1885-1959), President, First National Bank of Chicago; President, Federal Advisory Council, Board of Governors of the Federal Reserve System (an advisory group of banks)

William Adams Brown, Jr. (1894-1957), Department of State; previously Professor of Political Economy, Brown University

(Virginius) Frank Coe (1907-1980), Assistant Administrator, U.S. Foreign Economic Administration; later Secretary, International Monetary Fund (1946-1952); member of a spy ring that passed secrets to the Soviet Union

Emilio Gabriel "Peter" Collado (1910-1995), Chief, Division of Financial and Monetary Affairs, Department of State; later Executive Director, World Bank (1946-1947)

Joseph P. Dreibelbis (1899-1972), Assistant General Counsel, Board of Governors, Federal Reserve System; later Vice President, Bankers Trust Company

Henry H. Edmiston (1907-1996), Vice President, Federal Reserve Bank of St. Louis

Walter R. Gardner (1898?-1990?), Chief, International Section, Division of Research and Statistics, Board of Governors, Federal Reserve System; later an IMF official

Emanuel Alexandrovich Goldenweiser (1883-1953), Director of Research and Statistics, Board of Governors, Federal Reserve System; previously President, American Statistical Association (1943); one of the most influential career officials of the Federal Reserve

Alvin Harvey Hansen (1887-1975), Board of Governors, Federal Reserve System; previously and later Professor of Economics, Harvard University; introduced the economics of John Maynard Keynes in the United States

Frederick Livesey (?-1961), Adviser, Office of Economic Affairs, Department of State

Walter Clinton Louchheim, Jr., (1899-1973), Adviser on Foreign Investments, Securities and Exchange Commission

Ansel Frank Luxford (1911-1971), Treasury Department; Chief Legal Adviser; later a senior World Bank official (1946-1951), including Assistant General Counsel (1948-1951)

August William Maffry (1905-1982), Department of Commerce; later Vice President, Export-Import Bank of the United States (1945-1947); consultant, Economic Cooperation Administration (which administered the Marshall Plan) (1948-1951)

Raymond French Mikesell (1913-2006), U.S. Treasury Department; later Professor of Economics, University of Oregon

Emanuel E. "Duke" Minskoff (1909-1965), Treasury Department; later Director, Division of Foreign Assets Control, Treasury Department

Leo Pasvolsky (1893-1953), Supervisor, Division of Political and Economic Studies, Department of State; in charge of the Department of State's postwar planning; previously an economist and journalist; a major drafter of the United Nations Charter

Dorothy F. Richardson (ca. 1920?-?), Treasury Department; later (1945) married Solomon Adler, a member of the Soviet spy ring headed by Nathan Silvermaster, who worked at the Treasury Department from 1942-1945; Richardson was not accused of being a member

Janet Racolin Sundelson (1916-1949), U.S. Treasury Department; economist

John Parke Young (1895-1988), Chief, Division of International Finance, U.S. Department of State; technical consultant to China at Bretton Woods conference

Secretaries

Jacqueline Ambrose

Louis G. Ficks

Gladys George

Dorothy Landau

Ruth Lucas

Jo Morgan

Polly Morris

Irene Nielsen

513

APPENDICES

Lorna Rippel
Elsie F. Scharf
Linda M. Shanahan
Anne Tarshis
Myrtle E. Utech
Marian J. Vouk

Officers of the conference

Chairman: Harry Dexter White (U.S.)
Vice Chairmen
Lord John Maynard Keynes (UK)
Aleksei Smirnov (USSR)
Tingfu Tsiang (China)
Antonio Espinosa de los Monteros (Mexico)
Secretary: Frank Coe (U.S.)

Subcommittees

(The Steering Committee was concerned with the conference overall. The Agenda Subcommittee was concerned with the organization of the Bretton Woods conference. All other committees and subcommittees were concerned with the International Monetary Fund.)

STEERING COMMITTEE
Chairman: Harry Dexter White (U.S.)
Secretary: Frank Coe (U.S.)
Deputy Secretary: H.E. Brooks (UK)
Members: Antonio Espinosa de los Monteros (Mexico), John Maynard Keynes (UK), Aleksei Smirnov (USSR), Tingfu Tsiang (China)

AGENDA SUBCOMMITTEE
Chairman: Harry Dexter White (U.S.)?
Members: China, France, Mexico, Netherlands, USSR, United Kingdom, United States

SPECIAL COMMITTEE ON INFORMATION
Chairman: A.P. Morozov (USSR)
Reporter: August Maffry (U.S.)
Members: Octávio Gouvea de Bulhões (Brazil), John Deutsch (Canada), Sir

Theodore Gregory (India), Jacques Polak (Netherlands).

SUBCOMMITTEE FOR CONSIDERATION OF CERTAIN TECHNICAL MATTERS
Chairman: Walter Gardner (U.S.)
Members: Canada, Czechoslovakia, Netherlands, United Kingdom, Raymond Mikesell (U.S.)

SUBCOMMITTEE ON MANAGEMENT
Chairman: Sir Wilfrid Eady (UK)
Reporter: W. Eric Beckett? (UK)
Members: Te-Mou Hsi (China), Rodrigo Gómez (Mexico), Antonio Espinosa de los Monteros (Mexico), Jan Willem "Wim" Beyen (Netherlands), Fyodor Bystrov (USSR), George Bolton (UK), A.W. "Peter" Snelling (UK), Richard Brenner (U.S.), Ansel Luxford (U.S.)

SUBCOMMITTEE ON QUESTIONS OF IMMUNITIES[342]
Chairman: Unknown
Reporter: Unknown
Members: Unknown

SUBCOMMITTEE 1: PURPOSES, POLICIES AND SUBSCRIPTIONS
Chairman: Tingfu Tsiang (China)
Reporter: Octavio de Bulhões (Brazil)
Secretary: Emanuel "Duke" Minskoff (U.S.)
Members: Antonín Basch (Czechoslovakia), James Brigden (Australia), Fyodor Bystrov (USSR), Emanuel Goldenweiser (U.S.), Frederick Livesey (U.S.), Robert Mossé (France), Wynne Plumptre (Canada)

SUBCOMMITTEE 2: OPERATIONS OF THE FUND
Chairman: André Istel (France)
Reporter: Louis Rasminsky (Canada)
Secretary: Raymond Mikesell (U.S.)
Members: Elting Arnold (U.S.), [Edward?] Brown (U.S.), Emilio Collado (U.S.), N.I. Kuznetzov (USSR), August Maffry (U.S.), A.P. Morozov (USSR), Felipe Pazos (Cuba), Jacques Polak (Netherlands), Ts-Liang Soong (China)

---

[342] We are uncertain whether this was a separate subcommittee.

SUBCOMMITTEE 3: ORGANIZATION AND MANAGEMENT OF THE FUND

Chairman: Aleksei Smirnov (USSR)

Reporter: Antonio Espinosa de los Monteros (Mexico)

Secretary: Karl Bopp (U.S.)

Members: Raoul Aglion (France), Elting Arnold (U.S.), James Brigden (Australia), Edward or William Brown (U.S.), Walter Gardner (U.S.), Rodrigo Gómez (Mexico), Kuo-Ching Li (China)

SUBCOMMITTEE 4: ESTABLISHMENT OF THE FUND

Chairman: John Deutsch (Canada)

Reporter: Ervin Hexner (Czechoslovakia)

Secretary: Richard Brenner (U.S.)

Members: Hawthorne Arey (U.S.), Richard Brenner (U.S.), Daniël Crena de Iongh (Netherlands), Jean de Largentaye (France), Joseph Dreibelbis (U.S.), Walter Louchheim (U.S.), Redvers Opie (UK), John Parke Young (U.S.)

516

Appendix B

Schedule of meetings

The schedule of meetings is compiled from minutes or mentions in the transcripts. All times are local times. As a reminder, the American delegation arrived in Atlantic City on June 14, and many foreign delegates arrived on June 19, but the delegates aboard the *Queen Mary* did not arrive until June 23. The conference ended on June 30, when delegates took trains to Bretton Woods, New Hampshire, where the conference there began on July 1.

All meetings in Atlantic City occurred in the Claridge Hotel. Harry Dexter White's office was the Claridge Rooms, extensions 270-271. The Binnacle Room was a conference room in the hotel, since renamed. On the *Queen Mary*, Cabin 10, the location of many and perhaps all group meetings for which minutes were taken, was the room of Lord and Lady Keynes on the sun deck, which before World War II had been an area of the ship reserved for cabin class (first class) passengers.

There were some meetings at the conference for which there are no records or even good indications of when they occurred. For that reason, the Committee on Certain Technical Problems and the Agenda Subcommittee are absent from the schedule.

* Indicates meetings that have no minutes themselves but that other sources mention.

Thursday, June 8, 1944
1500   American Technical Group, first meeting / U.S. Department of the Treasury, Washington, D.C.

Wednesday, June 14, 1944
*Evening? American Technical Group, possible meeting / Claridge Hotel, Atlantic City, New Jersey

Thursday, June 15, 1944
1030   American Technical Group, second meeting / beach near Claridge Hotel

Friday, June 16, 1944
1000 American Technical Group, third meeting / Claridge Hotel
1600 American Technical Group, fourth meeting / Claridge Hotel

Saturday, June 17, 1944
*Unknown British delegation, informal meeting / *Queen Mary,* Cabin 10, mid Atlantic
1030 American Technical Group, fifth meeting / Claridge Hotel

Sunday, June 18, 1944
2130 American Technical Group, sixth meeting / Claridge Hotel

Monday, June 19, 1944
1030 British delegation, first meeting / *Queen Mary,* Cabin 10
1200 Allied shipboard delegations, first meeting / *Queen Mary,* Cabin 10
1700 British delegation, second meeting / *Queen Mary*
1800 Agenda Committee, first meeting / Claridge Hotel
2100 American Technical Group, seventh meeting / Claridge Hotel

Tuesday, June 20, 1944
Morning Subcommittee I, first meeting / Claridge Hotel
0930 Subcommittee II, first meeting / Claridge Hotel
1000 Subcommittee III, first meeting / Claridge Hotel
1000 Subcommittee IV, first meeting / Claridge Hotel
1030 British delegation, third meeting / *Queen Mary*
1130 Allied shipboard delegations, second meeting / *Queen Mary*
1530 American Technical Group, eighth meeting / Claridge Hotel
1600 Agenda Committee, second meeting / Claridge Hotel
1730 British delegation, fourth meeting / *Queen Mary*

Wednesday, June 21, 1944
Morning Subcommittee I, second meeting / Claridge Hotel
0915 American Technical Group, ninth meeting / Claridge Hotel
1000 Subcommittee II, second meeting / Claridge Hotel
1030 British delegation, fifth meeting / *Queen Mary*
1030 Subcommittee IV, second meeting / Claridge Hotel
1200 Subcommittee III, second meeting / Claridge Hotel
1215 Allied shipboard delegations, third meeting / *Queen Mary*
1600 Agenda Committee, third meeting / Claridge Hotel
1630 Allied shipboard delegations, fourth meeting / *Queen Mary*

1815 British delegation, sixth meeting / *Queen Mary*

Thursday, June 22, 1944
Morning Subcommittee I, third meeting / Claridge Hotel
0930 Subcommittee II, third meeting / Claridge Hotel
0930 Subcommittee III, third meeting / Claridge Hotel
0930 Subcommittee IV, third meeting / Claridge Hotel
1600 Agenda Committee, fourth meeting / Binnacle Room
1615 British delegation, seventh meeting / *Queen Mary*
1700 Allied shipboard delegations, fifth meeting / *Queen Mary*
2115 American Technical Group, tenth meeting / Claridge Hotel

Friday, June 23, 1944
Morning Subcommittee I, fourth meeting / Claridge Hotel
Morning Subcommittee IV, fourth meeting / Claridge Hotel
0930 Subcommittee II, fourth meeting / Claridge Hotel
0930 Subcommittee III, fourth meeting / Claridge Hotel
1000 Agenda Committee, fifth meeting / Claridge Hotel
1415 American Technical Group, eleventh meeting / White's office
*Evening? Steering Committee, first meeting? / Claridge Hotel

Saturday, June 24, 1944
*Morning British Commonwealth delegates, first meeting / Claridge Hotel
Unknown Conversation between Keynes and Pasvolsky / Claridge Hotel
1500 First Anglo-American meeting / Claridge Hotel
1600 Formal Agenda Committee, first meeting / Binnacle Room
Evening American Technical Group, twelfth meeting / [White's office]

Sunday, June 25, 1944
1000 American Technical Group, thirteenth meeting / White's office
1600 British delegation, eighth meeting / Claridge Hotel
1645 British Commonwealth delegates, second meeting / Claridge Hotel

Monday, June 26, 1944
1000 Formal Agenda Committee, second meeting / Binnacle Room
1030 American Technical Group, fourteenth meeting / White's office
*1030 Steering Committee, second? meeting / Claridge Hotel
1130 American Technical Group, thirteenth meeting / White's office
1130 Second Anglo-American meeting / Claridge Hotel
1500 Formal Agenda Committee, third meeting / Claridge Hotel

Tuesday, June 27, 1944
*Unknown Steering Committee, third? meeting / Claridge Hotel
1030 Formal Agenda Committee, fourth meeting / Claridge Hotel
1430 Subcommittee on Management, first meeting[343] / Claridge Hotel
1530 American Technical Group, fifteenth meeting / White's office
1630 Formal Agenda Committee, fifth meeting / Claridge Hotel

Wednesday, June 28, 1944
Morning? Special Committee on Furnishing Information, only meeting /
    Claridge Hotel
1030 Formal Agenda Committee, sixth meeting / Binnacle Room
*1245 Steering Committee, fourth? meeting / White's office
1430 Subcommittee on Management, second meeting / Room 206
1530 American Technical Group, sixteenth meeting / White's office
1630 Formal Agenda Committee, seventh meeting / Binnacle Room
*2130 Subcommittee on Management, third meeting? / Claridge Hotel

Thursday, June 29, 1944
1030 Formal Agenda Committee, eighth meeting / Binnacle Room
1530? Formal Agenda Committee, ninth meeting / Claridge Hotel

Friday, June 30, 1944
1030 Formal Agenda Committee, tenth meeting / Binnacle Room

---

[343] At the afternoon meeting of the Formal Agenda Committee on June 26
(chapter 45), its secretary, Frank Coe, announced a meeting of the Subcommittee
on Management later that day, but it seems not to have occurred.

Appendix C

Glossary

Agenda Committee (or Conference): The delegates to the Atlantic City conference when meeting as a whole. After all delegations arrived at the conference, the group was sometimes called the Formal Agenda Committee (or Conference) to distinguish it from the less complete group previously.

Alternate director: Official serving as Executive Director in the absence of the primary director.

Alternative: A proposed amendment to the Articles of Agreement.

Appointed directors: Executive Directors chosen by and representing single countries having large quotas, rather than elected by coalitions of countries each having a small quota.

Articles of Agreement: The agreements for the International Monetary Fund and the Bank for Reconstruction and Development.

Bank for Reconstruction and Development: The full name of this organization in the November 1943 U.S. proposal was the Bank for Reconstruction and Development of the United and Associated Nations. The Bretton Woods conference officially named the organization the International Bank for Reconstruction and Development (IBRD); it is now better known by its nickname, the World Bank.

Blocked balances: Funds in a foreign country that cannot be spent freely because of exchange controls. *See also* sterling balances.

Board, Board of Directors: Terms, especially in British usage, for what would become the Executive Directors.

Board of Governors: Highest authority of the IMF and World Bank, composed of officials appointed by every member government.

Bretton Woods: New Hampshire site of the conference immediately after Atlantic City to write the final agreements for the IMF and World Bank.

Capital transactions: Payments for capital-account transactions, that is, those involving financial assets or other investments, as opposed to current payments.

Chairman: British term for what became the IMF Managing Director.

Charges: Interest rates and fees on purchases (loans).

Commission: The three main bodies for conducting the work of the Bretton Woods conference. Commission I considered the IMF; Commission II, the World Bank; and Commission III, other means of international financial cooperation.

Committee: In the Atlantic City conference minutes, sometimes used to refer to the Agenda Committee, of which all delegates were members, other times used to refer to subcommittees, which had restricted membership.

Council: *See* General Council.

Councillors: British term for what became the IMF Governors.

Current payments: Payments for current-account transactions, that is, those involving goods and services, as opposed to capital transactions. Given a precise definition in the IMF Articles of Agreement.

Depository: Place where the IMF and World Bank hold gold and other assets.

Directorate: British term for what became the Executive Directors.

Drawings: *See* purchases.

Exchange controls: Restrictions on the use of a currency in international payments.

Elected directors: Executive Directors elected by coalitions of countries each having a small quota, rather than chosen by and representing single countries having large quotas.

Executive Committee, Executive Directors: A small body of officials supervising the day-to-day affairs of the IMF and World Bank. Includes some appointed directors and some elected directors.

Flimsy: Sheet of paper with a proposed amendment to the Articles of Agreement.

Formal Agenda Committee (or Conference): *See* Agenda Committee.

General Council: British term for what became the Board of Governors.

Gold convertible currency, gold convertible exchange: Financial assets that can be sold for gold, which implies that the assets are denominated in currencies that do not have exchange controls on capital transactions.

Governing Council: British term for what would be become the Board of Governors.

International Clearing Union: The British proposal, drafted by John Maynard Keynes, for a more ambitious body than the IMF.

International Stabilization Fund: The name the United States initially proposed for what became the IMF.

Joint Statement: "Joint Statement by Experts on the Establishment of an International Monetary Fund," also known as the Joint Statement of Principles, a draft proposal for the IMF published in April 1944.

Managing Director: Top manager of the IMF. The top manager of the World Bank is called the president.

Multilateral clearing: Use of a currency for payments with countries other than the issuing country.

Mutual Aid Agreements: A set of agreements among the Allies. The first was the Anglo-American agreement of February 28, 1942. Article VII of the Anglo-American agreement, whose language many of the other agreements imitated, committed the parties to work towards expanding production and employment and liberalizing trade after World War II was over.

Par (parity) value: Value, expressed in terms of gold, at which a country promises to maintain the exchange rate of its currency.

Preconference: The Atlantic City conference, considered as preparatory to the Bretton Woods conference.

Purchases: The IMF's term for loans. In economic reality, the same as loans; in terms of legal treatment, different in some respects.

Quota: Capital subscription. Voting power at the IMF and World Bank is linked to quotas.

Queen Mary: Ship on which many of the delegates from the United Kingdom and European governments in exile traveled from Britain to the United States.

Repurchases: The IMF's term for repayments of loans.

Remittances: Payments not in exchange for goods and services, especially payments by immigrants to family members in their country of origin.

Reporter (or Reporting Delegate): Delegate charged with summarizing the proceedings of a committee meeting.

Scarce currency: A currency whose stock at the IMF is exhausted. The IMF Articles of Agreement provided that the IMF could declare such a currency to be scarce and that member countries would then be allowed to discriminate against the issuing country in their trade policies and exchange controls.

Sterling balances: Assets denominated in pounds sterling, which during World War II and for many years thereafter could not be freely exchanged for U.S. dollars.

Transition (or transitional) period: Period during which an IMF member country could continue to apply exchange controls on current payments.

Uniform changes in par values: Simultaneous changes in the value of all currencies against gold.

United and Associated Nations: The United Nations were the World War II Allies that had declared war on the Axis powers. The associated nations were those that had severed diplomatic relations with the Axis but had not declared war, and such other countries as the Allies might wish to include. A number of the Allies were governments in exile of countries occupied by German and Japanese military forces.

Appendix D

Table of alternatives to IMF Articles

"Alternatives" was the term for proposed amendments to the draft IMF Articles of Agreement. At Atlantic City, because there was no agreed on draft proposal for the World Bank similar to the Joint Statement for the IMF, the conference only reached a draft proposal at the end of the conference and there was no time to propose alternatives. Below we summarize the major changes the alternatives proposed.

The sources for the table are U.S. National Archives, RG 56, Box 20, Folder A-11, "Check List of Pages in Doc. F-1," Document F-1 in the same folder, and the Atlantic City conference minutes. Roman numerals refer to articles of the draft IMF Articles of Agreement, Arabic numerals refer to sections, lower-case letters refer to subsections, and upper-case letters refer to alternatives. Alternative A is usually the American alternative and Alternative B is usually the British alternative. Some Atlantic City alternatives were dropped from the Bretton Woods draft Articles and others were renumbered, so occasionally a letter is missing from the list of alternatives. The capsule summaries of alternatives below emphasize how they differ from the Joint Statement and other alternatives, and are not necessarily comprehensive.

The list below is keyed to the Atlantic City reference scheme for alternatives, whereas in chapter 74 (Document F-1) the scheme is keyed to the Bretton Woods scheme. Parentheses here indicate Bretton Woods letters for alternatives that differed from the Atlantic City letters. Alternatives labeled as having been omitted at Bretton Woods were omitted from the first draft there but in some cases were reintroduced later.

I. Purpose and Policies of the Fund

Alternative A, United States — Minor changes in wording.

Alternative B, Australia — More emphasis on high employment and more tolerance for changes in exchange rates.

Alternative C (Bretton Woods Alternative F), Brazil — Promote international investment.

Alternative D (C), India — Add emphasis on growth in underdeveloped countries.

Alternative E (G), India — Promote settlement of wartime indebtedness.

Alternative F (D), Norway — More tolerance for changes in exchange rates.

Alternative G (E), Norway — More tolerance for changes in exchange rates.

II. Subscription to the Fund

II-1. *[[Total Amount]]*

Alternative A, United States — Add detail on countries eligible for membership, quotas, and time and place of payment.

Alternative B, Czechoslovakia — Allow grace period for payment of quotas. for countries whose currency has been disrupted by enemy occupation.

II-2. *[[Revisions to Quotas]]*

Alternative A, United States — Specify quota revisions every five years.

II-3. *[[Gold Subscription]]*

Alternative A, United States — Add detail on initial payment and payment when quotas are increased.

Alternative B, USSR — Reduce gold payment 50-75 percent for countries that have suffered from enemy occupation.

Alternative C (omitted at Bretton Woods), United Kingdom — Set thresholds allowing lower gold subscriptions for some countries.

Alternative D (C), United States — Reduce gold payment for countries that have suffered from enemy occupation, amount left blank.

III. Transactions with the Fund

III-1. *[[National Agency Dealing with Fund]]*

Alternative A, United States — Require IMF to deal only with the national agency dealing with it.

III-2. *[[Purchase of Another Member's Currency]]*

Alternative A, United States — Add detail.

Alternative B (omitted at Bretton Woods), Canada — Loosen conditions for purchase in certain cases.

Alternative C (B), Australia — Loosen conditions for purchase in certain cases.

Alternative D (C), Czechoslovakia — Change in wording to add precision.

Alternative E (D), France — Raise ceilings on IMF's holdings of a member's currencies in first and second years.

III-3. *[[Limitation on Operations]]*

Alternative A, United States — Restrict operations further.

III-4. *[[Scarce Currency]]*

Alternative A, United States — Make it optional rather than obligatory for a country whose currency is scarce to supply the IMF.

Alternative B, Netherlands — Change in wording to add precision.

III-5. *[[Obligations of a Purchasing Country]]*

Alternative A, United States — Change in emphasis from the IMF to bilateral dealings in currency.

Alternative B (transferred to IX-3 at Bretton Woods), United Kingdom — Elaboration to include a provision about holdings of currency obtained illicitly.

Alternative C (omitted at Bretton Woods), Czechoslovakia — Add a provision defining holdings of currency obtained illicitly.

III-6 *[[Purchase of Another Member's Currency with Gold]]*

Alternative A, United States — Strengthen obligation to acquire another member's currency through the IMF if as advantageous as other channels.

III-7. *[[Fund's Acquisition of Gold]]*

Alternative A, United States — Add a provision to return gold to a member under certain circumstances.

Alternative B, USSR — Add grace periods for countries that have been under enemy occupation.

Alternative C (omitted at Bretton Woods), United Kingdom — Strengthen IMF's ability to acquire gold from members whose reserves have increased; exclude from the calculation currencies that have only become convertible within the last financial year.

Alternative D (C), Belgium — Set the date of joining the IMF rather than the previous financial year as the basis for calculating increase in reserves.

Alternative E (D), Greece — Allow IMF to waive conditions concerning obligatory sales of gold to it.

III, proposed additional section. *Transferability and Guarantee of the Assets of the Fund*

Alternative A, United States — Safeguard IMF from exchange controls on current account of losses from failure of a designated depository.

III, proposed additional section. *Charges and Commissions*

Alternative A, United States — IMF may levy uniform service charges.

Alternative B, USSR — Limit charge to 1 percent except for countries that have borrowed more than 200 percent of quota.

III, proposed additional section. *Furnishing Information*

Alternative A, United States — Lengthy list of information members will supply to IMF.

(Alternative B — Not included at Atlantic City)

III, proposed additional section. *Consideration of Representations of the Fund*

Alternative A (omitted at Bretton Woods), United States — Members to consider IMF advice.

(Alternative A, United States — Not included at Atlantic City. Fund may warn a member about policies with balance of payments spillovers.)

(Alternative B — Not included at Atlantic City.)

Alternative C (omitted at Bretton Woods), USSR — IMF not to recommend fundamental changes in economic organization.

IV. Par Values of Member Currencies

IV-1. *[[Establishing Par Value]]*

Alternative A, United States — Par value may be expressed in terms of a gold convertible currency as an alternative to gold itself.

Alternative B (omitted at Bretton Woods), United Kingdom — Occupied countries may set provisional par values; IMF may reject a member's proposed initial par value.

IV-2; IV-3; IV-4. *[[Changes in Par Value; Fund's Approval of Change in Par Value; Latitude for Change in Par Value]]*

Alternative A (omitted at Bretton Woods), United States — Allow changes of up to 10 percent from initial par value as a matter of right.

Alternative B (omitted at Bretton Woods), Australia — IMF not to reject change in par value to meet a balance of payments deficit caused by severe shock in terms of trade.

Alternative C (omitted at Bretton Woods), Brazil — Add clause on loans from other international agencies.

Alternative D (omitted at Bretton Woods), USSR — Give latitude for changing par values that do not affect international transactions.

Alternative E (omitted at Bretton Woods), Greece — Greater emphasis on tentative nature of initial par values of countries that have been under enemy occupation.

IV-5. *[[Uniform Changes in Par Values]]*

Alternative A, United States — Add majority vote requirement for changes.

Alternative B (omitted at Bretton Woods), Canada — Add majority vote requirement for changes.

IV, proposed additional section. *Protection of the Assets of the Fund*

Alternative A, United States — Member will compensate IMF for devaluation of its currency with respect to gold or receive a refund for appreciation.

IV, proposed additional section. *Separate Currencies within a Member's Jurisdiction*

Alternative A, United States — A member with separate currencies in its territories need not change the par values of all concurrently.

Alternative B, Netherlands — Provisions of this article apply to all separate currencies within a member's territory.

V. Capital Transactions

V-1. *[[Use of Fund to Finance Capital Outflows]]*

Alternative A, United States — IMF may declare a member ineligible to use its resources if it uses them to finance large or sustained capital outflows.

Alternative B (omitted at Bretton Woods), Canada — Clarify wording.

V-2. *[[Capital and Current Controls]]*

Alternative A, United States — Make members' right to control capital flows more explicit.

VI. Apportionment of Scarce Currencies

VI-1.; VI-2. *[[Fund Warning of Scarcity; Rationing of Scarce Currencies]]*

Alternative A, United States — Representative of a country whose currency is scarce to participate in IMF report on the situation; IMF to consider general international economic situation when declaring a scarcity.

VII. Management of the Fund

VII-1. *[[Board and Executive Committee]]*

Alternative A, United States — Extensive detail on powers, voting, and operation of Board of Governors and Executive Committee.

Alternative B, United Kingdom — Detail on powers, voting, and operation of Board of Governors, Executive Committee, and Chairman.

Alternative C (omitted at Bretton Woods), Australia, Canada, or Netherlands? — Allocation of Executive Board seats to mid-sized and small economies.

VI-2.; VII-3. *[[Voting Power; Voting Procedures]]*

Alternative A, United States — Formula for voting.

Alternative B, United Kingdom — Quorum for the Board of Governors. Substitute for III-2 and III-3.

VII, proposed additional section. *The General Manager*

Alternative A, United States — General Manger to head IMF.

(Alternative B, United Kingdom? — Not included at Atlantic City. Duties and salary of General Manger.)

VII-4. *[[Publication of Financial Position]]*

Alternative A, United States — IMF to publish annual and quarterly reports.

VII, proposed additional sections. *Depositories; Form of Holdings of Currency*

Alternative A, United States — Members to designate depositories; currency not needed by IMF may be held as noninterest-bearing funds at depository

Alternative B, USSR? — IMF may to consider convenience for members for estalishing gold depositories.

Alternative C, Netherlands — About half the gold to be held in the IMF's headquarters country.

VII, proposed additional sections. *Location of Office; Relationship to Other International Organizations*

(Alternative A, United States — Not included at Atlantic City. IMF to cooperate with other international organizations.)

Alternative A, United States — Headquarters to be in country with largest quota.

(Alternative B, United Kingdom — Not included at Atlantic City. IMF may make arrangements with other international economic organizations and the United Nations.)

Alternative B , United Kingdom (omitted at Bretton Woods) — Headquarters to be decided at first meeting of Board of Governors.

VII, proposed additional section. *Distribution of Net Income of the Fund*

Alternative A, United States — Option of annual distribution of 2 percent.

VII, proposed additional section. *Miscellaneous Powers*

Alternative A, United States — IMF to have certain corporate powers.

VIII. Withdrawal from the Fund

VIII-1. *[[Procedure for Withdrawal]]*

Alternative A, United States — Withdrawal effective on date it is received.

Alternative B, Australia — Withdrawal from IMF will not trigger withdrawal from other international bodies.

VIII, proposed additional section. *Suspension of Membership or Compulsory Withdrawal*

Alternative A, United States — One-year suspension for failing to meet obligations, after which withdrawal unless standing is restored.

Alternative B (omitted at Bretton Woods), United Kingdom — IMF may suspend or compel withdrawal of a member immediately for failing to meet its obligations.

VIII-2.; VIII-3. *[[Liquidation of Obligations; Disposal of Withdrawing Member's Currency]]*

Alternative A, United States — Three-year deadline for liquidating obligations.

Alternative B, United Kingdom — Minor changes in wording.

VIII, proposed additional section. *Liquidation of the Fund*

Alternative A, United States — Procedures for liquidating the IMF.

(Alternative B, Belgium? — Not included at Atlantic City. To be inserted later.)

IX. Obligations of Member Countries

IX-1. *[[Gold Price]]*

Alternative A, United States — Add section: provisions of this agreement remain binding on member countries ineligible to borrow from the IMF.

IX-2. *[[Foreign Exchange Dealing]]*

Alternative A, United States — Members agree not to permit exchange rates outside of the parity range for their own currencies in their own territory.

Alternative B (omitted at Bretton Woods), United Kingdom — Obligation to purchase one's own currency at parity does not apply to capital transactions or prewar balances.

IX, proposed additional section. *[[Foreign Exchange Dealing, Continued]]*

Alternative A, United States — Obligation to purchase one's own currency at parity does not apply to capital and certain other transactions.

IX-3. *[[Current Transactions]]*

Alternative A, United States — Potentially widen scope for exchange controls.

Alternative B, United Kingdom — Potentially widen scope for exchange controls.

IX, proposed additional section. *Immunity of Assets of the Fund*

Alternative A, United States — IMF to be immune from national taxation.

IX, proposed additional section. *Immunity from Suit*

Alternative A, United States — IMF to be immune from lawsuits except when it consents.

IX, proposed additional section. *Restrictions on Taxation of Fund, Its Employees and Obligations*

Alternative A, United States — IMF exempt from national taxation.

X. Transitional Arrangements

X-1; X-2; X-3; X-4 *[[Entry into Force; Transition Period; Restrictions on Exchange; Adjustments during Transition Period]]*

Alternative A, United States — Members that have been occupied may maintain restrictions on current transactions; the IMF may recommend to such members to end restrictions, but will give them benefit of the doubt.

Alternative B, United Kingdom — IMF to report on restrictions on current transactions still in effect three years after IMF begins.

Proposed Article XI. Amendments

Alternative A, United States — Amendment by four-fifths of votes.

Alternative B, United Kingdom — Amendment by three-fifths of votes for some matters, unanimous votes for others.

Proposed Article XII. Interpretation of the Agreement

Proposed XII-1. *Interpretation*

Alternative A, United States — IMF to resolve disagreements between members.

Alternative B, United Kingdom — Executive Directors to resolve disagreements between members; right to appeal to Board of Governors.

Proposed XII-2. *Definitions*

Alternative A, United States — Various definitions.

Alternative C, USSR — Gold and convertible currency.

Alternative D (B), United Kingdom — Various definitions.

Proposed XII-3. *Effect on Other International Commitments*

Alternative A, United States — This agreement shall not hinder other commitments on nondiscriminatory reduction of trade barriers.

Proposed Article XIII. Putting the Fund into Operation

Alternative A, United States — Acceptance of membership; effective date of agreement; initial meeting of the IMF; initial par values

Alternative B, United Kingdom — Allow more discretion than U.S. amendment.

Proposed Article XIV. Execution of the Agreement

Alternative A (omitted at Bretton Woods), United States — Signatures and certified copies.

Index

The index is brief because the electronic version of the book offers the capability for word searches. Appendix A lists all the delegates. The glossary in Appendix C defines key terms. Page numbers can refer either to main text or to footnotes. For additional help finding discussions on a particular topic in or section of the draft IMF articles of agreement, use the table on page 30 to find the date when it was discussed and the table of contents to locate the chapter(s) corresponding to that date.

www.ingramcontent.com/pod-product-compliance
Lightning Source LLC
Chambersburg PA
CBHW070911100426
42814CB00003B/131